A KINGDOM UNITED: POPULAR RESPONSES TO THE OUTBREAK OF THE FIRST WORLD WAR IN BRITAIN AND IRELAND

In this, the first fully documented study of British and Irish popular reactions to the outbreak of the First World War, Catriona Pennell explores UK public opinion of the time, successfully challenging post-war constructions of 'war enthusiasm' in the British case, and disengagement in the Irish.

Drawing from a vast array of contemporary diaries, letters, journals, and newspaper accounts from across the UK, *A Kingdom United* explores what people felt, and how they acted, in response to an unanticipated and unprecedented crisis. It is a history of both ordinary people and elite figures in extraordinary times. Pennell demonstrates that describing the reactions of over 40 million British and Irish people to the outbreak of war as either enthusiastic in the British case, or disengaged in the Irish, is over-simplified and inadequate. Emotional reactions to the war were ambiguous and complex, and changed over time. By the end of 1914 the populations of England, Scotland, Wales, and Ireland had largely embraced the war, but the war had also embraced them and showed no signs of relinquishing its grip. The five months from August to December 1914 set the shape of much that was to follow. *A Kingdom United* describes and explains the twenty-week formative process in order to deepen our understanding of British and Irish entry into war.

Catriona Pennell is Senior Lecturer in History at the University of Exeter. She graduated from Trinity College, Dublin in 2008 with a PhD in modern British and Irish history. During her research, she was awarded two major scholarships: the R.B. McDowell-Ussher Fellowship from Trinity College, Dublin (2003–2006), and the R.H.S. Centenary Fellowship from the Institute of Historical Research (2006–2007).

D0911399

A Kingdom United

*Popular Responses to the Outbreak of the First
World War in Britain and Ireland*

CATRIONA PENNELL

OXFORD

UNIVERSITY PRESS

OXFORD

UNIVERSITY PRESS

Great Clarendon Street, Oxford, OX2 6DP
United Kingdom

Oxford University Press is a department of the University of Oxford.
It furthers the University's objective of excellence in research, scholarship,
and education by publishing worldwide. Oxford is a registered trade mark of
Oxford University Press in the UK and in certain other countries

First published 2012
First published in paperback 2014

Published in the United States of America by Oxford University Press
198 Madison Avenue, New York, NY 10016, United States of America

British Library Cataloguing in Publication Data
Data available

Library of Congress Cataloging in Publication Data
Data available

ISBN 978–0–19–959058–2 (Hbk)
ISBN 978–0–19–870846–9 (Pbk)

For my parents and in loving memory of Dada, my maternal grandfather—
J. A. Griffiths (1909–1994)

Preface

This book explores the way in which the peoples of the United Kingdom—England, Scotland, Wales, and Ireland—went to war in 1914. It is the first fully documented study of UK public opinion at the time and successfully challenges the myth of British 'war enthusiasm'. It explores what people felt, and how they acted, in response to an unanticipated and unprecedented crisis. It is a history of both ordinary people and elite figures in extraordinary times. It demonstrates that describing the reactions of over 40 million British and Irish people to the outbreak of war in 1914 as either enthusiastic in the British case or disengaged in the Irish is over-simplified and inadequate. A society as complex as the UK in the Edwardian era did not have a single, uniform reaction to such a major event as the outbreak of European war. Emotional reactions to the war were ambiguous and complex, and changed over time. By the end of 1914 the populations of England, Scotland, Wales, and Ireland had largely embraced the war. But the war had equally embraced them, and showed no signs of relinquishing its grip. In fact it would continue for another four years. However, the five months from August to December 1914 set the shape of much that was to follow. This book seeks to describe and explain that twenty-week formative process.

Catriona Pennell is a senior lecturer in History at the University of Exeter.

For more on the Russian rumour mentioned on p. 131, please see Catriona Pennell's article, 'Believing the Unbelievable: The Myth of the Russians with "Snow on their Boots" in the United Kingdom, 1914', *Cultural and Social History* 11, (2014), 69–88.

Acknowledgements

This book was made possible by the generous financial support of: the R. B. McDowell-Ussher Fellowship provided by the Trinity Trust at Trinity College, Dublin, 2003–2006; the Institute of Historical Research, London; the Executive of the Historial de la Grande Guerre in Péronne, France; and various grants awarded by the Dean of Graduate Studies at Trinity College, Dublin.

I gratefully acknowledge permission to quote from private papers granted by the Board of Trinity College and the Trustees of the Imperial War Museum. Extracts from the diaries of King George V are reproduced by permission of Her Majesty Queen Elizabeth II. Extracts from the papers of Norman Ellison are reproduced by permission of Liverpool Record Office, Liverpool Libraries. I am grateful to the following copyright holders for allowing me to reproduce extracts from the private papers under their jurisdiction: Lavinia Anson (Winifred Tower), C. R. C. Aston (Lt. Col. C. C. Aston), M. S. Bailey (Capt. Bruce W. S. Bailey), Judith Baines (Annie Purbrook), Simon Chater (Capt. A. D. Chater), Pauline Fenton (L. Wilson), David F. K. Hodge (Thomas Batty), Elizabeth King-Sloan (Misses Ada and Rhoda McGuire), Petra Laidlaw (Thomas Douglas Laidlaw), Arthur Lockwood (F. T. Lockwood), Thomas Pemberton (Lt. C. G. H. Bell), Fred Ponsonby (Arthur Ponsonby), R. B. Saunders (Robert Saunders), and Caroline Thompson (Lt. A. Thompson). It is worth noting that socio-cultural history projects, such as this book, are impossible without the continued donation of precious familial documents to local and national archives. Every effort has been made to trace the copyright owners of material used in this book; any omissions should be directed to the author.

I owe so much to my thesis supervisor, Professor John Horne. I thank him for his unending patience, advice, insight, and, above all, friendship. I have also been assisted in my research by a number of academic colleagues whose observations, suggestions, and criticisms have all been received with much appreciation. In particular I would like to thank Stephen Badsey, Adrian Gregory, Keith Grieves, Stuart Halifax, Tim Harding, Jacqueline Hayden, Nick Hiley, Keith Jeffery, Heather Jones, Spencer Jones, Jenny Macleod, Edward Madigan, Eunan O'Halpin, Mike Neiberg, Jane O'Mahony, Pierre Purseigle, Julian Putkowski, Gary Sheffield, Matthew Stibbe, Dan Todman, Calder Walton, and Michael Wheatley. The final stages of this book were completed at the University of Exeter, Cornwall Campus. I would like to thank my colleagues Alan Booth, Kate Conway, Laura Rowe, Richard Toye, and Nicola Whyte for reading drafts and offering support and ideas. I am extremely grateful to Rob Wilkinson for creating the map featured in Appendix III of this book. I would also like to thank Thérèse Sullivan for translating some of the W. P. Ryan Papers held at University College, Dublin. Any mistakes or oversights in this book are my responsibility alone.

Over the course of my research I have visited over seventy archives in Britain, Ireland, and abroad. I have been helped by a number of librarians and archivists and I would like to thank, in particular, Matt Olsen and Michael Hussey at the National Archives of the United States of America, Maryland Campus; Colin Harris at the Bodleian Library, Oxford; and Charles Benson and the late Anne Walsh at Trinity College, Dublin. I thank Christopher Wheeler and Stephanie Ireland at OUP for their patience and professionalism during this project.

This project has been the hardest, and most satisfying, task I have ever set myself. I could not have completed it without the support of my friends. Being a postgraduate at Trinity College, Dublin allowed me to become friends with some wonderful and inspiring historians—Jane Finucane, Richard Kirwan, Eve Morrison, Mary Muldowney, Clióna Rattigan, Claudia Siebrecht, and Daniel Steinbach. Outside of academia, I have been lucky enough to be surrounded by people who have tolerated my frequent disappearances, lack of contact, moments of panic, and, more importantly, been there to share in the 'eureka' moments. I would like to thank my friends and colleagues at the Refugee Youth Project in London, Oxford, and southern Lebanon for allowing me the flexibility to be a key member of the team, whilst concentrating full-time on my research. The Fakher-Eldin family, and Paul and Thérèse Sullivan have been families away from home. Thanks also to Nick and Amanda Jepson and Geni and David Reilly for hosting me during research trips to Essex and Scotland. I will always cherish the friendship and support offered to me by Fran Burke, Jane Delafons, Yousef Eldin, Sue Green, Susie Green, Lauren Hadden, George Higgs, Amy Iggulden, Sarah Lincoln, and Sasha Willmott, who all had an unfaltering belief that I would get this project completed. Special thanks to Cerion Barnes for his patience and support in the book's final stages. The greatest debt of gratitude must go to my family. My nephews and niece, Parker, Daisy, and Hugo, have been joyful distractions since their arrivals in 2004, 2007, and 2010 respectively. It is impossible to thank sufficiently my parents, Hilary and Paul Pennell, who have supported me well beyond the call of duty at every possible stage. My only aim with this book is to make you both proud.

Contents

List of Figures, and Map

FIGURES

MAP

List of Tables

Abbreviations Used in the Text

BEF	British Expeditionary Force
BSP	British Socialist Party
CID	Committe of Imperial Defence
DORA	Defence of the Realm Act
FA	Football Association
ILP	Independent Labour Party
INV	Irish National Volunteers
IPP	Irish Parliamentary Party
IRB	Irish Republican Brotherhood
NUWSS	National Union of Women's Suffrage Societies
POW	Prisoner of War
PRC	Parliamentary Recruiting Committee
RAMC	Royal Army Medical Corps
RIC	Royal Irish Constabulary
SWMF	South Wales Miners' Federation
UDC	Union of Democratic Control
UVF	Ulster Volunteer Force
VAD	Voluntary Aid Detachment
WSPU	Women's Social and Political Union

Abbreviations Used in the Notes

AMAE	Archive du Ministère Etrangères
BCA	Birmingham City Archives
BL	British Library
BMH	Bureau of Military History, Dublin
DRO	Devon Record Office
ERO	Essex Record Office
GMRO	Greater Manchester Record Office
GRO	Glamorgan Record Office
IWM	Imperial War Museum
LanRO	Lancashire Record Office
LRO	Liverpool Record Office
MALSL	Manchester Archives and Local Studies Library
MPP	Modern Political Papers, Bodleian Library
NA	National Archives
NAS, GRH	National Archives of Scotland, General Register House
NAS, WRH	National Archives of Scotland, West Register House
NDRO	North Devon Record Office
NLI	National Library of Ireland
NLS	National Library of Scotland
NLW	National Library of Wales
NWSA	North West Sound Archives
PRONI	Public Record Office of Northern Ireland
PWDRO	Plymouth and West Devon Record Office
ROLLR	Record Office for Leicestershire, Leicester and Rutland
SWML, HH	South Wales Miners' Library, Hendrefoelan House
SWML, SP	South Wales Miners' Library, Singleton Park
TCD	Trinity College, Dublin
UCD	University College Dublin
WGRO	West Glamorgan Record Office
WRO	Worcester Record Office

Introduction

The subject of this book is the way in which the peoples of the United Kingdom went to war in 1914. The outbreak of war on 4 August marked the start of a cycle of conflicts that would redefine and dominate British and world history in the twentieth century. It was, perhaps, *the* shaping moment of the twentieth century and produced consequences that we still live with today. Yet until now, the ways in which British and Irish people responded to war in 1914 have been largely unexplored. This is the first fully documented study of UK public opinion at the time. It seeks to explore what people felt, and how they acted, in response to an unanticipated and unprecedented crisis. By the end of 1914 the populations of England, Scotland, Wales, and Ireland had largely embraced the war. But the war had equally embraced them, and showed no signs of relinquishing its grip. In fact it would continue for another four years. However, the five months from August to December 1914 set the shape of much that was to follow. This book seeks to describe and explain that twenty-week formative process.

What follows is a history of both ordinary people and elite figures in extraordinary times. Over the last fifteen years, historians of Britain, France, Germany, and Austria have rewritten the history of the First World War from the 'bottom up', demonstrating the social and cultural significance of the conflict in fields as diverse as class and gender roles, welfare policy, psychiatry, and entertainment.[1] Likewise this book aims to reconstruct the feelings, emotions, and actions of the British and Irish people faced with the outbreak of war. Amongst 40 million people there can be no single 'experience': I explore a multiplicity of emotions and attempt to draw patterns and conclusions from the evidence. Probably no single account can do justice to the full range of responses. But one thing is certain: an entire population's feelings cannot be adequately described by the monolithic label of war enthusiasm.

---

[1] See Maureen Healy, *Vienna and the Fall of the Habsburg Empire: Total War and Everyday Life in World War One* (Cambridge, 2004), Margaret Randolph Higonnet and Patrice L. R. Higonnet, 'The Double Helix', in *Behind the Lines: Gender and the Two World Wars*, ed. Margaret Randolph Higonnet et al. (New Haven, 1987), Richard Wall and Jay Winter, ed., *The Upheaval of War: Family, Work and Welfare in Europe, 1914–1918* (Cambridge, 1988), Jay Winter and Jean-Louis Robert, ed., *Capital Cities at War: Paris, London and Berlin, 1914–1919*, 2 vols., vol. 1 (Cambridge, 1997), Jay Winter and Jean-Louis Robert, ed., *Capital Cities at War: Paris, London, Berlin, 1914–1919: Volume 2, A Cultural History*, 2 vols., vol. 2 (Cambridge, 2007).

GOING TO WAR

Over the course of these twenty weeks, the peoples of Britain and Ireland defined their position in relation to the conflict, voluntarily rallied around the national cause, enlisted, and said goodbye to loved ones. They sought domestic scapegoats in order to purge their fears of the external German enemy, notably in the form of enemy spies and aliens, responded to myth and rumour, and imagined and then actually encountered violence and loss. They had to adjust to economic dislocation and the breaking of daily routines and rituals. New government legislation, such as the Defence of the Realm Act (DORA) first passed on 8 August, giving the government wide-ranging interventionist powers during the war period, cemented the new reality that business could certainly not continue as 'normal'. By late August/early September the majority of the population were beginning to understand what was involved in modern warfare. But each week brought new revelations of the reality of the conflict.

Consequently, understanding how the British and Irish embarked on the war requires a detailed chronology that takes account of the constantly changing visage of the conflict. Reactions to the outbreak of war differ from responses after its outbreak. Crowds on 4 August, resigned editorials in the Liberal press in the following days, and the rush to the colours at the end of the month cannot be used as evidence of attitudes *before* the outbreak of war. Public opinion continued to evolve day by day, if not hour by hour. A fine-grained chronology permits a detailed and close-up analysis of the shifting views held in the public and private spheres. Yet for all this, the period from July to December 1914 also has an overall coherence. The First World War is recalled, above all, in terms of the stalemate of trench warfare and the appalling cost of trying to break it. Yet its opening months were characterized by a war of movement, with invasions, retreats, massive encounters on the battlefield, and some of the highest casualty levels of the entire conflict. This was the war that contemporaries in Britain and Ireland, as elsewhere, had to come to terms with down to the end of 1914.

The population of the UK in 1914 not only entered the war within a specific time period, but also within a defined space. This account takes a broad view of the UK, using sources from Wales, Scotland, and Ireland, as well as England, to examine regional variation in responses to the war. It thus refuses to be dominated by the south of England. For the first time the 'United Kingdom of Britain and Ireland' is examined as a totality in 1914. Unlike other accounts of Britain and the war, this book recognizes how intertwined Britain and Ireland were in wartime. At least until the Easter Rising of 1916, citizens in Ireland took to the war with as complex feelings and justifications as their compatriots across the Irish Sea. The majority of people—including those in Ireland—supported the onset of war in a spirit of seriousness and acceptance of duty. For clarity I have chosen to use the term 'Britain' and 'British' to refer to the three nations of England, Scotland, and Wales. However, I recognize that Scotland and Wales are not simply separate regions of the UK like Lancashire and the West Midlands so special focus is given to these areas to avoid 'flattening' them out. Ireland (north and south combined in that term) is treated separately. Irish politics was uniquely unstable within the United Kingdom in 1914 and therefore justifies a separate study. When I use the term 'United Kingdom' I am referring to all four nations. When I talk of Britain, the British people, and the United Kingdom in this book, I am not implying cultural uniformity but arguing that whilst differences existed between England, Scotland, Wales, and Ireland, there were also similarities of experience and response to the start of the First World War that made the kingdom, at this point, genuinely united.

'WAR ENTHUSIASM'

The moment of entry into the war of 1914–1918 deserves special attention. The long war that followed was so difficult to comprehend, both at the time and in the following decades, that many myths grew up to account for it. Popular reactions in 1914 were the subject of one of the most powerful such myths, and not only in the United Kingdom but also in France and Germany. Of course, 'myth' does not necessarily mean a falsehood. Often it is a highly selective, symbolic representation of an episode or event that endows it with a particular importance. Just as the French needed to generate a myth around the notion of the Union Sacrée and the Germans around the *Burgfrieden* (or 'fortress truce'), so the image of the outbreak of the First World War was cemented in Britain in the 1920s and 1930s as one of 'war enthusiasm'. In particular, the memoirs of politicians, such as David Lloyd George's, Liberal Chancellor of the Exchequer in 1914, used the luxury of hindsight to justify their decision to enter what became a horrific conflict by claiming it was enthusiastically supported by the majority of the population. Writing nearly twenty years after the event, Lloyd George recalled the reaction in central London to the announcement of war at 11 p.m. on 4 August. A crowd:

> extended from Trafalgar Square where it formed a dense mass, right along to the House of Commons, where its greatest number gathered about Downing Street opposite the War Office. Groups of young men passed along in taxi-cabs singing the *Marseillaise*. During the early part of the day there had been little disposition to demonstrate by the wearing of colours, but the tendency spread, and hundreds were buying Union Jacks. At seven o'clock in the evening, when Mr Asquith left the subsequent Council Meeting to go to the House of Lords, the crowds cheered him with extraordinary fervour. It was a scene of enthusiasm unprecedented in recent times.[2]

In Lloyd George's mind ordinary people were excited, noisy, and 'displayed marked tendencies towards mafficking', as during the riotous celebrations of the relief of the town of that name—Mafeking—from siege by the Boers during the South African War.[3] Moreover, he believed that it was these hysterical masses that had demanded

---

[2] David Lloyd George, *War Memoirs of David Lloyd George*, 4 vols., vol. 1 (London, 1933), 41.
[3] Ibid. 42.

war against Germany whilst British statesmen did their best to keep the country neutral.

Such a view of the events on 4 August also provided a cathartic explanation for those on the left. For pacifists, who believed that all wars were irrational, people who supported the war were also irrational. Caroline Playne (1857–1948), who wrote two histories of wartime public opinion in the interwar period, considered retrospectively that 'the whole period must be discredited, its preposterous time, and its deep-seated folly shown up in order that similarly perverse groups' mentality may be shunned by generations to come'.[4] Devastated by the war's outbreak she understood a population's support for war as an act of temporary madness. Only a psychotically induced breakdown could have permitted a country to enter four and a half years of slaughter with over 8.5 million men killed from all nations. As after the Crimean and South African wars, the myth of war enthusiasm was in large part an act of self-accusation by pacifists for failing to prevent the conflict, disguised by anger at the irrational mob.[5]

In reality, the responses of ordinary British and Irish people on 4 August were much more complex than the myth of war enthusiasm suggests. The crowds existed, yet other crowds opposed the war, and many more people were shocked and disbelieving, or at best reluctant in their acceptance. The belief that the war was made unavoidable by German violation of Belgian neutrality was not the same as a jingoistic anti-German fervour, though there were also various manifestations of deep feeling and occasional hysteria regarding the enemy. The central tenet of this book is that ordinary British and Irish people in 1914 did not back the war because they were deluded, brainwashed, and naïvely duped into an idiotic bloodbath, as the subsequent myth would have it.[6] Rather, their support was very often carefully considered, well-informed, reasoned, and only made once all other options were exhausted. By 4 August people supported the war, but only because they felt it was the right thing to do in the circumstances. They then proceeded to positively immerse themselves in the war effort and collaborate in its prosecution, but not necessarily in an overtly enthusiastic and jingoistic manner.

---

[4] Senate House Library, Special Collections: Playne Collection: Folder 156: Florence Lockwood 'Private Diary', 1921. See also Caroline E. Playne, *The Pre-War Mind in Britain* (London, 1928), Caroline E. Playne, *Society at War, 1914–1916* (London, 1931).

[5] For proponents of the 1854 'war enthusiasm' view see Kingsley Martin, *The Triumph of Lord Palmerston: A Study in Public Opinion in England Before the Crimean War*, 2nd ed. (London, 1963). See also William Laurence Burn, *The Age of Equipoise: A Study of the Mid-Victorian Generation* (London, 1964), 56. Regarding the South African War, see J. A. Hobson, *The Psychology of Jingoism* (London, 1901).

[6] A number of interwar and post-1945 memoirs recalled enthusiastic crowds embracing the war. See, for example, Geoffrey Marcus, *Before the Lamps Went Out* (London, 1965). War-hungry crowds also appeared in interwar fictional accounts of the conflict. Wilfrid Ewart, in his novel *Way of Revelation*, described 'a spectacle of a people drunk—drunk with sensationalism, with over-excitement, with lust for war' in London on the night war was declared. See Wilfrid Ewart, *Way of Revelation: A Novel of Five Years* (London, 1921), 107–9. The myth has also been sustained by some historians, such as Arthur Marwick, Peter Parker, and W. J. Reader. See Arthur Marwick, *The Deluge: British Society and the First World War* (London, 1965), 309, Peter Parker, *The Old Lie: The Great War and the Public School Ethos* (London, 1987), 151, W. J. Reader, *At Duty's Call: A Study in Obsolete Patriotism* (Manchester, 1988), 104.

Historians of France and Germany have dismantled the equivalent myths of war enthusiasm in 1914 in those countries. It is now over thirty years since Jean-Jacques Becker published his monumental study of French reactions to the outbreak of war, and that has been followed up with a number of more specific case studies for individual areas of France.[7] In *The Spirit of 1914: Militarism, Myth and Mobilization in Germany* (2000), Jeffrey Verhey has convincingly dispelled the widely held belief that the German population reacted with undifferentiated 'war enthusiasm' in the summer of 1914.[8] Other important German works have used the press to underline the diversity of reactions.[9] Taken together, this amounts to a new consensus that the populations of both France and Germany supported the war out of a sense of defiant duty, rather than a jingoistic desire for war.

This groundbreaking European scholarship only serves to highlight the gap in British and Irish historiography. Adrian Gregory has begun the work of reassessment, but images of war-hungry crowds are remarkably tenacious in the public mind.[10] It is still confidently asserted that Britons marched joyfully to war in August 1914. Writing about Britain's current operations in Afghanistan in *The Guardian*, Geoffrey Wheatcroft invoked 1914–1918 in referring to 'wars which our horrible politicians still take us into, and which inflict terrible sufferings on faraway innocents'.[11] He reaffirmed the sense that naïve and innocent Britons were 'duped' into war by arrogant and short-sighted politicians, thus echoing the very accusations Lloyd George polemically tried to counter in 1933. The British see the First World War as a uniquely terrible experience; as a result, the outbreak of this perceived national tragedy can only be understood in terms of a population 'gone mad', drunk on their own enthusiasm.[12]

This book will set aside the mythology and establish the real nature of responses to the outbreak of war in 1914 across the United Kingdom. It will examine public opinion, looking at the well known and powerful, but also at those whose ordinary lives were disrupted and often transformed by the unfolding drama. Feelings about the war were not only complex but changed over time, in three distinct phases. An initial phase of rallying around the flag during the war crisis and its immediate aftermath was followed by a second phase of confusion and disorder. But by September 1914, a 'war culture' was in place and resonated in many different

---

[7] Jean-Jacques Becker, *1914: Comment les Français sont entrés dans la guerre* (Paris, 1977). See also P. J. Flood, *France 1914–1918: Public Opinion and the War Effort* (London, 1990).

[8] Jeffrey Verhey, *The Spirit of 1914: Militarism, Myth and Mobilization in Germany* (Cambridge, 2000). Owing to France's centralized state system, Jean-Jacques Becker was able to make impressive use of eyewitness accounts returned by primary school teachers and prefects in certain departments of France thus producing a substitute for opinion polls. As equivalent sources are not available in Germany, Verhey based his study on newspapers and an analysis of crowd behaviour.

[9] See, for example, Jean-Jacques Becker and Gerd Krumeich, *La Grande guerre: Une histoire franco-allemande* (Paris, 2008), Thomas Raithel, *Das 'Wunder' der inneren Einheit: Studien zur deutschen und französischen Öffentlichkeit bei Beginn des Ersten Weltkrieges* (Bonn, 1996).

[10] Adrian Gregory, 'British "War Enthusiasm" in 1914: A Reassessment', in *Evidence, History and the Great War: Historians and the Impact of 1914–18*, ed. Gail Braybon (Oxford, 2003), Adrian Gregory, *The Last Great War: British Society and the First World War* (Cambridge, 2008).

[11] Geoffrey Wheatcroft, 'The Quality of Sacrifice', in *The Guardian*, 8 July 2009, 26.

[12] Dan Todman, *The Great War: Myth and Memory* (London, 2005).

social strata, remote from poets, elites, or politicians.[13] The people's war was born then and there, and this book charts its emergence, virtually day by day.

THE EVIDENCE

How is it possible to gauge popular reactions in Britain and Ireland to a war that erupted a century ago, in a time before opinion polls?

Newspapers provide an excellent foundation for establishing popular reactions to war in Britain and Ireland. Although any one newspaper in isolation is of limited value, taken together and treated with care, they remain an irreplaceable historical source. Problems, such as inherent bias, lack of authority, and inaccuracies, are outweighed, in my opinion, by the benefits of this source.[14] Used critically, newspapers contain multiple forms of public opinion, not only news stories and editorials, but letters from readers. They do more than merely report events, offering, in addition, analysis and criticism. Newspapers fuel conversation about politics, which in turn enables people to clarify their opinions as political actors. More importantly, newspapers are businesses reliant upon sales and advertising. They depend ultimately, not on political patronage, but on the opinions and beliefs of their readers; while editors and owners might seek to mould and at least influence the latter, the relationship also works in the other direction. W. T. Stead, the Victorian journalist, wrote of the mandate of the press being renewed every day, with the 'electorate' registering their votes by their daily purchases.[15] In short, the market mediates the relationship between the press and public opinion. Newspapers with different political and regional loyalties, therefore, offer a reliable representation of the varying British public perceptions of the war. Accordingly, over sixty local and national newspapers have been examined in the course of this study, as well as the satirical press.

But newspapers also do more than reflect opinion. They record public behaviour. This point is crucial. Much can be gleaned about public responses to war by asking what were people *doing* in autumn 1914? How were their feelings expressed in their behaviour? Newspapers and other sources inform us abundantly about this.

Popular collective behaviour—such as a protest or riot—is a blessing to the researcher of 'history from below', and in particular the researcher of popular opinion. The non-institutional political activity of ordinary people below the level of the social and political elites provides a significant expression of their attitudes and concerns.[16] Although the task of identifying the 'faces' of historical crowds is

---

[13] Stéphane Audoin-Rouzeau and Annette Becker, *1914–1918: Understanding the Great War* (London, 1999 trans. from French 2002).

[14] Jane-Louise Secker, 'Newspapers and Historical Research: A Study of Historians and Custodians in Wales' (PhD, University of Wales, 1999).

[15] J. O. Baylen, 'The "New Journalism" in Late Victorian Britain', *Australian Journal of Politics and History* 18 (1972), 384.

[16] For other studies of crowd behaviour, see Tim Harris, *London Crowds and the Reign of Charles II: Propaganda and Politics from the Restoration until the Exclusion Crisis* (Cambridge, 1987), Harvey J. Kaye, ed., *The Face of the Crowd: Studies in Revolution, Ideology and Popular Protest. Selected Essays of*

problematic, it is useful to dissect incidents of popular collective behaviour to understand what happened, why, who was involved, and what motivated them. In 1914, collective behaviour of this kind was particularly evident in xenophobic riots against actual or perceived Germans. The absence of such activity at crucial moments is also important: the focus of this book is by no means limited to the disaffected.

Acts and gestures should not overshadow the realm of the imaginary—what ordinary people *perceived* to be true. Stories of gruesome atrocities against Belgian and French civilians at the hands of the invading German army in 1914 were not merely a clever method of demarcating and vilifying the enemy for the consumption of naïve and 'sponge-like' populations.[17] The stories achieved their power because they were rooted in real events and because they resonated with wartime societies, clashing with a moral code established in the years preceding 1914, and provided a language in which to express some of the fundamental reactions to the outbreak of the war—that of fear, particularly the fear of invasion. Tracing such emotional reactions and perceptions provides yet another 'window' through which to view attitudes held in common by a wide range of people.[18]

Naturally, in wartime, communication was controlled by censorship and influenced by propaganda. Broadly speaking, although there was a degree of governmental control in the information released to the public in 1914, it was minimal. While the Press Bureau did exercise a considerable measure of control, it also sought a high level of cooperation with the press. 'Voluntary participation' best describes the relationship between the press and the government in matters of control and censorship.[19] Censorship and propaganda offices did not need to impose their views on editors, journalists, and cartoonists: they shared them, and decided to put their pens and brushes at the service of Britain and to fight against Germany in their own way. Although DORA regulations applied in part to the press, the government never had control of the press by law. An overall assessment of newspaper censorship in Britain during the First World War must conclude that it was far from draconian. Intellectuals, academics, artists, writers, and journalists volunteered as professionals to serve their country. This information flow was two-way: propaganda only had power to the extent that it modified pre-existing public opinion without overturning it. When common sense on the popular level diverged from state propaganda, the official message rang hollow or simply vanished. But when propaganda coincided with popular feeling, independently generated and independently sustained, then it had a real force.[20]

George Rudé (Hemel Hempstead, 1988), George Rudé, *The Crowd in History: A Study of Popular Disturbances in France and England, 1730–1848* (New York, 1964).

[17] John Horne and Alan Kramer, *German Atrocities, 1914: A History of Denial* (London, 2001).

[18] See also Joanna Bourke, *Fear: A Cultural History* (London, 2006), Georges Lefebvre, *The Great Fear of 1789: Rural Panic in Revolutionary France* (London, 1973), Clay Ramsay, *The Ideology of the Great Fear: The Soissonnais in 1789* (Baltimore, 1992).

[19] Deian Hopkin, 'Domestic Censorship in the First World War', *Journal of Contemporary History* 5 (1970), 153–4.

[20] Jay Winter, 'Propaganda and the Mobilization of Consent', in *The Oxford Illustrated History of the First World War*, ed. Hew Strachan (Oxford, 2000).

When I discuss the British and Irish 'people', who am I referring to? Do I mean everyone in the United Kingdom in 1914? Individuals all had opinions that are valid to this investigation. How do I account for them all? As mentioned, it is vital to avoid the danger of treating all inhabitants of the United Kingdom in 1914 as if they were the same. In an attempt to avoid this trap I have treated popular cultures in plural groupings: urban/rural, male/female, old/young, coastal/inland, Irish/British, national/local, public/private, elite/ordinary, and so on. I have tried to paint a picture of popular responses to various aspects of the war in its opening phases, such as the enemy, the national self, volunteering, philanthropy, the length of the war, and Britain's allies. Differences and divergences from the majority are noted throughout.

Owing to the United Kingdom's decentralized state system in 1914, sources equivalent to France's teachers' and prefects' reports, as used by Jean-Jacques Becker, are unavailable.[21] Additionally, as there was no perceived crisis in British civilian morale at this time, there was no encouragement for the police or military authorities to submit surveillance reports to central government on dissident activity. It was not until 1916, with new fears about strikes and war weariness, that such reports began to appear. However, this was not the case for Ireland. There, governmental concern about political and agrarian discontent, from the middle of the nineteenth century, meant that constabulary inspectors had to report to the Chief Secretary of Ireland on conditions in their districts. The 'CO 904' papers, as they are more commonly known, track paramilitary activity, demonstrations, parades, anti-recruitment campaigns, and meetings, as well as commenting on economic distress and unemployment, in an effort to combat the efforts of nationalist organizations to secure Irish independence in the 1914 period.

Without equivalent 'public morale' reports for England, Scotland, and Wales, I instead look at as many sources from as many places as possible, in order to sample 1914 society. I consulted over seventy archives during the course of this research. A mosaic of experiences emerges; the voices of a vast number of contemporaries are heard. A full cast of 441 diarists, correspondents, authors, poets, and elite figures appears in the *dramatis personae* in Appendix I, with brief contextual details where available. Appendix II provides a basic statistical breakdown of the gender, age, and pre-war occupation of my witnesses, 73 per cent were male: higher than the 48:52 ratio of men to women in England, Scotland, and Wales, and 50:50 ratio of men to women in Ireland in the 1911 census. All were born by 1909, and the earliest in 1846. Ninety-one per cent were adults in 1914, reflecting the lack of written source material from children.[22]

It is more difficult to conclude how representative my witnesses are in terms of social class, in part because of the lack of available information, but also because of the ambiguous nature of the concept itself. Edwardian society was undoubtedly a

---

[21] Becker, *1914: Comment les Français sont entrés dans la guerre.*
[22] Adult defined as aged 15 or above.

class society and a three-class hierarchy of 'upper', 'middle', and 'lower' was common usage amongst contemporaries in the pre-1914 period.[23] Railway carriages, churches, clothing, accents, public houses, educational systems, consumer goods, standards of living, working times, and wages, all served to embed a sense of precise station amongst Edwardians. Class division was more or less conspicuous, depending on geographical location. Southern towns with their large middle-class professional presence and the English countryside with its upper-class country house gentry had a more defined social hierarchy. Conversely, in more homogeneous enclaves such as the working-class districts of cities, rural communities, or industries such as mining, there was a stronger sense of equality amongst ordinary people, despite being under the rule of employers, landowners, or coal-owners.[24] In England, Wales, and Scotland, between 1870 and 1914, the size of the agricultural labour force had shrunk, whilst upper-class wealth had been sustained, and manual workers had concentrated in the export industries. However, in Ireland, agriculture remained dominant. This is roughly reflected in my witness sample. A total of 329 witnesses had an identifiable pre-war occupation. Excluding those fifty-five witnesses at either pre-school age, or studying at school or university, the lowest represented occupation was agricultural (1.5%). A further 7.7 per cent are clearly identifiable as working class, employed as mill or brewery workers, domestic servants, miners, or trade apprentices. Consequently, the vast majority of my witnesses were from the middle and upper classes, such as bankers, teachers, headmasters, military/naval personnel, politicians, religious ministers, and journalists. Naturally, the most literate classes are over-represented. Owing to the emphasis on middle-class people, I have highlighted those from a rural or working-class background wherever possible.

One of the main sources of these 'voices' is diaries and journals. Over 195 journals and diaries were utilized, ranging from the private diaries of King George V to the journals of Harry Miller, a schoolboy in Grimsby, Lincolnshire. Although contemporary written sources, such as diaries, tend to favour the middle classes, and elite papers tend to be male and urban, many voices can be discerned in the book—even if some are fainter than others—reflecting the variety of 1914 society presented at the last pre-war census in 1911.[25] Appendix III illustrates geographically where the diarists were located in 1914 to highlight the regional spread of sources consulted. Where location in 1914 was known, 103 witnesses were based in London, 176 were from English regions outside of the capital, and 107 were based in Scotland, Wales, or Ireland.[26] Despite the inevitable movement of some of these

---

[23] Bernard Waites, *A Class Society at War: England, 1914–1918* (Leamington Spa, 1987), 42.

[24] Paul Thompson, *The Edwardians: The Remaking of British Society* (St Albans, 1975, 1977), 296–7.

[25] For census breakdowns, see Census of England and Wales, 1911, Preliminary Report: Session 1911, Vol. LXXI, Cd. 5705; Census of Ireland, 1911, Preliminary Report: Session 1911, Vol. LXXI, Cd. 5691; Census of Scotland, 1911, Preliminary Report: Session 1911, Vol. LXXI, Cd. 5700. See also Emily Cockayne, *Hubbub: Filth, Noise and Stench in England, 1600–1770* (London, 2007), 7.

[26] Regions outside of the capital are broken down as follows: East Midlands (6); East of England (24); Jersey (1); North East (26); North West (31); Oxford/Cambridge universities (12); South East (35); South West (23); West Midlands (18).

witnesses over the course of the latter half of 1914, these statistics further indicate the geographical range of sources available for the study of public opinion at this time. Other sources included national, regional, and local newspapers; pamphlets; leaflets; magazines; committee minutes; records of universities; Working Men's Clubs; Mining Lodges and Trade Unions; memoirs; letters; photographs; police records; sermons; government records; and many more.

I supplemented contemporary sources with interviews taken retrospectively and a limited number of the witness statements of participants in the struggle for Irish independence, 1913–1921, who were interviewed in the 1950s. There are, of course, well-known pitfalls in using retrospective testimony, which may simply be 'old men drooling about their youth'.[27] There are limitations of the interviewee, the interviewer, and in the nature of interviewing itself.[28] However, these dangers do not invalidate retrospective testimony. I have controlled such sources by cross-referencing to published and unpublished official and private papers, as well as secondary literature. When nearly every interview with a First World War survivor undertaken by the Imperial War Museum Sound Archives begins with the question 'How did you feel on 4 August 1914?', these recollections are too valuable for this study to ignore.[29]

The regional and social diversity of the witness evidence used places a particular premium on localities, and makes it necessary to find the 'interface' between the local and the national level.[30] We cannot understand localities properly unless we understand the whole of which they form part; we cannot understand the nation properly unless we understand the localities that exist beneath it. A history of the United Kingdom looks very different depending on whether it was written from Belfast or Manchester, Cardiff or Aberdeen. Although it is not easy to find the interface owing to the obscurity over what is 'local' and what is 'national', earlier studies have demonstrated the benefits of this method.[31]

Equal weight is placed on 'national' and regional reactions to the outbreak of war. The sources utilized stretch from intimate personal records at the family and local level to those concerning national issues and national organizations. Where local evidence has been used to suggest patterns applicable to some larger region than the locality involved, I have attempted to corroborate this information from

[27] A. J. P. Taylor cited in F. M. L. Thompson, *The Rise of Respectable Society: A Social History of Victorian Britain, 1830–1900* (London, 1988).

[28] For more on the oral history, see Anthony Seldon and Joanna Pappworth, *By Word of Mouth: 'Elite' Oral History* (London, 1983), 16–35. See also Paul Thompson, *The Voice of the Past: Oral History* (Oxford, 1988), Paul Thompson and Natasha Burchardt, eds., *Our Common History: The Transformation of Europe* (London, 1982).

[29] The Imperial War Museum Sound Archive is the UK's foremost oral history collection relating to conflict in the 20th and 21st centuries. It holds approximately 9,200 recorded hours of First World War-related material resulting from interviews primarily conducted in the 1970s and 1980s. My thanks to Margaret Brooks from the Imperial War Museum for this information.

[30] Keith Robbins, 'Local History and the Study of National History', *The Historian* 27 (1990), 15–16.

[31] See, for example, David Fitzpatrick, *Politics and Irish Life, 1913–1921: Provincial Experience of War and Revolution* (Dublin, 1977), Pierre Purseigle, 'Beyond and Below the Nations: Towards a Comparative History of Local Communities at War', in *Uncovered Fields: Perspectives in First World War Studies*, ed. Jenny Macleod and Pierre Purseigle (Leiden, 2004).

other localities. Any negative cases to that pattern are noted. Reactions varied between town and country as well as regions. I have therefore developed an internally comparative approach. This is based on comparable areas of England and also on parts of Scotland and Wales and on Ireland, north and south. Such an approach allows me to disaggregate national opinion and take account of multiple responses—regional, English, non-English, etc. Within England I have chosen to compare Essex, Devon, Lancashire, London, and the West Midlands. Essex was selected for investigation as it was on the 'front' of the British home front in 1914. How did a rural county on the south-eastern coast react to the outbreak of a war being fought just across the Channel? Devon, another rural county, was chosen as a comparison to Essex. Were there similar fears of a German invasion on the south-western coast of Britain, more distanced from the fighting? Lancashire and the West Midlands were selected as major, though rather different, urban industrial centres of the United Kingdom in 1914. Lancashire, in 1911, had a population larger than that of London and was the centre of Britain's cotton industry. Alongside industrial Scotland and South Wales, Lancashire also provided insight into a region more divided by pre-war social class antagonism than others. London, as capital, was selected in order to provide a sense of reactions to the war at a 'national' level.

IMAGINING FUTURE WARS

In order to establish how the inhabitants of the UK responded to the outbreak of war, it is necessary to understand what the idea of war meant to them beforehand, for this was the standard against which new realities would be measured. How people thought in advance about war and who their enemy might be, helped shape their perceptions and experience when war came about, even if the realities of military conflict bore at best an indirect relationship (and at worst none at all) to what had been envisaged. Perhaps the most obvious discrepancy was in the ways the British and Irish imagined an army departing for war and the kinds of battle it might fight.

In comparison to the short-service, conscript armies of the continental powers, the British army was small, poorly organized, and isolated from Victorian society. National anxieties about its ability to defend the Empire or repel a foreign invasion came to a head during the South African War. A sense of a disaster narrowly averted triggered a tremendous upsurge of interest in the military in Edwardian Britain. The need for reform in the army was as evident as it had been after the Crimean War, and the process began during Conservative administrations. Yet, it was the Liberal-dominated governments after 1906 that carried through the reforms suggested in the three commissions on the state of the army.[32] Overseen by the Secretary of State for War, R. B. Haldane, significant improvements were made,

---

[32] Of these, the Esher Committee led to the establishment of the General Staff and the Army Council, and the Norfolk report of 1904 demanded expansion and improved training for Britain's auxiliary forces.

including the creation of the British Expeditionary Force (BEF), which could be deployed quickly to take part in an overseas conflict.[33] But the principle of expansion in the event of another big war was not among the lessons which the army digested in the aftermath of the South African War.[34] Haldane's 'citizen army'—the Territorial Force—launched in April 1908 was restricted to home defence in order to release the regular army to go overseas.

The principal voice of strategy before 1914 remained the Committee of Imperial Defence (CID), not the General Staff. The function declared in its title supports the view that Britain did not spend the years between 1900 and 1914 preparing itself for a land war on the European continent. If it had, it would have embraced the structures of the mass army, and specifically conscription.[35] The consensus of opinion rejected conscription as a solution to the United Kingdom's military problems. Military advocates of conscription, such as Douglas Haig and Lord Roberts, saw their desires for a conscript army blocked by fears of rising costs and a respect for liberal traditions. Despite constant attempts to entice the working classes, the National Service League, formed in 1902, never became a true mass movement. The Trades Union Congress and the Labour Party were consistently hostile to any form of conscription and the League remained a middle- and upper-class association. Support for conscription struggled to take root in Britain, a largely 'anti-militaristic' society that believed its island status necessitated a strong navy, not army.[36] Writings by scholars such as Norman Angell argued that militarism and expansionism did not offer any benefits because the increasingly pan-national system of economic markets made war an irrational act that would damage any combatant's 'great power' status.[37] Furthermore, it was argued that conscription would weaken the army by introducing to it poor physical types, and that there were grave dangers in training the populace to arms, as seen in revolutionary France. Some argued that conscription, together with continual preparation for war, was what held Germany back from achieving a flourishing economy.[38] The

---

[33] For more on the Haldane reforms, see John Gooch, 'Haldane and the "National Army"', in *Politicians and Defence: Studies in the Formulation of British Defence Policy 1845–1970*, ed. Ian Beckett and John Gooch (Manchester, 1981), John Gooch, *The Plans of War: The General Staff and British Military Strategy c.1900–1916* (London, 1974), John Gooch, *The Prospect of War: Studies in British Defence Policy, 1847–1942* (London, 1981), Edward Spiers, 'The Late Victorian Army, 1868–1914', in *The Oxford History of the British Army*, ed. David G. Chandler and Ian Beckett (Oxford, 1994), Edward M. Spiers, 'Between the South African War and the First World War, 1902–1914', in *Big Wars and Small Wars: The British Army and the Lessons of War in the Twentieth Century*, ed. Hew Strachan (London, 2006), Edward M. Spiers, *Haldane: An Army Reformer* (Edinburgh, 1980).

[34] Hew Strachan, 'Introduction', in *Big Wars and Small Wars: The British Army and Lessons of War in the Twentieth Century*, ed. Hew Strachan (London, 2006), 12.

[35] Hew Strachan, 'The Boer War and its Impact on the British Army, 1902–1914', in *'Ashes and Blood': The British Army in South Africa, 1795–1914*, ed. Peter B. Boyden, Alan J. Guy, and Marion Harding (London, 1999), 89, 96.

[36] Volker R. Berghahn, *Militarism: The History of an International Debate, 1861–1979* (Leamington Spa, 1981), 2.

[37] Norman Angell, *The Great Illusion: A Study of the Relation of Military Power in Nations to their Economic and Social Advantage* (London, 1910).

[38] John Gooch, 'Attitudes to War in Late Victorian and Edwardian England', in *War and Society: A Yearbook of Military History*, ed. Brian Bond and Ian Roy (London, 1977), 91.

years 1900 to 1914 witnessed a struggle between Conservatives and Liberals over the issue of military compulsion. With the anti-conscription Liberals in power from 1905 onwards, improvements to the quality and size of the British army had to be achieved via volunteerism and not compulsion.

A common spare-time occupation amongst the aristocracy and gentry was membership of the Volunteers, the Militia, and the Yeomanry. The Navy League, founded in 1895 to agitate for an increase in British naval strength, had around 100,000 members in 1914. By 1903, 2.7 per cent of all British males between the ages of 15 and 49 were in the Volunteer Force, the precursor of the Territorial Associations of the twentieth century. Owing to the high turnover of participants, over 8 per cent of the male population had undergone military training by the turn of the century, with at least 70 per cent of the Force coming from the working classes. The Volunteer movement played an important role in the social and recreational life of the country. Hundreds of thousands participated, as spectators or competitors, in rifle-shooting contests, 'sham fights', and military reviews. Volunteering was 'the spectator sport of mid-Victorian Britain'.[39]

Pre-war thinking about army organization was of limited value in one way, though the emphasis on volunteering in civic life was an important foundation for what was to come in the first half of the war. It is more prudent to consider pre-war attitudes to combat and violence as experienced and remembered in the past. Positive images of war and the army were prevalent in pre-1914 British society. The literate pre-war male generation had been brought up on the adventure stories of G. A. Henty, H. Rider Haggard, *Boy's Own* magazine, and best-selling accounts of the South African War which promoted an image of war as both honourable and glorious. Amongst the middle and upper classes a military spirit was promoted in public schools. Warfare was equated with sport, to be 'fought by gentlemen and won by the morally pure', and it was believed that team games instilled the essential qualities of a good military leader.[40] Schoolboys idolized military heroes produced by contemporary imperial and colonial wars. School cadet corps and youth organizations, which incorporated the motifs 'honour, duty, sacrifice, honesty', were established in this period. Chief among them was the Boy Scouts, an attempt by General Sir Robert Baden-Powell, a hero of the South African War, to turn 'boys from the slum . . . into worthy servants of Empire' through a range of outdoor pursuits.[41] Outside of formal education, certain currents of Edwardian thought depicted war as beneficial and desirable, linking it to popular ideas about Social

---

[39] Hugh Cunningham, *The Volunteer Force: A Social and Political History, 1859–1908* (London, 1975), 33, 46, 49–50, 68.

[40] Gerard J. De Groot, *Blighty: British Society in the Era of the Great War* (London, 1996), 31–4.

[41] Ibid. 32, 36–7. The 'Scouts' movement was phenomenally successful in the pre-war period, attracting 128,397 boys to its ranks in 1912. Although the reasons for its popularity are debatable – many working-class boys were attracted to the movement because of the opportunity to undertake outdoor pursuits rather than because of its promotion of empire—the 'Scouts' undeniably encouraged militaristic ideals and routine. See Bernard Porter, *The Absent-Minded Imperialists: Empire, Society, and Culture in Britain* (Oxford, 2004), 188, 208.

Darwinism. Under the principle of 'survival of the fittest', war was viewed as an opportunity to purify society and escape the ravages of 'luxury and sloth'.[42]

People had encountered violence, loss, and war before 1914. In the early hours of 15 April 1912, 1,522 passengers and crew drowned when RMS *Titanic* sank after hitting an iceberg on its voyage to New York. Communities in Southampton, whence it had departed, and Belfast, where it had been built, were deeply affected by this loss. On 14 October 1913 an explosion at Senghennydd colliery in Caerphilly killed 439 local men and boys. According to Bessie Davies, a local schoolgirl at the time, the outbreak of the First World War 'didn't seem such a disaster' in comparison to this tragedy.[43] These moments of localized 'rupture' were imprinted as tragic markers on the psyche of many ordinary people who used them as points of reference during the opening phases of the war in 1914. Prior to these two disasters, the British population had been exposed to the modern realities of warfare. The South African War had humiliated Britain despite costing three times more than the Crimean War, and involving four times as many troops.[44] People had watched their loved ones depart for war and other men return home wounded. The shock effects of the South African War had been magnified at home because it was a major media war with over seventy reporters at the front by early 1900.[45] It was also a highly political, contentious, and publically debated conflict. Public and political opposition amongst radical liberals had arisen over government policies during the war, including the use of concentration camps for Boer refugees and prisoners. The reportage of the Balkan Wars of 1912–1913 introduced the idea of modern warfare encompassing mass armies, machines, high casualties, atrocities, and entire civilian populations.

Developments in war had also led to attempts to regulate it. War increasingly came to be considered as a moral phenomenon and one in which ethical issues were of considerable importance.[46] The Hague Conventions were negotiated at the First and Second Peace Conferences in the Netherlands in 1899 and 1907 respectively, and along with the Geneva Conventions, were among the first formal statements of the laws of war and war crimes. The UK was signatory to both sets of international legislation. Although by no means universal, there was an understanding that war could either be prevented through pacific settlement or, if it did break out, be regulated to protect the innocent. Such a moral repugnance at war was especially strong amongst British Liberals and Labour supporters.

Since Crimea, the British army's major experience of war had been in the colonies, South Africa included. Characterized by incompetence at all levels in

---

[42] Glenn R. Wilkinson, '"The Blessings of War": The Depiction of Military Force in Edwardian Newspapers', *Journal of Contemporary History* 33 (1998), 98, 115. The phrase 'survival of the fittest' was first coined by the English polymath Herbert Spencer (1820–1903) in *Principles of Biology* (1864) in response to Darwin's *On the Origins of the Species* (1859).

[43] IWM, SA: 828, Reel 2 (1974).

[44] Iain Smith, *The Origins of the South African War, 1899–1902* (London, 1996), 1.

[45] Stephen Badsey, 'The Boer War as a Media War', in *The Boer War: Army, Nation and Empire*, ed. Peter Dennis and Jeffrey Guy (Canberra, 2000).

[46] Gooch, 'Attitudes to War in Late Victorian and Edwardian England', 93.

the early stages and tainted by scandal and brutality in the latter part, the South African conflict served as a wake-up call to the British military. The British drew most of their lessons from the opening period of conventional warfare, up until late summer 1900, with emphasis on mounted actions and gritty sieges heroic in a decidedly nineteenth-century manner, before it descended into the long and controversial guerrilla phase that eventually resulted in a British victory. In short, it was not the type of industrial war that was going to be experienced in 1914 and after. Post-South African War, the general opinion of the army was that frontal attacks were dangerous and costly, and should be avoided if possible. If one had to be made, the methods pioneered in Natal should be used, with close cooperation of infantry and artillery.[47]

The Russo-Japanese War (1904–5) provided further lessons for the British military, not least the incredible impact of fire power. Britain was fascinated with the war, owing as much to visceral imperialist sentiments as to a shared alliance with Japan, and the British armed forces made a greater effort to observe and to learn from the conflict than they had with any other foreign military campaign. The war seemed to confirm to the British much of what had been learned in the South African War. Frontal attacks were extremely costly and entrenchment offered excellent protection from artillery, making preparatory bombardments ineffective. Cover and concealment were crucially important. However, the aggressive Japanese won the war through a series of violent and bloody frontal attacks against Russian trenches. Continental opinion, particularly German and French, trumpeted this success as proof that the South African War lessons had been wrong, and that sheer willpower alone could break through trenches and fortresses, even if the cost was high.[48]

The experience of war in the colonies, and the observation of the Russo-Japanese conflict provided some valuable practical lessons for the British army and important reforms were implemented, despite restricted budgets and the predominance of the navy in British defence thinking. However, these improvements ensured that Britain would be better prepared for a future imperial, rather than continental, conflict.[49] The British still lacked a coherent military 'doctrine' on which to hang a future war and to base both training and tactics.[50] The British army could not anticipate with any accuracy against whom it might next fight or where it might next be deployed: the next war could be on home soil defending against an

---

[47] Lieutenant-General Frank Hickling, 'Introduction', in *The Boer War: Army, Nation and Empire*, ed. Peter Dennis and Jeffrey Grey (Canberra, 2000). See also Bill Nasson, *The South African War, 1899–1902* (London, 1999). Special thanks to Spencer Jones for his assistance in clarifying my understanding of the nature and military consequences of the South African War. See Spencer Jones, 'The Influence of the Boer War (1899–1902) on the Tactical Development of the Regular British Army 1902–1914' (PhD, University of Wolverhampton, 2009).

[48] Olivier Cosson, 'Les expériences de guerre du début du siècle: Guerre des Boers, guerre de Mandchourie, guerres des Balkans', in *Encyclopédie critique de la Grande Guerre, histoire et culture*, ed. Stéphane Audoin-Rouzeau and Jean-Jacques Becker (Paris, 2004).

[49] Spiers, 'Between the South African War and the First World War, 1902–1914', 21–2, 25.

[50] Shelford Bidwell and Dominick Graham, *Fire-Power: British Army Weapons and Theories of War 1904–1945* (London, 1982), 2.

invasion, on the continent, and/or in the colonies.[51] A lack of doctrine was due, in part, to a lack of introspection. The British, having gone from one major European war to another via a small war—or wars—on the way, had not had any breathing space to reflect, in contrast to their continental rivals. But for many in the British military, doctrine was to be resisted as it could act as a straitjacket.[52] The British army, therefore, did not respond to the rapidly increasing effectiveness of modern fire power by doggedly subscribing to the 'cult of the offensive' in the same way as their French and German counterparts.[53] The British interpretation of the 'offensive à outrance' was mixed. It certainly made some headway amongst higher levels of the army, but at a lower level was treated more circumspectly. On a doctrinal level, the South African conflict created few new ideas, and instead tended to reinforce existing concepts. The British retained their somewhat cautious and pragmatic approach to tactics, although at higher levels it was fashionable to ape continental thought. Additionally, a respect for fire power remained at brigade level and below. Training emphasized concealment, rapid skirmish movements, and rifle accuracy.[54] For those military (or civil) leaders who had contemplated the possibility of Britain's involvement in a continental war, few imagined that it would become a 'total' war of millions lasting over four years. Instead commanders and staffs of the British army believed that a future war would consist of a decisive opening battle to be fought four or five weeks after mobilization.[55]

Although they shocked contemporary opinion, recent wars also seemed remote. Given the naval competition with Germany, many assumed the key point in a future war would be a new Trafalgar.[56] Those who did contemplate a large land battle tended to think of it in Napoleonic terms: one decisive battle, admittedly bloody, but brief—a new Waterloo. Whilst images of Britain's future war varied depending on the individual, and these images often conflicted with each other, it would be fair to suggest that most people in Britain, regardless of rank or position, were anxious. The South African War had removed the complacency bred during the long years of peace and led to a loss in national self-confidence.[57] The expectation of war was increasingly a part of Edwardian consciousness.[58]

---

[51] Hew Strachan, *From Waterloo to Balaclava: Tactics, Technology, and the British Army, 1815–1854* (Cambridge, 1985), viii–ix.

[52] Strachan, 'Introduction', 1–4.

[53] As argued by Tim Travers, *The Killing Ground: The British Army, the Western Front and the Emergence of Modern Warfare 1900–1918* (Barnsley, 1987). For more on the 'cult of the offensive' debate, see Brian Bond, 'Judgement in Military History', *The RUSI Journal* 134 (1989), Antulio J. Echevarria II, 'The "Cult of the Offensive" Revisited: Confronting Technological Change Before the Great War', *Journal of Strategic Studies* 25 (2002), Michael Howard, 'Men Against Fire: The Doctrine of the Offensive in 1914', in *Makers of Modern Strategy: From Machiavelli to the Nuclear Age*, ed. Peter Paret (Oxford, 1986).

[54] Bidwell and Graham, *Fire-Power: British Army Weapons and Theories of War 1904–1945*. See also Jones, 'The influence of the Boer War (1899–1902) on the Tactical Development of the Regular British Army 1902–1914'.

[55] Bidwell and Graham, *Fire-Power: British Army Weapons and Theories of War 1904–1945*, 57, Bond, 'Judgement in Military History', 69.

[56] Jan Rueger, *The Great Naval Game: Britain and Germany in the Age of Empire* (Cambridge, 2007).

[57] Strachan, 'The Boer War and its Impact on the British Army, 1902–1914', 97.

[58] Samuel Hynes, *The Edwardian Turn of Mind* (Princeton, 1968), 53.

If Britain were to go to war, who did Edwardians believe would be their friends and enemies? Enemies obviously altered to some extent in relation to the fluidity of international alliances, and it was precisely the uncertainty about where the main enemy lay which exacerbated the sense of national insecurity. However, in the years immediately before 1914 the British, whether they admired or disapproved of their former enemy, no longer felt threatened by France.[59] In April 1904 Britain and France formalized their new 'entente' in a series of agreements. Beyond the immediate concerns of colonial expansion addressed by the agreement, the signing of the Entente Cordiale marked the end of centuries of intermittent conflict between the two nations, although both remained mutually suspicious. Since the 1830s the British had grown increasingly wary of Russian power in Eastern Europe and Central Asia, and it remained a significant long-term threat to British interests in the twenty years before the First World War.

However, international events between 1902 and 1911 began to identify Germany as Britain's potential future enemy. Although Anglo-German antagonism was fairly recent, it was particularly intense owing to the direct challenge to Britain's principal source of security, naval supremacy, and also to German reluctance to reach a settlement over spheres of colonial influence.[60] Many contemporaries believed that Germany was building a short-range battle fleet for no other reason than to scare the British whose national security relied on the primacy of the Royal Navy. The Entente with France arose, in part, because Germany would not do a Japanese-style deal with the British over colonies and because of its threat to France. In March 1905 the Germans interfered with the Anglo-French deal over Morocco in an attempt to show that nothing that affected Germany's interests could be done without its prior approval. As a result, Britain was pushed closer to its arch-rival Russia. In 1906, the new Foreign Secretary, Sir Edward Grey, began negotiations with Russia, and on 31 August 1907 the Anglo-Russian Convention was signed. Whilst this agreement carried with it no guarantees, the logic surrounding its signing was clear. Germany was becoming of increasing significance to British foreign policy. In part, it indicated Britain's need to cooperate with former enemies in order to prevent Germany from dominating in Europe.[61]

On 1 July 1911 Germany announced that it had sent a gunboat to the port of Agadir on the south coast of Morocco, ostensibly to 'protect' German residents. Rather than accept Germany's assertion that the matter was between Germany and France alone, Lloyd George made a vehement speech to bankers and merchants of the City of London at the Mansion House on 21 July, warning against further German expansion.[62] The speech was significant. Although war between Germany and Britain was not seen as inevitable it did indicate a deterioration of relations

---

[59] Robert and Isabelle Tombs, *That Sweet Enemy: The French and the British from the Sun King to the Present* (London, 2006), 460.

[60] Keith Neilson, *Britain and the Last Tsar: British Policy and Russia 1894–1917* (Oxford, 1995), xiii. See also Paul M. Kennedy, *The Rise of Anglo-German Antagonism 1860–1914* (London, 1980).

[61] David French, 'Allies, Rivals and Enemies: British Strategy and War Aims during the First World War', in *Britain and the First World War*, ed. John Turner (London, 1988), 23.

[62] *The Times*, 22 July 1911, 9.

between the two countries and the belief amongst certain Liberals that Germany had to be stood up to. Moreover, the speech highlighted tensions amongst Liberals about their foreign policy that would arise again in June to August 1914. Lloyd George was a leading radical and former 'pro-Boer' and his speech went against the tide of general Liberal opinion, which, on the whole, wanted to appease Germany and discard any commitment to France.

Fear at the apparent growing menace of Germany was inexorable, fed in particular by the naval race in which Britain sought to maintain its pre-eminence in the new, heavily armed Dreadnought class of battleship over the strong challenge from Germany.[63] This fear was heightened by Liberal attempts to economize; when, in 1909, it was suddenly realized that the Germans were going to be building ten Dreadnoughts to Britain's eight, panic ensued, especially palpable in 'military' towns such as Portsmouth. A by-product of the naval race was a new apocalyptic vision, this time entailing a failure of the Royal Navy to maintain its 'Command of the Sea' and a subsequent occupation of Britain by Prussian 'huns' who specialized in violating and murdering defenceless women.[64] Fear was also fuelled by alarmist speeches by Lord Roberts and his consorts in the National Service League. By 1906, pressure for a re-examination of the invasion issue led to an investigation by the CID. After sixteen meetings between 27 November 1907 and 28 July 1908, a final report and analysis was presented to the Cabinet on 22 October 1908. It concluded that naval supremacy had to be maintained, whilst two of the six BEF divisions would stay at home to repel any enemy attack. A final pre-war invasion alarm occurred in 1913 and the resultant CID report, in essence, reaffirmed the decision of the 1908 hearings.[65]

Although these discussions and investigations failed to achieve the propagandists' objective of enforcing conscription, they had a significant impact on British popular imagination. Parallel to the discussions about the potential for invasion within government circles, such scares 'captured press headlines, engendered graphic and harrowing works of fiction, and induced a state of near paranoia concerning the vulnerability of Britain's defensive preparations'.[66] One word could send 'a *frisson* of terror coursing down the middle-class spine—invasion'.[67] Since the mid-nineteenth century there had been an increasing awareness of the vulnerability of Britain to attack from across the Channel. The enemies in fiction reflected, to some extent, British foreign relations. Three major invasion panics in 1847–48, 1851–53, and 1859–61 were inspired by the fear of France, and were accompanied

---

[63] Arthur J. Marder, *From the Dreadnought to Scapa Flow: The Royal Navy in the Fisher Era, 1904–1919. The Road to War 1904–1914*, 5 vols., vol. 1 (Oxford, 1961).

[64] George Tomkyns Chesney, *The Battle of Dorking: Reminiscences of a Volunteer* (Edinburgh, 1871).

[65] Michael W. Ryan, 'The Invasion Controversy of 1906–1908: Lieutenant-Colonel Charles à Court Repington and British Perceptions of the German Menace', *Military Affairs* 44 (1980), 8. See also Rueger, *The Great Naval Game: Britain and Germany in the Age of Empire*.

[66] Ryan, 'The Invasion Controversy of 1906–1908: Lieutenant-Colonel Charles à Court Repington and British Perceptions of the German Menace', 8.

[67] Gooch, *The Prospect of War: Studies in British Defence Policy, 1847–1942*, 36.

by a flood of popular alarmist publications. But it was an article by Sir George Chesney in *Blackwood's Magazine* in May 1871 entitled 'The Battle of Dorking' that swopped one enemy for another and truly placed the possibility of a *German* invasion in the minds of contemporaries. It became a book, and caused such dismay amongst an already nervous public that Gladstone felt it necessary to make a speech against its alarmism. The story foretold the destruction of the Channel Fleet by a secret device, and the subsequent landing of 200,000 Prussians. The British forces were easily defeated, owing to antiquated equipment and obsolete tactics.

Over the next thirty years, this precedent was imitated by a myriad of writers, its popularity enhanced by the fact that invasion had now entered official discourse, with debates ranging from the construction of the Channel Tunnel in 1882–3 to the newspaper magnate Alfred Harmsworth's electoral campaign based on 'The Siege of Portsmouth' in 1895.[68] Many of the earlier accounts still presented the French as the putative foreign oppressor, but from the turn of the century the needle of anxiety switched direction to Germany. In *Riddle of the Sands*, published in 1903, Erskine Childers devised the ideal myth in which to convey the anxieties of a nation beginning to be alarmed about a menace from overseas. The espionage novel revealed in a stage-by-stage account the discovery of German plans to invade England.[69] The story seemed as if it ought to be true; and therefore caused a sensation when it came out, selling several hundred thousand copies.[70]

Riddle of the Sands was swiftly followed by William Le Queux's *The Invasion of 1910*, published in serial form in the *Daily Mail* in 1905. The story described a German invasion of the British Isles where the 'Uhlans' (or German cavalry) wreaked havoc in every town from Hull and York to Southend-on-Sea.[71] To boost sales, Alfred Harmsworth, now Lord Northcliffe, placed full-page advertisements in London dailies and in the larger provincial newspapers showing a map of the district the Germans were to be invading the next day in the *Daily Mail*. Another stunt was to send sandwich-men through London, dressed in Prussian-blue uniforms and spiked helmets, carrying notices of the Le Queux serial. The book was published in 1906, translated into twenty-seven different languages, and sold over one million copies.[72]

Other writers joined in the imaginary war against Germany; and most of them accepted the convention of an invasion as the basis of their arguments in favour of naval, military, or political measures. In Guy du Maurier's successful play, *An Englishman's Home*, the invaders were shown in the act of conquering the British Isles; in Saki's *When William Came*, the end-stage of the operation could be

[68] I. F. Clarke, *The Tale of the Future from the Beginning to the Present Day: A Check-list of those satires, ideal states, imaginary wars and invasions, political warnings and forecasts, interplanetary voyages and scientific romances—all located in an imaginary future period—that have been published in the United Kingdom between 1644 and 1960* (London, 1961), 24.

[69] Erskine Childers, *The Riddle of the Sands* (London, 1903).

[70] I. F. Clarke, 'The Shape of Wars to Come', *History Today* 15 (1965), 111.

[71] William Le Queux, *The Invasion of 1910 with a full account of the Siege of London* (London, 1906).

[72] Samuel R. Williamson, *The Politics of Grand Strategy: Britain and France Prepare for War, 1904–1914* (Cambridge, Massachusetts, 1969), 97.

observed in the detailed account of life under enemy rule in Hohenzollern Britain.[73] Such writings obviously caused a reaction in Germany; one German writer observed that the British were 'once more troubled by the idea of invasion— naturally by German armies only. German espionage is almost a standard feature of one section of the press.'[74]

Alarmist as these stories were, and manipulative in their desire to promote a political manifesto and boost sales, there can be no doubt that they expressed the fears of many Edwardians. The growth of German imperialism, the disputes with France and later with Germany, and the decision to abandon the traditional policy of isolation were all factors that helped to encourage an expectation of war in Britain. What is perhaps most indicative of pre-1914 attitudes is the fact that the possibility of invasion was difficult to ridicule. For example P. G. Wodehouse's story, *The Swoop! Or, how Clarence saved England*, was a failure. Wodehouse attempted to subvert the seriousness of a German invasion with comedy, in which the news of a German landing reaches a complacent nation in the *Stop Press* column of the newspapers and the British ignore the charging infantry, only noticing them in order to complain about the crowds. This farcical tale was unable to deflate the stories about the coming German invasion and the rumours of spies active throughout the country.

However, traditional scholarly focus on the rise of Anglo-German antagonism prior to the Great War has largely overshadowed the extent of Anglo-German connections and mutual cooperation. Ironically, if there were two European countries that had a sense of allegiance and cultural affiliation in the years immediately preceding the outbreak of war, it was Britain and Germany.[75] They were huge trading partners; British Liberals admired German efficiency; the British Left envied the massive organization of its Social Democrats and trade unions; and British intellectuals admired German universities. Germany's reputation in the British press in the pre-war period was not as negative as has often been claimed since 1914.[76] There is no question that an Anglo-German antagonism arose in the first decade of the twentieth century, but the years 1911–1914 saw more attempts to improve Anglo-German relations than further exacerbations of the rivalry.[77] Although Lord Haldane, the British war minister, failed in his mission to Berlin in February 1912 to resolve Anglo-German antagonism after the Agadir crisis, the very fact it was undertaken indicates that Britain and Germany hoped that at least a détente was possible. Following the Haldane Mission, the naval arms race virtually disappeared as a point of contention between Britain and Germany, although there was no formal agreement on naval armaments. Britain and Germany cooperated during the Balkan crises of 1912–1913 and reached mutually beneficial agreements

[73] Clarke, 'The Shape of Wars to Come', 111. The Hohenzollerns were the rulers of Germany.
[74] Ibid. 114.
[75] Dominik Geppert and Robert Gerwarth, 'Introduction', in *Wilhelmine Germany and Edwardian Britain: Essays on Cultural Affinity*, ed. Dominik Geppert and Robert Gerwarth (Oxford, 2008), 3.
[76] Martin Schramm, *Das Deutschlandbild in der britischen Presse, 1912–1919* (Berlin, 2007).
[77] Sean M. Lynn-Jones, 'Détente and Deterrence: Anglo-German Relations, 1911–1914', *International Security* 11 (1986), 124.

over the Portuguese colonies and the Baghdad railway in August 1913 and June 1914 respectively. This improvement in relations produced the false belief in both Britain and Germany that the July 1914 crisis could be resolved through Anglo-German cooperation and, furthermore, exacerbated the sense of surprise and shock at the outbreak of war in August.

1

Outbreak of War, July to August

Retrospectively, the summer of 1914 was portrayed as the culmination of the long Edwardian idyll that stood in contrast to the rupture and disharmony brought by the war.[1] In reality, the pre-war period was one of domestic unrest and mounting anxiety for the authorities. The challenges to authority posed by the labour movement, suffragettes, Ulster Unionists, and Irish Nationalists were threatening to make Britain ungovernable. This was the setting over which the war clouds gathered.

The Labour Party, formed in 1900, was increasing in power in the period before 1914 and had returned forty-two MPs at the December 1910 general election.[2] Trade unionism had long been a major economic and social force, and by 1914 the Trades Union Congress had 2.5 million members. With the organization of unskilled and general labourers, and with increased cost of living before the war, industrial unrest became particularly widespread and militant, peaking in 1912–1913. Several serious clashes took place between protestors, the police, and troops. Brigadier Vaizey, a schoolboy in 1914, recalled in 1978 how his father's head-horseman on their Tilbury Hall estate in Tilbury-juxta-Clare, Essex, believed the agricultural labour strike in nearby Ridgewell had triggered the European war.[3]

To upper-class Edwardian men, the campaigns of the suffragettes were as alarming as those of Labour in pre-war British society. Although by 1909 most suffragettes were members of the National Union of Women's Suffrage Societies (NUWSS)—the constitutional movement led by Millicent Fawcett—it was the militant organization, the Women's Social and Political Union (WSPU) founded by Emmeline and Christabel Pankhurst, that was attracting the most attention.[4] To keep the cause in the public eye and to attract new members, the tactics of the WSPU had become increasingly shocking. Rough treatment of suffragettes by both the police and the public led them to resort to attacks on property, including smashing the windows of West End clubs and acts of arson.

---

[1] Marwick, *The Deluge: British Society and the First World War* (London, 1965), 26. See also G. Dangerfield, *The Strange Death of Liberal England* (London, 1935, 1997), L. P. Hartley, *The Go-Between* (London, 1953).

[2] For more detail see Andrew Thorpe, *A History of the British Labour Party*, 3rd ed. (Basingstoke, 2008).

[3] ERO: SA 24/1002/1 (1978).

[4] Membership of the NUWSS exceeded 50,000 in 1914. See Martin Pugh, *State and Society: British Political and Social History 1870–1992* (London, 1994), 135.

However, the most serious challenge to parliamentary government in the period prior to the outbreak of war came from Ireland. In April 1912 the third Home Rule Bill began its passage through Westminster, its ultimate aim to establish a Dublin parliament for the whole of Ireland. By May 1914 it had been passed three times as required by the recently ratified Parliament Act of 1911. However, both the Unionists and the Conservatives used this two-year hiatus to build up resistance in Ireland. The dominant elite in Ulster—the Protestant minority led by Captain James Craig and Sir Edward Carson—feared a loss of power and status. Their campaign began with a declaration of adherence to the Union—the Ulster Solemn League and Covenant—to which 250,000 people put their signatures on 28 September 1912. They also established the Ulster Volunteer Force (UVF) of some 90,000 men, and embarked upon a series of illegal gun importations. The Ulster Unionists had the support of the leader of the opposition Conservative Party, Andrew Bonar Law, who pledged to support the Ulstermen even if they resorted to violence. A number of gun-running incidents in January 1914 forced the government to take the Ulster pledge more seriously. As a response to the establishment of the UVF, the Irish Nationalists formed their own Volunteer army—the Irish National Volunteers (INV). The emergence of these private armies raised the prospect that civil war would erupt if a Dublin parliament was set up. The situation was compounded by the Curragh incident in March when around fifty-seven British officers, stationed in Ireland, pledged they would resign rather than enforce the Home Rule policy in Ireland. This sent the ominous message that Westminster could not rely on the army to carry out its orders. King George V warned on 21 July that 'the cry of civil war is on the lips of the most responsible and sober-minded of my people'.[5] Five days later, on 26 July, a detachment of the King's Own Scottish Borderers fired on a crowd of Dublin civilians on Bachelor's Walk—suspected of being INV gun-runners—killing four and wounding many others. This sparked outrage in Ireland and was relayed to people in Britain under frightening, but accurate, headlines like 'Slaughter in Ireland'[6] and 'Fighting in Dublin'.[7] Winifred Tower, aged 20 and living with her parents on the Isle of Wight, believed this was the 'first blood of the civil war'.[8] The British government, in the summer of 1914, faced serious domestic discontent.

THE GATHERING STORM: 23 JULY – 4 AUGUST

Nonetheless, if domestic issues dominated, the British people were becoming increasingly anxious about the possibility of a future war prior to August 1914. However, war was scarcely visualized as an immediate contingency, especially when

[5] Cited in J. F. V. Keiger, 'Britain's "Union Sacrée" in 1914', in *Les sociétiés européennes et la guerre de 1914–1918*, ed. Jean-Jacques Becker and Stéphane Audoin-Rouzeau (Nanterre, 1990), 40.
[6] *Manchester Evening News*, 27 July 1914, 3.
[7] *Devon and Exeter Gazette*, 27 July 1914, 6.
[8] IWM, Docs: Tower, Miss W.L.B: P472, 27 July 1914.

we discount the benefit of hindsight. Any awareness of a possible 'future' war was accompanied by a sense that the *current* crisis would pass, just like previous altercations such as the Agadir crisis in 1911 and the recent Balkan crises. F. A. Robinson, a businessman from Cobham in Surrey, recalled that by late July the 'man in the street had been threatened with war so often that he was as optimistic as ever, and went about his daily work little dreaming what was in store'.[9] Throughout most of July, the European situation received little serious attention; the assassination of Archduke Franz Ferdinand, heir to the Austro-Hungarian throne, on 28 June 1914 by Bosnian-Serb nationalists in Sarajevo had resulted in a few editorials tracing the genealogy of the Hapsburgs and their tendency to meet with violent ends. Many British people viewed Austro-Serbian tensions as an internal affair of the Austro-Hungarian Empire. Harry A. Siepman, a London resident in 1914, had no idea where Sarajevo was, and thus doubted the necessity of Britain's involvement in a crisis stemming from that city.[10] The issue of Austro-Serbian relations paled in significance compared with the head-on clash between the Liberals and the Conservatives over Ireland.[11] Like Mr Britling, the character in H. G. Wells' 1916 novel, many ordinary people were 'mightily concerned about the conflict in Ireland, and almost deliberately negligent of the possibility of a war with Germany'.[12] It was not until 22 July—more than three weeks after the Sarajevo assassinations—that the possibility of a European political crisis was first mentioned as a potential source of economic instability in the financial pages of *The Times*.[13]

As a consequence, whilst diplomatically the temperature had been rising, especially since the evening of 23 July when Austria-Hungary had delivered its forty-eight hour ultimatum to Serbia, it was not until four days later that the seriousness of the situation became apparent to the British public. On 27 July *The Times* published the qualified acceptance of the Austrian ultimatum by Serbia on the evening of Saturday 25 July and, crucially, Austria-Hungary's immediate dismissal of the conciliatory Serbian response. The crisis led with the frightening headline 'Peace In The Balance'.[14] It was at this point that the political crisis in Ireland was eclipsed by the more serious conflict abroad. Christopher Addison, Liberal MP for Hoxton, Shoreditch, recorded in his diary on 27 July how 'everything, even Ireland . . . is now overshadowed by this Austro-Servian affair and the horrible fear of European complications'.[15] That day Edmund Gosse, librarian to the House of Lords, spoke with the Lord Chancellor, R. B. Haldane:

---

[9] IWM, Docs: Robinson, F. A: P401, 31 July 1914.
[10] Liddle: GS 1469: Harry A. Siepman (n.d.).
[11] D. C. Watt, 'British Reactions to the Assassination in Sarajevo', *European Studies Review* 1 (1971), 234.
[12] H. G. Wells, *Mr Britling Sees It Through* (Leeds, 1916, 1969), 121.
[13] Niall Ferguson, 'Political Risk and the International Bond Market between the 1848 Revolution and the Outbreak of the First World War', *Economic History Review* LIX (2006), 98.
[14] *The Times*, 27 July 1914, 8.
[15] Christopher Addison, *Four and a Half Years: A Personal Diary from June 1914 to January 1919*, vol. 1 (London, 1934).

[Haldane] said that Grey [the Foreign Secretary] was very anxious, and that he had received a telegram to announce the Kaiser's lightning return to Berlin. 'He can only be coming,' Haldane said, 'to declare war with somebody, certainly Russia, probably France, possibly us.' I said 'Then you think we can't keep out of it?' He answered 'Oh! I don't say that, but the position is suddenly very serious.'[16]

The Kaiser had indeed arrived back in Potsdam on 28 July, the day that Austria-Hungary declared war on Serbia. As the Hungarian ships on the Danube proceeded to bombard Belgrade, the German government and army fended off all attempts at mediation by the Entente powers. These rapid developments divided the British Cabinet. While Grey took the lead in seeking a diplomatic solution to the crisis in the form of a Four-Power Conference between France, Germany, Britain, and Italy, other Cabinet members threatened to resign if Britain went to war. Eyre Crowe, working in the Foreign Office and a strong proponent of anti-German policy, was frustrated by the indecision surrounding him.[17] This was compounded by the fact that only a handful of newspapers were explicit in their opinions. The Liberal *Daily News* and *Manchester Guardian* ran strong anti-war campaigns up until 4 August, as did the Socialist press such as the *Labour Leader* and the Glasgow *Forward*. Lord Northcliffe's papers, *The Times* and the *Daily Mail*, were equally anti-German from early in the crisis. However, the polemics of both sides were unrepresentative as much of the provincial press, both Liberal and Unionist, initially expressed a firm preference for neutrality. Paul Cambon, the French Ambassador in London, feared that the press, along with Radical MPs, would steer the British government away from a decision to intervene.[18]

At this point, and right up until the declaration of war on Germany on 4 August, many people believed that Britain should remain neutral. On 2 August, in a letter to the Scottish art critic Dugald MacColl, the English painter William Rothenstein, maintained that Britain had no reason to be involved in what he perceived was somebody else's argument.[19] Most arguments against British intervention were economic. At the root of Liberal anti-war ethos was the notion of free trade, which the war was anticipated to destroy. The grandfather of the historian A. J. P. Taylor, a prominent Lancashire tradesman, 'opposed the War, as he had opposed the Boer War that went before it. "Can't they see that every time they kill a German they kill a customer?" he moaned'.[20] Anti-war MPs John Morley and John Simon used financial arguments to support their stance, arguing:

that the Government should make an immediate declaration that in *no circumstances* would Great Britain be involved in war. They pleaded that their view was shared by a large and important body of opinion—'the great industrial centres of the North of

---

[16] BL: Ashley 5738, 27 July 1914.
[17] MPP Bodleian: Sir Eyre Crowe: MSS Eng e.3020, folios 9–10, 5 August 1914.
[18] Paul Cambon, *Correspondance 1870–1924: Tome Troisième (1912–1924)* (Paris, 1946), 71–3.
[19] University of Glasgow, Special Collections: Dugald Sutherland MacColl: Ms MacColl R218, 2 August 1914.
[20] Adam Sisman, *A. J. P. Taylor: A Biography* (London, 1994), 17. See also A. J. P. Taylor, *The Trouble Makers: Dissent Over Foreign Policy, 1792–1939* (London, 1993).

England . . . the banking and commercial authorities in London, including the heads of the Bank of England . . . ' all were 'adverse to any steps which might be construed into a resolve to take sides in the present dispute'.[21]

People feared war in areas where it would cause the most economic dislocation, highlighting the importance of locality in framing people's reactions to war. The Liberal press in Yorkshire were unanimously against the war owing to the negative economic impact it would have in the region. In Huddersfield people were anxious about the future of the local woollen industry. The fear in Grimsby, a town built around its fishing trade, was that a war between the German and British navies would destroy the local economy.[22]

For many people, and not just Liberal and Labour activists, the conflict on the continent was not 'Britain's fight' and they campaigned for Britain to remain neutral. Percy Woodhouse, Vice-Chairman of the Manchester Conservative and Unionist Association, urged the government not to break Britain's policy of neutrality, and solicited local representatives and dignitaries, such as Lord Derby (architect of the Pals Battalions scheme), reminding them that the country was under no obligation to take sides in the war.[23] On 2 August William George, a solicitor in Criccieth, Gwynedd, pleaded with his brother, David Lloyd George, to keep the country out of the conflict for similar reasons.[24] For others, Britain should remain neutral for strategic reasons. Enemies and allies were very fluid concepts in July and early August 1914, and at first Serbia was perceived as the key trouble-maker on the continent. In a private meeting with the Archbishop of Canterbury on 31 July the Prime Minister, H. H. Asquith, revealed his feelings about Serbia. To him it was a 'wild little State . . . for which nobody has a good word, so badly has it behaved' and that it 'deserved a thorough thrashing'.[25] Feelings of animosity amongst local people in Leicester to the Serbians 'causing trouble' on the continent were epitomized by a poster outside a newsagent's shop entitled 'To Hell With Serbia', a slogan that originated in Horatio Bottomley's *John Bull*.[26] The *Cambridge Daily News* (a Liberal paper) believed that 'no one will waste any tears over the castigation of a nation of regicides and cut-throats like the Servians'.[27] As late as July 1914, sympathy was expressed towards Germany (Britain's future enemy) and suspicion and antipathy towards Russia (its future ally). Whilst this was due to long-held animosity between the two nations, for some this was specifically because of race: Britain was more 'naturally' allied to Germany than the Slavs. On 1 August

---

[21] A. J. A. Morris, *Radicalism Against War, 1906–1914: The Advocacy of Peace and Retrenchment* (London, 1972), 394.

[22] *Grimsby Daily Telegraph*, 3 August 1914.

[23] LRO: 920 DER (17) 17/1, 4 August 1914.

[24] NLW: David Lloyd George: Mss 22517C, ff. 56–7, 2 August 1914.

[25] Lambeth Palace: Davidson Papers: British Conduct of the War: Volume 13 [Private papers], ff. 9–11, 31 July 1914.

[26] ROLLR: 1078, LO/424/375, Charles Albert Green (1987) and A. J. P. Taylor, '1914: Events in Britain', *The Listener* LXXII (1964), 80.

[27] *Cambridge Daily News*, 28 July 1914.

a group of academics from Oxford, Cambridge, and Aberdeen circulated a petition stating:

> We regard Germany as a nation leading the way in the Arts and Sciences, and we have all learnt and are learning from German scholars. War upon her in the interest of Servia and Russia will be a sin against civilisation.[28]

Anti-war sentiment was also expressed in letters to newspapers advocating neutrality, much of it strongly anti-Russian and often with an extremely powerful vision of war as a catastrophe for civilization.[29] King George V noted in his diary on 1 August how 'at this moment public opinion here is dead against us joining in the war'.[30] Politically, many people could not reconcile a Liberal government with war, particularly after Liberal opposition to the South African War. Richard Durning Holt, Liberal MP for Hexham, found it 'impossible to believe that a Liberal Government can be guilty of the crime of dragging us into this conflict in which we are in no way interested'.[31] Up until early August, the British Cabinet was bitterly divided over the European crisis, with most members strongly supporting neutrality in opposition to Grey and Asquith. Charles Hobhouse, Liberal MP for Bristol East, summarized the deep divisions and uncertainties within the Cabinet between Thursday, 30 July and Sunday, 2 August:

> At first [Lloyd George] was very strongly anti-German . . . but as the Liberal papers were very anti-war, he veered round and became peaceful. Churchill was of course for any enterprise which gave him a chance of displaying the Navy . . . McKenna[32] was for war if Belgian territory was violated, but against the dispatch of an expeditionary force. Harcourt[33], Beauchamp[34] and Simon[35] were for unconditional peace. The P.M., Haldane[36] and I for war if there was even a merely technical breach of the Belgium treaty. Pease[37] and Runciman[38] were strongly against war but not for unconditional neutrality. Burns[39] . . . was saying that this meant either unconditional neutrality or (leaning over the table shaking his clenched fists) war with both hands, naval and military.[40]

On Tuesday, 28 July Winston Churchill ordered the Royal Navy to Scapa Flow and its other war stations. The following day, Austria-Hungary's declaration of war against Serbia was published in *The Times*. All British naval, military, and colonial stations were warned that war was possible. Simultaneously, the London market

---

[28] *The Times*, 1 August 1914, 6.
[29] Gregory, 'British "War Enthusiasm" in 1914: A Reassessment', in *Evidence, History and the Great War: Historians and the Impact of 1914–18*, ed. Gail Braybon (Oxford, 2003), 74.
[30] Royal Archives, Windsor Castle: RA GV/PRIV/GVD/1914: 1 August.
[31] LRO: Durning Holt Papers: 920 DUR/1/10, 2 August 1914.
[32] Reginald McKenna, Liberal MP for North Monmouthshire.
[33] Lewis Harcourt, Secretary of State for the Colonies and Liberal MP for Rossendale.
[34] Lord Beauchamp (William Lygon), First Commissioner of Works.
[35] Sir John Simon, Attorney General and Liberal MP for Walthamstow.
[36] R. B. Haldane, Lord Chancellor and Liberal MP for East Lothian.
[37] Joseph Pease, President of the Board of Education and Liberal MP for Rotherham.
[38] Walter Runciman, President of the Board of Agriculture and Liberal MP for Dewsbury.
[39] John Burns, President of the Board of Trade and Liberal MP for Battersea.
[40] Edward David, ed., *Inside Asquith's Cabinet: From the Diaries of Charles Hobhouse* (London, 1977), 179.

began to shut down; eight firms failed by the close of business that day.[41] Asquith wrote to his confidante, Venetia Stanley, revealing that Britain appeared to be on a collision course with Germany. Only a 'miracle' could avert it at this late stage. The following day he believed the situation was 'as bad as can be'.[42] Ordinary people were aware of the increased seriousness in the situation. William Jones, who worked for the Birmingham Corporation in 1914, travelled in from Four Oaks to the city centre daily by train. He described each compartment as a 'little debating society' where news and current affairs were discussed amongst fellow passengers. He recalled the assassination of the Archduke:

> Of course no one thought that it would affect England at all at that moment, well not the ordinary people. But as we got forward into July a change took place and things began to look more serious . . . As we entered August things began to look very serious indeed.[43]

By the end of July, Norman Ellison, from West Kirby in Cheshire, recalled how 'the threat [of war] became more real'.[44] On Thursday, 30 July, Walter Waring, Liberal MP for Banffshire, described the situation in London as 'terribly black'. He warned his friends to postpone their visit as at the time of his writing 'everyone who can is leaving London as they say food riots are certain'.[45] This increasing desperation was reflected in two editorials in *The Times* entitled 'Lowering Clouds' and 'Waning Hopes'.[46] On Friday, 31 July, Russia's partial mobilization against Austria-Hungary, the day before, was reported in *The Times*. Shane Leslie, the Irish-born diplomatic aide and first cousin of Winston Churchill, described the 30 and 31 July as 'the lull before Armageddon'.[47] On 31 July came what *The Economist* called the 'final thunderclap'—the closure of the London Stock Exchange.[48] The same day, Dorothy Holman, a young woman in Teignmouth, Devon, recorded in her diary her surprise at the 'sudden' developments abroad: 'the papers are now nothing but war, war. Ulster has gone into oblivion so have all other subjects. It is so sudden, I never heard the vaguest suggestion of it till Sunday.'[49]

However, many still hoped that Britain would be brought back from the brink. Since 22 July there had been a sharp rise in the perceived probability of a Great Power war on the continent but Britain's involvement was not inevitable. Amongst the population, fear of war was a more apt description of feeling at this moment than certainty that Britain would be involved. On 27 July, Brien Cokayne, the

[41] Ferguson, 'Political Risk and the International Bond Market between the 1848 Revolution and the Outbreak of the First World War', 99.

[42] Michael Brock and Eleanor Brock, eds., *H.H. Asquith: Letters to Venetia Stanley* (Oxford, 1982), 132, 138.

[43] City Sound Archives, Birmingham Museum: R56 (1981).

[44] IWM, Docs: Ellison, Norman F,; DS/MISC/49 (1958).

[45] NAS, GRH: Waring of Lennel: GD 372/55/2-3, 30 July 1914.

[46] *The Times*, 30 July 1914, 9 and 31 July 1914, 12.

[47] NLI: Sir Shane Leslie: Ms 22,863, 30 and 31 July 1914.

[48] Cited in Ferguson, 'Political Risk and the International Bond Market between the 1848 Revolution and the Outbreak of the First World War,' 99.

[49] DRO: Dorothy Holman: 3830M/F9, 31 July 1914.

businessman, banker, and partner in the merchant and banking firm of Anthony Gibbs and Sons, believed that 'the general feeling seems to be that there will not be a war on the Continent, but it is by no means certain'.[50] Despite the feeling of ominous dread that hung over her small town near the Firth of Clyde, M. M. Goodwin, a young woman in 1914, felt the crisis would 'blow over'.[51] On 31 July Grey confided in Edmund Gosse that he had 'not lost all hope of a settlement'.[52] His sentiments were echoed by the Prime Minister the following day despite the Russian mobilization against Austria-Hungary the previous day and Germany's declaration that this signalled aggressive intent against itself. The *Daily Mail* called for 'extraordinary caution and restraint' to be shown by the British government. Although the situation was black, people should 'continue to hope, if only because no irrevocable step has yet been taken'.[53] *The Times* correctly highlighted the fact that mobilization would not necessarily lead to war and that there was still a chance of averting 'this supreme catastrophe'.[54] On 2 August Wilfred Scawen Blunt, the British writer and anti-imperialist, tried to convince his fellow writer Hilaire Belloc that Asquith would 'announce neutrality tomorrow, not perhaps a very *beau rôle*, but less absurd than the other'.[55] The historian Esmé Wingfield-Stratford (1882–1971) was unable to concentrate on his Saturday cricket game in Kent on 1 August:

> One must keep one's head and try to see things in proportion. There were two anchors of hope . . . So long as the army remained unmobilised, and Germany did not move, nothing *could* happen. The crisis was just a crisis; and the fact that nothing *had* happened might mean that the worst was already over: every hour now that the collapse was postponed increased the hope of recovery.[56]

This sense of distance from the impending crisis was compounded by the fact that many people were enjoying their Bank Holiday weekend between Friday, 31 July and Monday, 3 August. Charles Bell, from Wallasey near Liverpool, spent 3 August at the nearby resort of New Brighton where the 'attitude of the Bank Holiday crowd, might have been expressed by paraphrasing Drake's remark on Plymouth Hoe; 'Let us have a good Bank Holiday, and fight the Germans afterwards'.[57]

Although M. M. Goodwin 'waited and hoped and prayed that a miracle would happen and war would be averted', she reluctantly acknowledged that if the Triple Entente failed to resolve the crisis peacefully, Britain would have to be involved.[58] People were trying to balance hope and realism, and rationalize the situation in their minds. Whilst no one wanted war, people were steeling themselves to its

[50] Cited in David Kynaston, *The City of London, Volume II: Golden Years, 1890–1914* (London, 1995), 601.

[51] ERO: T/Z 25/668 (1966).

[52] BL: Ashley 5738, 31 July 1914.

[53] *Daily Mail*, 1 August 1914, 4.

[54] *The Times*, 1 August 1914, 9.

[55] Wilfred Scawen Blunt, *My Diaries: Being a Personal Narrative of Events, 1888–1914*, 2 vols., vol. 2 (London, 1920), 448.

[56] Esmé Wingfield-Stratford, *Before the Lamps Went Out* (London, 1945), 246.

[57] IWM, Docs: Bell, Lt C.G.H.: 92/13/1 (n.d.).

[58] ERO: T/Z 25/668 (1966).

eventuality. At 10 a.m. on Friday, 31 July the London Stock Exchange closed in a wave of financial panic, and a 'State of Imminent War' was declared in Germany.[59] The *New York Times* reported that Londoners now believed war was 'a probability . . . rather than a possibility'. Most people dealt with the increased tension with 'sober determination'. There was 'no flag-waving, no demonstrations, no music hall patriotism'. People understood the gravity of the situation but went about their business quietly. But the atmosphere in Britain was also 'gloomy', held in 'suspense', weighed down under the 'gravity of the menace', and 'anxious'.[60] The possibility of war hung over Britain like a dark storm-cloud. Imagery and headlines, such as a map of Europe entitled 'Under the Shadow of War', appeared across the British press indicating the sense of foreboding.[61] The ominous headlines were reflected in the language of both politicians and ordinary people. Many references exist in contemporary sources describing the period between 27 July and 3 August as 'black', 'dark', or a 'gathering storm'. Reverend James Mackay, a Wesleyan minister in Newcastle-Upon-Tyne, described the 'great dark war cloud' hanging over the whole community and the 'grave fears' of the local people.[62] On holiday in Westcliffe-on-Naze on 1 August, Hallie Eustace Miles, wife of the sportsman, writer, and food reformer Eustace Hamilton Miles, noted that: 'the air is full of whispers of coming trouble: and the rumours of War are becoming more and more alarming and more and more persistent'.[63] On 1 August, the Roman Catholic Bishop of Salford, Louis Casartelli, began circulating instructions for 'prayers for peace' to his clergy.[64] On the other side of the county, the East Lancashire Territorial Association viewed the deteriorating international situation with such concern that it called an emergency meeting the same day. As a result, it instructed a supplier who was holding 2,000 service uniforms on its behalf to send them immediately by train to Manchester. It also ordered a further 2,000 suits and 5,000 pairs of boots.[65]

Across the Bank Holiday weekend, war on the continent became inevitable as France mobilized against Germany in support of its Russian ally (Saturday), Germany invaded Luxemburg (Sunday) and declared war on France (Monday), and consequently issued an ultimatum to Belgium on Tuesday, 4 August, requesting free passage for its army. The only remaining question—but it was the vital one—was whether Britain would become involved. On 1 August, H. A. Gwynne, editor of the London *Morning Post*, believed that 80 per cent of the population were behind Grey in his efforts to uphold Britain's honour.[66] On 2 August the Sunday

[59] *The Times*, 1 August 1914, 8, 9.
[60] *New York Times*, 1 August 1914, 4, and 3 August 1914, 10.
[61] *Daily Mail*, 1 August 1914, 5.
[62] IWM, Docs: Mackay, Reverend James: Box 74/135/1, 3 August 1914.
[63] Hallie Eustace Miles, *Untold Tales of War-Time London: A Personal Diary* (London, 1930), 13.
[64] Salford Diocesan Archives, Burnley: 1914 Diary of Bishop L. C. Casartelli, 1 August 1914.
[65] K. W. Mitchinson, *England's Last Hope: The Territorial Force, 1908–1914* (Basingstoke, 2008), 221.
[66] Keith Wilson, ed., *The Rasp of War: The Letters of H. A. Gwynne to The Countess Bathurst, 1914–1918* (London, 1988), 19.

editor of *The Times* reported that the population of London had grasped the gravity of the situation:

> Nobody wanted war; nobody would shrink from war if the Continental position demanded it... Every one felt that the moment for a fateful decision was coming nearer and nearer, and that the clouds which were bursting over Europe might within a few hours affect our own country.[67]

King George V noted in his diary how crowds began gathering outside Buckingham Palace on the night of 2 August. They would do so each evening until 9 August.[68] From 2 August onwards, navigation of aircraft over Britain and its territorial waters was prohibited, except for those with naval or military orders. Certain classes of naval reserve and marine pensioners were mobilized. By 1 August defensive measures were already being put in place by the army and navy. Preparations for war were visible in Dover, Portsmouth, Aldershot, Woolwich Arsenal, Queensborough, and Cardiff. Mary Coules, daughter of a Reuters news editor, was in little doubt that something was wrong when her family left for their holiday in Worthing on 31 July: 'At Victoria station [London] we saw hundreds of coast-guardsmen—Naval reserve, I suppose—all with kit bags and straw hats... This was the first inclination we had of any likelihood of war'.[69] Grimsby saw 150 Austrians set sail for Hamburg; in Hull the local fishing fleet was recalled. In Barrow, the officials at the Armstrong Vickers shipbuilders cancelled their holiday that was due to start on 5 August. M. M. Goodwin began to worry when she saw that British vessels had steamed into the Firth of Clyde during the night. Her worries were amplified when horses, which were being commandeered by the army, began to disappear from the roads. When the Reserve were called up the following day she felt 'tears and fears that the worse was about to happen'.[70] Those who lived near a military or naval base or were in the army or Territorials were more aware of the prospect of war becoming a reality than others. On 2 August French Reservists left stations in London amid pathetic scenes of wailing, tearful, and fainting women who they left behind.[71] For Sydney Thomas, a Territorial encamped at Lark Hill near Salisbury, the situation was so serious that on 2 August he was compelled to write to his friend in Maidenhead begging her to take his wife and children in as evacuees from their home in Westcliffe-on-Sea, Essex. He was fearful of them being so close to Shoeburyness and Sheerness 'where fighting will surely take place if any attempt is made by the Germans to land in this country'.[72]

Some people took to the streets in protest. A large anti-war demonstration was held in Trafalgar Square on Sunday, 2 August. Those assembled passed a resolution in favour of international peace and solidarity, calling upon 'his Majesty's

---

[67] *The Times*, 2 August 1914, 5.
[68] Royal Archives, Windsor Castle: RA GV/PRIV/GVD/1914: 2–9 August.
[69] IWM, Docs: Coules, Miss M.: 97/25/1, 31 July 1914.
[70] ERO: T/Z 25/668 (1966).
[71] *Liverpool Echo*, 3 August 1914, 6.
[72] Liddle: DF Items: Defence: Threat of Invasion: Local Defence Volunteers: Item 5, 2 August 1914.

Government to take every step to secure peace on behalf of the British people'.[73] One of the key speakers, Keir Hardie, the Scottish socialist and Labour Party MP for Merthyr Tydfil, was championed in the *Daily News* the following day.[74] The atmosphere of this peace meeting was certainly dampened by the dreadful weather, which the Bishop of Salford thought a fitting accompaniment to the 'terrible war cloud which has burst over Europe!'[75] Political bias, both of eyewitnesses and the reporting press, makes it difficult to ascertain how popular the meeting was. Some middle-class youths heckled speakers. The *Daily Herald* dismissed them as 'a few rowdy clerks' and considered the meeting generally a success. The *Labour Leader* described it as the 'biggest Trafalgar Square demonstration held for years; far larger... than the most important of the suffrage rallies', and estimated that 15,000 people had attended.[76] According to the Conservative press, the meeting was disrupted, red flags were torn down and blows exchanged between socialists and their opponents. The Liberal *Daily Chronicle* stated that with the exception of these youths, the crowd gathered in the square was completely unanimous in passing a resolution which 'deplored the impotency to which the democracy of Germany had been reduced and in calling on the British government in the first place to prevent the spread of the war and in the second place to see that the country is not dragged into the conflict'.[77] Other anti-war protests were held on the same Sunday up and down the country, including crowds of around 2,500 in Birmingham, 4,000 at Ipswich, and 2,000 at Hyde near Manchester, amongst many others.[78]

When Germany declared war on France on 3 August 'all hope of peace... disappeared with a crash'.[79] In response, the British Cabinet sanctioned the mobilization of the British fleet and army. Haldane began sending mobilization telegrams to all Reservists and Territorials that afternoon. With no system of mass conscription in Britain and no previous experience of mass mobilization, Regulars looked to the press for instruction on where and when to report for duty. The distinctiveness of the British experience was evident to John Grover, an officer in training at Sandhurst in 1914, who recalled in 1973:

> No one had any idea what are the implications of a nation at war, in fact there'd never been such a war to my knowledge and the idea that this would be a national war to the extent of the complete mobilisation of the country I don't think had occurred to any of us. We thought it would be a quick clash as in 1870 when the Germans overran France so quickly.[80]

Using dramatic language, the *Daily Mail* described the situation as 'the end of an epoch... Existing landmarks are being swept away by the storm. Frontiers are

---

[73] *The Times*, 3 August 1914, 8.
[74] IWM, Docs: Spurrell, Lieutenant-Colonel Hugh W.: 92/36/1, 3 August 1914.
[75] Salford Diocesan Archives, Burnley: 1914 Diary of Bishop L. C. Casartelli, 2 August 1914.
[76] *Labour Leader*, 6 August 1914, 3.
[77] Cited in Gregory, 'British 'War Enthusiasm' in 1914: A Reassessment', 73.
[78] *Labour Leader*, 6 August 1914, 4–5.
[79] *Daily Mail*, 3 August 1914, 4.   [80] IWM: 46, Reel 2 (1973).

being obliterated, treaties torn up . . . Where peoples are not ready to defend themselves they will be trampled underfoot'.[81] Despite the absence of a formal alliance with France, British involvement was edging ever closer. Alice Henry, wife of the Irish botanist Augustine Henry, wrote from London on 3 August: 'Events have moved on terrifically and now England is embroiled and the hounds are loose . . . A general feeling between woe and depression'.[82]

Bank Holiday Monday was the point when many people began to accept the war as a reality. The Bishop of Salford wrote on that day that 'everybody's minds and mouths filled with this awful universal war'.[83] Like many others, Frank Lockwood, an apprentice lithographic artist from Linthwaite near Huddersfield, mentioned the war in his diary for the first time on 3 August.[84] Madame Tussaud's, which had reorganized part of their collection to reflect characters from the current crisis, did particularly good business on 3 and 4 August, suggesting that people were taking a newfound interest in contemporary events.[85]

By 3 August members of the Territorial forces were receiving, or expecting, their mobilization orders. Thomas Baker, from London, recalled how his friend arrived to participate in the Elstree Athletics Club Bank Holiday weekend race in his army uniform: 'He knew he'd have to report that night. So everybody knew that [war] was coming'.[86] A. M. Campbell's father, a captain in charge of the local Territorial battalion on the island of Islay, Argyllshire, received a telegram ordering his mobilization and assembly of all companies at battalion headquarters at Dunoon. An atmosphere of 'gravity and foreboding' prevailed over the household.[87] Harold Bartholemew, a soldier with the 8th Essex Cyclist Battalion, received his mobilization orders on the evening of 3 August. His response was to 'rush round' to his girlfriend's house where they stayed awake all night talking until he had to report to the Square in Braintree, Essex, at 9 a.m. Clearly they were both aware of the significance of Harry's mobilization and made the most of what they perceived was their last evening together for some time.[88]

At the beginning of the weekend, on Friday, 31 July, Grey had warned Cambon that the British government's decision to go to war, or not, depended upon the 'course of events – including the Belgian question, and the direction of public opinion'.[89] The obligation to France under the Triple Entente divided government and country, but Belgium was another matter, about which the Foreign Secretary spoke to the House of Commons on the afternoon of 3 August, referring explicitly to the German ultimatum to Belgium:

[81] *Daily Mail*, 3 August 1914, 4.
[82] NLI: Mrs Augustine Henry: Ms 7981, 3 August 1914.
[83] Salford Diocesan Archives, Burnley: 1914 Diary of Bishop L. C. Casartelli, 3 August 1914.
[84] IWM, Docs: Lockwood F.T.: 96/52/1, 3 August 1914.
[85] Lyn Macdonald, *1914—The Days of Hope* (London, 1987), 41.
[86] IWM: 8721, Reel 1 (1985).
[87] Liddle: DF Recollections: Box A-C: A.M. Campbell (n.d.).
[88] ERO: T/Z 25/625 (1966).
[89] Brock and Brock, eds., *H.H. Asquith: Letters to Venetia Stanley*, 138.

An ultimatum has been given to Belgium by Germany, the object of which was to offer Belgium friendly relations with Germany on condition that she would facilitate the passage of German troops through Belgium. [*Ironical laughter*] . . . We were sounded in the course of last week as to whether, if a guarantee were given that, after the war, Belgian integrity would be preserved . . . We replied that we could not bargain away whatever interests or obligations we had in Belgian neutrality. [*Cheers.*][90]

The fact that the German war plan required invading France through Belgium was broadly known, though no one could be certain it would be applied. But if Germany violated Belgium, Grey said, Britain must fight. He stressed the 'honour and interest' in sustaining the treaty guaranteeing Belgian independence, and raised the menace of one power dominating the continent. If Britain stayed neutral while Germany conquered, Britain would 'sacrifice our respect and good name and reputation before the world, and should not escape the most serious and grave economic consequences'. When he finished, the House applauded at length.[91] King George V noted in his diary, following the speech, that public opinion had been 'entirely changed' by Grey's words and that 'everyone is [now] for war and our helping our friends'.[92] Beatrice Webb, the British socialist, recorded in her diary on 5 August that 'the public mind was cleared and solidified by Grey's speech. Even staunch Liberals agree that we had to stand by Belgium'.[93] She was right: supporters of neutrality, who had been working feverishly to keep Britain out of the war since Austria-Hungary's declaration of war against Serbia on 28 July, dwindled rapidly on the afternoon of 3 August when a number of Liberals were won over by Grey's speech in the House of Commons.[94]

The German invasion of Belgium on 4 August erased any doubts about Britain's involvement in the war, for the government and the public. Of those still opposed to British intervention, the majority fell into line with national policy as the ultimatum expired. That evening, the village of New Mill near Huddersfield hosted a final anti-war meeting attracting 400 people. However, its resolutions recognized the inevitability of war. The purpose of the meeting was for posterity, to declare that the village had done its best to resist the war, but now steeled itself for the conflict.[95] As a leading figure in the Dunfermline Liberal Association told his local MP, Arthur Ponsonby, on 5 August: 'I think the majority of us are keen peace men, but we feel that now we are into war it is our duty to support the Government and to do everything in our power that will in any degree help to secure victory'.[96] Equally breakneck was the reversal in enemies: the pre-war language of enmity remained, but the targets changed. Although Serbia's attempt to assert national

[90] Great Britain, Parliamentary Debates, Commons, Fifth Series, Vol. LXV, 1914, 1809 [with House comments as found in original].
[91] Ibid.
[92] Royal Archives, Windsor Castle: RA GV/PRIV/GVD/1914: 3 August.
[93] Margaret I. Cole, ed., *Beatrice Webb's Diaries, 1912–1924*, 2 vols., vol. 1 (London, 1952), 25.
[94] Martin Ceadel, *Living the Great Illusion: Sir Norman Angell, 1872–1967* (Oxford, 2009), 601.
[95] *Huddersfield Examiner*, 5 August 1914.
[96] MPP Bodleian: Arthur Ponsonby: MS Eng hist c.660, folio 91, 5 August 1914 cited in Ceadel, *Living the Great Illusion: Sir Norman Angell, 1872–1967*, 160.

independence in June was often condemned, Belgium's right to defend its sovereignty in August was undisputed. Whilst Russia had been the enemy to civilization, and Germany its bastion, by 4 August, enemy and allied lines were clearly drawn. The invasion of Belgium had left no doubt in peoples' minds that Germany was the aggressor and, in order to uphold civilization, must be defeated.

Richard Durning Holt recorded his change of opinion about British neutrality on 9 August: 'I had thought we might and should have kept out of the war but when Germany decided on an unprovoked attack upon Belgium whose neutrality Germany equally with ourselves had guaranteed it seemed impossible for us to stand by'.[97] The invasion satisfied different opinions. For the diplomat, a treaty had been violated; for the strategist, a German invasion of Belgium gave it worrying access to the British Channel via Antwerp; for the religious, the courage of 'little Catholic Belgium' was inspiring; and for many more, the story of brave little Belgium standing up to a belligerent continental bully was reason enough for Britain to intervene. For Lady Kate Courtney, elder sister of Beatrice Webb and an active Quaker and pacifist, 'the German violation of Belgian neutrality was the rock on which all the anti-war feeling was shipwrecked', including her own.[98] The war could be recast for those who were less than eager. Instead of it being a war against German civilization, it was now a war for the defence of civilization against German 'barbarianism'. Responsibility for the war was clear and Britain could enter the war for just reasons and with clean hands.

THE STORM BREAKS

The British government's ultimatum demanded that the German army withdraw from Belgium (which had been invaded at 8 a.m. that morning) by 11 p.m. on 4 August. The time between the issue and expiration of the ultimatum was filled with tension, uncertainty, and anxiety. Contrary to their usual custom of picnicking in Epping Forest on the August Bank Holiday Monday, the Chapmans, a lower middle-class family from Leyton, London, stayed at home awaiting further news. Una, the daughter, recalled how ominous this day was: 'worried depressed, I felt it was the end of an era'.[99] At 11 p.m. GMT when the ultimatum had expired, Britain, which guaranteed Belgium's neutrality through a treaty of 1839, declared war on Germany. Grey wept as he informed the American Ambassador in London, Walter Hines Page, of the news.[100]

The official announcement of war was a shock for many people in Britain. Whilst some people had been expecting a European confrontation since as far back as the turn of the century, most had no idea. No less a person than King George V, on 8 August, in a letter to his son Bertie, revealed how 'little did I think when I saw

[97] LRO: Durning Holt Papers: 920 DUR/1/10, 9 August 1914.
[98] Liddle: DF 037: Lady Kate Courtney (1927).
[99] ERO: T/Z 25/601 (1966).
[100] Arthur S. Link, ed., *The Papers of Woodrow Wilson*, vol. 30 (Princeton, 1979), 370.

you last . . . only three weeks ago, that we should now be at war with Germany. It has all come so suddenly'.[101] Mrs A. Purbrook, a middle-aged woman from Hornchurch, Essex, recorded on 4 August 'just a week ago I don't think that, in spite of newspaper scares, any one of us, the uninitiated public, thought there would be war—and certainly they never really imagined that England would be in it. The final development has been most rapid'.[102] On 14 August the *Wiltshire News* reflected on the situation:

> Three short weeks ago the man who ventured to prophesy that the greatest war the world had ever known was about to begin would have been laughed at for his pains. Three weeks ago! Those of us who were not then thinking of our summer holidays, or the harvest, or talking placidly of the prospects of an early general election, had our eyes upon Ireland.[103]

Even those in the capital's financial sector were taken aback by the outbreak of war in 1914: for them it truly was 'a bolt from the blue'. They—like many ordinary members of the public—had evaluated the international crises before 1914 as local difficulties rather than milestones on the road to Armageddon.[104]

The language used by contemporaries reflected this surprise with words like 'shock', 'stunned', 'thunderbolt', 'whirlwind', 'bombshell', and 'unexpected'. For Beatrice Trefusis, an upper-class society lady in London, the outbreak of war was a bomb that had 'finally exploded'.[105] Phillip Leicester, a young man and Honorary Secretary of the Worcester Rifle Club, felt the outbreak of war was like the explosion of a 'Volcanoe [sic] on which we have slumbered for years'.[106] Dorothy Holman, a young woman who was considering entering the nursing profession, visited a hospital in Exeter on 5 August only to be told by the head district nurse that 'they were frightfully busy with premature babies caused by the shock of the war'.[107] Locals attending the opening ceremony of the annual Eisteddfod in Corwen, north Wales, on 5 August, knelt down in prayer 'in all their summer finery' when the announcement was made that Britain was at war with Germany.[108] The same day, Thomas Macmillan, an office clerk, was passing through one of Glasgow's main streets, Sauchiehall Street:

> The street was abnormally busy: people of all ages were walking rather aimlessly about and talking without reserve to those who would talk to them, while scattered here and there were groups, earnestly discussing the momentous news . . . I strolled down the street deep in anxious thought and, after purchasing a copy of one of the evening papers, editions of which were appearing hourly, I drifted into a Picture House . . . As I took my seat I felt as if some great misfortune had befallen me; and the longer I

---

[101] Royal Archives, Windsor Castle: RA GV/PRIV/AA59/290: 8 August 1914.

[102] IWM, Docs: Purbrook, Mrs A.: 97/3/1, 4 August 1914.

[103] *Wiltshire News*, 14 August 1914.

[104] Ferguson, 'Political Risk and the International Bond Market between the 1848 Revolution and the Outbreak of the First World War', 72, 101. See also Niall Ferguson, *The World's Banker: The History of the House of Rothschild* (London, 1998).

[105] Liddle: DF 129: B.M. Trefusis, 5 August 1914.

[106] WRO: Ref 705:185: BA 8185: Parcel 2: Phillip A. Leicester, 4 August 1914.

[107] DRO: Dorothy Holman: 3830M/F9, 5 August 1914.

[108] ERO: T/Z 25/680 (1966).

remained, the more did this strange feeling appear to be shared by those around me. All eyes were on the screen and all mouths were closed for perhaps the first time in such a place . . . With the singing of the National anthem I left the theatre and slowly wended my way homewards, through crowded streets. On reaching home I found all astir and sad to a degree. My mother and sisters were absorbed in anxious conversation and were counting the cost in lives, as women do, while my father and brother were together in another room which was littered with newspapers. Outside there was a steady hum of conversation, and newsboys were still shouting although it was past midnight.[109]

On 10 August Elizabeth Cadbury, wife of the chocolate magnate, practising Quaker and Liberal supporter, attended the first Sunday service of her local church in Northfield, Birmingham, following the outbreak of war. Although her personal beliefs were likely to make her distressed by the thought of European war she also observed that her fellow congregation was singing 'extraordinarily faint—no one seemed to have the heart to raise their voice'.[110] Even the King seemed anxious, according to Lieutenant General Douglas Haig, Commander of the First Army Corps of the BEF, who met with him on 11 August at a military display in Aldershot. On 13 August Haig revealed his own feelings about the situation: 'I felt the great uncertainties of the future lying before me and could not talk much . . . there must be great difficulties and uncertainties before each one of us'.[111]

The announcement of war in Walthamstow was met with a combination of worry and defiance. Cyril Royle, a teenager in Manchester in 1914, recalled how the news of the outbreak of war filled him with 'terror and dread'.[112] The *Cornish Guardian* on 7 August reported on the 'absence of gaiety' in Newquay since the declaration of war. In this moment of great anxiety, people 'did not feel like amusement'.[113] Thirty-five miles down the Lizard peninsula, there was a low turnout at the Newlyn carnival as people, concerned about the unfolding crisis, 'refrained from festivities'.[114] The Douglas family, in Sunderland, reacted to the news with dread and fear because of the possibility of their three sons being called up.[115] Mrs E. Mann recalled seeing the distressing sight of women on the platform of Huddersfield station on 4 August saying emotional farewells to their husbands and sons who, as Regulars and Territorials, were departing already.[116] Duncan Lorimer, a naval reservist, left Edinburgh station on the evening of 4 August and noted the emotionally charged and anxious atmosphere as soldiers and sailors bid farewell to their loved ones.[117] Nor was the outbreak of war welcomed by those men who had made the final decision. As the ultimatum approached, both Margot Asquith and her husband 'could not speak for tears', and on the stroke of midnight,

---

[109] IWM, Docs: Macmillan, Thomas: PP/MCR/C56 (1935).
[110] BCA: MS 466/432, Box 3: Cadbury Family Journal, 10 August 1914.
[111] NLS: Diary of Field-Marshal Haig: Acc 3155/98, 11, 13 August 1914.
[112] NWSA: 1994.0127: Dr Cyril Royle (1994).
[113] *Cornish Guardian*, 7 August 1914 cited in Stuart Dalley, 'The Response in Cornwall to the Outbreak of the First World War', *Cornish Studies* 11 (2003), 86.
[114] *Cornish Telegraph*, 6 August 1914 cited in ibid.
[115] Liddle: DF Recollections: Box D-I: Mrs G. Douglas (1970).
[116] Liddle: DF Recollections: Box J-M: Mrs E. Mann (1984).
[117] IWM, Docs: Lorimer, Surgeon Lt D.: 78/47/1, 4 August 1914.

the sound in the Cabinet Room where Asquith, Lord Crewe, and Sir Edward Grey all sat 'was as silent as dawn'.[118]

THE 4 AUGUST CROWDS

The London correspondent of the *Cambridge Daily News* described the reaction in London on the evening that the British ultimatum expired: 'the busy hive of the metropolis has not allowed itself to be perturbed into anything approaching a feverish excitement'. For the writer, 'exaggerated excitement' was not a feature of the crowds in London:

> It would be quite untrue to say that there was any war fever in London. The crowds in the streets are great—as great as they were at the time of the declaration of the Boer War. But the temper is really quite different...the people were not excited or demonstrative, but they were intensely interested.[119]

Robert Parker, working at Eastchurch Airfield, Kent, in 1914, was amongst the crowds in London that evening. He described the overarching mood of the crowds as 'anxious' not excited. People milled around to find out what was going to happen, rather than to celebrate the news when it arrived.[120] Another member of the London crowds recalled standing outside the gates of Buckingham Palace praying silently for the news of war not to be true.[121] The *Western Evening Herald* described the attitude of the London crowds as 'reassuring'. There was no excitement or panic. Determination to defeat Germany was not accompanied by malice. Although some people booed 'unfriendly' embassies, when a taxi-driver shouted 'Down with Germany' the crowd did not respond being 'in no humour for demonstrations of this kind'. A man distributing leaflets entitled 'Why Fight For Russia?' found they were either thrown away or returned to him.[122] Elizabeth Cadbury witnessed the crowds at various landmarks in London. They 'gathered together at any point where they thought there was a chance of hearing news, quietly and anxiously waiting. There seemed an extraordinary silence and sense of oppression over the whole of London'.[123] Men carrying placards bearing the motif 'Why War?' were able to parade 'unmolested' and only children, it appeared, felt patriotic enough to purchase the miniature Union Jacks on sale.[124]

Beyond London, Robert Roberts, a schoolboy in 1914, recalled the reaction of local people in Salford:

---

[118] Margot Asquith, *The Autobiography of Margot Asquith*, 2 vols., vol. 2 (London, 1922), 195–6. Margot Asquith does, however, also note Churchill's positive and jovial attitude to the war.
[119] *Cambridge Daily News*, 5 August 1914.
[120] IWM: 492, Reel 3 (1974).
[121] Mrs C. S. Peel, *How We Lived Then, 1914–1918: A Sketch of Social and Domestic Life in England During the War* (London, 1929), 16.
[122] *Western Evening Herald*, 4 August 1914, 4.
[123] BCA: MS 466/432, Box 3: Cadbury Family Journal, 6 August 1914.
[124] *Cambridge Daily News*, 5 August 1914.

The fourth of August 1914 caused no great burst of patriotic fervour among us. Little groups, men and women together . . . stood talking earnestly in the shop or at the street corner, stunned a little by the enormity of events.[125]

In Birmingham the people were described as calm and restrained.[126] In Newcastle-upon-Tyne, Reverend Mackay observed how 'there were no great demonstrations of excitement. The people took things very calmly.'[127] Mary Coules described the atmosphere amongst the crowds gathered at Worthing's bandstand as 'a queer, subdued flutter of excitement' rather than an outburst of uncontrolled enthusiasm.[128] Alfred Woodcock, an employee of a local brewery, recalled crowds blocking the streets in Walsall, West Midlands, on 4 August but does not describe them as loud, enthusiastic, or celebratory.[129] Activity only began as the ultimatum approached in the evening and crowds focused around particular places such as Territorial centres and newspaper offices. Although the declaration of war was greeted with cheering and the singing of the national anthem, the reaction was viewed at the time as a release of tension that had been building up over the past few days and not as one of enthusiasm and excitement.[130] In Cardiff, the feeling amongst the 4 August crowds that had gathered was described as 'wrought to a high pitch of intensity'. Like a kettle that had reached boiling point, the crowds sang patriotic songs and cheered in a sense of relief once the declaration of war was announced.[131]

In Croydon, just outside London, citizens greeted the declaration of war on 4 August with a sense of bewilderment. According to the Mayor there was no war fever, cheering, waving of flags, or singing of patriotic songs. The war was understood as something serious, not a cause for celebration. Instead of descriptions of cheering crowds, 'grave-faced knots of people' discussed the situation 'at every corner'. Even the activities of the Reservists in the street, prone to stir excitement and curiosity in other parts of the country, were recorded as being without incident.[132] The local Hampstead Heath paper reported that the usual holiday spirit had been dampened by the voices of 'news vendors shouting out the latest war news . . . Nowhere was there the slightest sign of 'Mafficking' and it was obvious to the observer that the idea of war was distasteful to all'.[133] A sober response on 4 August was also recorded in Leicester. Crowds only gathered as the Territorial regiments returned over the Bank Holiday from their camps, and these were not described as enthusiastic or excited.[134] In Peterborough, the declaration of war 'created no increase of excitement' and people's thoughts were dominated by the

---

[125] Robert Roberts, *The Classic Slum: Salford Life in the First Quarter of the Century* (Manchester, 1971), 186.
[126] *Birmingham Gazette*, 5 August 1914, 5.
[127] IWM, Docs: Mackay, Reverend James: Box 74/135/1, 4 August 1914,
[128] IWM, Docs: Coules, Miss M.: 97/25/1, 4 August 1914.
[129] City Sound Archives, Birmingham Museum: R167–8 (1982).
[130] *Bristol Times and Mirror*, 5 August 1914, 5.
[131] *South Wales Daily News*, 5 August 1914, 6.
[132] H. Keatley Moore and W. C. Berwick Sayers, *Croydon and the Great War: The Official History of the War Work of the Borough and its Citizens from 1914–1919* (London, 1920), 18–19.
[133] *Hampstead Record*, 7 August 1914, 2.
[134] F. P. Armitage, *Leicester 1914–18: The War-Time Story of a Midland Town* (Leicester, 1933), 12.

prospect of food shortages.[135] R. W. M. Gibbs, a mathematician later based in Oxford, was at the pier in Bournemouth when war was announced. He described the emotional reserve of the gathered crowds:

> The band on the pier played patriotic and martial airs. There was some cheering towards the end, but not nearly so much as one would have expected as the pier was packed with a bank holiday crowd. A gentleman who was with me and had recently returned from Colorado expressed surprise. He said 'An American crowd would have just gone crazy.'[136]

The estimated number of people gathered outside Buckingham Palace on the evening of 4 August varies between 1,000 and 10,000.[137] Considering that London was home to almost seven million people, even the top estimate implies less than 0.2 per cent of the total population were gathered in the vicinity of central London on 4 August. A useful control on these numbers is the estimated 100,000 Londoners who flocked to central London upon the news of the Armistice in 1918 and continued to do so for several days afterwards.[138] The King noted in his diary that the crowd that appeared at the Palace gates on 6 August was 'the largest yet' and on 9 August a 'gigantic crowd . . . quite 50,000' gathered, suggesting that 4 August was not as momentous as has since been claimed.[139]

Ferdinand Tuohy, a freelance journalist, was present amongst the crowds in Piccadilly Circus on Saturday 1 August:

> The theatres just emptying . . . on the pavement a London crowd of that day—young men, mostly what we liked to call 'bounders'; 'gay' women in longish dresses and picture hats . . . a few, frothy giggling flappers . . . 'Varsity Youth 'just down' and bent on a wonderful night.[140]

When special editions of newspapers announced that Germany had declared war on Russia:

> the whole of Coventry Street was agog. Upon ardent youth the effect was especially electrical . . . Down in the cafes and beer halls of Soho it was Bedlam, while wine and lager, but chiefly lager, flowed in unending gallons.[141]

It is unlikely that the composition of the crowds would have been significantly different three nights later. According to Lloyd George and the *Daily Mail*, the crowds in London on 4 August consisted mainly of young men, and this is supported by photographic evidence. The scene captured on 3 August shows a crowd of mostly middle-class young men in straw hats cheering the Royal Family as they appeared on the balcony of Buckingham Palace (see Figure 1.1).

---

[135] *Peterborough Citizen*, 5 August 1914.
[136] MPP Bodleian: R.W.M. Gibbs: MS Eng misc c.159, 18 September 1914.
[137] *New York Times*, 5 August 1914, 2, and *Evening Standard*, 5 August 1914.
[138] Gregory, 'British "War Enthusiasm" in 1914: A Reassessment', 72.
[139] Royal Archives, Windsor Castle: RA GV/PRIV/GVD/1914: 4, 6 and 9 August.
[140] Ferdinand Tuohy, *The Crater of Mars* (London, 1929), 2.
[141] Ibid. 3.

Fig. 1.1. Crowds outside Buckingham Palace, 3 August 1914

IWM, PA Collection No. 4203-02/Negative No. Q081832. Reproduced with the permission of the Imperial War Museum Photograph Archives.

Immediately prior to the expiration of the ultimatum, revellers were spilling out of theatres, on a Bank Holiday, perhaps fuelled by alcohol. This would have contributed to the heightened atmosphere led by 'cheering, shouting, flag-waving youngsters'. Most of the noise and cheering was made by 'the younger set'.[142] Having recently experienced war, the older generation's reaction to the outbreak of hostilities in August 1914 tended to be wary rather than excited. Percy Snelling, a Regular in 1914, recalled how British veterans of the South African War reacted to the outbreak of war very differently from younger soldiers. They believed war was a 'dangerous thing' and although they were willing to their duty 'they would have preferred not to'.[143]

Uncertainty, and anxiety to discover the latest news, formed one of the principal motives of the spontaneous gatherings. Newspaper offices and railway stations, where the national press arrived, were logical meeting points. In Newcastle-upon-Tyne crowds gathered at 11 p.m. in front of the Central Station and *Chronicle* offices.[144] People eager for information gathered around the offices of the *Worthing Gazette*. They remained after the ultimatum expired and the office workers had to encourage them to leave, announcing 'the uncertainty of receiving anything further' that night.[145] Similar scenes were reported at the offices of the *Devon and Exeter Gazette*

---

[142] Marcus, *Before the Lamps Went Out* (London, 1965), 318, 320.
[143] IWM: 314, Reel 12 (1974).
[144] IWM, Docs: Mackay, Reverend James: Box 74/135/1, 4 August 1914.
[145] *Worthing Gazette*, 5 August 1914.

in Exeter where crowds desperate for news were marked by their 'placidity' and 'sobriety'.[146] Clearly, interest in the war was not necessarily synonymous with excitement at its arrival. Other people were in London because they had been visiting on their Bank Holiday weekend or hoped to catch a glimpse of the King. Any signs of mobilization also drew the attention of crowds. The writer, Vera Brittain, about to start her studies at Oxford, was in Buxton on 4 August as part of an 'excited little group' which had gathered to watch the Territorials mobilize. Afterwards she walked home finding 'the Pavilion Gardens deserted, and a depressed and very much diminished band playing lugubriously to rows of empty chairs'.[147]

The crowds of 4 August 1914, in London and elsewhere, possessed many emotions—curiosity, apprehension, excitement, anxiety, shock, sadness, and silence. This is similar to the prevailing response to war in rural France. Concern and fear dominated rather than vibrant celebration.[148] Cheering at the moment of announcement was not necessarily an indication of enthusiasm for war but a release of tension, a climax to a week of not knowing. Reactions in Austria-Hungary to the outbreak of war have been described as the joyous release and relief at the end of weeks of anxiety and uncertainty—and the same could be said of Britain.[149]

In the opening decade of the twentieth century a fear had developed amongst liberal Edwardians of the emotional and irrational tendencies that patriotism could inspire. Whether or not the South African War really was a 'popular' war in Britain, it was widely assumed to have been so at the time. Newspaper reports of Mafeking Night (18 May 1900) described the joy and enthusiasm with which the news of the relief of the small British garrison town, besieged by Boer forces for seven months, was received across the United Kingdom. These reports were positive and non-accusatory; the crowds were described as carnival-like, innocently celebrating their nation's success in the appropriate way.[150] However, in the intervening years, descriptions of these patriotic demonstrations morphed into concerns that the British public had been dangerously out of control in its lust for war. Liberal intellectuals were shocked by the phenomenon of 'jingoism', which they now believed had characterized British responses to the South African War.[151]

The memory of such, apparently dangerous, overly patriotic responses was a constant point of reference in the August 1914 press on how people should behave. It was burnt into the public consciousness and used as a cultural yardstick to remind the British public of the limits of acceptable behaviour. The hysteria of Mafeking Night was deemed inappropriate and to be avoided at all costs. People

---

[146] *Devon and Exeter Gazette*, 5 August 1914, 7.

[147] Vera Brittain, *Testament of Youth* (London, 1933), 98.

[148] Jean-Jacques Becker, '"That's the Death Knell of Our Boys..."', in *The French Home Front, 1914–1918*, ed. Patrick Fridenson (Oxford, 1992), 29.

[149] Holger H. Herwig, *The First World War: Germany and Austria-Hungary, 1914–1918* (London, 1997), 35. See also Healy, *Vienna and the Fall of the Habsburg Empire: Total War and Everyday Life in World War One* (Cambridge, 2004).

[150] See, for example, *The North-Eastern Daily Gazette*, 19 May 1900, *Western Mail*, 19 May 1900, *The Pall Mall Gazette*, 19 May 1900, *Daily News*, 19 May 1900.

[151] Hobson, *The Psychology of Jingoism* (London, 1901), Paul Readman, 'The Liberal Party and Patriotism in Early Twentieth Century Britain', *Twentieth Century British History* 12 (2001).

were now called upon to be calm and unified. The experience of 1900 informed the descriptions of the crowds on 4 August:

> The gathering and demonstrations of crowds in the West End have been described as 'mafficking'. That is not a just description. When [Baden-Powell's] force was relieved London went mad and indulged in an orgy which, while it was spontaneous and touched all classes, and pervaded even the furthest suburbs, had many discreditable features. On Tuesday night [4 August] there was a certain amount of rowdyism, but it was not by any means of the same character.[152]

Robert Baden-Powell, the hero of Mafeking, issued an appeal published in the *Grimsby Daily Telegraph* 'to village lads to stop flag waving and to come forward to do something for their country'.[153] H. A. Gwynne wrote to his *Morning Post* correspondent in St Petersburg describing British public opinion:

> You have to bear in mind one thing: this war is not a 'Mafficking' war. We all feel it too deeply and too strongly. They do not even cheer the troops as they march through the streets. No bells are rung for a victory. There is no outward sign of rejoicing or grieving; but it is England at its very best, silent undemonstrative, but absolutely determined.[154]

These descriptions suggest, on one level, that whilst some characteristics of Mafeking Night were evident in 1914, egregious behaviour was absent. But on another level, these descriptions were also a warning: crowd behaviour in 1914 was not to get out of control. The descriptions of crowd reactions to the outbreak of war in 1914 were therefore not neutral. The response was both reportage and a public pronouncement: the British public knew the limits and crowd behaviour was to remain restrained. The reports were ideologically loaded interventions in a debate about how people might and should behave.

BEYOND THE CROWDS

As there was no radio or television in 1914 most people discovered that Britain was at war only the following morning, 5 August. It was then that the cook of the family of Mary Lees, in Wellington, Somerset, 'rushed into the dining room, she didn't knock the door, and my mother was there writing letters, and 'Oh Ma'am' she said, 'Oh Ma'am. War! War! War!'[155] Alice Remington, in Bay Horse, North Lancashire, awoke to the new reality because:

> of the noise of lorries going down the [main] road . . . one saw a lot of men in them and you began to wonder what it was all about. Then the news drifted through that all these lorries were going overseas and all the rest of it, and then it brought the war home, and then you found that the various people in the village who were reservists or

[152] *Cambridge Daily News*, 6 August 1914.
[153] *Grimsby Daily Telegraph*, 13 August 1914.
[154] Wilson, ed., *The Rasp of War: The Letters of H. A. Gwynne to The Countess Bathurst, 1914–1918* (London, 1990), 55.
[155] IWM: 506, Reel 1 (1974).

Territorials, they seemed to disappear and quite suddenly it came upon you this is the war, everyone's going.[156]

George Ewart Evans, the Welsh writer, discovered Britain was at war when a motor car with a newspaper placard blaring 'WAR DECLARED' fixed to its back drove through his village of Abercynon in South Wales.[157] Herbert Larner's family, like many families, was enjoying the Bank Holiday weekend at the seaside. He recalled how they discovered that Britain was at war when 'suddenly there was a rush of paper boys yelling "Special—War declared" running along Morecambe beach.'[158] The shouts of newsboys were the principal means by which people found out about the declaration of war.

A lack of up-to-date news in rural areas meant that the announcement of war often came as an even greater shock. Dai Dan Evans, a coalminer from South Wales, recalled 'Nobody expected the war to come, I mean from the little villages . . . [the declaration of war] was a shattering blow see. It came like a bolt from the blue as far as the mass of the people were concerned.'[159] William Johnson, on holiday in Saltfleetby, near Grimsby, was remote from all sources of news and had no idea about the extent of the crisis until he returned to London on 8 August.[160] Public notices announcing the outbreak of war were more common in rural areas than newspaper headlines and became a focal gathering point for the community to discover and then discuss the news. Grace Whitham, a mill-worker in Worsall, North Yorkshire, recalled how war was announced in the village by a notice on the church noticeboard. The entire mill left work to go and read it.[161] Beatrice McCann, a teenager in rural West Berkshire, discovered that Britain was at war with Germany when the postman cycled eight miles uphill from Hungerford to bring the news.[162] For some this delay in news created a sense of detachment. On holiday in Looe, Cornwall over the Bank Holiday weekend, Norman Edwards, a young man originally from Sutton Coldfield, felt that the war had nothing to do with him. It was only when he returned to his urban home that the reality of war set in with friends enlisting and the evidence of mobilization around him.[163] Alternatively the lack of news in rural areas compounded people's anxieties because it took them longer to find out what was actually happening.

However, apart from how people found out they were at war, there was little difference between urban and rural communities in the nature of the reaction, apart from volunteering. The war 'was greeted in rural communities, as elsewhere in English society, with a mixture of relief that the long weeks of rumour were at and end, and nervous apprehension about what lay ahead'.[164] In a letter to his son dated

---

[156] IWM: 511, Reel 1 (1974).
[157] George Ewart Evans, *The Strength of the Hills: An Autobiography* (London, 1983), 12–13.
[158] ERO: T/Z 25/687 (1966).
[159] SWML, HH: SWCC AUD/263: Dai Dan Evans (1972).
[160] IWM, Docs: Johnson, William W.: PP/MCR/47, 8 August 1914.
[161] NWSA: 2000.0694: Grace Whitham (2000).
[162] Liddle: DF Recollections: Box J-M: Beatrice McCann (n.d.).
[163] City Sound Archives, Birmingham Museum: R48 (1981).
[164] Pamela Horn, *Rural Life in England in the First World War* (Dublin, 1984), 24.

15 August, Robert Saunders, headmaster of the local school in the small Sussex village of Fletching, described the prevailing mood: 'Another week of excitement, everyone restless and ready to discuss war news on the slightest provocation ... Every night there is a rush for the evening papers which arrive at 9 p.m., then [the] doctor and his wife come in to compare notes and discuss the war generally.'[165] The writer, Rudyard Kipling, was holidaying in Kessingland, Suffolk, on 7 August and commented how calmly the local people reacted to the outbreak of war: 'they don't howl or grouse, or get together and jaw but go about their job like large horses ... the simple Suffolker doesn't panic. He just carries on all serene.'[166]

Some anti-war protests were made following the official declaration of war on 4 August. Three members of the government resigned: John Burns (President of the Board of Trade), John Morley (Lord President of the Council), and Charles Trevelyan (Secretary to the Board of Education).[167] Burns received a number of letters from his constituents in Battersea, as well as from non-constituents across England, in support of his actions.[168] However, for Burns and Morley, resignation was their first and final act of protest. Lord Morley assured his colleagues in the House of Commons on 4 August that he would watch them 'in tactical silence from a long way off' and pledged to 'do nothing, by speeches or letters, to embarrass them in any way in carrying out what they consider to be proper and necessary'.[169]

Opposition to the war was not widespread in August 1914. In general, both the Socialist and Labour leadership came out in favour of its prosecution. The British Socialist Party (BSP) executive announced its cautious support although there was anti-war 'internationalist dissent' both in London and Glasgow. On Clydeside, the BSP, under the leadership of John Maclean and William Gallacher, conducted a strong anti-war agitation. They were aided by the pacifist Independent Labour Party (ILP), and the two organizations held a large peace demonstration on Glasgow Green on 9 August attended by around 5,000 people. However, the press universally boycotted the event and the 'Stop the War' campaign barely got off the ground.[170] Similarly, a meeting of the ILP, held in Loanhead, near Edinburgh on 4 August, had to be brought to 'a hasty conclusion' owing to the number of interruptions received by people who supported the King and Sir Edward Grey. Accusations of Grey being 'the greatest scoundrel on God's earth' were intolerable to the gathered audience.[171]

Although official government censorship took time to be instituted, ordinary people immediately and voluntarily dealt with anti-war opinion. The Lord Provost

---

[165] IWM, Docs: Saunders, R.: 79/15/1, 15 August 1914.

[166] Thomas Pinney, ed., *The Letters of Rudyard Kipling*, vol. 4 (London, 1999), 248, 250.

[167] Prior to the declaration of war, David Lloyd George (Chancellor of the Exchequer), Lord Beauchamp, and Simon had all declared that they would resign on the outbreak of war. However, they were all persuaded to stay.

[168] BL: John Burns: Add 46303, ff. 12–13, 4 August 1914.

[169] BL: Ashley Papers 5738, 4 August 1914.

[170] *Forward*, 15 August 1914.

[171] *Edinburgh Evening News*, 5 August 1914, 3.

of Glasgow, D. M. Stevenson, who had publicly expressed his doubts about the basis for war throughout early August, was lambasted in the press once the official declaration was announced. A number of citizens even demanded his resignation from the council.[172] On 6 August, Keir Hardie, who four days earlier had confidently addressed a large anti-war crowd in Trafalgar Square, was shouted off stage by his own constituents in Aberdare, for expressing the same opinions. Emrys Hughes, his future son-in-law, witnessed the commotion:

> As Hardie rose, the silence changed into pandemonium and it was evident that a well organised opposition had captured the back of the hall. A bell began to clang, there was a lot of shouting which culminated in the singing of the national anthem, *Rule Britannia* and other patriotic songs. The men in the front rows got on their seats and shouted back at the disturbers and there were two or three fights. It was evident there was going to be no meeting that night, and that Hardie would not be allowed to speak . . . There was booing and shouting on all sides, the sound of a revolver shot and an ugly rush but we managed to get out onto the street unhurt and walked along followed by the mob still singing and shouting all the time . . . On we went up the main street—the crowd dwindling away and ultimately breaking up.[173]

The MP, Arthur Ponsonby, was a strong opponent of the war although he did not resign from the government in August. However, his opinions were not shared by his constituents. On 7 August he received a letter from William Donaldson who told him that:

> the feeling [in Stirling] . . . is universal, in approval of what the Government has done. Everybody is convinced that Mr Asquith and Sir E Grey did all they could to secure peace . . . The feeling is also universal that Germany overstepped all limits and that things had come to such a pass that British armed intervention was absolutely necessary.

Later that month Ponsonby attempted to organize a meeting with local Liberal Associations in Dunfermline but was told that if his attitude was to be critical he would not be well received.[174] On 8 August, James Ramsay MacDonald, MP for Leicester and leader of the ILP, gave his first anti-war speech following the official declaration of war when he addressed a Labour group at the Trades Hall in Leicester. The response from local political opposition was swift. At a hastily convened public meeting in the Market Place the next day, members of the Corporation, in a demonstration of cross-party solidarity, roundly rejected MacDonald's views before a large crowd of outraged townspeople.[175] Once the commitment to war had been made, those who had reservations about Britain's involvement had to put them to one side.

[172] Glasgow City Archives, Mitchell Library: Lord Provost's Letter Books: G1/1/22, August 1914 and *The Glasgow Herald*, 28 August 1914.
[173] NLS: Emrys Hughes: Dep 176/Box 7 (n.d.).
[174] MPP Bodleian: Arthur Ponsonby: MS Eng hist c.660, folio 99–100, 7 August 1914 and folio 106–13, 19 August 1914.
[175] Ben Beazley, *Four Years Remembered: Leicester During the Great War* (Derby, 1999), 15.

STORM DAMAGE

The immediate impact of the outbreak of war was characterized by disruption and dislocation. Shane Leslie accompanied the American Attaché to the deserted German Embassy in London on 11 August. His description of the scene they found evokes the kind of chaos and panic that accompanied the outbreak of war: 'All in pathetic confusion: rosary in bedroom, toys, letters...forgotten in a rush.'[176]

A variety of scheduled events were cancelled owing to the outbreak of war including, amongst many, the Shrewsbury Flower Show—held every year since 1885 and scheduled for 19 and 20 August 1914—and the Welsh Counties Hunters' Society Show, scheduled for 8 August.[177] As many people were on holiday at the seaside when war was declared there was a rush to get home on the crowded trains, many of which were delayed. This compounded the already tense atmosphere and brought home the reality of war.

The war was made immediately apparent in other ways. On 4 August Thomas Baker, a gardener in Buckinghamshire, observed how 'all sorts of transports started to move...I've never seen so many horses appear...after a few days...several brigades of troops were parked around Stanmore' in Greater London.[178] 'Quiet little Hereford' was overrun with troops and equipment.[179] Beatrice Trefusis, in London, recorded in her diary on 5 August how 'Everyone's plans are cancelled—everything is suddenly changed. The first visible sign of anything unusual here is the appearance of a few yeomanry men who have come here and are buying all the available horses in the neighbourhood for the Govt [sic], and rushing off with them'.[180] Sonny Cracknell and his friends in Colchester were frequently late for school because of the number of soldiers who marched from the barracks in Clacton to Colchester every day at 8 a.m. blocking the road.[181] W. Eaves, in Plymouth, described on 8 August how 'trenches are being dug all along the coastlines...and this evening I was confronted by a barbed wire entanglement and a redoubt of sandbags'.[182] Sentries appeared at strategic points across the country. The writer, Virginia Woolf, described how Lewes, Sussex, was practically 'under martial law' within a week of the outbreak of war.[183] Between 7 and 10 August Eleanor Roberts, visiting London from America, made frequent references in her diary to the number of soldiers parading, Territorials marching back to barracks, confiscated horses and motor cars, and 'long lines of artillery and

[176] NLI: Shane Leslie: Ms 22,863, 11 August 1914,
[177] *Daily Mail*, 8 August 1914, p.4 and Carmarthenshire Archives Service, Carmarthen: United Counties Hunters' Society Show Minute Book: D/UCHS/2, 8 August 1914.
[178] IWM: 8721, Reel 1 (1985).
[179] WRO: Ref 705:185: BA 8185: Parcel 2: Phillip A. Leicester, 5 August 1914.
[180] Liddle: Domestic front: DF 129: B.M. Trefusis, 5 August 1914.
[181] ERO: SA 8/482/1 (n.d.).
[182] PWDRO: Letter on outbreak of war: Acc 511/1, 8 August 1914.
[183] Nigel Nicolson, ed., *The Question of Things Happening: The Letters of Virginia Woolf, Volume 2: 1912–1922* (London, 1976), 51.

ammunition wagons, with their horses picketed near... ready to leave at a moment's notice'.[184] Miss N. Cordal, a domestic servant in Lowestoft, recalled that within a few days of the announcement of war the harbour was 'packed with ships' like never before. The war soon brought changes closer to home and she was eventually 'let go' from her position as her employers attempted to economize.[185]

Economically, the war was expected to have large, and distressing, effects. The financial expert, Sir Charles Addis, feared the economic, and other, consequences of a German defeat. On 9 August he decried the:

> hateful war. Even victory is only *less* hateful than defeat and *less* hurtful. But hurtful and hateful our victory must be. After all Germany stands for a great deal of what is best in civilisation. If she is wiped out the damage moral and intellectual as well as economic will be enormous.[186]

In the House of Commons, the radical MP Josiah Wedgwood foresaw disruption of trade and industry, with consequent social upheaval. Ramsay MacDonald warned that 'there are places like West Ham, where the whole population will encamp on the doorstep of the workhouse before the month is over'.[187] In early August 1914 the War Office advised local military and civilian authorities to start preparing for outbreaks of disorder that might erupt owing to the foreseen sudden increase in unemployment and food prices.[188] To meet the anticipated distress, relief committees were set up and large sums donated by the public. Within twenty-four hours of its establishment on 7 August the Prince of Wales' National Relief Fund had raised £250,000.

Fears of immediate economic dislocation expressed by Liberals were realized very quickly in August 1914. Although *The Times* called for those 'who cannot fight' to learn 'to sit still' and restrain from flocking to withdraw money, amass food stores in their houses, or rush about the country seeking sanctuary, panic was soon visible, particularly in London.[189] Here the population caused a considerable strain on the Bank of England as they rushed to spend, stock up, and protect their savings. In consequence, the Bank Holiday had to be extended to Thursday, 6 August in order to give the Bank of England the breathing space it required. The government printed an issue of £1 and 10s. in paper notes and then boldly reduced the bank rate from 10 per cent (the rate it had reached on 1 August) to 6 per cent. As early as 1 August the *Daily Mail* reported food prices in the capital rising and large quantities being bought by hospitals for backup supplies. On 3 August the paper reported the rush to buy food and how many shops had been cleared out. 'The amount of

---

[184] ERO: SA 1324/1, Eleanor Roberts' diary, 7–10 August 1914.

[185] ERO: T/Z 25/596 (1966).

[186] Letter from Sir Charles Addis, 9 August 1914 cited in David Kynaston, *The City of London, Volume III: Illusions of Gold, 1914–1945* (London, 1999), 10.

[187] Cited in Armitage, *Leicester 1914–18: The War-Time Story of a Midland Town*, 16.

[188] DRO: Lord Lieutenant of Devon: Protection of Vulnerable Points: 1262M/L147, August 1914.

[189] *The Times*, 1 August 1914, 6.

business', reported one London shopkeeper, was 'unprecedented'.[190] A wealthy Kensington resident recorded the scenes she had witnessed in London on 5 August:

The well-to-do people in London have, in quantities lost their heads. They are buying enormous stores of food, as if for siege provisions, despite the requests for days in the Press that they would not selfishly put-up the prices. One woman rang up Barker's Stores, Kensington, at 4am on Saturday, Aug 1, and ordered from the night watchman £65 worth of provisions, groceries, coal etc. Taxis today are laden with provisions people are taking home. Some of the big stores have run out of fish. Smaller shops refuse to quote prices for meat, and will not undertake to deliver foods at regular customer's houses on account. They are selling provisions over the counter at fancy prices. Bacon is scarce, and sugar, groceries and butter have risen in price. One grocer would not undertake to deliver our ordinary small orders, but finally did so . . . Among the very poor there is indignation at rich people laying in siege stores, and they say burglars, and people who may starve later, are marking the houses where it is done, in order to raid them later on. We are neither withdrawing money to hoard, or ordering any food more than our customary daily needs for a household of eight women.[191]

The financial panic spread beyond London. On 4 August the Committee of the Edinburgh and District Trades' Council passed a motion protesting against Cuthbert's Co-Operation Association for raising the price of foodstuffs in the town. The motion was withdrawn when the Association revealed it had been compelled to raise prices in an attempt to discourage people from buying large quantities.[192] On 4 August, the artist, Augustus John, urged his partner, Doriella McNeill, to 'get in at once a supply of flour and potted goods, tea etc for a month or two. It looks as if we'll need them . . . In a week or two there'll be no money about and no food'.[193] On 5 August members of the Liverpool Labour Representation Committee and Labour Party reported that local workers were already 'suffering from excessive charges for necessaries of life'.[194] In August, Alice Nash, near Hull, had been left in charge of her younger brothers and sisters whilst her mother was away. On hearing the declaration of war Alice felt the appropriate action was to spend all the 'emergency money' left by her mother on food, resulting in enough supplies to last six weeks or more.[195] The cook in Lillian Levi's house in Glasgow went so far as to hoard lumps of sugar in her pillowcase.[196]

The war had an immediate and negative impact on trade and employment. By 2 August Birmingham was suffering considerably and there was great uneasiness on the Newcastle coal exchange. In the Fifeshire coalfield alone nearly 20,000 men were said to be unemployed on 4 August. A few days later the industry and transport services of Liverpool were almost at a standstill, and the Yorkshire woollen

[190] *Daily Mail*, 1 August 1914, 6 and 3 August 1914, 7.
[191] IWM, Docs: Diary of a London lady (anonymous): Misc 29 (522), 5 August 1914.
[192] NLS: Edinburgh and District Trades' Council, Minutes: Acc 11177/16, 4 August 1914.
[193] NLW: Augustus John: Mss 22777D, ff. 48–9, 4 August 1914.
[194] LRO: Liverpool Labour Representation Committee and Labour Party: 331 TRA/6/3, 5 August 1914.
[195] Liddle: DF Recollections: Box N-S: Alice Nash (n.d.).
[196] IWM, Docs: Levi, Mrs Lillian: 86/68/1 (n.d.).

industry was in a serious state of depression. The war had an immediate and devastating effect on Cornwall's three main industries—china clay, tin mining and fishing—exacerbating pre-war trends in tin mining and bringing new issues of restricted markets and a reduced labour force for china clay and fishing.[197] Although employment was already on a downward curve in July 1914, the war brought instant disaster, particularly for the cotton trade owing to the suspension of all imports and exports. Burnley, which was producing 75 per cent of its normal output in July, sank to 25 per cent in August, a trend that would continue for the remainder of 1914. On 6 August Louis Rooke wrote to his son, Leonard, who was about to depart for Egypt on active service, apologizing that he would not be able to see him off owing to the 'terrible dislocation' of his soap brokerage business in Liverpool.[198] On 10 August, Cecil Jackman, a businessman, described the economic situation in London: 'the . . . luxury trades like feathers fancy boxes etc are done and there will be many women out . . . Printing is depressed. Furniture and clothing temporarily collapsed. Clerks out in numbers'.[199] Although on 8 August Alex Morton, owner of Morton Sundour Fabrics Ltd in Dentonhill, Carlisle, appealed to his suppliers to continue with business 'as normal', by 11 August a notice was posted outside the factory informing workers that they would now all be working on short time owing to the dislocation of the textile industry.[200] By 13 August, Nellie May, in Caterham, Surrey, was at her 'wits end' trying to keep her female staff employed at her textile business. 'I *must* do it somehow if only on half-time—things are much too bad to think of pleasure'. Four days later the situation had deteriorated further: 'there is *no* business doing and little or no work for my girls . . . I think the most I can hope for is 1 months business and that [is] probably extremely uncertain'.[201]

Rural areas also suffered. As early as 12 August, George Sturt commented on the difficulties experienced by businesses in Farnham, Surrey as a result of the disruption of supplies and the commandeering of horse power, which had led to much short-time working, including his own workshop:

> The builders are in want of materials: the gravel company cannot get trucks (railway) to send their gravel away, and scarce know how to keep their men at work. Half the motor cars, and more than half the horses in the neighbourhood have been commandeered by the military. The milkmen cannot get their milk delivered.[202]

At Little Waltham in Essex, a labourer recalled how several of his fellow workers were members of the Reserve and were called up out of the harvest field.[203] The

[197] *West Briton*, 17 August 1914.
[198] Liddle: GS 1382: Major Leonard Frank Rooke, 6 August 1914.
[199] GRO: Correspondence to Bruce Family: D19/41, 10 August 1914.
[200] NAS, GRH: Morton of Darvel papers: GD 326/24/1, 8, 11 August 1914.
[201] GRO: Correspondence to Bruce Family: D19/41, 13, 17 August 1914.
[202] E. D. Mackerness, ed., *The Journals of George Sturt, 1905–1927*, 2 vols., vol. 2 (London, 1967), 699.
[203] ERO: T/Z 25/803 (1966).

sudden disappearance of farm-workers at harvest-time created significant difficulties for farmers who had been employing them.

The panic over food and money was indicative of more general confusion and anxiety in the immediate days and weeks following the announcement of war. R. W. M. Gibbs was surrounded by people panicking in his boarding house in Bournemouth:

> Nobody seemed to quite realise what had happened. One American gentleman staying at the boarding house who had been for some days very successfully courting a very pretty girl, suddenly announced his intention of dashing off to Switzerland to fetch his wife and family . . . Several old ladies were very agitated with regard to financial matters and rushed about trying to cash cheques.[204]

Walter Hines Page described the scenes at the American Embassy in London on 6 August as 'bedlam turned loose' as 'crazy [American] men and weeping women were imploring and cursing and demanding' to be safely repatriated. One American woman was so distressed about not being able to return home that she had allegedly 'cut her throat'.[205] Political figures and religious and community leaders tried to calm and steer their constituencies and congregations. James McCarthy, the Bishop of Galloway, South-West Scotland circulated a prayer to be read at all masses in the diocese on 16 August. It acknowledged the horror of war, the distress, dislocation, suffering and upheaval that it caused, and urged people to remain calm in the 'common calamity'.[206]

Despite prior anticipation in some quarters and a more generalised apprehension, the actual outbreak of war took both the government and people by surprise. Although immediate steps were taken to regulate certain aspects of British wartime society, such as the control and incarceration of 'enemy aliens' and propping up the insurance and financial markets, other aspects of state provision were slow to develop. The government's response to anxieties about food production and supplies was left wanting. Despite some precautionary measures, such as the taking over of the railways (on 4 August) to control food distribution and the buying up of sugar supplies in the West Indies to compensate for the loss of imports from Central Europe, the government's attitude was to rely on exhortation and persuasion rather than direct action. On 3 August they established the Cabinet Committee on Food Supplies, their policy being 'not to interfere with ordinary trade at all, but to leave the traders to conduct their own business'.[207] Relief provision was also ad hoc, and took time to become centralized and organized. In this vacuum, and through fears of impending distress, local projects sprang up spontaneously. Yet nowhere was this chaos more visible than in Britain's embryonic voluntary recruitment system.

---

[204] MPP Bodleian: R.W.M. Gibbs: MS Eng misc c.159, 18 September 1914.
[205] Link, ed., *The Papers of Woodrow Wilson*, 367, 370.
[206] Scottish Catholic Archives, Edinburgh: Diocese of Galloway: DG 6/4/5, 16 August 1914.
[207] Reginald McKenna cited in David French, 'The Rise and Fall of "Business as Usual"', in *War and the State: The Transformation of British Government 1914–1919*, ed. Kathleen Burk (London, 1982), 19.

Conventionally, the 'rush to the colours' has been taken as prime evidence of the supposed 'war enthusiasm' in August 1914. However, the fine chronology of recruitment tells a different tale.[208] The monthly enlistment rates for the regular army and Territorial Force in Britain from August to December 1914 show that September, not August, emerges as the month with the strongest recruitment (462,901 men) not just in 1914 but for the whole war, representing 9 per cent of the overall enlistment in the army. This is not to deny that an intensification of volunteering took place at the outset of war. Despite logistical and promotional issues surrounding voluntary recruitment at the outbreak of war, around 113,000 men volunteered between 4 and 24 August, which was symptomatic of the mood of national emergency. Men were also responding, in part, to the appeals made by Lord Kitchener which appeared in _The Times_ on 7 and 28 August. But mass recruitment came later, in the first week of September—when 188,327 men volunteered in just seven days.

This qualified picture of volunteering at the outset of the war is confirmed and partly explained by the hesitancy with which contemporaries turned their shock at the outbreak of war into the major step of joining the armed forces, with huge potential consequences for their personal lives, families, and careers. In Glasgow, Thomas Macmillan, tossed a coin with his brother over which one of them would enlist; whoever won the bet would get to stay at home to look after their ageing parents. Thomas lost and he enlisted shortly afterwards.[209] James Stewart Roy, a lecturer in English at the University of St Andrews, recalled his mother's reaction to him wanting to enlist in October 1914:

> My mother came over to me and laying her hands on my shoulder said in her calm quiet voice like one speaking after much thought: 'My dear boy, I have never ventured to broach the subject but I know how deeply you have been feeling and the struggle that has been going on inside you. But you must allow no consideration for me to stand in the way of what you believe to be your duty. Whatever you do I shall accept your decision. I know that you will have reached your decision after much prayerful consideration. Let nothing stand between you and what you believe to be your duty. And remember, should you decide to go I shall be in good keeping.' . . . I knew how much these words had cost her.[210]

Many of the men, like Roy, who sought their parents' approval would have eventually enlisted. However, it highlights the consideration put into the decision, and the time taken over it. Alan Dorward, a student of philosophy at Trinity College, Cambridge, deliberated for weeks over whether or not he should enlist. In his diary entry for 25–27 August he recorded how discouraging his mother was, adding to his indecisiveness. Eventually it was his doctor who made the decision for him: owing to a medical condition he was deemed unfit for active service.[211]

[208] Gregory, 'British "War Enthusiasm" in 1914: A Reassessment', 80.
[209] IWM, Docs: Macmillan, Thomas: PP/MCR/C56 (1935).
[210] NLS: James Stewart Roy: Acc 5415 (n.d.).
[211] Later Chair of Philosophy at the University of Liverpool, 1928–1954. University of Liverpool, Special Collections: Dorward Diaries, Diary 10: D446/10/10, 25–27 August 1914.

Some soldiers who sought approval of their decision were met with encouragement. W. J. Parr, a vicar in Lechlade, Gloucestershire approved his son's request to join the Royal Naval Division on 28 August 1914: 'We can offer no opposition to your doing anything that may be of loyal service to your Country ... Do whatever you think is best and offer where the need is greatest.' However, a week later he added that this decision had been 'rather a wrench' for him.[212] A. J. H. Marshall, the headmaster of a school in Southampton, congratulated Sapper William Thomas, a former pupil, on his decision to enlist on 4 October:

> You have done the right thing in enlisting. The country needs young men of your stamp just now. The old school motto—'DUTY' is a glorious one, and I am glad to tell you that a goodly number of old boys are serving their country.[213]

Others were met with disapproval. In a letter dated 10 September, Alan Gardner, on active service with the Young Men's Christian Association, berated his family for not being enthusiastic about him enlisting.[214] Many letters exist from soldiers to their mothers or partners asking them to be brave and not downhearted, highlighting the negative impact enlisting had on those who remained at home.[215] From Aldershot on 6 August Charles Carrington, author of the noted post-war memoir *A Subaltern's War*, described to his parents how 'every family in the district is upset' because of the orders to mobilize.[216] On the 8 September, aged 17 years, he enlisted with the 1st Birmingham Battalion of the Royal Warwickshire Regiment. Some mothers tried to stop their sons from enlisting. In a letter to his wife dated 25 August F. N. Blundell, an officer with the Lancashire Hussars encamped at Prescot, Merseyside, noted how 'the mothers of Little Crosby are up in arms against the idea of enlistment'.[217] In an interview with the Archbishop of Canterbury on 2 December, General Campbell, the Head of the Recruiting Department at the War Office revealed his concerns about the interference of women in the volunteering process who were holding back potential recruits.[218] General Campbell's concerns were not unfounded. Martha Lord, a schoolgirl from Todmorden, West Yorkshire in 1914, recalled in 1990 her mother's reaction to her 17-year-old brother Edward's desire to enlist:

> He was working at the bobbin mill ... he wanted to go ... and his friends were joining up. And me mother kept telling him she didn't want him to go you know. She understood what was ... better than he did because there'd been the Boer War during me mother's lifetime ... About end of October ... they came, a sergeant ... to the bobbin mill ... and one of the neighbours came running to our house and she said

[212] Liddle: GS 1226: Jackie W. Parr, 28 August 1914 and 7 September 1914.
[213] Liddle: DF: Education & Children & Students, Item 35, 4 October 1914.
[214] Liddle: GS 0607: Alan Gardner, 10 September 1914.
[215] Liddle: GS 0069: John Bagnall-Bury, 5 November 1914 and GS 1732: H.R. Wight, 5 December 1914.
[216] Liddle: GS 0273: Charles E. Carrington, 6 August 1914. Charles Edmonds, *A Subaltern's War* (London, 1929).
[217] LanRO: Letters of Captain F.N. Blundell: DDBL acc. 6519, 25 August 1914.
[218] Lambeth Palace: Davidson Papers: Recruiting Campaigns: Volume 341 [Great War], ff. 257, 2 December 1914.

'Mrs Clarke . . . there's a sergeant come and two soldiers with him and they've set up some boxes and he's going to speak to the men as they come out and try to recruit them. They're coming out of work, it's dinner time.' And me mother got her shawl on and hurried down and he [the sergeant] were talking to these men and telling them to come, you know, and to be patriotic and serve their country. . . . . And he had his hand on me brother's shoulder . . . And, like a mother would do, she just went up to him and she knocked his hand off his shoulder and she said 'you're not having my lad.' And she got hold of his [Edward's] arm and pulled him away.[219]

Martha's mother was unable to stop her son from volunteering—he ran away and enlisted soon after this incident and died on the Somme in 1916. L. Wilson enlisted in Hull in 1914 although his mother had vowed that 'none of my lads will ever enlist'. On hearing that he had volunteered she 'broke down and sobbed broken heartedly'.[220] It was not only mothers who were devastated by their son's enlistment. In early December, Sir Alfred Dale, Vice-Chancellor of Liverpool University, received an angry letter from the father of a student who had sought Dale's advice about enlisting. Although the student wanted to fulfil what he perceived to be his duty, his father strongly disagreed.[221]

Other men delayed enlisting because of familial or business commitments. George Singles, a regular soldier, was working at the recruiting office in Whitehall in early August 1914. He described to his mother how he was 'sitting here like a stuffed mummy waiting for a few more straggling' volunteers to turn up. 'They are all grumbling as most of them have had to leave good jobs.'[222] William Jones, a clerk in the Gas Department of Birmingham Corporation in 1914, did not enlist until August 1915 because he was the sole carer for his mother and their home, owing to the death of his father in 1913. He also had commitments to his local church.[223] A. Stuart Dolden, a solicitor's clerk in London, was forced by his employers to wait until November before joining up, and was then 'absolutely shattered' to be turned down because his chest measurement was two inches under regulation.[224] Men were also delayed by the process of settling their affairs and securing post-war employment.

Between 11 and 31 August 1914 the lowest daily national returns occurred on 23 August (2,571 men), 16 August (3,215), and 22 August (5,922).[225] There are external factors which help to explain the low levels of recruiting during the third week of war. Many thought that Secretary of State for War Lord Kitchener's call for 100,000 men was the sum total required. It was announced on 25 August 1914, that the first 100,000 had almost been secured. It was not until 28 August that Kitchener appealed for a further 100,000 men, giving a further boost to

[219] NWSA: 2001.0740: Martha Lord (1990).
[220] IWM, Docs: Wilson, L.: 86/30/1 (n.d.).
[221] University of Liverpool, Special Collections: Letter Book of Vice-Chancellor Sir Alfred Dale: S 2341, Letter 642–3, 4 December 1914.
[222] Liddle: GS 1479: George Herbert Singles, August 1914.
[223] City Sound Archive, Birmingham Museum: R56 (1988).
[224] A. Stuart Dolden, *Cannon Fodder: An Infantryman's Life on the Western Front, 1914–18* (Poole, 1980), 11.
[225] NA, Kew: NATS, 1/398.

recruitment.[226] At a local level there had been confusion about how and where to enlist. The actual process of enlistment was not necessarily easy, as the pre-war machinery struggled to cope with the vastly increased numbers. Stories appeared in the press of men who had waited all day at recruiting offices returning home unaccepted, simply because there were no doctors to examine them. New recruits were faced with a system in utter chaos. Similar experiences were reported up and down the country as the army's administration sagged under the weight of volunteers in August and September 1914. In the early weeks of the war, age and height regulations were carefully adhered to, and the medical examination was relatively thorough, leading to a high number of rejections which distorts volunteering (will-ingness) and enlistment (final result) statistics. Finally, there was much concern and confusion in the early weeks of the war over pay and allowances, especially for married men. During August 1914 separation allowances were still paid monthly in arrears, and it was not announced until 28 August 1914 that they would definitely be paid to new recruits.[227] For Elizabeth Lee, a young woman in Kent, the chaos of the first week of war was summed up by the lack of a properly organized recruiting system. She recalled how 'there was troops marching, chaps joining up all in their regular clothes, some using broom handles, you know, for imaginary guns and drilling going on in every odd bit of field . . . the chaos that there was getting [the men] ready'.[228]

***

A range of witnesses have testified to their feelings in response to the build-up and outbreak of war in July/early August 1914. Urban/rural, male/female, upper/middle/working class, elite/non-elite, and young/old have supported the view that shock, tension, anxiety, dread, and defiance characterized British popular responses in the days that immediately followed the announcement of war. Even those in positions that necessitated a 'finger' on the European pulse, such as politicians and financiers, were, to a large extent, shocked by the outbreak of hostilities. No major differences appear in the first phase of the chronology between regions, although military towns and naval ports did experience more concentrated activity. There is also a suggestion that these areas, used to sending their young men away as reservists at times of national emergency, responded to the outbreak of war in 1914 more calmly as regular contact with the military and navy had instilled in them a readiness and willingness to fight when war came.[229] Overall, local and individual concerns, such as the future of local business and the dislocation of families, were as omnipresent as the broader issue of increasingly unstable European politics. Dislocation and uncertainty featured in all aspects of life, including how people responded to the call for volunteers. The outbreak of war had sent shockwaves through all communities: for many men it would take time for the dust to settle before life-changing decisions, such as volunteering, could be made.

---

[226] *The Times*, 28 August 1914, 6.

[227] John Morton Osborne, *The Voluntary Recruiting Movement in Britain, 1914–1916* (New York, 1982), 8–9, Peter Simkins, *Kitchener's Army: The Raising of the New Armies 1914–1916* (Manchester, 1988), 31–78, 106.

[228] IWM: 779, Reel 3 (1976).

[229] Dalley, 'The Response in Cornwall to the Outbreak of the First World War', 87.

Resignation and defiance were additional notable characteristics of the public mood in the period immediately following the outbreak of war. In a letter to his New York manager, William Thomson, dated 10 August, George MacKenzie Brown—who directed Thomas Nelson and Sons publishing house in partnership with the Scottish novelist John Buchan—described the public mood:

> Almost everybody in Great Britain seems satisfied that there was no other course open to us but to go to war, and the people are taking it very quietly and with determination to see the thing through.[230]

On the whole, those who had strongly disagreed with the war, regardless of religious or political beliefs, had resigned themselves. In a letter to A. N. Monkhouse, the writer and journalist, Walter Dixon Scott, the literary critic, revealed how: 'The whole thing is blind idiocy. Perhaps worse—there's knavery too. But we're evidently in it for now.'[231] He died of dysentery on the troop-ship *Aquintania* near the Dardanelles, three weeks after landing on 23 October 1915. Despite the prospect of a 'ghastly list of casualties' following the fall of Namur in late August 1914, Neville Chamberlain, member-elect of Birmingham City Council since 1911 and Chairman of the Town Planning Committee, defiantly stated that the country must 'stick it out' and 'win in the end'.[232]

Aspects of the war that would become strong features of the remainder of 1914, appeared already in these early days. A volunteer spirit, an obsession with spies, a fear of enemy infiltration, and a sense of national community in wartime were becoming the basis of British wartime society. By 10 August contemporaries were complaining of a lack of war news and this vacuum was quickly filled with fear, anticipation, imagination, and rumour. The reality of war was sinking in; by 18 August, the Archbishop of Canterbury was receiving requests from his clergy for prayers for the dead.[233] The war was taking over people's lives. On 21 August, Lydia Middleton, wife of Thomas Middleton at the Board of Agriculture in London, told her son how 'it is hard to believe that the war has only lasted for seventeen days. It feels like seventeen weeks at least'.[234] By 23 August Lady Mabel Napier from Northumberland, wrote to her sons telling them how she could 'think and talk of nothing but the war, and all news is awaited for anxiously'.[235] Evidence of war was appearing everywhere, including its harsh realities. As Asquith wrote to his wife, Margot, on 18 August 'the curtain is lifted'.[236]

---

[230] Cited in Imogen L. Gassert, 'Collaborators and Dissidents: Aspects of British Literary Publishing in the First World War, 1914–1919' (DPhil, University of Oxford, 2002).
[231] MALSL: Walter Dixon Scott: MISC/391, August 1914.
[232] University of Birmingham, Special Collections: Neville Chamberlain's Political Journal, 1913–1920: NC 2/20, 24 August 1914.
[233] Lambeth Palace: Davidson Papers. Prayers and Special Services: Volume 367 [Great War], ff. 88.
[234] Liddle: DF 091: Mrs Lydia Middleton, 21 August 1914.
[235] Liddle: DF 094: Lady Mabel Napier, 23 August 1914.
[236] MPP Bodleian: Margot Asquith: MS Eng c.6691. ff. 161–2, 18 August 1914.

2

The National Cause

Once the shock of the outbreak of war had subsided, the first question people asked themselves was why Britain was at war. How did the British people construct a positive image of the national self in 1914? How did they define the national cause? What was emphasized and why? How selective was the resulting vision? Was a new moral order created? If so, who was included and who excluded? What defined appropriate and inappropriate behaviour? Finally, who disagreed with Britain being at war?

WHY ARE WE AT WAR?

Explaining why Britain was at war involved constructing heroes, victims, scape-goats, and villains, however simplistic or idealistic. It was not enough to vilify the enemy: what Britain stood for in wartime had to be defined. Often these ideas were latent in peacetime but came to the fore once the nation was in crisis. Values, beliefs, and codes of behaviour that were inherent and implicit in Edwardian society, became explicit.

The decision to go to war in August 1914 left the Liberal government in a difficult position. Radical members of the Liberal Party, such as David Lloyd George, had campaigned against the South African War and were deeply suspicious of Conservative 'jingoism'. The Liberal Party had won the 1910 electoral campaigns based on a manifesto to reduce military spending. They now had to modify their pre-war pacifism, and did so by investing in the belief that Britain was fighting a 'holy war' for idealistic aims, such as freedom, liberty, and justice, above and beyond the mere object of beating the enemy. 'Poor little Belgium' relieved Liberals of unbearable embarrassment following 'a reversal of life-time commitments' against war.[1] Addressing Parliament on 6 August, Asquith emphasized efforts made by Grey—who kept much of his diplomacy secret, even from most of the Cabinet—to secure peace in the face of German aggression. Despite this, he went on, war had been forced upon Britain since it was its duty and honour to protect the rights of small nations, such as Belgium, and remain loyal to its old ally France. If

---

[1] Stuart Wallace, *War and the Image of Germany: British Academics 1914–1918* (Edinburgh, 1988), 59.

Britain had given into Germany's demands to remain neutral, the government would have been tarred 'with dishonour . . . and [would have] betrayed . . . the interests of this country'. According to Asquith, Britain was fighting first 'to fulfil a solemn international obligation . . . not only of law but of honour', an obligation that 'no self-respecting man could possibly have repudiated', and second to 'vindicate the principle that small nationalities are not to be crushed, in defiance of international good faith, by the arbitrary will of a strong and overmastering Power'. He concluded that Britain entered the war with a clear conscience, to defend civilization in the face of unbridled aggression.[2]

The major ideas expressed in this speech—national honour, rule of law, justice, the rights of small nations, fair play, and anti-bullying—were reiterated in pamphlets, literature, lectures, newspaper editorials, and speeches throughout 1914, all grappling with the question of why Britain was at war. Soon after the outbreak of the war, Charles Masterman, head of the War Propaganda Bureau, invited twenty-five leading British authors to Wellington House to discuss ways of best promoting Britain's interests during the war.[3] The novelist Arnold Bennett first contributed to the propaganda effort with *Liberty: A Statement of the British Case*, which appeared originally as an article in the *Saturday Evening Post*. Rudyard Kipling's hymn of dedication to the war, 'For All We Have and Are', appeared in *The Times* on 2 September, for which the editors donated £50 to the Belgian Relief Fund on his behalf.[4] British academics and intellectuals rallied behind Britain's cause. Three weeks after the outbreak of war, spontaneously and without government interference, members of the Oxford History School published what they felt was an authoritative version of the British case against Germany. *Why We Are At War: Great Britain's Case* inaugurated a long series of 'Oxford pamphlets' written by some of the best-known history tutors in Oxford at that time.[5] For the historians, Britain's obligation to France was as important as Belgium in Britain's decision to go to war.[6]

The war was justified to the British public in three ways. First, Germany, which was seen as a growing menace to peace for years, was made responsible for the war. Britain had striven for peace until the last moment, but its duty was to stop Prussian militarism. Connected to this idea was Britain's national honour. It could not stand by and let Germany dictate an aggressive foreign policy. Finally, this meant standing by both Belgium and France whose annihilation would be a disaster for British interests as well as honour. Such sentiments were articulated across the class spectrum. The topics of lectures given to the Manchester and District Branch of the

---

[2] *The Times*, 7 August 1914, 7.
[3] Including Arnold Bennett, Arthur Conan Doyle, G. K. Chesterton, John Galsworthy, Thomas Hardy, H. G. Wells, amongst others.
[4] *The Times*, 2 September 1914, 9.
[5] Harmut Pogge von Strandmann, 'The Role of British and German Historians in Mobilizing Public Opinion in 1914', in *British and German Historiography 1750–1950: Perceptions and Transfers*, ed. Benedikt Stuchtey and Peter Wende (Oxford, 2000), 351.
[6] Wallace, *War and the Image of Germany: British Academics 1914–1918*, 60–1.

Working Men's Club and Institute between August and December included why Britain's war was just and fair and why Germany needed to be crushed.[7] For Rupert Brooke the war meant that:

> Honour has come back, as a king, to earth
> And paid his subjects with a royal wage;
> And nobleness walks in our ways again;
> And we have come into our heritage.[8]

The government published a White Paper to substantiate this position, which contained a selection of the diplomatic correspondence between 22 July and 4 August. It aroused widespread interest and reprints were made in more popular form, such as Sir Edward Cook's *Why Britain is at War: The Causes and the Issues*.[9] After reading the White Paper, Lord Emmott, First Commissioner of Public Works,[10] told his daughter, Gwen, on 8 August that despite his doubts, 'having read the white book through I have no more doubt of the justice of this war than of my own existence'.[11] The equivalent French publication, the *Livre Jaune*, also provoked widespread interest amongst the British press and population when it was released in early December.[12] The evidence of German atrocities gathered and published in the British press throughout 1914 further substantiated Britain's righteousness. On 12 December, the Liberal journalist Harold Spender tried to convince the dissident former-MP John Burns of Britain's just cause, using such evidence:

> I have just read the *Belgian White Paper* and I am bound to say that it is a pretty black record of . . . violence. It is far more damaging than the other *Papers*. The German case in regard to Belgium does not exist, and I adhere to the view that we must stand by Belgium, especially after all our pledges.[13]

Most crucial of all was explaining the war in order to create a mass army by volunteering. The recruitment campaign was, therefore, the most important forum on which the national cause was defined. Britain's moral crusade had to be explained to the very men who were required to fight. All the political parties were anxious to cooperate in this campaign. Uniting under a single recruiting organization cemented this collaboration and stabilized a flawed and inadequate pre-war system of recruitment.[14] The first preliminary meeting of the

---

[7] GMRO: Records of the Manchester and District Branch of the Working Men's Club and Institute Ltd: G20/13, August to December 1914.

[8] Rupert Brooke, '*1914*': *Five Sonnets* (London, 1915). The sequence of poems was first published in the short-lived journal *New Numbers* Issue 4, December 1914.

[9] St Deiniol's Library, Hawarden: WW1 Pamphlet Collection: Box C: *Why Britain Is At War* (1914).

[10] Lord Emmott replaced Lord Beauchamp in this position in early August 1914. Lord Beauchamp was appointed Lord President to replace Lord Morley who had resigned in protest over the war.

[11] IWM, Docs: Peel, Captain H.: P391, 8 August 1914.

[12] AMAE, Paris: Correspondance politique et commerciale 1897–1918: Nouvelle Série: GUERRE 14–18; Dossiers divers: Vol 1715, ff. 151–2, 2 December 1914.

[13] BL: John Burns: Add 46303, ff. 147–8, 12 December 1914.

[14] Osborne, *The Voluntary Recruiting Movement in Britain, 1914–1916* (New York, 1982).

Parliamentary Recruiting Committee (PRC) was held on 27 August. It undertook many important roles, including the publication of recruiting material, such as pamphlets and posters, and the organization of meetings at local and national level.

Around 13 million PRC leaflets and over a million PRC posters had been issued by January 1915.[15] The latter concentrated on patriotic themes encapsulated in 'for King and Country' or liberal and humanitarian values such as 'freedom, fairness, anti-(Prussian) militarism, defence of the underdog ('plucky little Belgium'), and so on'.[16] Private Thomas McIndoe, who fought with the 12th Battalion Middlesex Regiment, recalled the impact of Alfred Leete's famous Kitchener poster, first issued in September 1914, on his decision to enlist: 'It was seeing the picture of Kitchener and his finger pointing at you—any position that you took up the finger was always pointing to you'.[17] Official PRC leaflets published in 1914 answered the question of why Britain was at war. Men were asked to fight in defence of the nation, to honour international promises and the rule of law, to halt the spread of German aggression, to avenge the atrocities in Belgium, and to prevent such violations happening on British soil. In a reversal of a rational cost-benefit analysis of war, whereby the destruction of war outweighs any benefit, men were asked to contemplate the cost of a British defeat, and thereby a German victory. The equation was simple; without enough recruits, the BEF would not be strong enough to withstand the advancing German army with their sights set on England. Could any man live with the guilt of knowing that their lack of patriotism contributed to a German victory?

Public recruiting meetings were another significant feature on the PRC's agenda. It is difficult to judge how much these meetings stimulated recruitment, but they were certainly considered an important part of the PRC's strategy in 1914. Different formats were tried across the country from cinema shows to military pageants where bands paraded through the streets. Frank Lockwood was involved in a scheme to encourage volunteering in his home county of Yorkshire. On 28 October an illuminated tram, which ran between Huddersfield and Marsden, was accompanied by a military band playing patriotic songs drawing carriages bearing messages of 'Your existence is at stake' and 'Your Country needs you'.[18] Some men did enlist because of these recruitment drives. Sixteen-year-old George Coppard was caught up in the heady excitement: 'news placards screamed out at every street corner, and military bands blared out their martial music in the main streets of Croydon. This was too much for me to resist and, as if drawn by a magnet, I knew I had to enlist straight away.' Lying about his age, he enlisted with the Royal West Surrey Regiment on 27 August.[19]

---

[15] R. Douglas, 'Voluntary Enlistment in the First World War and the Work of the Parliamentary Recruiting Committee', *Journal of Modern History* 42 (1970), 568.
[16] Porter, *The Absent-Minded Imperialists: Empire, Society, and Culture in Britain* (Oxford, 2004), 257.
[17] Max Arthur, *Forgotten Voices of the Great War* (London, 2006), 32.
[18] IWM, Docs: Lockwood F.T.: 96/52/1, 28 October 1914.
[19] George Coppard, *With A Machine Gun To Cambrai* (London, 1969, 1986), 1.

In September the War Office wrote to London Variety Theatres asking them to display recruiting posters and to present patriotic war tunes.[20] Recruitment songs performed at Music Halls emphasized the benefits of enlisting ('Ten bob a week, plenty grub to eat') and endorsed the positive values of Britain at war to an urban working class enjoying inexpensive entertainment.[21] Traditional songs, such as *Land of Hope and Glory* (composed in 1902) and *The Red, White, and Blue* confirmed Britain's superior qualities—freedom, greatness, and bravery—and called for British men to do their duty and fight to protect the nation's values. Recruiting songs in abundance called for men to fight for 'home and right', to 'answer Duty's call' for 'Old England stands for Justice, Truth/For Freedom, Honour, Right'.[22] Songs were also written in honour of Belgium.[23] *England's Debt*, a song written for Oxford Belgian Day—a local fundraising day in honour of the beleaguered country—on 7 November took a more sombre approach, recalling the atrocities inflicted upon the Belgian people and forcing the British people to understand the disastrous price of a German victory.[24]

However, in 1914, public recruiting meetings were the mainstay of the PRC's campaign where local dignitaries and political figures, likely to inspire trust and a sense of duty, took to the platform to appeal to men to enlist. The Vice-Chancellor of Liverpool University, Sir Alfred Dale, appealed to university graduates on 2 September:

> It is the duty of every man to consider not why he should offer himself for service, but why he can hold back. The need is urgent, the cause is great. The man who is free to give himself but fails to give, whatever the issue of the struggle may be, will look back hereafter on his great refusal with sorrow or with shame.[25]

At a recruiting meeting in Brighton on 7 September, Rudyard Kipling argued that, as Germany was fighting to overthrow the civilized world, more British men were needed to 'check this onrush of organised barbarism'.[26] The language of the speeches given at such meetings was formulaic. Positive qualities of Britain as a nation were emphasized, alongside the prospect of Germany winning the war. Appeals were made to avenge the atrocities in Belgium, to halt Prussian militarism, and to stand up for freedom, honour, and international law. To substantially increase the distribution of the message, these speeches were often reprinted in the newspapers, both locally and nationally, the following day, whilst editorials

[20] Andrew Horrall, *Popular Culture in London c.1890–1918: The Transformation of Entertainment* (Manchester, 2001), 192.

[21] *Come On And Join* reprinted in Max Arthur, *When This Bloody War Is Over: Soldiers' Songs of the First World War* (London, 2002), 3.

[22] For example, *Recruiting Song* and *A Recruiting Song For Those Who Might Join And Don't*: John Johnson Collection, Bodleian Library, Oxford: Great War, Box 21, 1914.

[23] Arthur, *When This Bloody War Is Over: Soldiers' Songs of the First World War*, 13–14.

[24] *England's Debt*: John Johnson Collection, Bodleian Library, Oxford: Great War, Box 21, 1914.

[25] University of Liverpool, Special Collections: Letter Book of Vice-Chancellor Sir Alfred Dale: S 2341, Letter 276, 2 September 1914.

[26] *The Times*, 8 September 1914, 10.

called for more and more men.[27] As the recruitment process was local, linguistic and religious communities, particularly in Wales and Scotland, were accommodated.

The nation did not stand alone in the righteousness of its cause. Quite apart from earthly allies, the support of God was enrolled, thus opening up for a society in which Christian belief still predominated a vast repertory of religious and spiritual values with which to frame the conflict. On 21 August the Archbishop of Canterbury, Randall Davidson, gave a service of intercession at Canterbury Cathedral. Although he regretted that war had come about at all, he felt that:

> Our conscience as a Nation State and people is, as regards this war, wholly clear. We might, I suppose, *for a time*, have stayed outside it. But it would have been at the loss of England's honour, England's chivalry to weaker peoples, England's faithfulness to plighted word. Could any of us have asked God's blessing upon that?[28]

Rhetoric like this was replicated from pulpits throughout Britain. On 16 August Reverend Canon F. J. Foakes-Jackson told his congregation at Westminster Abbey that Britain was fighting 'for liberty, for the rights of small nations against what we believe to be the tyranny of arrogance'.[29] Violet Clutton, in London, was particularly reassured by a service she attended at Westminster Abbey on Sunday 9 August:

> We had a perfectly splendid sermon which I think just expressed the feelings of all of us at this time. It pointed out that we have everything to be thankful for in that we have a just cause to fight for and that our hands are not soiled with bringing about the war; rather have we done all in our power to prevent it . . . we are fighting, not for our own gain but to protect the weak against the strong, and above all to keep our word that we would stand by our allies. It pointed out that in a true Christian one of the highest principles must ever be to keep an oath or compact, and as with individuals, so with nations, we have bound ourselves to stand by France [and Belgium] . . . It concluded by saying that for good and for ill it was necessary now that we should see it through to the end.[30]

Biblical allusions to the Good Samaritan, Naboth's Vineyard in 1 Kings, divine righteousness, and God's protection of the weak, were used to dispel quasi-pacifist qualms and justify, amongst religious communities, the decision to go to war.[31] Catholic leaders were inspired to support the war because of the feeling of camaraderie with poor Catholic Belgium. The Bishop of Salford, Louis Charles Casartelli, who had been trained at the University of Louvain, was devastated by the destruction of its historic library on 26 August. The tragedy moved him to support

---

[27] *The Times*, 28 October 1914, 9.

[28] Lambeth Palace: Davidson Papers: Sermons (1914–1917): Volume 548 [Sermons], ff. 34–42, 21 August 1914.

[29] Reverend Canon F. J. Foakes-Jackson, 16 August 1914, in *Sermons for the Times, No. 1. Four Sermons on War* (1914).

[30] DRO: Violet Clutton: 6258M/Box 1, Vol I, 9 August 1914.

[31] For example, the sermon by Reverend Samuel Hemphill, delivered on 9 August 1914, in *Sermons for the Times, No.4: Sermons on the Holy War* (1914). See also Dafydd Densil Morgan, '"Christ and the War": Some Aspects of the Welsh Experience, 1914–1918', *Journal of Welsh Religious History* 5 (1997), 74.

Britain's cause in the war more forcefully and vocally.[32] Widespread support of war by the Established and Nonconformist churches, alongside three prominent Nonconformist Carmarthenshire MPs, undoubtedly had an effect on opinion, and subsequently recruitment, in Wales.[33] Methodist ministers in Cornwall preached that the war was a just crusade and that it was a necessary purge of the human soul. They openly supported the war and tried to inspire this patriotic feeling amongst their congregations.[34] Leaders of the Scottish Presbyterian Churches also delivered sermons and addresses in support of Britain's war effort. In interpreting the outbreak of war, preachers emphasized Germany's breaking of treaty pledges and invasion of neutral Belgium. Germany was the aggressor and Britain had entered the war in self-defence, to preserve its liberty and empire.[35] Lucien Wolf, the Jewish journalist and historian, addressed the Jewish Historical Society of England on 7 December. He called for the 'whole Jewish community' to rally behind the war effort 'until the power of what is called German Militarism is crushed'. Only then could Jews across Europe live without menace to their political, civil, and religious rights.[36] Scriptural language was commandeered for militaristic use, and religious leaders, of all denominations, became recruiting officers.

Few religious leaders voiced any opposition to the Great War once it had broken out. The invasion of Belgium had particularly shocked and united Christian opinion in Britain. This act was understood as a flagrant violation of the principles of international law, the gradual building up of which Christians had been at pains to support as the best hope for future peace and international order. Christ's care of the downtrodden and weak, David defeating Goliath, and stories of the early Christian communities persecuted by the might of the Roman Empire were all evoked to support the moral necessity of Britain's intervention on behalf of Belgium.[37]

No section of British society was denied the opportunity to engage with the justifications for war in 1914, including its youngest members. As the future generation, the war was being fought on the behalf of children, and therefore they had to be educated about the national cause. Justifications of the war as a moral crusade became common in juvenile literature and, within days of the declaration of war, writers were busy explaining to their young readers just why the nation was at war. One of the earliest was Elizabeth O'Neill's *The War, 1914: A History and an Explanation for Boys and Girls*, published in the autumn of 1914. Her justification for war neatly summarized how most authors explained the war to children as a chivalric struggle against the forces of evil:

---

[32] Salford Diocesan Archives, Burnley: 1914 Diary of Bishop L. C. Casartelli, 29 August 1914.

[33] Robin Barlow, 'Some Aspects of the Experiences of Carmarthenshire in the Great War' (PhD, University of Wales, 2001), 36.

[34] Dalley, 'The Response in Cornwall to the Outbreak of the First World War' *Cornish Studies* 11 (2003), 88–9.

[35] S. J. Brown, '"A Solemn Purification by Fire": Responses to the Great War in the Scottish Presbyterian Churches, 1914–1919', *Journal of Ecclesiastical History* xlv (1994), 84.

[36] St Deiniol's Library, Hawarden: WW1 Pamphlet Collection: Box B: *Jewish Ideals and the War: An Address* (1914).

[37] Alan Wilkinson, *The Church of England and the First World War* (London, 1996), 30–1.

The war of 1914 was different from other wars in this, that no one but the Germans can say that Germany was in the right. The Allies, as all the world knows, were fighting for justice and right against a country and an emperor who seemed almost mad with pride. The soldiers of the Allies went out to battle not as soldiers have often gone to war, because it is the business to be done, but rather like knights of old, full of anger against an enemy who was fighting unjustly, and full, too, of a determination to fight their best for justice and right. This is one more reason which has made the Great War of 1914 so wonderful a thing.[38]

Two pamphlets produced by the Victoria League, a society promoting friendship amongst the people of the British Empire, were adapted for children. J. H. L. Ridley's *Why We Are Fighting* was adapted from Cook's *Why Britain is at War*. In simple language, evoking the importance of promises made between friends, Ridley explained that 'although Britain loves peace, she declared war on Germany because Germany had broken her word . . . Boys and girls, you have been brought up to keep your promises, and if we want one of you to do a thing we put you on your word of honour'.[39] W. J. Pimcombe's *Britain and Gallant Belgium* explained why Britain had to stand up for freedom and the rights of small nations.[40] Children were encouraged to take the leaflets home to read to their parents, perhaps in a belief that adults were more likely to absorb a message communicated by their children rather than an anonymous representative of the state. Children were literally bringing the gravity of the situation home: could their parents answer the call and protect their offspring in a time of national crisis?

These assumptions and values were diffused throughout the British population, the majority of whom understood that Britain was at war to defend international law, civilization, justice, morality, and freedom, to defeat what was perceived to be a power-hungry and barbaric nation intent on the destruction of Europe, to uphold friendships and international agreements, and to maintain Britain's position in world affairs. Britons were not brainwashed into believing that they were fighting a just cause, in defence of international law and national honour. The content of contemporary diaries and letters demonstrate that ordinary people expressed the same ideas and used the same language employed in official speeches and pamphlets. This holds true across all regions and most levels of society. Ordinary people used 'big words' like honour, justice, defence, righteousness, and therefore the high diction of 1914 was speaking to a mood, not dictating it.

Prior to the official declaration of war on 4 August many hoped Britain would stay out of the conflict, believing it was not its fight. However, once war was declared and the initial shock had worn off, the majority accepted that Britain's cause was 'the Cause of the Right against Wrong'.[41] For the British public, the violation of Belgium was a just reason to be at war with Germany. Indeed, the more

[38] Elizabeth O'Neill, *The War, 1914: A History and an Explanation for Boys and Girls* (London, 1914), 14–15.

[39] NLW: George Eyre Evans, *Aberystwyth War Book*: XD 523 E90, *Why We Are Fighting* (1914).

[40] NLW: George Eyre Evans, *Aberystwyth War Book*: XD 523 E90, *Britain and Gallant Belgium* (1914).

[41] DRO: Fursdon Family Correspondence: 5242M/Box 27/18, 4 September 1914.

wrongs Germany seemed to commit, the more righteous Britain became. On 8 August, in reaction to the German besiegement of Liège, Violet Clutton recorded in her diary: 'The more dishonourably the Germans behave the more justification we shall have in thrashing them soundly.'[42] Ulric Nisbet, a former student of Marlborough College, agreed:

> Our country was 100 per cent right and Germany was 100 per cent wrong. We were fighting for King and Country and Empire, and 'gallant little Belgium'. We were fighting to uphold the principles of justice and freedom, and international morality and to smash Kaiserism and German militarism.[43]

In a letter to the publishing house Macmillan on 16 December, the anthropologist J. G. Frazer, believed the war had highlighted 'the English spirit at its best and the German spirit at its worst'.[44] For Ada McGuire from Wallasey, Cheshire, the extreme situation of being at war made her reassess her world view: 'It is hard to realise what a love one has for one's country till that country is threatened and threatened by such a foe!'[45] On 6 August Thomas Macmillan and his fellow workers in Glasgow, agreed that the war was justified 'not so much on account of the violation of treaties and the invasion of Belgium as from a genuine feeling of alarm that the swaggering, and heartless bullies who directed the German fighting machine would not know where to stop'.[46]

The reasons why Britain was at war permeated the minds of the British population regardless of class or region. On 6 August, Georgina Lee—the eldest daughter of the English pastoral painter Henry William Banks Davis and a solicitor's wife in London—recorded in her diary that England was 'championing the cause of a small people and a great ally threatened with disaster'.[47] Britain had gone to war to defend both Belgium and France from the aggressiveness of Germany. Ten days later she amended this interpretation, adding that Britain was fighting for 'the future welfare of our country'. For if Britain did not take part in the war, and do 'her full share on the battlefields' she would not be entitled to any 'spoils of war' or 'advantageous conditions of peace'.[48] In a letter dated 23 August to her cousin Rose, Nellie Barry, from Mortimer, Berkshire, affirmed 'the perfect righteousness' of Britain's cause and concluded that Britain would have ended up friendless amongst nations if it had gone back on its promises to France and Belgium.[49]

Within four days of the declaration of war, Mr W. Eaves of Plymouth perceived the war to be about national honour and prestige. On 8 August he wrote to his friend:

> Whether it be long or short, both you and I rejoice to have lived so long to witness the traditional esprit de corps of England thrust into life anew and to mark the

---

[42] DRO: Violet Clutton: 6258M/Box 1, Vol I, 8 August 1914.
[43] IWM, Docs: Nisbet, Captain H.U.S: 78/3/3.
[44] BL: Macmillan Papers: Add 55139, ff. 42, 16 December 1914.
[45] IWM, Docs: McGuire, Misses A. & R.: 96/31/1, 28 August 1914.
[46] IWM, Docs: Macmillan, Thomas: PP/MCR/C56 (1935).
[47] Gavin Roynon, ed., *Home Fires Burning: The Great War Diaries of Georgina Lee* (Stroud, 2006), 7.
[48] Ibid. 14.
[49] Liddle: DF 009: Jessica Howard Barry, 23 August 1914.

impenetrability of the bonds which bind the Empire together. The old spirit lives, as we have always insisted and our prestige . . . will now be ensured for another century at least.[50]

According to D. P. Blades, the editor of *The Student*, Edinburgh University's student publication, August 1914 would 'be hailed as a great month in our nation's great history, the month which issued in a new era of national development and national consciousness'. The British people were now 'knit together in a great project of sacrifice'. According to Blades the war was not one of self-preservation or material gain. It was 'for the vindication of abstract principles, for the preservation of national traditions, national honour and national ideals . . . Honour and justice and truth are to be vindicated'.[51] For the artist Augustus John, the war was an opportunity to restore Britain from a period of decadence and self-interest. On 27 October he wrote: 'It ought to do people a world of good. I'm sure the country will benefit. People were getting too silly'.[52] His sentiments were echoed by Ada McGuire, from Wallasey, Cheshire, in a letter to her sister on 28 August who felt that the war would 'awake England from the pursuit of pleasure and selfishness into which her people were sinking'.[53]

As the war was understood to be about upholding national honour, combined with the destruction of an abhorrent enemy, a negotiated peace was impossible. As the wife of Major D. G. Johnson, serving in China, explained to her husband in a letter dated 21 September:

> I think this war is the most awful calamity that has ever befallen the world, but I am Patriot enough to see that Peace at any Price is not possible if we want to remain a nation, and that until our armies have utterly crushed the Germans there can be no Peace with Honour.[54]

Britain had to be victorious for all of these aims to be achieved. Elizabeth Cadbury had demonstrated in favour of neutrality prior to Britain's official declaration of war on 4 August. However, once war was declared she put herself solidly behind the war effort because, in her opinion, a lasting European peace settlement could only come about if Britain was victorious.[55] For A. H. D. Acland, Liberal MP for the Chiltern Hundreds, a victorious Germany was difficult for him to even contemplate.[56] For some people the desire for a British victory took time to develop. Owing to his hatred of war, Dr James Maxwell of Bromley, Kent, was at first apprehensive about 'asking for victory to our army'. However, by late November his opinions had solidified: 'the longer it goes on, the more I feel the awful *injustice* and *cruelty* of the war and in every prayer I ask for victory'.[57] As stories of German atrocities reached

[50] PWDRO: Letter on outbreak of war: Acc 511/1, 8 August 1914.
[51] University of Edinburgh, Special Collections: D. P. Blades, 'Editorial,' *The Student* XII (1914), 3–4.
[52] NLW: Gwen John: Mss 22305D, ff. 117–19, 27 October 1914.
[53] IWM, Docs: McGuire, Misses A. & R.: 96/31/1, 28 August 1914.
[54] Liddle: GS 0861: Major General D.G. Johnson, 21 September 1914.
[55] BCA: MS 466/432, Box 3: Cadbury Family Journal, 27 September 1914.
[56] DRO: Journal of A.H.D. Acland: 1148M, add 23/F29b, August 1914.
[57] University of Birmingham, Special Collections: Dr James Laidlaw Maxwell: DA 26/2/1/6/49, 25 November 1914.

Britain, via newspapers, soldiers on leave, and Belgian refugees, indignation to-wards Germany increased, along with the desire to see it defeated absolutely. On 24 September, after much consideration about the validity of stories of German atrocities in Belgium, R. W. M. Gibbs concluded that the British war effort was justified and that not 'one man out of a hundred has any doubts but that our action was justified'.[58]

THE ALLIES

Solidarity with foreign allies was central to the British understanding of war in 1914 because a sense of duty to Belgium and France was understood to be a major reason why Britain had entered the war. The Triple Entente Declaration signed on 4 September, and published in *The Times* two days later, officialized this sense of alliance. The document was an unratified attempt to ensure that the French, Russian, and British governments did not seek a separate peace with Germany. Logically, the British press featured more stories about Allied successes than German. Some people were aware that the former may have been exaggerated so as not to destabilize morale. However, most appeared to accept these early success stories at face value and held high hopes for the BEF in its supporting role to the larger Allied armies.

The sentiment behind the Declaration found a broad echo in the minds of the British people. On 8 September, a letter to *The Times* appealed for Allied flags to be displayed in as many places as possible around London 'to symbolise the solidarity of the Allies . . . and to help us realise the common brotherhood uniting the armed forces of the Powers who are combating Austro-Prussian militarism and avenging its atrocities in Belgium and Bosnia'.[59] A week later, Vera Brittain recorded the sense of strength and comfort this gave her, since it was 'much finer to be fighting with Allies than to fight alone; to be united with so many nations is tremendously moving'.[60] Once the shock of war had worn off, the novelist, Mrs Humphry Ward, remembered Britain's loyalty to France: 'I am with her, heart and soul, and to see her wiped out by Germany would put out for me one of the world's great lights'.[61] The British public invested much hope in France and Russia, whose strength and commitment were celebrated.[62] The alliance reassured Britons that they were not alone in the war, and was a source of strength to be drawn on, particularly in times of difficulty. A sense of unity with the British Empire was also celebrated. Beatrice Trefusis, a London resident, recorded her joy at the response of the British

[58] MPP Bodleian: R.W.M. Gibbs: MS Eng misc c.159, 24 September 1914.
[59] *The Times*, 8 September 1914, 9.
[60] Alan Bishop, ed., *Chronicle of Youth: Vera Brittain's War Diary 1913–1917* (London, 1981), 109.
[61] Janet Penrose Trevelyan, *The Life of Mrs Humphry Ward* (London, 1923), 263.
[62] See the following examples in *Punch*: 'Well Met!' (France), 19 August, 161 and 'Hail! Russia!,' 16 September 1914, 243.

Dominions in her diary on 11 August: 'It is thrilling to read today of all the offers from the Colonies—including a million bags of flour from Canada. They must see that we are in the right in declaring war. Their messages are whole-hearted and also do one good to read'.[63] Georgina Lee was also moved and invigorated by the loyalty of the colonies, in particular India, and the Dominions which sent troops and supplies.[64] Recruiting literature used the 'United Empire' to shame British men into enlisting and to further emphasize Britain's just cause. A leaflet published in October asked why 'from every corner of the Empire offers of men, money and supplies have poured in?' The answer was simple: 'Because all the peoples and races over whom the Union Jack flies know that the fight for British freedom against German aggression is "a just cause" to be prosecuted to "a successful end"'.[65]

National anthems of the Allied countries were printed in full and reproduced in song collections to be performed at patriotic gatherings. On 28 August, Georgina Lee noted one such performance: 'The house was draped in red, white and blue, and the performance was much leavened with patriotic display...the *Marseillaise* was sung by the House, everybody standing...It was the first time since the beginning of the War that we had felt in anything like a mood for laughing'.[66] Flags of the Allied countries were displayed together, and this made Vera Brittain 'feel cold with excitement'.[67] On arriving home from the annual Cambridge Officers' Training Corps camp at Aldershot in August, Hugh Spurrell found local people from his hometown of Carmarthen:

> wearing allied flags and some sported the little tin medals of generals who had fought in the South African War. I wore the flags of the allies for a few days, but soon found that the number was too great. Besides this, there was some difficulty in deciding on the proper colours for the flag of Montenegro. So I gave up the habit and kept war maps instead.[68]

The alliance and its celebration through displays and songs, underlined the feeling that at least Britain was not alone. Allied objects were soon commercialized. A. W. Gamage Ltd, the London department store, produced a catalogue of Allied merchandise, including silk flags of all sizes, bunting, badges, rosettes, favours, and buttonhole badges—all available in the Allied colours.[69]

Member countries of the alliance took on different roles in the minds of ordinary people. Belgium was viewed more as victim than partner, a crucial role in helping British people understand why Britain was at war. However, it was more difficult to situate Russia positively in relation to Britain's national cause owing to pre-war rivalries. The Labour and Liberal parties were particularly opposed to the autocratic and anti-Semitic Tsarist regime. They were suspicious of Russia and shared the views of the German Liberals and Left that Russia was the real enemy. There was a public outcry in Britain following the bloody Russian pogroms of 1903–1906

[63] Liddle: DF 129: B.M. Trefusis, 11 August 1914.
[64] Roynon, ed., *Home Fires Burning: The Great War Diaries of Georgina Lee*, 32.
[65] John Johnson Collection, Bodleian Library, Oxford: Great War, Box 3, October 1914.
[66] Roynon, ed., *Home Fires Burning: The Great War Diaries of Georgina Lee*, 25.
[67] Bishop, ed., *Chronicle of Youth: Vera Brittain's War Diary 1913–1917*, 109.
[68] IWM, Docs: Spurrell, Lt-Col Hugh W.: 92/36/1 (n.d.).
[69] Flintshire Record Office: Bryn-y-pys Estate Wartime Papers: D/BP/510.

which left around 2,000 Jews dead, and many survivors sought refuge in Britain. Despite the Entente of 1907, negative feelings towards Russia still existed. Consequently, once war broke out some people continued to view Russia as enemy, rather than ally. Harry Miller, son of Jewish émigrés living in Grimsby, Lincolnshire, felt on 7 August that 'the only two nations that deserved to be wiped out entirely are the Russians and the bloodthirsty Servians'. In late October he still felt bitter towards Russia: 'Russia is still as bad and heartless as she was before this war started. The Belgians had England to flee to, the Poles have fled to other parts of Russia, but the poor Jew bears the brunt of everything and has nowhere to go.'[70] Arnold Bennett recorded in his private journal on 6 August that 'Russia is the real enemy, and not Germany'.[71] Yet publicly, in his pamphlet *Liberty: A Statement of the British Case*, he attempted to ease people's minds about 'the alleged barbarism of Russia' by emphasizing that Britain's ally was first and foremost France, and that an alliance with Russia was accidental.[72]

Yet once the war was engaged, a dramatic shift took place regarding people's perceptions of Russia, although some doubters remained. From Hendon, Laura Erwine wrote to Hanna Sheehy-Skeffington, the Irish suffragette and pacifist, explaining how she did not 'understand the anti-Russian feeling. Russian art and culture and individual Russians are infinitely more attractive than Germans!'[73] Very quickly Russia 'the barbarian' became Russia 'the saviour'. Its past wrongs were forgotten when Russia's mass army had early victories against the Germans. Despite the halting of the Russian invasion of East Prussia in late August, confidence in the Russian performance on the Eastern Front was sustained throughout 1914, with the press praising Russian victories.[74] Cartoons in *Punch* depicted Russia as a great bear or steamroller attacking the Germans from the east whilst the French and British resisted from the west.[75] The necessities of war quickly transformed past enemies into contemporary allies.

The Anglo-French victory against the Germans at the Battle of the Marne (6–10 September) was one of the single most important events in the war, and a turning point in military history. It halted the Germans in their advance on Paris and left the Schlieffen Plan—based on a speedy defeat of France to avoid a war on two fronts—in tatters. The German army had failed to gain its quick victory in the West and four years of stalemate ensued. The BEF played only a small part in the battle when compared with the titanic struggle between the very much larger French and German armies. It was nonetheless an important part, as it struck a blow at a sensitive place in the German front, contributing to the German decision to abandon the field of battle and withdraw to the north.

However, the French, with seventy divisions on the Western Front, had taken the weight of the fighting and withstood relentless German assaults. It should have

[70] IWM, Docs: Miller, H.: 02/38/1,Box 1, Item 1, 7 August 1914.
[71] Arnold Bennett, *The Journals* (Middlesex, 1932, 1971), 377.
[72] Arnold Bennett, *Liberty: A Statement of the British Case* (London, 1914), 42–4.
[73] NLI: Sheehy-Skeffington papers: Ms 22,667/1, 15 September 1914.
[74] Liddle: GS 0251: A.S.G. Butler, 9 December 1914.
[75] See for example, *Punch*, 16 September 1914, 233.

been a moment when the British celebrated their French ally for its strategic triumph against the Germans. This is not how the victory was reported in the British press. On 8 September *The Times* described the battle as an Allied success: the Germans were in retreat because of 'vigorous action by the French troops, powerfully aided by the British Army'. The following day the headline read 'A British Victory', and the remainder of the article referred to Allied forces fighting the Germany army. When victory was confirmed on 12 September, the 'French left operating from the north' had defeated the Germans 'in conjunction with the British forces in the south'. Anglo-French troops had operated 'jointly'. Note how the French were not referred to as an army and that this article gives a sense of balance and equality in their performance. Such bias went beyond *The Times*. In his dispatch dated 10 September, the Commander-in-Chief of the BEF, Sir John French, described how the enemy was 'falling back before the British Army'.[76] Understandably, this riled the French. The following day, Paul Cambon complained to the French Minister of Foreign Affairs, Théophile Delcassé, that all that could be inferred from British press reports was that French 'soldiers withdrew without fighting and that all the weight of resistance against the Germans has fallen on the English troops'. Whilst the British press was full of information on the BEF, accounts of battles, prisoners and guns taken, he felt there was nothing on the French army apart from 'dry' official communications: 'Our retirement of Charleroi was not without danger and would deserve to be told. As General French speaks only about [British] operations, one could believe that the French Army did not exist any more or that it did not do anything'.[77]

Nor was the Marne celebrated as a French victory in contemporary diaries and letters. The silence of these sources speaks volumes. On the whole, only negative opinions about France were recorded, particularly when the slow progress of the BEF began to register. For certain Cabinet members this was earlier rather than later. On 20 August, in a letter to his brother William, Lloyd George revealed his frustration with the French armies: '[They] have made a bad start. For the moment it looks as if they were outclassed in sheer brain power'.[78] In a letter to his stepmother, Mary, Austen Chamberlain, who had only recently taken over his late father's West Birmingham seat in the House of Commons, expressed disappointment with the French performance up to 2 September: 'the French are not showing as much resisting power as one could have hoped'.[79] For those not privy to sensitive information, frustration towards the French began to appear in early October. In a letter to his mother in Pembrokeshire, Lawrence Colby, in Southampton awaiting departure to the front, confided that the disillusioning retreat from Mons was due to the French not having enough men, 'their mobilisation

[76] *The Times*, 8–10, 12 September 1914, 8–9.

[77] AMAE, Paris: Papiers Delcassé: Lettres de Diplomates III: Paul Cambon, ff. 333–4, 12 September 1914.

[78] NLW: William George (Solicitor) 9: WG 2870, 20 August 1914.

[79] University of Birmingham, Special Collections: Letters to Mary Chamberlain from Austen Chamberlain: AC 4/1/1139, 2 September 1914.

arrangements being defective', to stem the German advance at the frontier.[80] Mrs D. G. Johnson reported to her husband in China that a British General, on leave from the front with 'shattered nerves', had reported 'that the French have nothing like the men they said they had and that they leave nearly all the ... movements to our troops'.[81] On 4 November Beatrice Trefusis visited a group of wounded Belgian officers in Chagford, Devon. She recorded in her diary how one officer had spoken 'bitterly about the French' in whom he had 'no confidence' and felt 'could have done much more than they have'. Without the BEF 'the Belgian and French armies would have been done for at the beginning'.[82] In a letter to the Town Clerk of Rutherglen, Glasgow, H. Gulliver, a contributor to the relief of Belgian refugees, praised the bravery and self-sacrifice of Belgium. However, he had less admiration for the conduct of France in the war: 'I have it on reliable authority that the French mobilization was slow and bad—almost as bad as in 1870 ... France has to struggle against carelessness and corruption still'.[83]

Reactions towards France were ambiguous, veering between silence and criticism on the performance of its armies. The French armies were commended by ordinary British people in tandem with the BEF, but rarely on their own account. Newspapers acknowledged French successes usually as an 'Allied' rather than specifically French victory. British victories, however, were claimed as such. It was obviously easier for the British to blame the French for the lack of Allied progress than their beloved BEF. Yet feelings went deeper than that. Britain had always, and still does, have a difficult and ambiguous relationship with France. On hearing that the BEF had successfully landed in France, Georgina Lee noted the irony that English armies had previously landed in France as enemies: now they were fighting alongside each other in a battle for the latter's survival.[84] Without really knowing how they felt about France before the war, it was difficult for British people to suddenly celebrate their partnership. In August 1914 Britain was confronted with its relationship with France—and was struggling to come up with an answer. However, the main issue, particularly in relation to the Marne, was that an acknowledgement of France's victory would mean downplaying the tiny part played by the BEF. At this stage Britain only had a small army on the Western Front—mass enlistment was in its embryonic stages. It was therefore necessary to inflate Britain's role. The rhetoric of the national cause had presented the war as a momentous battle for Britain's survival. To maintain the centrality of the war in people's minds, the British army had to be central to winning the war effort. Russian victories on the Eastern Front could be celebrated as they posed no threat to Britain's performance; but where the BEF was fighting, victory had to be shared with the French, or better still, be Britain's alone.

[80] NLW: Ffynnone2: Additional Material: 2422, 4 October 1914.
[81] Liddle: GS 0861: Major General D.G. Johnson, 11 October 1914.
[82] Liddle: DF 129: B.M. Trefusis, 4 November 1914.
[83] Glasgow City Archives, Mitchell Library: Rutherglen Town Clerk's Papers on Belgian Refugees: RU/4/5/163, 3 December 1914.
[84] Roynon, ed., *Home Fires Burning: The Great War Diaries of Georgina Lee*, 18.

A NEW MORAL ORDER

As in France, the opening months of the war were crucial for suggesting how Britons should appropriately respond to the conflict. Normality appeared to be suspended. New values, qualities, and expectations of how to behave suggest that a new moral order was being constructed in 1914. A pamphlet appealing for assistance with Llandudno's Local War Relief Fund referred to this new moral order as 'new responsibilities' that everyone had to undertake 'in the attainment of the purpose for which our Country is now fighting'.[85] If one could not enlist, then acting in solidarity with fellow non-combatants and the needy was the appropriate way to behave.

In August 1914 the British population and its political representatives were faced with a choice: to either band together collectively in a time of need or not.[86] Differences were set aside and Britain's understanding of the righteousness of its cause manifested itself in positive behaviour. Considering the pre-war divisions in the United Kingdom, a political truce for the duration of the war was a decision to be celebrated.[87] In his political journal Neville Chamberlain, Austen's half-brother, contrasted the situation on 6 August with that of five days earlier: 'The Cabinet were utterly divided and up to Saturday proposed to do nothing . . . [now] the spirit of the country could not be better'.[88] On 28 August Richard Durning Holt noted the extraordinary change that had come over Parliament: 'the feeling almost unanimous and several bills passed through all stages by 6 o'clock which at any other time would take a couple of full days to get second reading alone'.[89]

A decrease in crime also signified how the British population understood the seriousness of the situation and the need to unite behind a common cause. In his Annual Report to the City Council for the year 1914, the Chief Constable of Edinburgh, Roderick Ross, concluded that the remarkable absence of serious crime since the outbreak of war was because:

> The great issue for which we are presently fighting has absorbed the attention of even the criminal and has had the effect of restraining his hand from crime, or it may be that he has left his accustomed haunts and gone forth to fight his country's battles. If this is so, and from what I learn there seems considerable truth in it, it certainly says much for the criminal that he has in the hour of common danger responded, like his better-behaved fellows, to the call of his King and Country.[90]

[85] Flintshire Record Office, Hawarden: Printed Wartime Leaflets: D/M/7074, 1914.

[86] What John Horne has termed 'the choice of 1914'. See John N. Horne, *Labour At War: France and Britain, 1914–1918* (Oxford, 1991).

[87] Kelger, 'Britain's Union Sacrée' in 1914' in *Les sociétiés européennes et la guerre de 1914–1918*, edited by Jean-Jacques Becker and Stéphane Audoin-Rouzeau (Nanterre, 1990).

[88] University of Birmingham, Special Collections: Neville Chamberlain's Political Journal, 1913–1920: NC 2/20, 6 August 1914.

[89] LRO: Durning Holt Papers: 920/DUR/1/10, 28 August 1914.

[90] Edinburgh Central Library: Chief Constable's Annual Reports: HV 8198, February 1915.

In early November, Hallie Eustace Miles recorded in her diary how 'the one-ness of Everything and Everybody [sic] is beautiful. We all seem tuned to the same key, and marching to the same rhythm. There is hardly ever a drunken person to be seen nowadays. Burglaries are rare. So is hooliganism. Everyone is living a better and cleaner life'.[91]

Examples exist across the classes of women helping out according to their means. At one end, Lady Helena Molyneux, Countess of Sefton, busied herself with various relief projects throughout 1914 in Lancaster and London, from visiting wounded soldiers to learning bandaging.[92] At the other, in Nelson's Printing Works in Edinburgh, Lady Betty Balfour noticed on 26 August that the female machinists spent every moment off the machines knitting 'war socks'.[93] Solidarity with the soldiers, wounded, disabled, refugees, and other war victims became the civilian substitute for action in combat.[94] For Ada McGuire in Wallasey, Cheshire, the war made her, along with many other non-combatants, want to demonstrate her loyalty and support to the British war effort.[95] She did so by supporting a variety of relief organizations set up in Britain at the outbreak of the war. The British people rallied behind the Belgian refugees arriving in Britain. By October over 100,000 of the latter had arrived and, with echoes of Edwardian society's philanthropic values, the Local Government Board reported how 'it is characteristic of our national ways that the duty of attending to the refugees should have been undertaken by voluntary organisations'.[96] The same month, Dr James Maxwell commented to his son that 'the whole country is active on behalf of Belgium, everybody desiring to do something on their behalf'.[97] Although the support of Belgian refugees was one of the major altruistic efforts in the war, the British people also supported a number of other worthy causes, both domestic and international, to show their loyalty to the British war effort.

People generously donated money to the Prince of Wales' National Relief Fund and gifts to Princess Mary's Fund.[98] On 2 August King George V and Queen Mary visited Devonshire House in Piccadilly to 'see the Ladies who are collecting the 300,000 socks and belts which Mary will send to the troops at the front'.[99] Mrs Caroline Ann Oates, of the Gestingthorpe Estate in Essex, donated around £1,681 (£130,000 in today's money) between August and December to such causes as the Serbian Relief Fund, the Belgian Relief Fund, the Victoria League, the Primrose

---

[91] Miles, *Untold Tales of War-Time London: A Personal Diary* (London, 1930), 26–7.

[92] LRO: Diaries of the Family of Molyneux of Sefton: 920 SEF/4/17, 13 August 1914.

[93] NAS, GRH: Balfour of Whittingehame Papers: Lady Betty Balfour: GD 433/2/348, 26 August 1914.

[94] John Horne, 'Social Identity in War: France, 1914–1918', in *Men, Women and War*, ed. T. G. Fraser and Keith Jeffery (Dublin, 1993), 122.

[95] IWM, Docs: McGuire, Misses A. & R.: 96/31/1, 28 August 1914.

[96] Session 1914–1916, Vol. VII, Cd. 7750: First Report of the Departmental Committee Appointed by the President of the Local Government Board to Consider and Report on Questions Arising in Connection with the Reception and Employment of the Belgian Refugees in this Country.

[97] University of Birmingham, Special Collections: Dr James Laidlaw Maxwell: DA 26/2/1/6/45, 22 October 1914.

[98] Mary, Princess Royal, was George V's eldest daughter, aged 17 in 1914.

[99] Royal Archives, Windsor Castle: RA GV/PRIV/GVD/1914: 2 October.

League, War Loans, and comforts for soldiers.[100] On 27 October Mrs Johnson told her husband how the British public responded to Lord Roberts' appeal for field glasses for the troops:

> He got 15,000 on *one* day, and many more afterwards. He asked for saddles and had to cry 'Enough' in a few days and when the appeal was blankets and sweaters it literally *snowed* them, and the response *to every* subscription is too marvellous for words.[101]

Across Britain women began to learn first aid; in Boreham, Essex, they started bandaging lessons in the local vicarage on 20 August.[102] Activities ranged from large monetary donations, to small gestures such as the distribution of mugs of tea to soldiers on route marches to Clacton in Essex.[103] Edinburgh University Student Representative Council agreed on 30 November to set up a fund to raise money to supply and equip a motor ambulance for the front.[104] Flag days were celebrated, people adopted 'lonely' soldiers to correspond with, and women knitted furiously.[105] Mary Coules, from London, noted in her diary how everybody had 'developed a craze for knitting socks—all our conversation was punctuated by "purl, plain, plain, purl!"'[106] This activity had its origins in pre-war traditions of philanthropy, but the energy with which it was undertaken in 1914 was entirely novel, and satirized in the national press.[107] In a letter to her son, Phil Heath stationed in Plymouth with the Royal Garrison Artillery, his mother, in Exmouth, told him how his father was 'coming in useful as a general pattern. I try socks on his feet and Hilda [her daughter] flings shirts over his head and for some time I have been trying to snatch a suitable moment for putting his arm in a sling, but that has not been successful at present'.[108]

Patriotic fund-raising events and concerts were held across Britain. Madame Lucie Barbier, a Parisian singer and pianist who had moved to Aberystwyth in 1909 and set up the University's Musical Club, organized a number of concerts in aid of Belgian and domestic relief funds in October and November 1914.[109] In Oxford, William Watkin Davies, a student at St John's College, recalled the 'Belgian Day' held on 7 November: 'The whole town was decorated with yellow, red and black, the . . . Belgian colours, which also happen to be the St John's colours. Numbers of ladies paraded the streets selling rosettes and others collecting for the need of the

---

[100] Dominic Webb, 'Inflation: The Value of the Pound 1750–2005' (London, 2006). Since 1914 prices have increased 77 fold. ERO: Estate and Family Records: Oates Family of Gestingthorpe: Accounts of Mrs Caroline Ann Oates: D/Doa/A8, Account Book Account book of Mrs Caroline Ann Oates, 1904–1915.

[101] Liddle: GS 0861: Major General D.G. Johnson, 27 October 1914.

[102] ERO: Diary of Reverend Denys Yonge: D/DU 358/26, 20 August 1914.

[103] ERO: SA 8/482/1 (n.d.).

[104] University of Edinburgh, Special Collections: University Student Representative Council Minutes: Da 60–9, 30 November 1914.

[105] NWSA: Resource Pack, Memories of the Great War 1914–1919 (1992).

[106] IWM, Docs: Coules, Miss M.: 97/25/1, August 1914.

[107] See, for example, 'The Ruling Passion', *Punch*, 25 November 1914, 429, which depicts a waitress so obsessed by her knitting that she continues at work.

[108] Liddle: GS 0735: Lt-Col C.P. Heath, Letter 41, 6 September 1914.

[109] NLW: Lucie Barbier: Mss 22694D, ff. 134–7, 15 October to 26 November 1914.

refugees. Cambridge has collected £500 in this manner, and it was our desire to surpass the sum'.[110]

Schools across Britain involved themselves in the war effort, not only through education and the singing of patriotic songs in assembly but by a variety of relief efforts. On 4 September the boys of Holy Trinity School in Barnstaple busied themselves collecting blackberries to make jam to send to the 'Jam Committee' of their local Distress Fund.[111] On 16 December the children of Huntshaw Church of England National School sent a parcel containing 'sixteen pairs of socks, five long mufflers and eight pairs of mittens together with cigarettes to the value of ten shillings' to the soldiers of the Devonshire Regiment, via the Mayoress of Exeter.[112] Miss D. L. Cockhill, a schoolgirl in Dovercourt, Essex in 1914, recalled how her fellow classmates 'wore red, white and blue hair-ribbons, and patriotic badges and sang patriotic songs' because they 'were proud of our country going to the aid of gallant little Belgium'. Other activities that local schools engaged in included writing letters to wounded soldiers, holding sales and concerts in school premises, and even closing the school completely to allow for the billeting of soldiers.[113]

People went so far in their effort to display their loyalty through relief efforts that they provided a source of good-natured humour for cartoonists in *Punch*. Eight cartoons appeared in *Punch* between August and December 1914 that incorporated the theme of solidarity and relief. Seven of them ridiculed people's overzealous efforts to 'support' British soldiers at home and abroad. The first of these cartoons appeared on 30 September indicating that retrospective humour was derived from these once the initial shock had worn off and people were 'settling' into the war.[114] Earlier, this would perhaps have been inappropriate and not appreciated by *Punch's* readers. The cartoons ridiculed the intention behind the relief effort, suggesting that those zealously involved in knitting did not fully appreciate the realities of war.

There is little evidence to suggest that charitable behaviour slowed down in late 1914, although support for Belgian refugees did wane. On the whole, people were as committed to relief efforts in December as they were in August and September. There are some exceptions. On 14 December P. H. Pilditch, a Territorial stationed in Boxmoor, Hertfordshire, recorded how local people were less willing to billet the soldiers:

> The majority of the people I saw, rich and poor, were unwilling to put themselves out in the slightest degree to put up the men. It made me absolutely wild . . . They make me feel ashamed to be of the same nationality.[115]

---

[110] NLW: W. Watkin Davies: 47, 7 November 1914.

[111] NDRO: Holy Trinity Boys' School, Barnstaple, School Log Book 1904–21: 1903C/EEL, 4 September 1914.

[112] NDRO: Huntshaw C.E. National School, Barnstaple, School Log Book 1893–1915: 3073C/EFL, 15 December 1914.

[113] ERO: T/Z 25/650 (1966), PWDRO: Prince Rock Girls' School, Plymouth, School Log Book 1909–1932: Acc 1524/2, 19 October 1914, ERO: D/Q 49/I2/a2.

[114] *Punch*, 30 September 1914, 277.

[115] Liddle: GS 1268: P.H. Pilditch, 14 December 1914.

As the war went on, Richard Durning Holt became disillusioned with Britain's charitable response as he felt it was counter-productive; 'a great encouragement to many not to help themselves'.[116] Apprehensiveness also developed in the labour movement as some feared that knitting circles were taking away income from paid labourers, therefore adding to unemployment. However, any unease that existed about Britain's relief efforts did not appear to signal disenchantment with the war, rather it was rooted in practical economic concerns.

British people were motivated to express their loyalty to the nation through relief work for a variety of reasons. Non-combatants felt a sense of duty and understood the necessity of the situation, even if they were averse to war in general. People volunteered for relief work in an effort to make their response to the war equal to the soldiers' sacrifice. Those who could not fight, particularly women, could contribute by supporting the troops and comforting their families in a time of need. It would also shield non-combatants from accusations of 'not doing their bit'. In a letter thanking Mrs Cyrus Braby for the blanket and gloves she had sent him, Corporal Upton, in training in Aldershot in December 1914, reassured her that 'anybody who tries to make our troops life a bit easier are doing as much as a soldier at the front and may God help you in your splendid work'.[117] As casualty lists increased, people on the home front had to make Britain worth dying for. William Watkin Davies summarized a sermon given at St Mary's Church, Oxford on 29 November: 'This winter we see young men every day cheerfully laying down their lives for their country. Then let us who cannot fight devote ourselves to the task of making the country better worth dying for!'[118]

People were also driven by more self-protective reflexes. Many women described 'war effort' gatherings—such as a working sewing party—as a form of social support. Here they could discuss the war, and their personal involvement in it, and seek reassurance from other women in a similar position. Such work also distracted them from the horrors of the conflict.[119] Elsie Russell, in Jedburgh on the Scottish Borders, involved herself in relief efforts as it was a comforting tonic to the depressing casualty lists.[120] Walter Dixon Scott told a friend on 10 August why he felt British non-combatants were rallying behind the war effort:

> We're in a horrid mess and huddle closer. But it's more than that. Death's in the air and we begin to realise in its bare elements the astonishing fact of life.[121]

Fear, anxiety, and the cold realities of war had brought people together in a common cause of survival, alongside a sense of patriotism and duty.

Civilian efforts would always be subordinate to the soldier who, at the top of this new moral order, was exalted for his ultimate act of solidarity—volunteering to

---

[116] LRO: Durning Holt Papers: 920/DUR/1/10, 4 September 1914.
[117] Liddle: DF 017: Mr and Mrs Cyrus Braby, 7 December 1914.
[118] NLW: W. Watkin Davies: 47, 29 November 1914.
[119] Peel, *How We Lived Then, 1914–1918: A Sketch of Social and Domestic Life in England During the War* (London, 1929), 22, 24.
[120] Liddle: GS 0251: A.S.G. Butler, Letter A3, 22 September 1914.
[121] MALSL: Walter Dixon Scott: MISC/391, 10 August 1914.

fight, and possibly die, for his country. The entire home front was morally subordinated to the fighting soldier.[122] He was revered as a symbol of honour and bravery and embodied all that the nation was fighting for and against. A man in uniform fighting for Britain was a hero. In a letter to his fiancée in Edinburgh, J. M. McLachlan, in Cumberland, recalled the sight of a soldier who was about to return to the front after a period of leave. Although everybody was sorry to see him go they thought him 'no end the hero'.[123]

Whilst their soldiers were still alive, women expressed their pride alongside caution and sorrow. On 8 November, George Hope's mother congratulated her son, a soldier on the Western Front, for retrieving a body of a fellow soldier from the field so it could be properly buried. Although incredibly proud of him she added, 'I do entreat you not to be rash or take unnecessary risks. Remember how precious your life is, to me, to your wife and tiny children'.[124] The dual identity of 'mother' and 'female' created a tension for women with sons serving, torn between their desire to protect (as mothers) and their need to be protected (as women). However, if a soldier died in battle, his sacrifice had to be understood as heroic. Mrs Johnson of Daylesford, Gloucestershire, dwelled on the recent death of her brother-in-law, Jack, on the Western Front. However, she comforted herself that 'to "die for your country" is the greatest of all honours so we need not fear that he did not *know* that'.[125] On 23 October, whilst trying to persuade his mother that he should enlist, Anthony Eden, the future prime minister, argued that seeing as he had to die at some point 'why not now by the most honourable way possible, the way that opens the gate's of Paradise—the soldier's death?'[126] There was no sense that a soldier had died unnecessarily or without honour. For if a soldier's death was believed to be an unnecessary waste then what were all the others still fighting for?

Despite his opposition to the war, Keir Hardie was careful to avoid criticizing those who enlisted. In his weekly column in the *Merthyr Pioneer*, he announced: 'The lads who have gone forth by sea and land to fight their country's battles must not be disheartened by a discordant note at home'.[127] Criticism of soldiers was therefore rare and shocking. On 17 September John Beech, a labourer from Burton-on-Trent, was fined for 'using language calculated to provoke a breach of the peace'. In front of friends, he criticized the British army and declared that the Kaiser ought to be on the throne at Buckingham Palace. A 'quarrel and fight ensued'.[128]

In the new moral order civilians were expected to do their duty and to make significant sacrifices. This meant behaving appropriately: maintaining normality,

---

[122] Higonnet and Higonnet, 'The Double Helix', in *Behind the Lines: Gender and the Two World Wars*, ed. Margaret Randolph Higonnet, Jane Jenson, Sonya Michel, and Margaret Collins Weitz (New Haven, 1987), 31–47.
[123] Liddle: GS 1022: Captain J.M. McLachlan, 15 September 1914.
[124] NAS, GRH: George Hope papers: GD 364/1/Bundle 22, 8 November 1914.
[125] Liddle: GS 0861: Major General D.G. Johnson, 19 October 1914.
[126] University of Birmingham, Special Collections: Avon Family Letters: AP 22/1/143, 23 October 1914.
[127] *Merthyr Pioneer*, 15 August 1914, 1.
[128] *Western Evening Herald*, 18 September 1914, 3.

helping the needy, and banding together in community relief and solidarity efforts. Civilians were expected to demonstrate stoicism, selflessness, and endurance, and to go without luxuries, comforts, and frivolity. Peacetime pleasures like theatre comedies and trips to the seaside were avoided in favour of donations to war charities and patriotic concerts. Those members of society that were seen to be behaving inappropriately, or activities believed to be encouraging inappropriate behaviour, were open to criticism. The national 'enemy within', who were at risk of subverting the war effort by their lack of understanding or inappropriate behaviour, were singled out and admonished as anomalies to the British war effort.

Appropriate civilian behaviour in 1914 centred on equality, gender, and sacrifice. The first and most obvious targets were those men who did not share equally in the sacrifice made by others who had enlisted. Commonly referred to as 'skulkers' or 'shirkers', from late August they were ridiculed in the press and chided by ordinary people. Macleod Yearsley, in London, recalled seeing in *The Times* on 27 August a sardonic advert: 'WANTED – PETTYCOATS for able-bodied young men in this Country who have not yet joined the Army'.[129] In late November Augustus John wrote to his sister Gwen, in Paris, angered by the slowing down of recruitment. He knew exactly who was to blame:

> It is the middle classes, the bourgeoisie, shopkeepers etc who hang back . . . It makes me so *mad* to go into a drapers shop and see the smug young cowards behind the counter asking what is your pleasure?

And exactly how to fix it: 'The best thing the G[erman]'s could do for the country would be the Zeppelin raid. Nothing short of bombs dropping on their shops will round the shopkeepers'.[130]

Civilian pastimes that were perceived to be holding men back from enlisting were also criticized. Cartoons in *Punch* ridiculed members of the upper class who continued to play sports, such as golf and cricket, without thinking about enlisting.[131] Association football, the most popular pre-war civilian sport, was targeted in the first few weeks of war. The Football Association (FA) came under fire from a hostile press whose contributors were incensed by the decision to continue to play the scheduled league games despite the crisis. They argued that, owing to the voluntary enlistment system, the FA should suspend games and encourage its players and supporters to enlist. Members of the public joined in castigating professional competitions for encouraging young men to 'shirk' their duty.[132] In a letter to his fiancée in Edinburgh, J. M. McLachlan, in Cumberland, cursed those men who had not enlisted yet had the audacity to continue to play football:

[129] IWM, Docs: Yearsley, P. Macleod: DS/MISC/17 (1938).
[130] NLW: Gwen John: Mss 22311D, ff. 53, late November 1914.
[131] See for example *Punch*, 14 October 1914, 322.
[132] Colin Veitch, '"Play Up! Play Up! Play Up! and Win the War!" Football, the Nation and the First World War, 1914–1915', *Journal of Contemporary History* 20 (1985, 1985), 370–1.

I think it's simply rotten the way all those strong well-trained blighters are fooling about playing football just now. And it's even worse that they get such big crowds to go and watch them—wasting their money on that when it's so much needed for other things.[133]

Whilst representatives of cricket, hockey, and rugby gradually began to suspend games and encourage their players to enlist, the FA remained hesitant. After consultation with the War Office the FA opened its grounds for military drill and recruiting. It was also announced that a battalion of football players and followers had formed in Glasgow and that recruiting rallies would be held at football grounds during the half-time interval on match days.[134] These acts, however, did not quell the protests which reached a peak on 8 September 1914 when F. N. Charrington, an East End Temperance worker, sent a telegram to the King, asking for the playing of football to be banned during the war.[135] In November *The Times* reported bitterly that recruitment drives at football league matches were unsuccessful, despite large crowds. On 21 November, only six volunteers came forward from the crowd at a game between Cardiff and Bristol Rovers, whilst at the Arsenal ground in London, a call for recruits yielded only one man.[136] It was not until 24 April 1915 that professional football finally came to end with the 'Khaki Cup Final' played between Chelsea and Sheffield United at Old Trafford, Manchester.

Equality was another key value in the new moral order. Civilians were expected to make an equal economic sacrifice in 1914. Those who sought to benefit financially from the unique wartime economic conditions were highlighted as enemies of the national cause. At the outbreak of war those who sought to hoard food or increase prices to profit from panic-buying were labelled as 'profiteers'. On 5 August Georgina Lee criticized such activities in London: 'An enormous rise in prices, which is most unfair for the rest of the community. I hear of one woman who ordered £500 worth of groceries at Harrods, and another who actually bought over the counter £45 worth. Her chauffeur stood by, carrying off parcels in relays to her motor cars'.[137] Edrica de la Pole, in Tremar, Devon, had little sympathy for hoarders and profiteers describing them as: 'Motor Hogs and greedy Hogs at that...they are buying from *six months* to *two years supply* which is wicked nonsense. Many tradesmen are refusing to supply any abnormal orders which is creditable to them'.[138] On 18 September anti-Semitic feeling reared its ugly head when the *Devon and Exeter Gazette* speculated that second-hand clothes buyers making a profit out of new recruits who were selling their civilian clothes once issued with their new uniform were 'mainly Jews'.[139] Hilda Davison, in Sunderland, recalled her local grocer coming round the back streets at night, offering

[133] Liddle: GS 1022: Captain J.M. McLachlan, 6 October 1914.
[134] Horrall, *Popular Culture in London c.1890–1918: The Transformation of Entertainment*, 197–8.
[135] Veitch, "'Play Up! Play Up! Play Up! and Win the War!" Football, the Nation and the First World War, 1914–1915', 371.
[136] *The Times*, 23 November 1914, 6.
[137] Roynon, ed., *Home Fires Burning: The Great War Diaries of Georgina Lee*, 6.
[138] PWDRO: Diary of Edrica de la Pole: Acc 1306/22, 5 August 1914.
[139] *Devon and Exeter Gazette*, 18 September 1914, 7.

potatoes at 2/8 per stone—four times above the normal price. The family 'were weak enough to buy them', adding to this tradesman's wartime fortune. Yet, whilst the grocer was clearly out to make a profit, the Davison family were driven by fear and panic of not having sufficient supplies.[140]

There were repercussions for those who dared to profit from the war. If it was felt that the authorities were not dealing properly with profiteers, people, spontaneously, did so themselves. On 4 August, Miss G. West, in Selsey, Gloucestershire, reprimanded her neighbours, who earlier that day had lectured her on the wrongs of hoarding, when she found them, later that afternoon, stocking up on vast quantities of meat and margarine.[141] On 7 August a crowd gathered outside the premises of Mr Price, a grocer, in Swansea, protesting against his alleged raising of prices. Two inspectors, three sergeants, and twelve constables were unable to calm the crowd, who were throwing stones and shouting. It was only when the local Catholic priest, Father Harrington, attended the scene that the crowd could be persuaded to disperse quietly.[142] However, the authorities showed little sympathy to Mr Price; on 27 October his application to the Town Council for more than £356 in compensation (approximately £27,000 in today's money) under the 1886 Riot (Damages) Act was thrown out in disgust.[143]

Equality in wartime was not just economical. All aspects of the way people lived had to be seen to be fair, including well-being, health, sacrifice, suffering, loss, grief, as well as material goods.[144] The appropriate moral behaviour of women was a key issue in 1914 because they had to ensure that the 'home' the men were fighting—and dying—for was maintained. The sacrifice the men were making in battle had to be respected via the appropriate behaviour of their women. Women were expected to behave with deference, sobriety, and devotion whilst their men were away. As Violet Clutton recorded in her diary on 3 November women and girls could 'serve their country best by leading quiet lives, thus setting an example of self-restraint and uprightness at home'.[145] Women who made an unequal sacrifice to the war, such as Mrs Martha Ainsworth, from Loughborough, who, by 28 September had six sons fighting at the front (and a seventh already killed in action), were celebrated in the local press (see Figure 2.1).

Those women who were not perceived to be fulfilling their national duty were criticized heavily because this was believed to be a slight on the male sacrifice. Concerns were raised about an increase in women drinking owing to the absence of their husbands and the separation allowance that gave them an independent income. Women were also criticized for loitering around military camps. In his

[140] Liddle: DF 040: Miss H.W. Davison (1981).
[141] IWM, Docs: West, Miss G.M.: 77/156/1, 4 August 1914.
[142] GRO: Chief Constable of Swansea, Reports to Watch Committee: D/D Con/S 2/3/3, 25 August 1914.
[143] Webb, 'Inflation: The Value of the Pound 1750–2005.' WGRO: Watch Committee Minutes: TC 4/Watch/11, 27 October 1914.
[144] Jay Winter, 'Paris, London, Berlin 1914–1919: Capital Cities at War', in *Capital Cities at War: Paris, London and Berlin, 1914–1919*, ed. Jay Winter and Jean-Louis Robert (Cambridge, 1997), 10–13.
[145] DRO: Violet Clutton: 6258M/Box 1, Vol II, 3 November 1914.

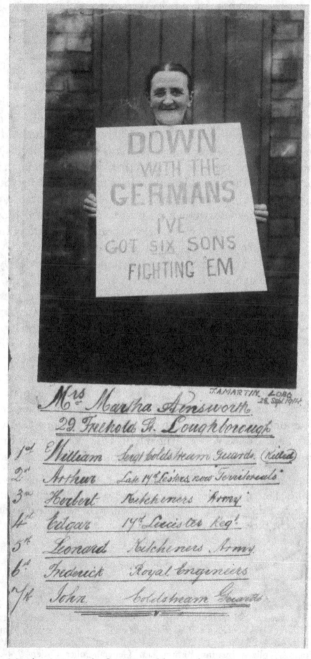

Fig. 2.1. Mrs Martha Ainsworth, from Loughborough, 28 September 1914

ROLLR: Newspaper Cuttings Book (Police): DE 3831/252, 1914. Reproduced by permission of The Record Office for Leicestershire, Leicester and Rutland.

annual report for the year 1914, the Chief Constable of Edinburgh, Roderick Ross, noted how the concentration of large numbers of troops in the county had increased the number of girls and young women 'frequenting the vicinity of the various camps . . . in circumstances which certainly do not conduce to their moral welfare'. He welcomed the formation of Women Patrols, a national movement under the auspices of the Standing Committee of the National Union of Women Workers of Great Britain and Ireland. As a way of dealing with the issues of loitering and temperance, organizations set up alcohol-free clubs where soldiers' wives could meet and be entertained.[146] Over 400 miles away, the Lord Lieutenant of Devon, Lord Fortescue, raised similar concerns in a letter to his deputy, Sir William Acland, on 28 October. He admitted that 'every loose woman in the town is placing herself gratis at the disposal of any man in uniform . . . High Street, Exeter is like Piccadilly Circus'. He too hoped that rescue workers and 'other good women' would be able to direct these women back onto a moral path. However, it is interesting to note that soldiers were not held responsible for leading these women astray; instead 'the women are . . . thrusting their wares on men who have little wish to traffic with them'.[147] The Archbishop of Canterbury was also deeply concerned with the problem of alcohol and female morality. He corresponded with both Lord Kitchener and Lord Roberts about the issue in late October and presided over a conference entitled 'Alcohol and the War' at Caxton Hall, Westminster on 12 November. He called for abstinence from alcohol for the duration of the war as a way of sharing 'in the self-denial of those who are gallantly serving their country at the front'.[148]

The fear of an increase in drunken women was over-stated. Even certain senior police officers felt it was exaggerated.[149] The evidence does not support the fears of temperance workers or officials who were campaigning against the perceived 'tide' of immorality amongst separated women.[150] According to Chief Constable Ross of Edinburgh City Police, those women who did turn to alcohol in wartime did so not as a celebration of their new-found freedom but out of loneliness or anxiety:

> I consider they are more to be pitied than blamed. With very little to relieve the otherwise dull monotony of their lives, grown lonelier doubtless through the absence of their husbands, I do not wonder that these women, to relieve the natural anxiety which must ever be present in their minds, and to break the weary tedium of waiting, have found a certain solace in the Public House.[151]

---

[146] Edinburgh Central Library: Chief Constable's Annual Reports: HV 8198, February 1915.

[147] DRO: Lord Lieutenant's Papers, 1881–1928: 1262M/L129, 28 October 1914.

[148] Lambeth Palace: Davidson Papers: Control of Alcoholic Consumption in Wartime: Volume 374 [Great War], ff. 42–4, 23 October, ff. 50–2, 28 October, and ff, 89, 12 November 1914.

[149] West Midlands Police Museum, Birmingham: General Police Orders Book, 1913–1915: 1991.1226, 7 December 1914.

[150] See Devon and Cornwall Constabulary and Force Museum, Exeter: Chief Constable's Annual Report (City of Exeter): A2004.00176, January 1915 and DRO: DCC Devon Police 1/1/16, 25 November 1914.

[151] Edinburgh Central Library: Chief Constable's Annual Reports: HV 8198, February 1915.

His assessment was confirmed by a case reported in the *Western Evening Herald* on 27 October. A woman charged with drunken behaviour in Westminster argued that she had turned to drink because one son was killed at Mons and another was away at the front. She had got drunk because she was so distraught.[152]

Yet what counted was that despite evidence to the contrary, people perceived female drunkenness to be a frightening problem. Just as members of the public were keeping an eye on anyone 'suspicious', they were also willing to report 'immoral' women to the authorities. Whilst the reality of the situation was that women were not inebriated, the perception was exaggerated, highlighting what was at stake in the defence of the nation. It was a two-frontal defence, on both the home and fighting front. The morality of the home front had to be exemplary in order to make the soldiers' sacrifice abroad worthwhile. Drunken women were showing disrespect to the sacrifice of the fighting soldier. The new moral order of British society in 1914 not only expected people to make the biggest sacrifice that they could, but also to appreciate and understand the sacrifices made by others. Certain members of society failed to grasp the severity of the situation and the magnitude of the sacrifices men at the front were being asked to make. Despite the sense of unity in crisis amongst all society, regardless of class, some tensions did remain, and surfaced over the issue of appropriate moral behaviour.[153]

In his diary entry for 25 to 27 August, Alan Dorward—from a wealthy family—recorded his mother's reaction to his desire to enlist: 'She says why not let all the unemployed and ignorant people go, instead of a brilliant philosopher like me?'[154] For the upper classes, cartoons also focused on how these men and women begrudged the (minor) impact the war was having on their privileged lives. For example, on 4 November *Punch* featured a cartoon depicting two gentlemen fox-hunting. Their anger at the Kaiser stemmed from the rather trivial issue of the decreasing quality of their horses owing to the number requisitioned by the army.[155] In reality, the new moral order of 1914 meant that sacrifices had to be made, respected, and equal. The majority of British people understood this and acted accordingly. The minority who failed to do so were soon 'outed' by their peers or concerned authorities. Under war conditions Britain became a self-regulating society where members of the public understood the rules and were willing to enforce them.

THE LIMITS OF DISSENT AND DOUBT

Protest during the first five months of war, in the sense of being anti-war, was small and relatively unorganized. Of the three major potential sources of disorder—

---

[152] *Western Evening Herald*, 27 October 1914, 3.
[153] *Punch*, 26 August 1914, 187 and 30 September 1914, 279.
[154] University of Liverpool, Special Collections: Dorward Diaries, Diary 10: D446/10/10, 25–7 August 1914.
[155] *Punch*, 4 November 1914, 385.

labour, suffragettes, and Ireland—the first two chose by and large to support the war (the case of Ireland will be discussed separately). Although British trade union leaders and some of their followers had taken part in demonstrations against the war before the official declaration on 4 August, once Britain was at war with Germany the unions responded to this *fait accompli* with an 'industrial truce'. Very few official public anti-war meetings were held in England, Scotland, or Wales once war was declared and those that were, such as the BSP and ILP joint meeting on Glasgow Green held on 9 August, were met with little support from the general public.[156] The response of the labour movement was in sharp contrast to the political agitation and strike action witnessed between 1910 and 1912. To those who felt that a class war was looming on the horizon in the pre-war period, 'the first two years of the Great War must have been immensely reassuring'.[157] Workers and industrialists sought to avoid disputes. In the year 1914, 972 strikes occurred (mostly in the first six months of the year) compared to 1,459 in 1913.[158] Less than 6 per cent of the 451,000 strikers for the year were involved in action between 4 August and 31 December 1914.[159] Between September and December 1914, just under 161,500 working days were lost to strikes accounting for around 1.6 per cent of the annual total.[160] From Dumfermline, Scotland, the American consul wrote that 'the outbreak of war has caused a united and complete loyalty of all classes'.[161]

Two days after the declaration of war the NUWSS announced that it was suspending all political activity until the war was over. Similarly, the leadership of the WSPU began negotiating with the British government. On 10 August the government announced it was releasing all suffragettes from prison. In return, the WSPU agreed to end their militant activities and help the war effort. Christabel Pankhurst appeared at the London Opera House with a speech on the 'German Peril' in September; one month earlier she had been one of the Home Secretary's number one public enemies. Along with her mother Emmeline, they became familiar figures on recruiting platforms, and dissident suffragette newspapers stopped printing.[162] A handful of suffragettes opposed the war. Helena Swanwick severed her long association with British suffragettes such as Millicent Garrett Fawcett and the Pankhursts because of their unconditional support for the war. Even Sylvia Pankhurst went against her family and disagreed with the war. She could not bring herself to support the British government's call for women's war service when that same government still refused women full citizenship.[163]

Where dissent was expected, it tended not to germinate in the first months of war. The 1914 Annual Report of the Edinburgh and District Trades' Council

---

[156] See Chapter One.

[157] R. Geary, *Policing Industrial Disputes: 1893 to 1985* (Cambridge, 1985), 48.

[158] David Silbey, *The British Working Class and Enthusiasm for War, 1914–1916* (London, 2005), 21.

[159] NA, Kew: LAB 34/14 and LAB 34/32.

[160] Silbey, *The British Working Class and Enthusiasm for War, 1914–1916*, 21.

[161] National Archives of the United States, Maryland Campus: American Consulate, Dumferline: M367, Roll 18 (763.72/1228), 5 November 1914.

[162] Martin D. Pugh, 'Politicians and the Woman's Vote, 1914–1918', *History* 59 (1974), 360.

[163] Karen Offen, *European Feminisms 1700–1950: A Political History* (Stanford, 2000), 260–1.

responded angrily to the 'unfair attacks made upon the Scottish workers' who had been accused of being 'drunkards and shirkers' and failing to support the war effort.[164] The war found the official Labour and Socialist movement in Glasgow, as elsewhere in the country, without a united policy. According to John Maclean although there was a general mood among the militant workers in Glasgow of anti-war feeling, there was no unified direction or centre of resistance.[165] Yet many Scottish Labour representatives accepted the 'gallant little Belgium' thesis and spoke out openly in support of the war.[166] In Western Scotland 25 per cent of the male workforce had volunteered for the British army by December 1914. 'Red Clydeside'—the urban areas of Glasgow on the banks of the River Clyde—has become associated with early and sustained opposition to the war. However, the Clyde Workers' Committee was formed in 1915, with William Gallacher as its head, in response to the Munitions Act which forbade engineers from leaving the company they were employed in. The first strike did not occur until February 1915. Moreover, opposition to the war has to be distinguished from hostility to the way in which wartime measures of economic reorganization were imposed.[167] Although some individual socialists protested against the war, no significant collective political action appeared in 1914. James Murray, a riveter on Fairfield Shipyard in Glasgow at the outbreak of war, enlisted in the army despite being a socialist. He felt 'sufficiently patriotic to offer my services to the Army in that first week. Over and above that, I felt this would be a great adventure, and would probably permit me to exercise and improve my knowledge of French and German'.[168]

Owing to their recent turbulent history, miners in South Wales were looked upon as most likely to cause trouble at the outbreak of war. They did not get off to a good start. Before the official declaration of war the Admiralty asked the South Wales Miners' Federation (SWMF) to cut short the August Bank Holiday and return to work. Experiments in the 1860s and 1870s had convinced the navy that they were reliant on Welsh coal, which allegedly generated more steam power and was relatively smokeless. But the SWMF refused to comply on 1 and 3 August, and very few miners turned up for work on 4 August.[169] This refusal was seen as unpatriotic by many, and condemned in the press. A cartoon appeared in the *Western Mail* that day appealing to the patriotic virtues of Welsh miners. 'Dame Wales' dressed in traditional Welsh national costume, called upon the miners to return to the pits to provide coal for the Admiralty (see Figure 2.2).

Was this refusal to work the Bank Holiday an expression of opposition to the war? Anthony Mòr-O'Brien believes that the decision was based on Labour values and the miners felt they had no reason to get involved with a war on the

[164] NLS: Edinburgh and District Trades' Council, Annual Reports: Acc 11177/38, March 1915.
[165] Tom Bell, *John Maclean: A Fighter for Freedom* (Glasgow, 1944), 26–7.
[166] NLS: Draft copy of *The ILP in Bo'ness, 1903–1932* by James Livingstone: Acc 1087/1 (n.d.).
[167] I. Donnachie, C. Harvie, and I. S Wood, eds., *FORWARD! Labour Politics in Scotland 1888–1998* (Edinburgh, 1989), 21–2.
[168] IWM, Docs: Murray, James: P457 (1976).
[169] SWML, SP: South Wales Miners' Federation Minute Book, 1913–1915: WML SWCC: MNA/NUM/3/1/2/3.

DAME WALES: Welshmen! In the hour of danger our Navy asks for coal. It shall not ask in vain. We will show the world that the blast of my horn, resounding in the hills of Wales, can be responded to by men as patriotic as any the world can boast!

THE CALL OF PATRIOTISM.

Fig. 2.2. 'The Call of Patriotism'
Western Mail, 4 August 1914, 8. Reproduced with the permission of Media Wales.

continent.[170] However, it would appear more likely that the miners refused to work the Bank Holiday because they had fought hard for their rights, as demonstrated by the strikes in 1910–1912, and valued any time off from their hard and demanding job. Len Jeffreys, a miner from Cross Keys, Newtown, confirmed this view in 1972: 'There was opposition to [the Admiralty's request] . . . but it was confined to the reaction to being asked to work extra time see, and having just got the eight hour day see then the reaction was well damn if we lose this now it means losing it forever'.[171] When asked this question in 1973, Will Coldrick, a miner from Abersychan, answered 'Oh I should say generally speaking the miners were in favour of the war and you didn't get much of a hearing if you were anti-war'.[172] Therefore, their refusal to work on 4 August was more an expression of their rights as hard labourers, than a political decision about the war. Once war was declared,

---

[170] Anthony Mòr-O'Brien, 'Patriotism on Trial: The Strike of the South Wales Miners, July 1915', *Welsh History Review* 12 (1984), 84–5.
[171] SWML, HH: SWCC AUD/271: Len Jeffreys (1972).
[172] SWML, HH: SWCC AUD/339: Will Coldrick (1973).

an Admiralty request that the miners work on 16 August (a Sunday) was agreed immediately by the Executive Council of the SWMF and throughout 1914, a number of Welsh miners enlisted in the army.[173] C. B. Staunton, a pre-war labour activist who had an antagonistic relationship with the British authorities, declared in early August, 'In times of distress and trouble, I stand with my country'.[174]

Where dissent did occur it had limited impact in 1914. As discussed, three Liberal MPs resigned following the declaration of war on 4 August. One of the most outspoken opponents of the war outside the government was Ramsay MacDonald. According to his daughter he was opposed to the war 'because he considered that the country had drifted into militarism, not for the protection of civil liberties and the quality of life, but owing to long-standing status and commercial jealousies between the Powers which could . . . have been settled around the conference table'.[175] His anti-war speech to a Labour group at the Trade Hall, Leicester, given on 8 August, led to accusations of treason and cowardice. *John Bull* featured a vitriolic cartoon against MacDonald and Keir Hardie on 17 October accusing them of being enemy aliens.[176] On a visit to Edinburgh the press depicted him as 'a wild irresponsible person, if not a traitor'.[177] Yet despite his opposition to the war, MacDonald still visited the front in December 1914 and, like Hardie, paid tribute to the courage of the troops.[178]

Ponsonby and MacDonald joined with two other politicians, Charles Trevelyan and Fred Jowett of Bradford, to form the Union of Democratic Control (UDC) on 5 September 1914. These men were joined by a number of prominent intellectuals and activists: J. A. Hobson, Norman Angell, Bertrand Russell, E. D. Morel, and Helena Swanwick. The UDC would eventually become the leading anti-war organization in Britain.[179] During the first few weeks of the war the UDC focused on challenging the standard reasons as to why Britain was at war. The main issue was 'secret diplomacy', and its members were convinced that there should be parliamentary control over foreign policy. Its practical task was to show that there had been nothing in German policy before the war to excite alarm. Morel did this in a pamphlet for the ILP *How the War Began*, which was published in late 1914. Germany was presented as an aggrieved power, whilst Austria-Hungary was portrayed as fighting a defensive war. The dissenters also challenged the idea that Belgium was the moral reason why Britain had entered the war. For the UDC, the war had been started by the ententes with France and Russia, not by the German invasion of Belgium.[180]

---

[173] SWML, SP: South Wales Miners' Federation Minute Book, 1913–1915: WML SWCC: MNA/NUM/3/1/2/3.
[174] Mòr-O'Brien, 'Patriotism on Trial: The Strike of the South Wales Miners, July 1915', 86.
[175] Jane Cox, ed., *A Singular Marriage: A Labour Love Story in Letters and Diaries: Ramsay and Margaret MacDonald* (London, 1988), 377.
[176] *John Bull*, 17 October 1914, 15.
[177] NLS: Arthur Woodburn: Acc 7656/Box 4/Folder 2 (n.d.).
[178] Lord Elton, *The Life of James Ramsay MacDonald* (London, 1939), 269–71.
[179] Martin Swartz, *The Union of Democratic Control in British Politics During the First World War* (Oxford, 1971).
[180] A. J. P. Taylor, *The Trouble Makers: Dissent Over Foreign Policy, 1792–1939*, 132–9.

After the first few weeks of fighting descended into deadlock, the UDC turned their attentions from arguments about why the war had broken out to how the war should be ended. 'Peace by Negotiation' (or peace without victory) became the central theme around which British anti-war groups rallied. This idea was supported by those who urged a rapid end to the Great War—socialists in the ILP, the BSP, Quakers and other Christians opposed to military violence, Liberal politicians, and trade union organizers. Healthy rearrangement, even rebalance, of world forces, leading to an eventual unity of nations, had to contain the principle of equity, not victory, otherwise threats to world security would perpetuate themselves. A 'fight to the finish' and the crushing of Germany would only lead to its desire for revenge (and another war) in the future. Instead the immediate suspension of war would provide an opportunity for a happy balance in international relations and curb the desire to wage war to settle disputes.[181] However, the UDC, particularly after its existence was made public on 10 September, remained a minority organization in 1914, and its members, such as Norman Angell, had to defend it from a barrage of hostility. Although by the end of November, Angell had decided that he could not leave his UDC colleagues in the lurch and abandon it completely, he stood by them publicly whilst also trying to moderate their activities in private. Individually, his statements became less strident and he announced his support for the war whilst also planning to volunteer with the ambulance corps at the front.[182]

The socialist anti-war perspective was neatly summarized in cartoons published in *Forward* in August 1914. Many socialists viewed the war as a form of militaristic madness let loose on Europe.[183] Workers of the world were being forced to fight for the benefit of wealthy exploiters and capitalists, in a war from which the worker would have no gain.[184] Ultimately, socialists did not see enemies amongst their fellow man: war itself was the enemy.[185] During the first three months of war the playwright and socialist, George Bernard Shaw, produced *Common Sense About The War*, a socialist analysis of the war published as a supplement to the *New Statesman* on 14 November. He charged that the war, fomented on both sides by fanatical militarists, had been avoidable. England, driven by imperialism and militarism, had long prepared for war while deluding Germany that Britain would stay out of a continental struggle.[186]

As Shaw anticipated, his pamphlet generated a fury of outrage and derogation amongst the British press and public.[187] He was denounced as a traitor, former friends cut him off, and booksellers and librarians removed his works from their

[181] H. Weinroth, 'Peace by Negotiation and the British Antiwar Movement, 1914–1918', *Canadian Journal of History* X (1975), 369–71.

[182] Ceadel, *Living the Great Illusion: Sir Norman Angell, 1872–1967* (Oxford, 2009), 153.

[183] *Forward*, 15 August 1914, 5.

[184] *Forward*, 8 August 1914, 5.

[185] *Forward*, 22 August 1914, 5.

[186] Samuel A. Weiss, ed., *Bernard Shaw's Letters to Siegfried Trebitsch* (Stanford, 1986), 180.

[187] Jonathan Atkin, *A War of Individuals: Bloomsbury Attitudes to the Great War* (Manchester, 2002), 85.

shelves. Even socialist colleagues, like Robert Blatchford, editor of *The Clarion*, were angered by his tract. Significantly, opposition to Shaw's work emerged spontaneously from the grass roots. People were not being instructed from above, by the government or military authorities, to reject Shaw's opposition to the British war effort. They concluded themselves that this type of opinion had no place within the new moral community of Britain at war in 1914. Newspapers were also self-censoring. Major British newspapers rejected Shaw's wartime correspondence as unpalatable, including C. P. Scott, editor of the *Manchester Guardian*. In November he explained to Shaw that, in normal circumstances, his work would have been published but that, crucially, wartime was not like normal times. Too many readers would find his work 'highly disturbing' and 'one's duty now is to encourage and unite people and not to exercise and divide'.[188]

The views were echoed amongst a minority of the general population who were of similar religious or political backgrounds. The humanistic–aesthetic opposition to the war amongst the Bloomsbury literary circle has been well documented.[189] For Dr John Johnston, a socialist-Christian doctor from Addlington, Lancashire, the war was wrong on religious grounds. He could not understand how Christian men were willing to kill each other at the bidding of their rulers. The war was yet another illustration of 'the inhumanity of man to man'.[190] Despite what was being preached at the pulpits, Christianity could not be aligned with war. A. Maude Royden from London, a member of the Christian Union, shared Johnston's opinions. In a letter dated 17 December to Albert Murray in Oxford, who would later be imprisoned as a conscientious objector, he wrote: 'I . . . find it somehow *impossible* to believe that it is just as right to fight as to forbear . . . I find it perhaps a perfect thing for the noblest trojan to do; but a disloyal thing for a Christian'.[191] Thomas Macmillan, who lived in a working-class area of Glasgow, attended his local church on the first Sunday after the declaration of war (9 August) and noted how at the close of the service, just as the congregation sang the national anthem, 'several young men walked out of the church in protest'.[192]

Individuals who did express anti-war feeling were aware that they were in the minority and 'that the war would be carried on without them'.[193] The historian and pacifist, Goldsworthy Lowes Dickinson (1862–1932), lecturing at Cambridge in 1914, felt a 'sense of alienation from common opinion' owing to his anti-war stance and retreated into a near solitary existence.[194] Some war-resisters were subjected to outright abuse. Alfred Evans, a piano maker from Southall, Middlesex, was ignored by his fellow workers for being anti-war and was later imprisoned in

---

[188] Dan H. Laurence, ed., *Bernard Shaw: Collected Letters, 1911–1925*, 3 vols., vol. 3 (London, 1985), 239–40, 249–50.

[189] See Atkin, *A War of Individuals: Bloomsbury Attitudes to the Great War*.

[190] Bolton Archives and Local Studies Centre, Bolton: Diaries of Dr John Johnston: ZJO/1/35, 23 August 1914.

[191] Liddle: CO Files: A.V. Murray: CO 066, 17 December 1914.

[192] IWM, Docs: Macmillan, Thomas: PP/MCR/C56 (1935).

[193] Robert Donnington and Barbara Donnington, *The Citizen Faces War* (London, 1936), 37.

[194] E. M. Forster, *Goldsworthy Lowes Dickinson* (London, 1934), 157, 163.

1916 as a conscientious objector. A practising Catholic he recalled how, soon after the outbreak of war, his fellow communicants ignored him and 'spat on the ground' as he left mass for being opposed to the war.[195] Children, often more sensitive than their parents to social convention, were conscious that an anti-war stance was against the 'norm' in 1914. Jennie Lee, the British socialist and a schoolgirl in 1914, began to notice a few weeks into the war that her parents (socialist members of the ILP) were not acting like other parents:

> They were opposed to the war. This was awkward. It was worse than that, it was frightening . . . secretly I was ashamed. Children are sticklers for convention. They hate their family to seem in any way 'queer'. Yet here we were meeting each Sunday evening in the open-air miles outside the town because the local authorities and someone called DORA [sic] refused to give us permission to hold meetings in the usual places like ordinary people.[196]

There were also people who were not part of the official left-wing, anti-war movement who had issues with the overly optimistic and gushing statements about Britain, its cause, and its success in the war. In a letter to his wife Margot on 18 August, Asquith expressed his frustration with the reports about Allied successes: 'I am disgusted with the optimism of the press and other people, believing all this nonsense about great Belgian victories and the Germans already demoralised or starving and committing suicide'.[197] Charles Sorley, who fought and died in the First World War, found 'questions of national honour' to be 'childish and primitive' and hoped that 'all journalists etc., who say that war is an ennobling purge etc, etc., could be muzzled'.[198] Pro-war opinions were not clear cut. What was expressed in public was always more nuanced in private. In September, the same month that he had attended the Propaganda Bureau's Wellington House meeting, Bennett described the war as 'grotesque, a monstrous absurdity' in his article 'Let Us Realise' for *Harper's Weekly*.[199] A month earlier he had confided in his journal that he felt war was a 'mistake on our part'.[200] Yet Bennett resolved, like many people in Britain, that whilst war was unwanted, by August it was unstoppable. As resistance was useless it was better to develop a 'stolid attitude' towards the conflict, to knuckle down and get on with the business of winning it.[201]

There was no significant opposition to the war in 1914. This was not as a result of censorship, oppression, or threats to those who wanted to dissent, at least from the government. Liberal democratic British society allowed room for the expression of reasonable dissent. Any censorship that did exist tended to emerge spontaneously

[195] IWM: 489, Reel 3 (1974).

[196] Jennie Lee, *To-Morrow is a New Day* (London, 1939), 38.

[197] MPP Dudlelan: Margot Asquith: MS Eng c.6691, ff. 161–2, 18 August 1914.

[198] Jean Moorcroft Wilson, ed., *The Collected Letters of Charles Hamilton Sorley* (London, 1990), 187, 211.

[199] Atkin, *A War of Individuals: Bloomsbury Attitudes to the Great War*, 85.

[200] Bennett, *The Journals*, 377.

[201] Atkin, *A War of Individuals: Bloomsbury Attitudes to the Great War*, 85.

from the grass roots. Peace rallies were broken up by members of the public in Edinburgh and Aberdare, and many people denounced individual pacifists to the police. In August 1914 a Monmouthshire collier complained about the activities of a fellow-worker; in Newton-le-Willows, a vicar denounced a 'pro-German English socialist of the most rabid type' who was 'far more dangerous than any German spy'; and Miss Boston, a member of the ILP, walked out in disgust from a meeting addressed by her leader, Ramsay MacDonald, whose speech, she claimed, was 'mischievous, calculated and could do vast damage'.[202] Fred Allan, from Glasgow, wrote on a number of occasions in October to the Secretary for Scotland, T. McKinnon-Wood, complaining about the 'absolutely disloyal articles and references in the recent issues of the Glasgow Socialistic Weekly "FORWARD"', and demanding that the authorities took action. A report from the Lord Advocate concluded that:

> scurrilous and offensive as many of the statements made, they cannot ... be regarded as treasonable or seditious, or as constituting an offence under the Defence of the Realm Act ... At worst there is only offensive and bitter *criticism* ... any action taken ... would only serve to secure notoriety and advertisement for the newspaper without any corresponding public advantage.[203]

In sum, he felt that Mr Allan was taking the passages in *Forward* far too seriously.

***

Dissent was limited in 1914 because the majority of the population rallied around the national cause. As in other wars, in 1914 people were brought face to face with the 'demands and meanings of Britishness' and chose, on the whole, to do what was being asked of them.[204] The population understood that Britain was at war to defend honour, liberty, and the rights of small nations. The commitment of ordinary people to the British cause was reflected in their behaviour. A new moral order was established in 1914 based on volunteerism, self-sacrifice, and equality of sacrifice. Consequently, official suppression of dissent was not required, as the authorities' best ally was a supportive population. It was convenient for the authorities to stand aside and let the 'tide of public opinion do the work they could not easily do themselves'.[205] In 1914 the bulk of the British population considered pacifism an inappropriate response to war. Only nationalist Ireland was perceived as the biggest source of potential dissidence. However, would it be enough to break the unity behind the national cause?

---

[202] NA, Kew: HO 45/10741/263275, ff. 3, 9, 27 August; ff. 365, 350, 154, 1 September, and ff. 8, 2 September 1914 cited in Hopkin, 'Domestic Censorship in the First World War,' 166.

[203] NAS, WRH: *Forward* Socialist newspaper: HH 31/5/2, October 1914.

[204] Linda Colley, *Britons: Forging the Nation 1707–1837* (London, 1992), 281.

[205] Hopkin, 'Domestic Censorship in the First World War', *Journal of Contemporary History* 5, no. 4 (1970), 165.

3

The Enemy

National identity is never more sharply defined than in times of conflict. In peacetime 'banal' indicators, such as currency, a football team, or an anthem, cement feelings of belonging to a wider (and often imagined) national community.[1] War accelerates and intensifies the need to know who and what you are in order to defeat a dangerous enemy. When societies go to war, their world-view becomes polarized into 'us' versus 'them'. The positive collective self—the nation and its allies—is directly juxtaposed with the enemy. The latter exists both as an external threat to the very survival of the nation and as an internal, covert menace in the form of spies and foreign nationals—termed 'enemy aliens' in 1914.

At the outbreak of war, the majority of British people believed that Germany was their enemy and this feeling, in turn, compounded a 'mighty sense of righteous exaltation' about Britain and its cause.[2] In many respects, the image of the enemy was the negative reverse side of the values identified with the nation. For example, the construction of 'Brave Little Belgium' could only be achieved with the parallel widespread belief in the 'evil Hun'. But how precisely was this perception of Germany as the enemy constructed? What was the relationship between the actions of the external enemy—Germany and its enemy allies—and the internal enemy—enemy aliens and spies?

THE EXTERNAL ENEMY

The majority of the British people were repulsed by perceived German militarism and barbarianism. Germany was seen as a huge military machine, with large armies that were sweeping across Europe, leaving destruction in their wake. According to J. Herbert Lewis, Liberal MP for Flintshire in 1914, 'Germany has developed a militarism that is essentially barbaric. May Heaven save our land from its clutches.'[3] According to the American Ambassador in London:

> [The British people] regard the German Emperor and the system of government that he stands for as they regarded Napoleon, a world pest and an enemy of civilisation, and

---

[1] Michael Billig, *Banal Nationalism* (London, 1995), and Benedict Anderson, *Imagined Communities: Reflections on the Origin and Spread of Nationalism* (London, 1991).
[2] Marwick, *The Deluge: British Society and the First World War* (London, 1965), 49.
[3] NLW: J. Herbert Lewis: B28, 7 September 1914.

that there can be no permanent peace till he and his system are utterly overthrown . . . I send you this as the opinion universally held here.[4]

Germany was understood to be so driven by militarism that it had caused the outbreak of war. Many German sources cited in the British press supported these conclusions. One example was the infamous book by the German General Friedrich von Bernhardi. A strong advocate of military aggression, Bernhardi argued that Germany had to expand or face certain decline on the world stage.[5] The book was regarded by many as evidence of Germany's responsibility for the outbreak of war. Eleanor Peart, in Wales, believed it to be 'exactly true' highlighting Germany's pre-war 'devilish ideas'.[6] German militarism was seen as the opposite of British self-perceptions—a nation fighting for the survival of civilization.

It was, however, the atrocities committed by the German armies in Belgium and France that confirmed for the majority of people that Germany was a barbaric nation driven by bloodthirsty militarism, and which helped fashion the predominant stereotypes of the enemy.[7] Over 3 per cent of cartoons published in *Punch* between August and December 1914 depicted the atrocities. Two examples—'The World's Enemy' and 'God (and the women) Our Shield'—graphically captured the destructive and violent atrocities committed by the German troops in Belgium. They illustrate the idea that the German military and its leadership, in the form of the Kaiser, were directly responsible for the carnage and atrocities on the battle field.[8]

Not everyone believed that Germany was capable of such barbarianism. Beatrice Trefusis felt it necessary to distinguish between the perpetrators of atrocities within the German army and the majority of the German population.[9] The Principal of Glasgow University, Sir Donald MacAlister, was in Germany at the outbreak of the war and on his return wrote in the *Glasgow Herald* of the kindness shown to him and his family by all the Germans they encountered during their evacuation.[10] Charles Sorley had also been travelling in Germany when war broke out. He later volunteered with the British army, and in October, from his training camp in Aldershot, he wrote to the Master of Marlborough College:

They are a splendid lot [the Germans] and I wish the silly papers would realize that they are fighting for a principle just as much as we are. If this war proves (as I think it will) that you can kill a person and yet remain his greatest friend—or, less preferably, be killed and yet stay friends—it'll have done a splendid thing.[11]

---

[4] National Archives of the United States, Maryland Campus: American Embassy, London: M367, Roll 371 (763.72/19/722), 10 September 1914.

[5] Friedrich von Bernhardi, *Germany and the Next War* (New York, 1912).

[6] NLW: Dolaucothi: Estate and family records of the Johnes and Hill-Johnes of Dolaucothi, Carmarthenshire: D L8699, 18 October 1914.

[7] Horne and Kramer, *German Atrocities, 1914: A History of Denial* (London, 2001).

[8] *Punch*, 19 August 1914, 167 and 9 September 1914, 233.

[9] Liddle: DF 129: B.M. Trefusis, 12 September 1914.

[10] *Glasgow Herald*, 17 August 1914.

[11] Wilson, ed., *The Collected Letters of Charles Hamilton Sorley* (London, 1990), 196.

On 26 November the *Western Mail*, a Cardiff-based paper, featured a large photo of German soldiers giving their food to Belgian refugee children—hardly the image of a barbaric enemy.[12] However, these were minority voices and incidents. In 1914, belief in rumours that German soldiers were cutting off the hands of Belgian babies, mutilating women, and crucifying their enemies was widespread amongst the British people. Although belief was never absolute and had waned by late autumn, it was a powerful and frightening representation of the enemy. In Dorothy Owen's eyes the Germans were simply 'wicked' because of their treatment of Belgian refugees.[13] Stories of atrocities meant that to Annie Mary Howell, a schoolgirl in Bermondsey in 1914, 'the Germans . . . were somebody terrible . . . the wickedest of the wicked'.[14] When Henry Dotchin, interviewed in 1985, was asked how he felt about the Germans during the First World War he replied: 'I hated them. There you are. And I'm not going to say that I didn't.'[15] The nationwide belief in atrocity stories compounded the belief that the British people were fighting on the right side: for poor, mutilated, violated little Belgium. Additionally, people were forced to confront the 'realities' of war and realized that Germany was the enemy and had to be defeated.

The German's perceived responsibility for the war and their ability to commit such atrocities meant that they were seen as immoral and unlawful. Such judgements were made according to contemporary liberal definitions and norms, such as those ratified under the 1907 Hague Convention on Land Warfare. British academics immediately mobilized around the themes of law-breaking and immorality. Within academic publications, such as those written by members of the Oxford History School, the British case for war was presented in moral terms; Britain was answering the call of 'Right' and coming to the aid of 'Poor Little Belgium'. Moreover, Britain was defending international law against an enemy that was driven by a lust for violence and militarism.[16] Many arguments highlighted how there was 'proof' that Germany had been planning war long before the assassination of Archduke Franz Ferdinand in June 1914.[17]

In an attempt to offset the image of Germany's militarism and its huge armies, so as not to terrify the British public, Germany was also ridiculed. Humour effectively reduced the enemy to a manageable size in the minds of the British people, while laughing at their worst fears helped to contain their anxiety. *John Bull*, the *Daily Mirror*, the *Daily Graphic*, and the *Daily Mail* all included humorous images belittling the German enemy.[18] *Punch*, in particular, delighted in humiliating the enemy and emphasizing its inferiority through satire.[19] The cartoon shown in

---

[12] *Western Mail*, 26 November 1914, 8.   [13] IWM: 4190, Reel 1 (1963).

[14] IWM: 613, Reel 1 (1975).   [15] IWM: 8846, Reel 4 (1985).

[16] For example, see *Prussia's Devilish Creed* by Alex M. Thompson (London, 1914) seen at WGRO: D/D Z 276/77.

[17] Wallace, *War and the Image of Germany: British Academics 1914–1918* (Edinburgh, 1988), 60–6.

[18] See W. K. Haselden, *The Sad Experiences of Big and Little Willie during the First Six Months of the Great War* (London, 1914), and other collections held at the Centre for the Study of Cartoons and Caricature, University of Kent at Canterbury.

[19] *Punch*, 19 August, 162, 7 October, 298, and 4 November 1914, 378, 387 (for just a few examples).

"KAISER BACK TO THE FRONT."
(ATTEMPTED ILLUSTRATION TO A RECENT POSTER OF THE EVENING PRESS.)

Fig. 3.1. 'Kaiser back to the Front'
Punch, 30 December 1914, 544. Reproduced with the permission of The Board of Trinity College Dublin.

Figure 3.1 ridicules an incompetent Kaiser with his head on back to front, suggesting that he does not know whether he is coming or going: hardly the image of a terrifying enemy.

These cartoons resonated with the general public. On 24 November Elizabeth Cadbury recorded in her diary a visit to a sick friend, Ursula, in Birmingham. She noted how 'the Kaiser plays a large part in her imagination, and after looking through the pictures in *Punch*, she said that though people thought the Kaiser was such a wicked man, still he was good for something and this was to make people laugh'.[20]

Not everyone accepted the stark delineation between Germany-Wrong and Britain-Right. In a sermon given at Canterbury Cathedral on 21 August, the Archbishop, Randall Davidson, called for restraint, understanding, and generosity in people's treatment of the enemy.[21] The same day, George Rose, an Essex artist,

[20] BCA: MS 466/432, Box 3: Cadbury Family Journal, 24 November 1914.
[21] Lambeth Palace: Davidson Papers: Sermons (1914–1917): Volume 548 [Sermons], ff. 34–42, 21 August 1914.

recorded in his diary how the organizers of a local patriotic concert were going to exclude all German music 'but public opinion was too strong' against the idea and the original programme remained intact.[22] On 14 September William Watkin Davies recorded in his diary: 'They [Germany] are a great, a magnificent nation, and it would be an enormous calamity if anything happened to reduce their output of civilising influences'.[23] Even Winston Churchill, who referred to the German fleet as 'rats in a hole', was told to rein in his language by the King.[24] Such people soon became weary of polemics. In late September, George Rose was sickened by a biased sermon delivered at his local church in Greensted. He resented how the service had put him 'into a rage of uncontrollable hate', and he resolved never to attend 'these blasphemous orgies of sloppy sentimentality'.[25] In a letter to the *Manchester Guardian* dated 25 September, Charles Eshborn, from Rusholme, Lancashire, ridiculed those 'narrow-minded' people who had banned the music of German composers, such as Beethoven and Mendelssohn.[26]

On 30 December, the Oxford mathematician, R. W. M. Gibbs, speculated over the impression a Martian, who had landed from outer space, would get of Britain's enemy from the reports in the press. He concluded:

> I don't think the Martian would have much sympathy for 'the enemy' . . . for he would soon discover what a scoundrel he is . . . He indulges in the most abominable practices. He uses explosive bullets, prods out the eyes of the wounded, cuts off the breasts of women and the hands and fingers of children. What he lacks in courage, he makes up in cunning and cruelty. A favourite trick is to hoist the white flag and when 'we' advances innocently to take him prisoner, the blackguard flies at him. 'The enemy' takes a malicious pleasure too in wrecking cathedrals and very beautiful buildings and shelling Red Cross wagons. Added to all this, he is an atrocious liar . . . So I think the stranger from Mars would conclude that the sooner 'the enemy' was beaten the better.[27]

Some people disliked Germany and blamed it for the war and the barbaric acts committed during its course; other people felt a degree of sympathy with the nation and its people. Other people felt outright hatred. A friend of Arthur Butler described to him in October how he sometimes could not sleep 'for being in a frenzy of hate' over the Germans.[28] Professor Schuster, a naturalized German and Chair of Physics at Manchester University, returned from abroad with his family in mid-September (having been away since before the war) to find that their milkman had made a number of serious allegations about him being an enemy spy.[29] Eventually the case came to court in mid-October where they were exonerated.

[22] ERO: Diaries of George H. Rose: D/DU 418/15, 21 August 1914.
[23] NLW: W. Watkin Davies: 46, 14 September 1914.
[24] MPP Bodleian: H.H. Asquith: Royal Correspondence: MSS Asquith 4, ff. 22–3, 22 September 1914. Churchill's comments were later featured in a cartoon published in *John Bull* on 31 October 1914, 15.
[25] ERO: Diaries of George H. Rose: D/DU 418/15, 27 September 1914.
[26] Liddle: GS 0526: Charles Eshborn, 25 September 1914.
[27] MPP Bodleian: R.W.M. Gibbs: MS Eng misc c.162, 30 December 1914.
[28] Liddle: GS 0251: A.S.G. Butler, Letter A15 (n.d.).
[29] See *The Observer*, 8 October 1914.

A statement of the Schusters' innocence appeared in the editorial of the *Manchester Guardian* on 19 October. However, on the same day the family received an anonymous letter from a member of the public:

> If that arch-fool, McKenna [Liberal Home Secretary, 1911–1915], does not very soon intern for the war in concentration camps with the filthy pig German swine soldier prisoners every damned hog of a German in England, whether naturalised or not, the people will take matters into their own hands and such bloody traitors as yourself... will be all wiped out. Germans have proved themselves in this war, from their filthy Kaiser downwards, to be blasphemous, traitors, liars, spies, assassins, outragers [sic] of women and girls, brutal, lustful, devils from Hell, and naturalisation in England is only a cloak to carry on their hellish brutalities. You are a German and the above applies to you as to every other German on the face of the earth. The whole bloody race must be wiped out. I'll get you, you damned beast and spy.[30]

The reaction was extreme: but the basic emotion of combined fear and hatred was widespread.

Just as the Allies were an extension of the collective self of the nation, so the minor enemy allies—Austria-Hungary and the Ottoman Empire—stood in parallel relationship to the principal foe. However, neither could compete with Germany as Britain's absolute enemy. Once people realized that Austria-Hungary could not have targeted Serbia without German approval, as they did in the crisis of late July/early August, Austria-Hungary faded from the picture. Both public and private sources made little or no comment about Austria-Hungary being an enemy during this period and ordinary people did not distinguish between Austrian and German internees in Britain.

The Ottoman Empire was more visible as an enemy ally following its entry into the war on 5 November 1914. Its position as enemy tapped into a long history of Liberal stereotyping of Turkey as backward, barbaric, and oppressive towards its Christian subjects. On 16 December *Punch* produced a special supplement entitled 'The Unspeakable Turk'—a compendium of cartoons depicting Turkey as a barbarian since the late nineteenth century.[31] These cartoons focused in particular on massacres committed by the Ottoman Empire against its minority Christian communities from 1842 onwards, ironic considering Russian pogroms were ignored. This was the selective vision of moral turpitude in wartime. Once Turkey entered the war it was ridiculed for being Germany's stooge.[32] However, there was little popular echo to the press images. Perhaps this was because Turkey did not present a real threat. The Ottoman Empire was commonly referred to as the 'sick man of Europe'.[33] This worn-out anachronism did not conjure up frightening images of potential invasion, and its navy would never be able to attack Britain. There were few Turkish immigrants in Britain before the war, and they were therefore less visible targets. British people understood this and their focus remained on Germany.

---

[30] Liddle: DF 114: Florence Schuster, 19 October 1914.
[31] Supplement to *Punch*, 16 December 1914.
[32] *Punch*, 11 November 1914, 391.
[33] M. E Yapp, *The Making of the Modern Near East, 1792–1923* (London, 1987), 92–3.

The absence of Austria-Hungary and Turkey in contemporary sources serves to underline the absolute predominance of Germany as the enemy in 1914.

THE INTERNAL ENEMY

Beyond the usual need for out-groups by which to define oneself in contrast to, there was the emotion of a combined fear and hatred in war which made it imperative to find—and invent where it did not exist—the figure of the enemy, so that such feelings could be discharged. Hence, in Britain, there was the imaginary formulation of the enemy within, as in every other belligerent society. This took two forms—the enemy alien and the spy—both with deep pre-war roots.

In 1911 there were over 53,000 German immigrants in Britain, the highest number for fifty years. The majority lived across London, their occupations including hairdressing, baking, and waiting tables. Hostility towards them was often intertwined with anti-Semitic feeling. From the late nineteenth century up until 1914 the Jewish population in Britain had increased from around 60,000 to 300,000, and consisted mainly of East European Jews fleeing anti-Semitic Russia.[34] Anxiety over this level of immigration, particularly of Russian Poles, led to the Aliens Act of 1905. This hostility increased when Anglo-German diplomatic relations deteriorated during the opening years of the twentieth century. Economic fears were now bolstered by a conspiracy theory that Germans were in Britain in order to 'take over' control of the country.[35] F. H. Hunt recalled in 1980 how German brass bands used to visit his hometown of Kirton, Lincolnshire, before 1914: 'In the general belief that they were spies, we boys had no compunction in hindering their playing by ostentatiously sucking lemons in front of them. Any foreign visitor . . . automatically came under suspicion of spying for Imperial Germany'.[36] James Pratt shared similar suspicions about German musicians who visited Aberdeen in the summers before 1914:

> [They] were really spies in disguise . . . busy collecting information . . . about what was happening; fortifications; everything of that sort . . . At that time the Germans were infiltrating into British industry in a most remarkable manner . . . if the Germans had waited another five, ten years they wouldn't have needed to have had a war because they so controlled our industries that we couldn't have fought.[37]

Just as the fear of invasion surfaced in popular culture, fear of enemy spies also featured in popular novels and increased in intensity during diplomatic crises such as the Moroccan Crisis in 1905–6.[38] However, pre-war anti-German feeling was

---

[34] Joanna Bourke, *Working-Class Cultures in Britain, 1890–1960* (London, 1994)
[35] Panikos Panayi, '"The Hidden Hand": British Myths About German Control of Britain During the First World War', *Immigrants and Minorities* 7 (1988), 192.
[36] Liddle: GS 0818: F.H. Hunt (1986).   [37] IWM: 495, Reel 2 (1974).
[38] Such as Childers, *The Riddle of the Sands* (London, 1903), Le Queux, *The Invasion of 1910 with a full account of the Siege of London* (London, 1906), William Le Queux, *Spies of the Kaiser, Plotting the Downfall of England* (London, 1909), Louis Tracy, *The Invaders* (London, 1901).

not present throughout the United Kingdom, and Germans continued to settle unmolested in British towns and cities. Many naturalized Germans were willingly sponsored for citizenship by their native-born neighbours, and men and women of German origin frequently intermarried and held positions of respect in their neighbourhoods.[39] Although some hostility existed, it was nothing in comparison to the suspicion and fear of the German enemy within which developed during the opening months of the First World War.

Since the turn of the twentieth century, populations had begun to be categorized by nationality.[40] People understood that their fellow residents were either national or non-national. As a reaction to the increase in immigration, the 1905 Aliens Act had officially termed British non-nationals as 'aliens', and in 1914 German and Austrian residents in Britain became 'enemy aliens'. The mere fact of their nationality seemed to make them a dangerous threat to the survival and success of Britain in the war, and on 5 August the Home Secretary, Reginald McKenna, introduced the Aliens Restriction Bill to 'remove or restrain the movements of undesirable aliens'.[41]

Civilian internment was not a new phenomenon in 1914. In the late nineteenth and early twentieth centuries the Spanish in Cuba and the British in South Africa had interned non-combatants in 'concentration camps'. However, what was different in 1914 was the sheer scale of the problem. Universal military service in continental European armies meant there was a huge reserve of men that could be called upon to fight. Each enemy alien that Britain detained was one less recruit for the German army.[42] Although universal internment of all males of military age did not take place in Britain until May 1915 after the Lusitania riots, the first wave of arbitrary arrests and internment began on 24 August when around 4,500 German reservists were rounded up.[43] Between 28 August and 16 September 6,700 Germans were arrested, bringing the total number of civilian internees to 10,500.[44] According to the Under-Secretary for Scotland, D. D. Cubitt, in Scotland the Scottish police were too successful. In September he appealed to the War Office to provide stricter instructions about who they should be interning owing to their overzealousness.[45] By 20 September the War Office begged the Home Office

---

[39] IWM: 95, Reel 1 (1973). See also Laura Tabili, '"Having Lived Close Beside Them All The Time": Negotiating National Identities Through Personal Networks', *Journal of Social History* 39 (2005).

[40] In 1858, passports became a standard document issued solely to British nationals. Until 1915, they were a simple single-sheet paper document and included a photograph of the holder. The British Nationality and Status of Aliens Act 1914 was passed on the outbreak of the First World War. At this time a new format was introduced, a single sheet folded into eight and containing a cardboard cover. It included a description of the holder, as well as a photograph, and had to be renewed after two years.

[41] Hansard Parliamentary Debates, 5 August 1914.

[42] Matthew Stibbe, 'The Internment of Civilians by Belligerent States during the First World War and the Response of the International Committee of the Red Cross', *Journal of Contemporary History* 41 (2006), 8.

[43] Nicoletta F. Gullace, 'Friends, Aliens, and Enemies: Fictive Communities and the Lusitania Riots of 1915', *Journal of Social History* 39 (2005), 355.

[44] Panikos Panayi, *The Enemy Within: Germans in Britain During the First World War* (Oxford, 1991), 81, 95.

[45] NA, Kew: HO 45/10729/255193.

to stop the arrests as there was no more room to house the prisoners. The accommodation problem had become so acute by December that McKenna had to agree to the release of over 1,000 prisoners on parole.[46] Civilian internees were held in makeshift, temporary camps based 'on board ships, some in barracks, some in large buildings... and some in huts' around the United Kingdom until the system was formalized in 1915.[47]

Any organizations or associations connected with Germany were closed down and it became illegal to trade with the enemy. Jeremiah O'Leary, an Irishman working in London, recalled how the German gymnasium in Highbury was shut down by the government in 1914. Ironically it went on to be used by another 'internal enemy': the North London Company of the Irish Nationalist Volunteers.[48] Letters in *The Times* and the *Daily Mail* demanded that all German waiters be sacked. Neville Chamberlain noted in his diary on 4 August how 'the hotel service is crippled, nearly all the waiters having left to go back to service in Austria-Hungary, Germany and Switzerland'.[49] Some newspapers implored their readers to boycott German and Austrian waiters, and if any professed to be Swiss to demand to see their passport.[50] Universities and schools had to get rid of their German and Austrian staff.[51] In some cases employees themselves demanded the resignation of their alien colleagues. On 20 October the miners from Lewis Merthyr Lodge in South Wales resolved that 'no persons shall descend their pits' until Mr Sholback, a German head electrician, was 'shifted from the colliery'.[52] To protect themselves, Germans anglicized their names, people got rid of their dachshunds, and in Essex butchers changed the name of 'German Sausage' to 'Dunmow Sausage'.[53] On 19 August *Punch* featured the 'spot-the-difference' cartoon shown in Figure 3.2.

This German grocer replaced any symbols of the enemy country, such as a dachshund, his pipe, and German delicacies with overtly English items—a terrier, a cigarette, and stilton cheese. Ironically, some British citizens who had germanized their names before the war found themselves in a difficult position in August 1914. On 12 August William George Newman, a watchmaker from Great Totham,

[46] David French, 'Spy Fever in Britain, 1900–1915', *The Historical Journal* 21 (1978), 367–8.

[47] NA, Kew: FO 369/714, 4 December 1914.

[48] NA, Dublin: BMH Witness Statements: J.J. O'Leary: WS, 1,108 (1955).

[49] University of Birmingham, Special Collections: Neville Chamberlain's Political Journal, 1913–1920: NC 2/20, 4 August 1914.

[50] Peel, *How We Lived Then, 1914–1918: A Sketch of Social and Domestic Life in England During the War* (London, 1929), 40.

[51] University of Liverpool, Special Collections: Annual Reports of the University: R/LF 371 A1, 1908–1914 and ERO: T/Z 25/626 (1966).

[52] SWML, SP: Lewis Merthyr Lodge Minute Book, 1913–1915: SWCC MNA/NUM/L/48/2, 20 October 1914.

[53] James Munson, ed., *Echoes of the Great War: The Diary of the Reverend Andrew Clark, 1914–1919* (Oxford, 1985), 17. Anti-German feeling among the British people prompted the Royal Family to abandon all titles held under the German crown and to change German-sounding titles and house names for English-sounding versions. On 17 July 1917, a royal proclamation by George V provided that all agnatic descendants of Queen Victoria would be members of the House of Windsor with the personal surname of Windsor.

A QUICK CHANGE OF FRONT.

Fig. 3.2. 'A Quick Change of Front'

Punch, 19 August 1914, 159. Reproduced with the permission of Punch Limited.

Essex, was arrested for being an enemy alien. Five days later he was released without charge when it was revealed that he was born at Borley, Essex and not Berlin. He had been claiming that he was German since 1913 'for trade purposes as the German watch and clock makers are supposed to be the best workmen'.[54]

An extension and intensification of this all-consuming concern with enemy aliens in Britain was an obsession with enemy spies and espionage. Naturally, genuine espionage took place on British soil during the war—the most infamous case being Carl Hans Lody who was shot at dawn on 6 November 1914.[55] Yet, the threat of German spies in Britain during the First World War was minimal.[56] Once again, perception was more powerful than reality. In 1914 the British public, and certain members of the elite including Vernon Kell, head of MI5, perceived the threat of enemy spies to be much bigger than it actually was, despite efforts by those in power to contain the situation.

Immediately after the outbreak of war anything German, and anyone thought to have the least sympathy with the Germans was accused of espionage. On 11 August Violet Clutton, in London, recorded in her diary 'where ever one goes nowadays one hears of nothing but Germans, Germans, Germans from everyone, German

---

[54] ERO: Essex Police Records: First World War: The War: Suspects, 1914–1918: J/P 12/6 and *Essex County Standard*, 22 August 1914, 7.

[55] NA, Kew: WO 94/103.

[56] Thomas Boghardt, *Spies of the Kaiser: German Covert Operations in Great Britain during the First World War Era* (Basingstoke, 2004). See also Christopher Andrew, *The Defence of the Realm: The Authorized History of MI5* (London, 2009).

spies and the wicked Kaiser who began it all'.[57] No one was immune from accusations of espionage. One such victim was the novelist D. H. Lawrence who had returned to Britain and married his wife, Frieda, in July 1914. Frieda's German parentage and Lawrence's pacifism meant they were viewed with suspicion in wartime Britain and lived in near destitution.[58] On 4 September, at the bandstand in Clacton-on-Sea, an argument ensued between an audience member and the timpanist after the latter failed to stand during the playing of the national anthem. The *Essex County Standard* reported the following day that despite the conductor's best efforts to explain to the gentleman concerned that the drummer was unable to stand, it was still felt necessary to distribute leaflets 'explaining that every member of the band was British and that it was not want of loyalty that explained the sitting position of the tymphanist [sic]'.[59] General D. G Johnson was told by his concerned wife on 27 October that there was a spy in the Cabinet, either Lord Haldane or Reginald McKenna.[60]

Historians have retrospectively described this period in terms of 'spy-fever', and justifiably so since this was also the terminology of contemporaries who used words like 'spy-mania', 'spy-scares', 'spy-obsession', and 'hunt-the-alien' campaigns in their diaries and letters.[61] Basil Thomson, Assistant Commissioner at Scotland Yard in charge of the Criminal Investigation Department in 1914, recalled a decade later:

> In August 1914 the malady [the spy-scare] assumed a virulent epidemic form accompanied by delusions which defied treatment. It attacked all classes indiscriminately, and seemed even to find its most fruitful soil in sober, solid and otherwise truthful people.[62]

'Fever' is an appropriate description for this atmosphere because not only does it describe the hysteria or delirium similar to that felt by an intensification of temperature (how Thomson interpreted the reaction to spies in the interwar period), but it also suggests a malady within the body (which is perhaps how contemporaries understood the spy problem). The enemy within could subvert the national cause and weaken the immunity of Britain from foreign attack.

On the day that the UK went to war, it was reported to the Metropolitan Police that secret saboteurs had blown up a culvert near Aldershot and a railway bridge in Kent. On inspection, both were found to be intact.[63] But the rumour-mill had begun in earnest. By 6 August the *Daily Mail* and *The Times* were reporting arrests and charges against suspected spies as 'London is said to be full

[57] DRO: Violet Clutton: 6258M/Box 1, Vol I, 11 August 1914.

[58] George J. Zytaruk and James T. Boulton, eds., *The Letters of D.H. Lawrence: Volume II, June 1913–October 1916* (Cambridge, 1981). Later in the war they were accused of spying and signalling to German submarines off of the coast of Cornwall where they lived. In late 1917, after constant harassment by the military authorities, Lawrence was forced to leave Cornwall at three days' notice under the terms of the Defence of the Realm Act.

[59] *Essex County Standard*, 5 September 1914, 5.

[60] Liddle: GS 0861: Major General D.G. Johnson, 27 October 1914.

[61] French, 'Spy Fever in Britain, 1900–1915'. See also BCA: Sir Richard Threlfall Papers: MS 347A/122, 12 October 1914.

[62] Basil Thomson, *Queer People* (London, 1922), 10, 37.

[63] Andrew, *The Defence of the Realm: The Authorized History of MI5*, 53.

Teutonic Barber. "SHAFE, SIR?"
Customer. "YE-ES——— THAT IS, NO!———I THINK I'LL TRY A HAIR CUT."

Fig. 3.3. 'Teutonic Barber'

Punch, 16 September 1914, 239. Reproduced with the permission of The Board of Trinity College, Dublin.

of German spies'.[64] Rumours spread about German barbers, acting as enemy agents, cutting 'your throat . . . instead of your hair' and were graphically depicted in *Punch*. The cartoon shown in Figure 3.3, published precisely at the moment when the Germans were being pushed back from the Marne towards the Channel coast (increasing fears of a German invasion of Britain), depicts a Kaiser-like barber menacingly sharpening his razor ready for his next British customer.

Rumour often became reality for unsuspecting victims. On 7 August the *Western Mail* reported that a German hairdresser named Otto Kruger, living in Abercynon, Rhondda Cynon Taff, was charged under the Official Secrets Act.[65] According to *The New York Times*, by 17 October all of England was buzzing with talk of the 'spy menace'.[66] Spies were believed to have been heard of, seen, or captured across the United Kingdom including in Yorkshire, Plymouth, Dorset, Essex,

---

[64] Michael MacDonagh, *In London During the Great War* (London, 1935), 15.
[65] *Western Mail*, 7 August 1914.   [66] *New York Times*, 17 October 1914, 1.

Sunderland, Shrewsbury, Surrey, Lincolnshire, East Scotland, and London.[67] Scottish police spent all of September 1914 searching for a reported German airbase in the remote Highlands.[68] William Le Queux, the famous spy-author, felt so personally threatened by spies near his home in Shepperton-on-Thames that he hounded his local police and Scotland Yard for protection.[69] As well as reports in the press, rumours about spies spread by word of mouth. Beatrice McCann who lived near Hungerford in 1914 recalled how a German student had been staying with her family before the war broke out. The news spread like 'wildfire' through her village and he was eventually interned on the Isle of Man.[70] Between 8 and 17 August, Edrica de la Pole, from Tremar, Devon, had been told about three different spies being caught in a remote area of east Devon.[71] A London resident, and former Special Constable, recalled how he had heard about the rumour of Prince Louis of Battenberg being a German spy because 'a policeman told me that his brother was to be in the firing squad'.[72]

The presence of enemy spies in Britain was confirmed for many people by soldiers on home defence duty. Cecil Holt, serving with the 6th Cyclist Battalion Royal Sussex Regiment in Norfolk, regularly lavished his sister, Iris, in Lewes, Sussex, with exciting espionage stories.[73] Richard Orlebar was serving with the 3rd Battalion Bedfordshire Regiment in Felixstowe in December 1914. He described in detail to his parents, in Herefordshire, a 'great spy hunt' although they were yet to catch their man.[74] Visual evidence also confirmed to ordinary people the 'reality' of the spy threat. Precautions against the subversion of vulnerable points in Britain by enemy agents acted as a self-fulfilling prophecy. With such increased and visible police activity, it is unsurprising that ordinary people became convinced that German spies were around every corner. On 19 August Violet Clutton observed how, in London: 'Every day more and more spies are being arrested for attempting to blow up bridges, cut communications, explode the Gas Works or poison the water supply. Wish every German had been turned out days ago.'[75] Annie Brunton, also in London, recorded in her diary how she had heard from a friend that 'two spies were caught poisoning the water and were shot' in Farnborough, Hampshire on 23 August.[76] Activities such as sketching or photography were

---

[67] Liddle: GS 0735: Lt-Col C.P. Heath, Letter 37, 13 August 1914, Liddle: EP 085: Mark Ward, Letter 5 (1914), Munson, ed., *Echoes of the Great War: The Diary of the Reverend Andrew Clark, 1914–1919*, 9, 19–20, 26, Liddle: GS 1507: L.F.S. Sotheby, Letter 5, 22 December 1914, IWM, Docs: Scott, Major W.S.: 99/12/1, 19 August 1914, IWM, Docs: McDonald, Lieutenant D.: 01/29/1 (1914), IWM, Docs: Miller, H.: 02/38/1, 9 August 1914, IWM: 517, Reel 1 (n.d.) and 495, Reel 2 (1974), IWM: 617, Reel 7 (1975).

[68] NAS, WRH: German Aircraft in Scotland: HH 31/6, File 1, September 1914.

[69] NA, Kew: MEPO 3/243.

[70] Liddle: DF Recollections: Box J-M: Beatrice McCann (n.d.).

[71] PWDRO: Diary of Edrica de la Pole: Acc 1306/22, 8–17 August 1914.

[72] Peel, *How We Lived Then, 1914–1918: A Sketch of Social and Domestic Life in England During the War*, 41.

[73] Liddle: AIR 224: A.H. Morton, August and September 1914.

[74] Liddle: GS 1205: R.A.B. Orlebar, 1 December 1914.

[75] DRO: Violet Clutton: 6258M/Box 1, Vol I, 19 August 1914.

[76] NLI: Diary of Annie Brunton: Ms 13,620/2, 23 August 1914.

treated suspiciously. Miss Gladys Dolby New, a student at Liverpool University in 1914, recalled in 1989 how she and her art coach were arrested by two soldiers whilst out sketching near the Mersey estuary. They were released when her work was not deemed good enough to aid the Germans.[77] Suspicious lighting and possible signalling were vigilantly policed and anyone seen at night along a coastal area with a lantern was likely to be arrested.

The restriction on reliable and up-to-date news exacerbated the belief that spies were present. Sir George Aston believed that the British army had to assemble secretly in August 1914 because Britain was 'a land teeming with the enemy's spies in all walks of life'.[78] Similarly Mabel Barthorpe, in London, believed 'the secrecy of our troops is wonderfully kept and necessary with so many spies about'.[79] Any negative 'scare' stories published in the press, such as the rumour that the BEF had been annihilated at the front in August 1914, were blamed on the presence of spies in Britain.[80]

People were convinced that spies surrounded them and amateur spy-catchers abounded. Hallie Eustace Miles recorded in her diary on 31 October 'I *know* I travelled in a 'bus with two German spies today, and it was such an awful feeling, as if a dark shadow was present'.[81] Rumours about spies were acted upon and those thought to be spies were actively accused. Of particular note is the degree to which ordinary people accused others of being enemy spies, and reported them to the authorities. The level of self-vigilance was not coerced from above by the police or government (although their actions certainly would have helped legitimize it); ordinary people took it upon themselves to deal with spies. In his report for the year ending 31 December, the Chief Constable of Edinburgh City police, Roderick Ross, described how he had received 'a lot more letters and reports, anonymous and otherwise, since the outbreak of the war' from loyal citizens 'who are energetic in at once communicating anything of a suspicious nature which may have come to their notice'.[82] The Lord Lieutenant of Devon received a number of letters from concerned local residents about the spies in their midst. One such example was written in November by an Exmouth resident, G. S. Stevens:

In common with all other British subjects I am greatly troubled at the number of spies in our midst, and I think it is the duty of every loyal person to report anything which seems to them at all suspicious. Herr Hengl and his family occupied a house in Morton Road, Exmouth for several weeks and then took an unfurnished house in Phillipps Avenue next to this house, where I am at present, on a visit. Upon re-taking possession of the house in Morton Road, the owner has found a saucepan hidden away in a cupboard which has evidently been used for other than domestic purposes. There also appears to have been a hole dug in the back garden. In the back garden of the house in Phillipps Avenue Herr Hengl was seen apparently digging a hole earlier in the day

[77] Liddle: DF Recollections: Box N-S: Miss Gladys Dolby New (1989).
[78] Sir George Aston, *Secret Service* (London, 1930), 52.
[79] DRO: Fursdon Family Correspondence: 5242M/Box 27/18, 17 August 1914.
[80] IWM, Docs: Robinson, F.A.: P401, 18 August 1914.
[81] Miles, *Untold Tales of War-Time London: A Personal Diary* (London, 1930), 24.
[82] Edinburgh Central Library: Chief Constable's Annual Reports: HV 8198, February 1915.

upon which he was removed. He has bought *new* furniture for the house, but, rather curiously *brought* a number of stuffed birds—very ordinary looking birds—is it possible they may be the receptacles of incriminating papers? Yesterday, at about 2 o'clock (I think) I saw a carrier pigeon steadily flying over the roof of this house—apparently in a beeline for the mouth of the river. It disappeared from my view at once. I saw Herr Hengl pacing 7 paces from the right hand wall of his garden, his back about 5ft from the house soon after his arrival. The policeman to whom I reported this thought he might be measuring for a clothes line![83]

By mid-September, in London alone, the police had received nearly 9,000 reports from the public of suspicious Germans.[84] Ninety were deemed to be worthy of investigation; none proved to have any foundation.[85] By 15 September the Chief Constable of Birmingham City Police, Charles Rafter, was exasperated by groundless accusations that were wasting police time. In a general order to his force he demanded that 'all reports made by Officers about aliens will in future be made in writing and not by word of mouth, so that accurate information will be obtained and misleading intelligence not sent in'.[86]

This intense atmosphere also encouraged people to 'shop' someone they disliked. A. R. Williamson, Second Officer of SS *Santaren* which docked in Cardiff on 15 November, used the frenetic atmosphere as a chance to remove the unpopular Chief Engineer by accusing him of being a German enemy spy.[87] For other suspects, they were simply guilty of being or looking 'different', increasing the sense that spy-catching resembled a witch-hunt. John Macleod, a soldier with the Cameron Highlanders, was accused of being a German spy by fellow soldiers because he had shaved badly and had cuts on his face.[88] Ernest Cooper, a solicitor from Southwold, Suffolk recalled how 'old women in trousers soon began to worry the authorities'.[89] The Chief Constable of Devon reported to the Home Office that he had received 'several complaints' about the monks of Buckfast Abbey, Devon, who were reported to either be spies themselves or harbouring German aliens.[90] Choosing to live 'outside' of society in the service of God had laid them open to suspicion.

For soldiers and policemen on home defence duty, the combination of being told that spies were in their midst, leading to anticipation and a heightened atmosphere, and the boredom they inevitably experienced whilst guarding railway bridges and alike, perhaps induced them to accuse innocent people of being enemy aliens. A member of the Royal Naval Division, stationed in Norfolk in October 1914, recalled how occasional 'spy scares' varied the monotony of naval life.[91] On

[83] DRO: Lord Lieutenant's Papers, 1881–1928: 1262M/L112, 25 November 1914.
[84] French, 'Spy Fever in Britain, 1900–1915', 365.
[85] Hew Strachan, *The First World War, Volume One: To Arms* (Oxford, 2001), 106.
[86] West Midlands Police Museum, Birmingham: General Police Orders Book, 1913–1915: 1991.1226, 15 September 1914.
[87] Liddle: RNMN/Williamson: A.R. Williamson, 15 November 1914.
[88] Liddle: GS 1027: J.D. MacLeod, 10 August 1914.
[89] IWM, Docs: Cooper, Ernest Read: P121, August/September 1914.
[90] NA, Kew: HO 45/23540.
[91] IWM, Docs: Anonymous memoir of a member of the Royal Naval Division: Misc 254: Item 3484 (n.d.).

28 August, Cecil Forester, later 7th Baron Forester of Willey Park, Shropshire and aged 15 in 1914, recorded in his diary how his family car was stopped by Lake Vyrnwy by a 'Policeman who thought we were German spies!!'[92] This was not an isolated occurrence as *Punch* deemed it suitable material to be ridiculed on 26 August.[93] In Dover, it was reported that 'an attempt had been made to tamper with the water supply...A sentry, on night duty at the reservoir, had fired at an intruder, who, it was said, had emptied a mysterious bottle, containing typhoid germs, or some virulent poison, into the tanks'.[94] Mabel Rudkin's house was near the waterworks and she heard the shots ring out:

> On the following day, a notice was sent to every householder, directing that all drinking water should be boiled for at least two hours...I obediently boiled (had I not heard the shots?) but though many defied the order, ascribing the intruder and his bottle to the over-wrought imagination of the sentry, boilers and non-boilers fared equally well. No case of illness occurred which was traced to contaminated water.[95]

After weeks of talking about spies to his sister in Sussex, Cecil Holt finally snapped: 'I have to wait till about 3 a.m. before I can go round the guard. I mean to catch some of them tonight somehow. I am in the mood for damning somebody'.[96]

The British population in 1914 appeared to suffer from an acute case of 'spy-fever'. Anybody who was thought to have the slightest German connection was treated with suspicion. In this broad sense it shared some features of a medieval witch-hunt. Those who did not conform to or preserve British society in wartime had to be purged.[97] Florence Schuster had been abroad since before the outbreak of war. When she arrived in Manchester in September 1914 and saw evidence of 'spy-fever' she thought ordinary people had 'lost their heads'.[98] Her family would later fall victim to the 'spy fever'. Nowhere in Britain was untouched by this obsession with spies. Moreover, although it was supported by articles in the printed press, it was in no way driven by newspapers alone. A fundamental characteristic of British 'spy-fever' in 1914 is that it emerged spontaneously at the grass roots. By the end of September 1914 *Punch* injected some humour in its portrayal of the treatment of aliens in Britain, suggesting that perhaps the fear was exaggerated.[99] This was mirrored in other contemporary satirical publications, where even those suffering from German measles were unwelcome in British wartime society.[100]

---

[92] Liddle: GS 0569: Lord Cecil Forester, 28 August 1914.
[93] *Punch*, 26 August 1914, 179. An overzealous policeman incurs the wrath of an angry British motorist after an inappropriate line of questioning that enquires as to the relationship he has with the lady in the passenger seat.
[94] Mabel Rudkin, *Inside Dover, 1914–18: A Woman's Impression* (London, 1933), 45.
[95] Ibid.
[96] Liddle: AIR 224: A.H. Morton, August 1914.
[97] Christina Larner, *Witchcraft and Religion: The Politics of Popular Belief* (Oxford, 1984), 124.
[98] Liddle: DF 114: Florence Schuster, September 1914.
[99] *Punch*, 30 September 1914, 271, 21 October 1914, 347, 18 November 1914, 428.
[100] Walter Emanuel and John Hassall. *Keep Smiling, More News by Liarless for German Homes.* (London, 1914), 7.

VIOLENCE AGAINST THE ENEMY WITHIN

It would be surprising if the fear and hatred directed to constructing the figure of the enemy within had not also resulted in violence. Racial tension is sadly not a new, or obsolete, phenomenon in Britain.[101] Racial violence 'breaks out against the background of underlying hostility towards an out-group, exacerbated by recent developments, and sparked off by a particular incident'.[102] Just as Muslims are becoming the victims of racial tension in the current 'War on Terror', particularly after the latest terrorist attack or foiled plot, Germans in Britain during the First World War came under attack at particular low points of the conflict, such as the sinking of the *Lusitania* in May 1915. However this hostility was based on long-term Germanophobia that existed prior to 1914 and had intensified during the war.

Episodic acts of violence against those deemed to be enemy aliens and their sympathizers occurred in 1914 and marked the moment when language and imagination turned into acts of violence. These riots, all of them against civilians rather than prisoners of war (POW), had a clear chronological concentration, as illustrated in Table 3.1. I shall return to the issue of reactions amongst the British public to German and Austrian POW soldiers later in this section. Each of the major incidents followed a similar pattern. Once a victim was identified, crowds built up around a particular target—usually a shop belonging to the victim—and over the course of a few hours cheering, booing, and patriotic singing would develop into stone throwing, smashing of windows, the destruction of property, and looting. The police and/or military authorities would be required to disperse the crowds of varying sizes. The incidents often continued late into the night, starting up again the next evening if the riot lasted more than one day.[103]

Although these riots were limited and did not involve the majority of the British population, it is as a symptom rather than an act that they are important. There are a variety of explanations as to why anti-German riots broke out in the autumn of 1914. Sylvia Pankhurst viewed the riots as a indication of the economic dislocation caused by the war. In her opinion the trades were under attack and not the nationality of their owners.[104] The riots can also be situated in a wider context of racial violence in Britain, including pre-war anti-Semitic feeling.[105] As noted, following the outbreak of war, anti-Semitism, at times, merged with anti-German feeling, although it is difficult to draw a clear line between anti-alienism

---

[101] Colin Holmes, *Anti-Semitism in British Society, 1876–1939* (London, 1979), Colin Holmes, *A Tolerant Country? Immigrants, Refugees and Minorities in Britain* (London, 1991), Panikos Panayi, 'Anti-Immigrant Violence in Nineteenth and Twentieth Century Britain', in *Racial Violence in Britain in the Nineteenth and Twentieth Centuries*, ed. Panikos Panayi (London, 1996).

[102] Panayi, 'Anti-Immigrant Violence in Nineteenth and Twentieth Century Britain', 19.

[103] More detail about particular riots can be gained from the work of Panikos Panayi (1989; 1996) and Kit Good (2002), mentioned above as well as NA, Kew: 45/10944/257142 and NLW: George Eyre Evans, *Aberystwyth War Book:* XD 523 E90.

[104] E. Sylvia Pankhurst, *The Home Front: A Mirror to Life in England during the First World War* (London, 1932, 1987).

[105] Panayi, 'Anti-Immigrant Violence in Nineteenth and Twentieth Century Britain'.

Table 3.1. Major outbreaks of anti-German violence in Britain, August to December 1914**

Place	Start date	End date	Victims	Approx no. of crowds	Make-up of crowds
Peterborough	Fri. 7/8	Sat. 8/8	2x German pork butchers' shops; 1x Englishman defending them at local pub	3,000	Young men (labourers and manual workers)
Keighley	Sat. 29/8	Tues. 1/9	3x German butchers' and bakers' shops;	5,000	Striking engineers (labour dispute since May 1914); Irishmen; young girls
			1x English factory owner;		
			1x English butcher's shop		
Aberystwyth	Wed. 14/10	Wed. 14/10	1x German professor returning to Aberystwyth University	2,000	Working men and women
Saffron Walden, Essex	Fri. 16/10	Sat. 17/10	1x English family who were accommodating two Germans	2,000	Young men
Deptford, London	Sat. 17/10	Mon. 19/10	Number of German shops (bakers, butchers, confectioners); Austrian owned pub	5,000– 6,000	Men, women, and children
Crewe	Sat. 24/10	Sun. 25/10	3x German shops	1,000	Labourers as ringleaders; large no. of women and girls as spectators

* Sources include: NA, Kew: HO 45/10944/257142; NLW, Aberystwyth: XD 523 E90; Kit Good, 'England Goes To War, 1914–15' (PhD, University of Liverpool, 2002); Panikos Panayi, 'Anti-German Riots in London during the First World War', *German History* 7 (1989); Panikos Panayi, 'Anti-German Riots in Britain During the First World War', in *Racial Violence in Britain in the Nineteenth and Twentieth Centuries*, ed. Panikos Panayi (London, 1996).
* *NB:* Minor outbreaks of violence also occurred in the East End of London, Neath, Sunderland, Durham, Essex, North Devon, Liverpool, and Birmingham during the autumn of 1914.

and anti-Semitism.[106] When Lord Rothschild implored *The Times* on 31 July 1914 to tone down its leading articles supporting British involvement in the war, both the Foreign Editor, Henry Wickham Steed, and his proprietor, Lord Northcliffe, regarded this as 'a dirty German-Jewish international financial attempt to bully us

---

[106] Holmes, *Anti-Semitism in British Society, 1876–1939*, 122.

into advocating neutrality'.[107] F. Ashe-Lincoln, a schoolboy in Plymouth in 1914, recalled that:

> there was a tremendous amount of anti-Semitism. Jews were attacked right, left and centre and all Jews were described as being 'Germans' . . . We [he and his brother] had at one time to get special protection from our school, from the Head Master, because of the number of attacks that were made on us. Our clothes were torn, and so on. They accused all Jews of being 'Germans' and the depth of feeling against Germans was so intense in [the First World] war, and any Jew was regarded as being good game.[108]

The violence can also be explained by theories of community formation; violence towards Germans, outside the national community, helped to define those who belonged. These explanations are valid. However a closer look at these riots, particularly the cluster in October, can reveal more.

A logical explanation for the riot that broke out in Peterborough on 7 August is the heady excitement and tension caused by the lead-up to and outbreak of war. Smaller riots also occurred in the East End of London soon after the outbreak of war, again possibly for the same reasons.[109] This was despite the *East London Observer* calling for its readers on 8 August 1914 to behave 'justly, and like a gentleman and a friend' towards its German community.[110] The fact that the Peterborough riot occurred on a Friday and Saturday could be connected to pay-day and/or weekend drinking getting out of hand. The Keighley riot on 29 August stands out as the anomaly. However, an ongoing labour dispute in the area since May 1914 between factory engineers and their employers provides some explanation as to why tempers were running high. Clearly that is why a factory owner—Sir Prince Smith—was targeted and, when the police intervened, a butcher's shop—owned by the son of a policeman—was also destroyed.[111] The involvement of Irishmen was perhaps because it provided an opportunity to momentarily refashion an Irish identity that had always been cast in opposition to England.[112] Crowd psychology was clearly involved: people were caught up in the behaviour of a group, perhaps triggered by an angry minority.[113] A letter to the *Liverpool Echo* on 27 October argued that 'the mobs in these cases are always led by a very few men—often roughs'.[114] The perpetrators of the violence were usually young males, who, in the Keighley case, were angry strikers, and in the other cases possibly angry for other reasons, such as the strain of wartime conditions or the fact that they were stuck in Britain whilst the real action was going on abroad. The riots often broke out at night and alcohol as a contributory factor to the actions of the mobs must

---

[107] Cited in Niall Ferguson, *The Pity of War* (London, 1999), 195.
[108] Liddle: DF Recollections: Box J-M, F. Ashe-Lincoln, (n.d.).
[109] Panayi, 'Anti-German Riots in London during the First World War', 186.
[110] Strachan, *The First World War, Volume One: To Arms*, 105.
[111] Good, 'England Goes To War, 1914–15'.
[112] Gullace, 'Friends, Aliens, and Enemies: Fictive Communities and the Lusitania Riots of 1915', 354.
[113] Verhey, *The Spirit of 1914: Militarism, Myth and Mobilization in Germany* (Cambridge, 2000), 75–87.
[114] *Liverpool Echo*, 27 October 1914, 4.

also be acknowledged. The fact that the British recruitment system was based on volunteering and not conscription, unlike France and Germany, meant there were still young men in the country who could get involved in rioting throughout 1914.

However, the cluster of major riots between 14 and 24 October followed immediately on news of the fall of Antwerp, and thus of Belgium, on 10 October (see Appendix IV). For the French, the moment of greatest danger had followed the arrival of the main German invasion force in France between 21 and 23 August. French public opinion became particularly alarmed around 29 August when the official communiqué for that day reported how the French troops 'remained on the Somme': they were supposed to still be in Belgium and the Nord.[115] Paradoxically, the moment of real concern for the British was when the Battle of the Marne was over, as it deflected the war away from Paris towards the Channel coast, and thus towards Great Britain. From mid-September until the First Battle of Ypres in November, which blocked the Germans from the coast and prevented a new advance, the sense of threat to Britain mounted. The fall of Antwerp, to which Churchill, as First Lord of the Admiralty, had despatched the Royal Naval Division, resulted in the Belgian government being forced into exile and the remnants of the Belgian army slipping down the coast to join the Allies. Moreover, it marked the culmination of the threat of invasion for the British.

For centuries, defending the Low Countries (modern-day Netherlands and Belgium) from foreign occupation was essential to British security. In the early 1580s, they were described as the 'counterscarp' (the outer defences of a fortress) to Elizabeth I's kingdom.[116] Possession of the Low Countries would open up another front in the war and allow rival navy facilities to operate in the Channel. Belgian independence and neutrality were perceived therefore as vital to prevent an invasion of Britain. Consequently the fall of Antwerp was seen as a disastrous result for Britain. Reports of the fall of Antwerp were published in the British national press within twenty-four hours. In a letter to her sister dated 12 October, Ada McGuire, in Liverpool, told her how the family 'have all been nearly in tears over this Antwerp business'.[117] On 13 October, Reverend J. B. Armour, a Presbyterian minister visiting his son in South Shields, recorded how the previous day had been extremely depressing owing to the news of the fall of Antwerp: '[It] is a very bad loss... and forebodes a very long war'.[118] Violet Clutton immediately made the connection between the fall of Antwerp and the increased possibility of a German invasion of Britain: 'The fall of Antwerp... is dreadful... I'm afraid it makes an invasion much more possible as they have at last got a sea front town to make their base... It is a terrible possibility'.[119] More frightening news was to follow over the next

---

[115] 'La situation, de la Somme aux Vosges est restée aujourd'hui ce qu'elle était hier', 29 August 1914, cited in *Les Communiqués officiels depuis la déclaration de la guerre. Du 15 au 31 août* (Paris & Nancy, Berger-Levrault, 1914) (series: Pages d'histoire, 1914, no. 7), 29.

[116] Gary Sheffield, *Forgotten Victory: The First World War, Myths and Realities* (London, 2001), 40–1.

[117] IWM, Docs: McGuire, Misses A. & R.: 96/31/1, 12 October 1914.

[118] PRONI: Reverend J.B. Armour: D/1792/A3/5/26, 13 October 1914.

[119] DRO: Violet Clutton: 6258M/Box 1, Vol II, 11 October 1914,

fortnight with reports of a German advance towards Calais and violent clashes between Allied and German forces on the French and Belgian coast.

The depressing turn of events in Belgium was personified for the British people by the arrival of thousands of Belgian refugees at British ports. These refugees were full of terrifying stories of German atrocities and German military strength. The British people immediately rallied providing relief and assistance—enhancing the positive image of the collective self. Simultaneously some people reacted with expressions of anger at German residents in Britain—the scapegoats for the external enemy who had caused this disaster. In both Aberystwyth and Deptford the arrival of Belgian refugees on the evening that violence broke out added fuel to the smouldering fire of Germany's war crimes.[120] In Saffron Walden, the house where two Germans were being harboured was very close to the local hospital where wounded British soldiers were recovering. Home Office instructions to police in Porthcawl, South Wales on 31 October to remove posters calling for people to 'Remember Antwerp' suggest that the authorities were aware that this event was a significant trigger for violent actions towards Germans.[121]

The peak period when alien activity is mentioned in contemporary sources is between October and November 1914. On 3 October *The Globe*, a Unionist newspaper, printed a speech by Lord Charles Beresford, a major anti-alien campaigner, that blamed the sinking of three British ships on 22 September upon 'assassins in the shape of spies'.[122] The nervousness that this speech inspired was compounded one week later by the fall of Antwerp. Government reassurances on 9 October that all dangerous aliens had been rounded up only served to cause more anxiety. Within seven days the *Evening News* and the *Daily Mail* had begun a campaign to boycott German workers.[123] Between 26 October and 21 November Reverend Andrew Clark, diarist and Rector of Great Leighs in Essex, mentioned spies or espionage on six separate occasions.[124] In late October the press began a campaign calling for the internment of all aliens, and Prince Louis of Battenberg, the First Sea Lord, resigned soon afterwards. King George V recorded his reaction to Battenberg's resignation: 'the Press and Public have said so many things against him being born a German and that he ought not to be at the head of the Navy, that it was best for him to go. I feel deeply for him, there is no more loyal man in the Country.'[125] In a letter to a naturalized German employee dated 4 November, Mr W. Muirsmith advised that he resign because 'British feeling against aliens has become acute and will I expect become more so. It is growing daily'.[126] On 5 November the entire staff of Lerwick Post Office on the Shetland Islands, Scotland,

---

[120] Panayi, 'Anti-German Riots in London during the First World War', 187.; NLW, Aberystwyth: XD 523 E90.

[121] NA, Kew: HO 45/10944/257142.

[122] NA, Kew: HO 45/10765/267450.

[123] Panayi, 'Anti-German Riots in London during the First World War', 186.

[124] Munson, ed., *Echoes of the Great War: The Diary of the Reverend Andrew Clark, 1914–1919*, 25–34.

[125] Royal Archives, Windsor Castle: RA GV/PRIV/GVD/1914: 29 October.

[126] NAS, WRH: Aliens Working in the UK: GD 431/4/8, Bundle 2, 4 November 1914.

were rounded up and interned in the County Buildings. Rumours spread that they had been leaking information about the British Fleet to German spies. However, they were all released without charge, or explanation, on 7 November.[127] According to Michael MacDonagh, *The Times* journalist, October and November was the peak period for spy-fever in Britain because the public were suffering 'from the first bewildering shock of being at war'.[128] The public had been without reliable news from the front for months. Moreover, their 'quick victory' had not been realized and they were becoming impatient. By November Britain had endured a string of unexpected and sudden German victories. People began to search for explanations. That Britain still had enemy aliens in the country who were subverting the war effort fitted nicely, and was supported by a number of Cabinet members. Over the course of late October and early November the Home Secretary was challenged for not doing enough about the spy problem.

Obsession with spies during late October was an expression of a deep sense of fear felt amongst the British population that Britain would not win the war. On 26 October, *The New York Times* dedicated an editorial to the arrest and internment of enemy aliens in Britain. According to the paper 'these arrests, often of older men who have been in the community for years, shows how the British spirit is unconfident and nervous'.[129] When Britain suffered defeats and saw the ramifications of these defeats, such as the arrival of Belgian refugees, this tension and fear overflowed into outright violence. It is no coincidence that the worst anti-German violence erupted during the tense month of October when little was known about the position of the BEF and Belgium had fallen, allowing the Germans to advance rapidly towards Calais. Therefore, although people expressed confident assertions that Britain was 'right' and militarily stronger than Germany, there were significant levels of doubt and fear that in fact Germany was not going to be easily defeated and that Britain was at risk of a German invasion or subversion from within. As people saw the reality and ramifications of war with Germany—perceived to be a militaristic and barbaric enemy—they directed their anger at the cost of war towards the enemy alien within, and expressed their fear and uncertainty about Britain's progress in the war by obsessing over the enemy spy within.

Unlike German and Austrian civilians in Britain, German POW soldiers experienced little hostility towards them on their arrival in Britain. Curiosity was the dominant popular reaction in August and September 1914.[130] Once interned, people could 'visit' prisoners in the POW camps. This was in a similarly voyeuristic manner to people 'visiting' Belgian refugees. Beatrice Trefusis, a London resident, lived near a large detention camp of German prisoners on Frith Hill. She recorded in her diary on 11 October how 'people go in hundreds to gaze at them as if they were animals at the zoo!'[131] Michael MacDonagh described in September how this

---

[127] NAS, WRH: Arrest of Post Office Staff at Lerwick: HH 31/17, November 1914.
[128] MacDonagh, *In London During the Great War*, 32.
[129] *New York Times*, 26 October 1914, 10.
[130] Heather Jones, *Violence Against Prisoners of War: Britain, France and Germany, 1914–1920* (Cambridge, 2011), 74.
[131] Liddle: DF 129: B.M. Trefusis, 11 October 1914.

curiosity developed into 'friendliness to the point of giving [German POW in Frimley] cigarettes, apples, cakes and bottles of ginger beer'.[132] It is difficult to understand exactly why violence was reserved solely for German civilians in Britain and not German prisoners. It may be because so few prisoners were captured by the British in 1914—only around 10,000, half the amount of British prisoners claimed to have been interned by the Germans by December 1914.[133] It is also due to timing. The first arrivals of prisoners of war in Britain occurred in August and September 1914. At that stage, the British people were still getting used to war and all it entailed. Their hatred towards the enemy was developing. By October, it had been cemented and along with the disastrous news from the Western Front, certain pockets of opinion bubbled over into outright violence. German civilians were more visible, vulnerable, and close-to-hand scapegoats than the securely interned and guarded prisoners of war.

A number of the reactions towards the 'enemy' evident in Britain in 1914 were common to the other major belligerents, France and Germany. For example, panic over enemy spies within, internment of enemy aliens, and concerns over the poisoning of reservoirs are well documented in Germany and France at this time.[134] However the timing and peak moments of these concerns differ. Unlike Britain, violence towards German civilians in France occurred immediately after the declaration of war between 5 and 8 August 1914. The memory of Germany's last invasion of France, forty years previously, was raw. By late August, France's worst fears were confirmed as the German army advanced into its territory, committing atrocities as it went and eventually occupying the majority of the north-east. A link can be seen between the level of hostility felt towards the enemy and how strongly civilians felt emotionally involved in the conflict. The French were immediately involved in the protection of their nation, and simultaneously civilians took to the task of ridding their country of the German enemy within, whilst their soldiers fought the German enemy without. As France had a system of conscription, by October 1914—when violence in Britain was being committed by both men and women—French women were the main perpetrators of violence towards German prisoners.[135] In Britain, fear and hatred of the enemy developed throughout August and September 1914, peaking in October when both young men were still around to be involved in violent behaviour, and when the British understanding of the seriousness and brutality of war was confirmed by the disastrous fall of Belgium.

Some people did protest about the outbreaks of violence. However, as noted in Table 3.1, those who openly defended German victims often became targets themselves and remained in the minority. Alfred Whiting, a schoolboy in Walthamstow in 1914, lived near a bakery owned by an elderly German couple.

---

[132] MacDonagh, *In London During the Great War*. 26–7.
[133] Jones, *Violence Against Prisoners of War: Britain, France and Germany, 1914–1920*, 61.
[134] Becker, *1914: Comment les Français sont entrés dans la guerre* (Paris, 1977), Verhey, *The Spirit of 1914: Militarism, Myth and Mobilization in Germany*.
[135] Becker, *1914: Comment les Français sont entrés dans la guerre*.

He was on friendly terms with them and they used to provide him and his friends with cakes on their way home from school. When Alfred saw a man smashing the windows of their shop he rushed to try and stop him, without success. The couple were later removed and interned.[136] Others voiced their concerns in private. James Lewis was deeply disturbed by the destruction of a German pork butcher's shop in Waterloo, Liverpool, and the looting that followed. He was a classmate of the owner's son.[137] Eve Travis recalled standing in the crowds as a German butcher's shop (also in Liverpool) was destroyed. 'I can remember crying me eyes out . . . [with] me mother—we were both crying because we knew these people as friends.'[138] A condemnatory letter featured in the *Liverpool Echo* on 27 October:

> I am ashamed to see English people making violent attacks on individual people, who cannot defend themselves . . . Leave the German and Austrian spies in England to the police. Public action is only a hindrance. Surely we cannot fight brutality with brutality. We would make ourselves just as bad as those concerned.[139]

Not everyone ostracized German and Austrian enemy aliens. German immigrants had successfully integrated into British life over the course of sixty years. British people had German friends, neighbours, employees, and colleagues. They shopped at German-owned shops. Some people had German family, either by blood or marriage, including the British Royal family. It is therefore unfair to argue that every British person vehemently hated every German. It was certainly easier to hate 'Germany', an anonymous and distant country, than particular Germans. For example, Dolly Shepherd's uncle-in-law was German. Her opinion was that Germans 'were quite alright'.[140] John Riddey wrote to his sister in Moreton-on-Marsh on 1 November asking after their German governess: 'I hope noone [sic] will dare to attempt to duck Fraulein in the pond. I'd duck him in if I was big enough.'[141] Asquith expressed sympathy towards German enemy aliens in a letter to his wife, Margot, dated 14 September, after a visit to a POW camp in Aldershot.[142] Some soldiers stationed at POW camps developed a sympathetic attitude towards the Germans. Wilbert Spencer wrote to his mother in Surrey describing his duties at Deepcut camp in Surrey. To him the Germans were 'an awfully nice lot of fellows' who had invited him to Berlin after the war.[143]

For some people sympathy with enemy aliens went beyond rhetoric. On 31 August the Home Office recorded that many destitute enemy aliens forced out of their jobs in Birmingham were 'being looked after by friends'.[144] The Archbishop of Canterbury worked tirelessly to help destitute enemy aliens and their families, to the point where he was criticized.[145] When Professor Hans Eggeling, Chair of

---

[136] ERO: SA 4/689/1 (n.d.).   [137] NWSA: 2001.1016: James Richard Lewis (2001).
[138] NWSA: 2001.0746: Eve Travis (2001).   [139] *Liverpool Echo*, 27 October 1914, 4.
[140] IWM: 579, Reel 5 (1975).   [141] Liddle: GS 1352: John R. Riddey, 1 November 1914.
[142] MPP Bodleian: Margot Asquith: MS Eng c.6691, ff. 171–2, 14 September 1914.
[143] Liddle: GS 1515: Wilbert Berthold Spencer, 1914.
[144] NA, Kew: HO 45/10729/255193.
[145] Lambeth: Davidson Papers: Treatment of Internees and POWs, 1914–15: Volume 351 [Great War], ff. 1–125, August to December 1914.

Sanskrit and Comparative Philology at Edinburgh University, submitted his resignation to the University Senate on 5 November owing to his nationality, a 'sense of
loss and warm feelings' were expressed by his colleagues.[146] Significantly, his
resignation was met with protest from fellow members of staff, an action that
would have put them at risk of accusations of being 'German sympathisers'.[147] Joan
West, in Selsey, Gloucestershire, took pity on a Polish girl who had been forced to
resign as a local governess. Despite being an Austrian Pole, and therefore technically
an enemy alien, the West family were convinced that her sympathies lay with the
Allies and accommodated her over the Christmas holidays.[148] The Scottish Socialist newspaper *Forward* made a sarcastic reference to Britain's defence of its culture
on 5 December.[149] Playing on the contemporary arguments of so-called civilized
and cultured Britain fighting Prussian militarism, the cartoon highlighted leftist
criticisms of British policy towards alien enemies. The 1914 British Nationality and
Status of Aliens Act stated that 'the wife of an alien shall be deemed an alien',
resulting in British women, like the woman depicted in the cartoon, being pun-
ished alongside their husbands of German origin, whilst foreign women who
married a British subject received British citizenship.[150] The husband, although
German, had lived in Britain since he was a baby; but was now ostracized owing to
the outbreak of war. Societies were also established to help destitute enemy aliens
across Britain, including Birmingham, London, and Manchester.[151] Caroline
Playne was actively involved in The Emergency Committee for the Assistance of
Germans, Austrians and Hungarians in Distress, a society supported by the
Archbishop of Canterbury amongst others. By the end of September they claimed
to have dealt with over 700 cases.[152] In early September, Norah Woodman was
invited to become matron of St Giles' Home in central London, a former workhouse that was being used to house destitute aliens during the war. The only

[146] University of Edinburgh, Special Collections: University of Edinburgh Senatus Academicus,
Minutes: Da 31/8, 5 November 1914.
[147] University of Edinburgh, Special Collections: University of Edinburgh Court, Minutes: Da 23/
5, 8 and 22 September 1914.
[148] IWM, Docs: West, Miss G.M.: 77/156/1, 30 December 1914.
[149] 'A Triumph for British Culture', *Forward*, 5 December 1914, 1. The caption reads: Extract
from a letter—'. . . Though his father took him from Germany when he was a baby, he is still an 'Alien
Enemy.' His Scottish-born wife can get nothing for she married an Alien Enemy, though a German-
born woman, who has married a Scotsman, is entitled to relief. . . He is too ill (sciatica) for the
concentration camps—no fear of him assisting Germany, so why should Britain feed him? He can get
no work, being an 'Alien Enemy,' and, if he did, the Boss need not pay him wages . . . The factory will
put him out. Even the Co-operative Societies will not assist the appeal of the Alliance for foods to help
such as he . . . What a triumph for our Culture and Christianity!'
[150] Gullace, 'Friends, Aliens, and Enemies: Fictive Communities and the Lusitania Riots of 1915',
345.
[151] BCA. MS 466/432, Box 3: Cadbury Family Journal, 2 December 1914 and MALSL: Minutes
of the Committee of the Society for the Relief of Really Deserving Distressed Foreigners: M294/2/1/2,
11 and 19 August 1914.
[152] Senate House Library, Special Collections: Playne Collection: Folder 10: Interned/Enemy
Aliens, Papers & Cuttings (November 1914) and Folder 155: Reports of the Emergency Committee
for the Assistance of Germans, Austrians and Hungarians in Distress, 1914–1919 (1914).

instructions she was given were 'to be *kind* and *tactful* and not to look at them with "Spy, you are discovered" expression'.[153]

***

Fear, anxiety, uncertainty, and sympathy with Belgian refugees fuelled anti-German feelings in Britain in the first five months of war. The war defined who belonged to the national community. Blood-ties and race began to undercut pre-war bonds of neighbourliness, familial affection, and even marriage itself. Liberal notions of inclusion, based on law and citizenship, were replaced by the more popular and emotive concepts of belonging. Citizenship was no longer defined by character, community, or law, but by blood and ethnicity. Friends, neighbours, and innocent aliens became enemies and outsiders. The war, and in particular stories of atrocities, helped forge bonds around innocent victims of German violence, and strengthen belief in the Allied cause. Simultaneously it rationalized and exacerbated a growing hatred towards ethnic Germans.[154]

However, it is unlikely that public opinion, whilst suspicious and anti-German, pushed the government to take harsher measures against enemy aliens. Aside from sporadic acts of violence following the fall of Belgium, public opinion was more tolerant at the local level. It was only when the situation became uncertain and frightening, particularly when it was feared that the Germans were edging closer to the Channel coast, that anti-German feeling manifested itself in violence. However, this is not to downplay the fact that in 1914 Germany was the enemy, and any members of that nation were unquestionably outside British national wartime society.

[153] Liddle: DF 145: Norah B. Woodman, 4 September 1914.
[154] Gullace, 'Friends, Aliens, and Enemies: Fictive Communities and the Lusitania Riots of 1915', 345–50.

4

Encountering Violence: Imagined and Real

On the morning of 4 August 1914, Germany invaded neutral Belgium. The biggest invasion force of modern times—one million men (five armies made up of sixteen corps)—had violated both French and Belgian territory. Attempts at resistance met with brutal force. Within days the Allied press were reporting atrocities—some exaggerated, many later to be proved accurate—committed by the German troops against innocent civilians. These included rape, pillage, the deliberate destruction of buildings, the use of women and children as human shields, and mass executions. In total, around 6,500 Belgian and French civilians perished between August and October, the majority between 5 and 31 August.[1]

The opening stages of war were characterized by unprecedented violence and huge losses. The clashes between the German and French armies were devastating as the Germans swept to the Marne. Total French casualties for the first month of the war were 260,000, of which 140,000 were sustained during the climatic final four days of the Battle of the Frontiers (14–24 August).[2] This explosion of violence extended to the British. The size of the original BEF that embarked for France on 9 August consisted of four infantry divisions and one cavalry, totalling around 81,000 men. However, in the first five months of the war this small army was involved in some of the most crucial and bloody areas of fighting on the Western Front. For the British experience, this period was bracketed by the Battle of Mons at the end of August and the First Battle of Ypres in November, with little respite in between. By the end of 1914 the British force was devastated; about one-third were dead and many more would never fight again. A conservative casualty estimate for the period August and November sets the figure at 89,864—larger than the size of the original BEF who embarked for France in early August, and four times higher than the total number of British military deaths in the South African War, Britain's most recent experience of conflict.[3]

The casualty figures were far from abstract for contemporaries. News about big battles and ever-increasing casualty lists, published in the British press, drew the attention of all sections of Britain's home-front society.[4] Despite Britain's military

---

[1] Horne and Kramer, *German Atrocities, 1914: A History of Denial* (London, 2001), 1, 9–86, 435–9.

[2] David Stevenson, *1914–1918: The History of the First World War* (London, 2005), Barbara W. Tuchman, *The Guns of August* (London, 2000).

[3] Brigadier-General J. E. Edmonds, *Military Operations: France and Belgium, 1914*, ed. Historical Section of the Committee of Imperial Defence, 2nd ed., 2 vols., vol. 2, *History of the Great War Based on Official Documents* (London, 1925), Major General Sir Frederick Maurice, *History of the War in South Africa, 1899–1902*, 4 vols. (London, 1906–1910).

[4] Audoin-Rouzeau and Becker, *1914–1918: Understanding the Great War* (London, 2002), 22.

investment and consequent losses being substantially smaller than those of the French, this did not mean that the experience of violence was any less intense. The British population was a part of the harsh reality of the conflict in its opening weeks and months. New tolerance levels of brutality were established between August and December that perhaps set the bar for the rest of the conflict.

How did contemporaries imagine and experience the violence of war? The first section establishes what people knew about the opening movements of the war. The second addresses fear of invasion in Britain, particularly along the vulnerable east coast, reactions to atrocity stories, and the myths that appeared in wartime as a result of these fears. The final section examines the reactions to experiences of violence, in particular the bombardment of the north-east coast of Great Britain on 16 December 1914, and civilian encounters with Belgian refugees and military casualties—the primary victims of violence.

WHAT PEOPLE KNEW

British people had imagined and experienced violence before the war. Pre-war popular fiction on future wars and invasion had provided frightening images of what war involved. Descriptions of the siege warfare of the Napoleonic and Crimean Wars contained some of the grotesque details that would become familiar characteristics of war in 1914.[5] However, many historians of the First World War argue that a 'conspiracy of silence' was in place to prevent or inhibit realistic descriptions of the experience of trench warfare. This filter theory largely holds true with regard to the contemporary newspaper press.[6] Although censorship in Britain during the war was far from repressive, the Press Bureau, in cooperation with patriotic newspaper proprietors and journalists, did exercise a considerable measure of control to ensure no information useful to the enemy was published. Unfavourable news was passed over or delayed. News of particular battles and troop movements was censored, while details of specific local regiments were rigidly suppressed. If any information was provided, it was usually after the event. On 13 October Reverend Yonge, from Boreham in Essex, wrote 'War news is scanty, intelligence nil. Too much secrecy makes one ill.'[7] Interestingly, status did not guarantee access to sensitive information. On 31 August Lord Stamfordham, the King's Private Secretary, revealed to Lord Derby that 'we get no news as to who has been killed or wounded'.[8]

Correspondence between Lord Murray, Private Secretary to Sir Edward Grey, and Lord Northcliffe, editor of *The Times*, during the first week of December highlights the tension between the press and the government over the issue of

---

[5] Todman, *The Great War: Myth and Memory* (London, 2005), 7.

[6] Eric F. Schneider, 'What Britons Were Told About the War in the Trenches, 1914–1918' (DPhil, University of Oxford, 1997), 218.

[7] ERO: Diary of Reverend Denys Yonge: D/DU 358/26, 13 October 1914.

[8] LRO: Papers of the 17th Earl of Derby: 920 DER (17) 33/Buckingham Palace 1914–15, 31 August 1914.

publishing war news. Northcliffe felt 'part and parcel of a foolish conspiracy to hide bad news'.[9] Alfred Milner, the German-born British statesman, felt that the concealment of negative information, particularly casualty lists and defeats, only acted to demoralize people who felt like they were being kept in the dark.[10] Yet, there were severe punishments for those believed to be spreading 'false news', another form of perceived inappropriate behaviour acting against the moral order of 1914. A meeting of the South Wales and Monmouthshire Branch of the National Union of Journalists on 17 October recorded how a Swansea journalist had been detained for violating DORA regulations by spreading 'reports likely to create alarm among the civilian population in the defended harbour'.[11] On 10 December Harold Weering, from Falmouth, received an eight-week prison sentence for spreading a report that German warships were at St Ives Bay, West Cornwall; the same day Edwin Single, from Jersey, was court-martialled for spreading false news that 250,000 German soldiers had broken through to Calais.[12] On 28 December Kate Hume, a 17-year-old girl from Dumfries, was tried before the Edinburgh High Court for publishing two forged letters alleging that her sister, a field-nurse, had died after her breasts had been cut off by German soldiers who left her to bleed to death on the floor of the Belgian hospital at Vilvorde. The offence was considered serious enough to warrant immediate imprisonment.[13]

War correspondents experienced many difficulties when attempting to report what was happening on the Western Front. While they did not necessarily 'routinely peddle falsehoods', they were hampered by a number of factors, including the difficulty of witnessing any fighting and the reliance upon eyewitness accounts after the battle was over.[14] Although the content of their despatches suggest that correspondents were aware of the necessities of modern warfare and the emergence of lethal weaponry, most emphasized perceived German losses and military setbacks while frequently ignoring or qualifying British and Allied combat failings and casualty levels. An analysis of articles in *The Times* that dealt with the war on the Western Front between 22 August and 12 September reveals that any reports of Allied defeats or retreats were tempered by emphasizing higher German losses. Newspaper correspondents were patriots as well: they did not want to be seen to be aiding the enemy or demoralizing their home population. Moreover, articles were always a few days, or sometimes a week, behind the actual event. Details were vague and the content was ambiguous.

However, the lack of reliable published information did not diminish people's thirst for news. People were not blithely reading the newspapers without critique,

---

[9] NLS: Murray of Elibank Papers: Acc 8803, ff. 140–1, 1 December 1914.

[10] Wilson, ed., *The Rasp of War: The Letters of H.A. Gwynne to The Countess Bathurst, 1914–1918*, (London, 1988), 28–9.

[11] GRO: Minute book for the National Union of Journalists, South Wales and Monmouthshire Branch, 17 October 1914–30 June 1917: CL/NUJ 3, 17 October 1914.

[12] *Devon and Exeter Gazette*, 11 December 1914, 7, and *Lancashire Daily Post*, 11 December 1914, 4.

[13] *The Times*, 30 September 1914, 5, 7 December 1914, 6, 29 December 1914, 3, 30 December 1914, 5.

[14] Gerard Cronin, 'Representations of Combat: The British War Correspondents and the First World War' (PhD, Trinity College, Dublin, 1998), 106, 121.

and many became weary and sceptical of the perceived newspaper bias, optimism, and ambiguity. As a result, people attempted to piece together war events via inference from newspapers, guesswork, discussion (with each other or wounded soldiers), and correspondence (with other civilians and soldiers serving at home or abroad). Word of mouth was particularly important. Violet Clutton concluded that the most common form of information gathering was '"I was told so-and-so by some one who knows a friend of a high official at the Admiralty or War Office" as the case may be'.[15] Letters of serving soldiers published in the press were also eagerly consumed by the public. National newspapers like *The Times* and *Daily Mail*, provincial papers like the *Scotsman* and *Western Mail*, and, above all, local papers, featured columns of front-line soldiers' correspondence. The *Evesham Journal* in October summarized a letter from one recruit at the front:

> Sometimes the slaughter is terrific. It is often impossible to bury the dead and the stench from their decomposing bodies is very bad indeed. Sometimes . . . the bodies lie on the ground over the space of a mile as thick as sheaves after the self-binder in the harvest field. Sometimes explosions lift men eight or nine feet into the air and then they simply go to pieces.[16]

Indeed, so common had the practice become that, by early 1915, it posed a problem for the War Office for violating censorship and DORA regulations.[17]

Whilst some politicians were privy to secret information, ordinary people sought to try and understand what was going on in France independently. A schoolboy in Corwen, North Wales remembered how his father: 'had a map hanging on the wall and he used to point out how the war was developing and how near the Kaiser's army was, and when the Allies were moving forward he used to put a red little flag up and black ones for the German army. It was all very alarming'.[18] Between 22 August and 12 September *The Times* featured twenty maps illustrating Allied and German troop movements on the Western Front. On a number of occasions *Punch* satirized the attempts of ordinary people to follow the latest war developments in this way.[19]

Soldiers' letters from overseas were censored by the army, but letters from soldiers in training in the United Kingdom were not. The mechanisms for postal censorship, like many other restrictions on traditional freedoms in wartime, had been put into place over the five years before the war but were only gradually enforced in the first few months, before becoming institutionalized in the course of the next year.[20] The 'conspiracy of silence' was therefore not all-encompassing and the British population were not entirely in the dark. Through personal correspondence, civilians knew at least something of the violence of war. On 8 November

---

[15] DRO: Violet Clutton: 6258M/Box 1, Vol. I, 7 August 1914.
[16] Cited in Horn, *Rural Life in England in the First World War* (Dublin. 1984), 44.
[17] Schneider, 'What Britons Were Told About the War in the Trenches, 1914–1918', 101.
[18] ERO: T/Z 25/680 (1966).
[19] For example, *Punch* 26 August 1914, 191, 23 September 1914, 262, and 14 October 1914, 323.
[20] See NA, Kew: CAB 16/27 'Press and Postal Censorship in Time of War: Report and Proceedings' (1913). Very little survives regarding the management of the enormous operation of postal censorship during the First World War in Britain.

Ralph Verney, son of the Liberal MP for North Buckinghamshire and serving with the Rifle Brigade in France, wrote to his wife, Nita, in London: 'the German infantry are allowed to get within 200 yards of our trenches . . . we then open up on them with rapid fire and machine guns, and simply mow them down till it is quite sickening'.[21] On 20 November Edward Hulse, serving in France, wrote to his mother describing life on the front line:

> It is damp, very cold and unpleasant . . . we are only 150 yards from the enemy's trenches . . . we have not changed our boots or socks even, and far and away the worst part is the cold in one's feet at night, which makes sleep impossible for more than half an hour or so at a time.[22]

He was killed in action in 1915. Whilst some soldiers simply avoided writing or talking about the subject, many were eager to explain, and had an audience who would listen. Although some soldiers perhaps exaggerated their experiences to confirm their status as 'warriors', it does not detract from the fact that civilians were being exposed to grotesque details that challenged their pre-1914 understandings of war.

Tales from the front filtered back in other ways too. Violet Clutton read an uncensored, hand-delivered letter sent from a nurse serving in Le Mans, France, dated 25 September. The lengthy letter goes into graphic detail about the desperate conditions in the military hospitals and the difficulties faced in trying to deal with such horrific injuries: 'I can't possibly explain to you how really awful it is . . . on Sunday we had 1,114 wounded through, Monday and Tuesday over 1,000, Wednesday more. Some of the cases are . . . really too awful'.[23] Soldiers home on leave or wounded also provided graphic descriptions of life at the front. On 5 December Hallie Eustace Miles spoke with a relative home on leave from the Household Brigade. 'He has been in the thick of the fighting, and, as there was no Cavalry work going on, he had to go with the rest of the Cavalry into the trenches. Such a horrible time, he says it was! The worst part of all was hearing the crys [sic] and groans of the wounded and dying, and not being able to leave the trenches to help them.'[24] Beatrice Trefusis, in London, had spoken with:

> several returned wounded officers—and none of them want to go back . . . Several have gone off their heads, from the strain. It is dreadful, too, to hear of the neglect of wounded—both officers and men, due to the hospitals being so understaffed. Willie Holbech, who died from wounds the other day, was 5 days without having his wound dressed. It became septic.[25]

Other soldiers home on leave described the deteriorating conditions in the trenches as the first winter approached including the mud, freezing temperatures, and

---

[21] David Verney, ed., *The Joyous Patriot: The Correspondence of Ralph Verney, 1900–1916* (London, 1989), 156.

[22] Sir Edward Hamilton Westrow Hulse, *Letters Written from the English Front in France between September 1914 and March 1915* (Privately Printed, 1916), 32–3.

[23] DRO: Violet Clutton: 6258M/Box 1, Vol II, 19 October 1914.

[24] Miles, *Untold Tales of War-Time London: A Personal Diary* (London, 1930), 29.

[25] Liddle: DF 129: B.M. Trefusis, 15 November 1914.

flooding. In a letter dated 15 October, Lydia Middleton, in London, described how a family friend, serving in France, 'had spent a week in a trench half full of water and when he got out his legs were so sodden and soft that he couldn't walk'.[26]

Injured and convalescing servicemen in Britain were a visual reminder of what modern war could do. Amputees, men deafened by the guns and explosives and sometimes shell-shocked, soldiers whose bones had been crushed, and men with ghastly face wounds, could all be noticed by civilians. As early as 29 August Annie Brunton saw two invalided soldiers leaving Victoria Station in London: 'One with his arm bound up and the other, a boy of about 18 with cotton wool and bandages over his eye. Poor child—he looked as though he had been crying . . . he may have been in pain'.[27] On 1 October King George V and his wife visited wounded officers in King Edward VII's hospital in London. He commented in his diary how 'we saw each of the 30 there, some of them are rather bad'.[28] Mabel Rudkin, in Dover, witnessed the arrival of 'laden hospital ships, bearing their mangled, ghastly burdens'.[29] William McIvor, aged 12 in 1914, accompanied his father (who had volunteered to transport the wounded in his car) to meet the incoming hospital trains from Birkenhead, Cheshire: 'In many cases the men had come straight from the front line. It was my first sight of casualties, serious and otherwise and my reaction of feeling utterly sickened and shocked was, I suppose, natural'.[30]

Gathering these pieces of information about life on the front line allowed people to imagine what it was like for their soldiers. When conditions were bad in Britain, people thought of what it must be like in France and Belgium. On 19 November Dr James Maxwell, in Bromley, Kent, wrote to his son in America complaining about the British weather. But he added 'where one thinks of our brave fellows in France, living in the trenches, in such weather, it is too terrible'.[31] On 22 November Ada McGuire wrote how much she pitied 'the poor chaps in the trenches in this weather. They must be so uncomfortable.'[32] When snow began to fall in Grimsby, Lincolnshire, in December Harry Miller's first thought was how freezing it must be for the soldiers in France.[33] Whilst civilians could not experience first hand the life of a soldier in 1914, nothing suggests that they were not willing or able to reach some level of empathy. The gulf between 'home' and 'front' was not as wide as commonly believed.[34]

---

[26] Liddle: DF 091: Mrs Lydia Middleton, 15 October 1914.
[27] NLI: Diary of Annie Brunton: Ms 13,620/2, 29 August 1914.
[28] Royal Archives, Windsor Castle: RA GV/PRIV/GVD/1914: 1 October.
[29] Rudkin, *Inside Dover, 1914–18: A Woman's Impression* (London, 1933), 46.
[30] Liddle: DF Recollections: Box J-M: William McIvor (1978).
[31] University of Birmingham, Special Collections: Dr James Laidlaw Maxwell: DA 26/2/1/6/48, 19 November 1914.
[32] IWM, Docs: McGuire, Misses A. & R.: 96/31/1, 22 November 1914.
[33] IWM, Docs: Miller, H.: 02/38/1, December 1914.
[34] For more on communication between the home front and the fighting front, please see Joanna Bourke, *Dismembering the Male: Men's Bodies, Britain and the Great War* (London, 1996), 20, Helen B. McCartney, *Citizen Soldiers: The Liverpool Territorials in the First World War* (Cambridge, 2005), 36, Jay Winter, *Sites of Memory, Sites of Mourning: The Great War in European Cultural History* (Cambridge, 1995).

Individual accounts of life at the front may have slaked the thirst of civilians for news of the fighting, but they could not provide a reassuring overview of the military situation. Rumour and scaremongering flourished. As James Brady confirmed in Rochdale, Lancashire: 'Because, by and large, we depended on rumour and unsubstantiated comment, a good deal was left up to the imagination and the whim and bias of the romantics—ready to let fantasy run riot'.[35] A rumour does not necessarily have to be a calculated 'implantation' from above in order to spread. Seeds of rumour take root when the evidence on an important topic is ambiguous. Rumours attempt to structure uncertainty.[36] As Beatrice Trefusis noted on 21 August: 'One has so little news from authentic sources, that one seizes any odd rumours with glee—crumbs to live on'.[37] In the opening months of war the vacuum of news was filled by apprehension, rumour, and fear crystallizing, in particular, around the possibility of a German invasion.

IMAGINING INVASION

Contemporaries did not know the precise sequence of military events in the autumn of 1914 until some time afterwards. Thus the possibility that the German invasion would extend to Britain remained a real one until after the Battle of Ypres in November. Although Britain had never experienced invasion, this did not make the threat irrelevant. British identity has been forged over 300 years by these very threats of an enemy 'other' invading British sovereign territory.[38] Invasion anxiety climaxed in the decade before 1914 and the CID met regularly between 1906 and 1913 to establish a cohesive plan in case of invasion.[39] Such pre-war fears had a significant impact on British popular imagination. Alarmist invasion stories were doubtless manipulative in their desire to promote conscription and boost newspaper sales, but they expressed the fears of many Edwardians. For James Lewis, aged 13 in 1914, the outbreak of the war 'seemed . . . to be only the culmination of the boys' stories I'd read, so many of which featured fictitious invasions of Britain by the Germans'.[40]

In the autumn of 1914 the British military authorities were extremely agitated over the possibility of invasion. Out of all the documents prepared by the government on the issue during the course of the war, around half appeared between 15 September and 1 December 1914.[41] Whilst the war was still one of movement, home defence was a key issue.[42] On 14 September, Maurice Hankey, Secretary to

---

[35] IWM, Docs: Brady, J.: 01/36/1 (1980).

[36] G. W. Allport and L. J. Postman, *The Psychology of Rumor* (New York, 1947).

[37] Liddle: DF 129: B.M. Trefusis, 21 August 1914.

[38] Colley, *Britons: Forging the Nation 1707–1837*, 3–6.

[39] For more detail on this topic please refer to K. W. Mitchinson, *Defending Albion: Britain's Home Army, 1908–1919* (Basingstoke, 2005), Howard Roy Moon, 'The Invasion of the United Kingdom: Public Controversy and Official Planning, 1888–1918' (PhD, University of London, 1968).

[40] NWSA: 2001.1016: James Richard Lewis (2001).

[41] Moon, 'The Invasion of the United Kingdom: Public Controversy and Official Planning, 1888–1918', 535.

[42] Viscount Sandhurst, *From Day to Day, 1914–1915* (London, 1928), 118.

the CID, argued that confidential instructions for the population should be prepared in the event of a raid, even if invasion was improbable. At the CID meeting of 7 October, a newly appointed sub-committee presented Hankey's proposals in a paper: 'Instructions to Local Authorities in the Event of Belligerent Operations in the United Kingdom'.[43]

In 1914 invasion preparations and home defence measures were taken all along the east coast of Britain from Scotland to Sussex. While the authorities tried to keep these preparations out of the public eye—to avoid scaremongering, people witnessed them, stoking fear and anxiety. I have discussed how the population of the south-east of England, specifically in the agricultural county of Essex, coped with the threat of a German invasion in 1914 in detail elsewhere.[44] Perhaps the most overwhelming evidence regarding the sense that there was a real possibility of invasion is an engraved stone plaque set into the old boundary wall of Orford House in the village of Ugley. Erected around 1919, it reads:

These and many similar arrows were painted to direct non-combatants inland across country—avoiding main roads to facilitate the movement of troops in the event of a successful landing by the Germans on the East Coast, 1914–1918.[45]

It highlights the seriousness with which the issue of invasion was perceived in 1914. For the people of Essex, just as their introduction to war had been framed by the fear of an enemy landing, their commemoration uniquely expressed relief that it never became a reality.

Invasion was important for British experience in 1914. First, the German invasion of Belgium justified Britain's entry into the war. It immediately became '*the* burning international question' and for Britain in particular, 'Brave Little Belgium' became shorthand for the moral issues of the war.[46] Historians debate whether Britain would have entered the war without a German invasion of Belgium. But the latter made entry inevitable and did so on terms that maximized support for what was perceived as a moral crusade. Thus Jim Davies, an 18-year-old actor in London's West End in August 1914, recalled that the invasion of Belgium was precisely what made Britain enter the war.[47] On 20 August David Lloyd George revealed to his brother that 'nothing but Belgium would have induced me to throw in my lot with the war party'.[48] As the war progressed 'the small state was

---

[43] Moon, 'The Invasion of the United Kingdom: Public Controversy and Official Planning, 1888–1918', 540.

[44] Catriona Pennell, '"The Germans Have Landed!": Home Defence and Invasion Fears in the South East of England, August to December 1914', in *Untold War: New Perspectives in First World War Studies*, ed. Heather Jones, Jennifer O'Brien, and Christoph Schmidt-Supprian (Leiden, 2008).

[45] From photograph taken of the plaque at Ugley, 24 June 2004 (author's own). Orford House was the main residence of the former Orford House Estate. Construction started on the house in 1706, and was originally commissioned by Edward Russell, First Lord of the Admiralty under King William III.

[46] Sophie de Schaepdrijver, 'Occupation, Propaganda and the Idea of Belgium', in *European Culture in the Great War: The Arts, Entertainment, and Propaganda, 1914–1918*, ed. Aviel Roshwald and Richard Stites (Cambridge, 1999), 267.

[47] IWM: 9750, Reel 2 (n.d.).

[48] NLW: William George (Solicitor) 9: WG 2870, 20 August 1914.

elevated to the status of living embodiment of the right-against-might values that the West was ostensibly fighting for'.[49] Second, anxiety over invasion along the east coast or concern elsewhere counterbalanced any outbursts of 'national' enthusiasm. Finally, it should be noted that fear of a possible invasion was not unusual in British history. However what was different in 1914, compared with invasion scares since the Spanish Armada, was that people began to believe that it was a definite possibility. The fine line between perception, anticipation, and reality had become blurred. Evacuation preparations and invasion plans were drawn up ready to be used if required; people seriously considered, and disagreed over, the issue of armed self-defence; and, for the population of Ugley, the relief that invasion did not occur between 1914 and 1918 justified the erection of a plaque along the very route they would have fled down.

British people feared a German invasion because of the atrocities they believed the German army was capable of. Atrocities were not a new concept for British people in 1914.[50] Publications such as E. D. Morel's *King Leopold's Rule in Africa* (1904) and Samuel Clemens' *King Leopold's Soliloquy* (1907) published harrowing images of the victims of Belgian atrocities.[51] Such pictures were popular features of missionary lectures in Britain from the 1890s onwards. Audiences at these meetings were composed of 'local missionary auxiliaries, chapel congregations, working men's meetings, and, in the broadest sense, the British public'. The report of Roger Casement—British civil servant and Irish nationalist—on the conditions of Africans on the Upper Congo was received as irrefutable proof of the Congo Free State's brutal labour practices. He also brought back photos of mutilated slaves which were circulated in books and lantern-slide lectures.[52] Developments in international law, particularly the Hague Conventions of 1899 and 1907 which provided regulations, amongst other things, for the conduct of belligerents and neutral powers towards each other and other nations, also meant people were more aware of the moral boundaries that, in theory, could not be crossed in occupation and warfare. Atrocities had therefore been used to mobilize public opinion around a particular cause before the outbreak of war; in 1914 they would do so again. Just as Russia had gone from enemy to ally, Belgium went from perpetrator to victim. The language of atrocities remained the same (and even severed hands, a prominent feature of the Congo campaign, were integrated into British propaganda), but the targets swiftly changed. Although Britain's general respect for Germany before the war meant that reformist campaigns avoided mobilizing against imperial Germany's atrocities in South West Africa, these feelings died amongst the British side when the Germans became 'the Huns' in August 1914.

---

[49] Schaepdrijver, 'Occupation, Propaganda and the Idea of Belgium', 268.

[50] Kevin Grant's work on the major British reform campaigns against forced labour and atrocities highlights how the language of atrocity had entered the British public sphere prior to the outbreak of war. See Kevin Grant, *A Civilised Savagery: Britain and the New Slaveries in Africa, 1884–1926* (London, 2005).

[51] Samuel Clemens, *King Leopold's Soliloquy* (London, 1907), E. D. Morel, *King Leopold's Rule in Africa* (London, 1904).

[52] Grant, *A Civilised Savagery: Britain and the New Slaveries in Africa, 1884–1926*, 40, 57.

As discussed, the theme of German atrocities quickly became a common, and national, feature of war reports in 1914. While the reality of these atrocities can no longer be challenged, such stories and images were important for mobilizing British opinion, particularly at the start of the war, because they justified Britain's involvement, placing it clearly on the 'right' side.[53] The theme helped construct the image of Germany as the enemy. Additionally, atrocity stories—and those who disseminated them (mainly Belgian refugees and wounded soldiers)—brought the British people face to face with the horrors and brutality of war in 1914.

German atrocities in Belgium had an additional resonance in Britain because they suggested the horrors that might happen on British soil should the Germans invade. At a recruiting meeting in Bognor a British MP translated the Belgian experience into local terms:

> If the German troops were to land in Bognor, we would see women and children flocking into Chichester, driven by these Uhlans, wounded men shot as they ran into streets, women bayoneted and outraged. That was the outlook if a raid took place upon the sacred soil of our shores.[54]

As Ada McGuire wrote on 11 October:

> If they [the Germans] do come here they will have no mercy on us, and oh! their cruelty is appalling. There are children in Waterloo and Birkenhead who have no hands... Two little Belgian girls [whose] parents were dead and their nurse had been found bayoneted at their side *but* both children had had their arms chopped off from above the elbows!! Now that is a fact. Poor wee mites... That is, I suppose, only one of many cases and some of the things are too dreadful to mention. Laura says if the Germans come here she will commit suicide.[55]

At a service at his local church in Essex, George Rose reflected on what had happened to Rheims Cathedral in France, moved to tears by the idea that it could happen to his place of worship: 'I looked up to the rich stained glass windows... What if the roof were off and the windows suddenly struck blind... as the Cathedral at Rheims. Yet Rheims was greater than this, and as dearly loved'.[56] By mid-August the language of 'atrocity' had become commonplace in news reports. A typical story published in the *Daily Mail* on 31 August carried the headline: 'Holocaust of Louvain—Terrible Tales of Massacre'.[57] The contents of these stories were similar—graphic, brutal and terrifying—and permeated into British imaginations. Dorothy Bing believed that the German enemy ate Belgian babies, by sticking them on a bayonet and roasting them.[58] Rudyard Kipling, in Burwash, Sussex, relayed some of the horrific stories he had heard discussed by

---

[53] Horne and Kramer, *German Atrocities, 1914: A History of Denial*.

[54] Cited in Ibid. 185–6.

[55] IWM, Docs: McGuire, Misses A. & R.: 96/31/1, 11 October 1914.

[56] ERO: Diaries of George H. Rose: D/DU 418/15, 6 December 1914.

[57] *Daily Mail*, 31 August 1914, 8, Horne and Kramer, *German Atrocities, 1914: A History of Denial*, 177.

[58] IWM: 555, Reel 2 (1974).

Belgian refugees arriving in Folkestone to the American publisher Frank N. Doubleday on 11 September:

> Germany is running this war... without the faintest regard for any law human or divine... They cut the hands off a surgeon whom they took prisoner in order that he might never practise again. A Belgian officer... told her that women and girls were *publicly* raped in Belgium by the command of their officers... The Belgian refugees who are pouring into Folkestone all bring their talk of unbelievable horrors which they have suffered or witnessed.[59]

One typical example of perceived German brutality described, in September, how a German soldier smashed a child's head with the butt of his rifle and how German troops 'dragged away women with children in their arms to march them at the head of their columns'. Some women were tied up in leather stirrups and used as horses.[60]

Stories of German atrocities were not just confined to newspapers. Eyewitness accounts often made the stories go from rumour to reality. On 11 September Walter Hines Page informed the Secretary of State in Washington that 'a trustworthy woman' had told him 'that there are wounded English soldiers now in an English hospital whose noses were cut off while they lay wounded on the field. Hundreds of such stories are told by apparently credible persons'.[61] On 22 October Lawrence Parsons, commander of the 16th (Irish) Division, met, at the War Office in London, a wounded officer who told him that 'he had been shot when wounded by a German officer and that he had seen a German cut off a child's hands'.[62] Until R. W. M. Gibbs spoke with his milkman he had disbelieved the atrocity stories. However, the milkman's brother-in-law, who was recovering in a local hospital from injuries sustained at the front, had provided confirmation. Gibbs concluded that he would 'as soon take the word of a wounded soldier, as that of a journalist whose stock in trade consists of second-hand rumours and censored despatches'.[63] Wounded soldiers confirmed German acts of atrocity in Birmingham, Brighton, Stroud, Worcester, and London.[64] On 27 October Mrs Johnson, from Daylesford, wrote:

> we hear our troops are warned to be specially on the look out for atrocities. That they are only too true is confirmed... Maugie Arnold's husband, who has just returned [wounded] from the front... helped rescue a crowd of women and children who had been bricked and barricaded into a house which was then set on fire. He said several of

[59] Pinney, ed., *The Letters of Rudyard Kipling*, 253–4.
[60] *Daily Citizen*, 7 September 1914.
[61] National Archives of the United States, Maryland Campus: American Embassy, London: M367, Roll 14 (763.72/838), 11 September 1914.
[62] NLI: Lawrence Parsons' Diary: Ms 21,524, 22 October 1914.
[63] MPP Bodleian: R.W.M. Gibbs: MS Eng misc c.159, 30 September 1914.
[64] University of Birmingham, Special Collections: Letters from Mary Chamberlain (neé Carnegie) to Austen Chamberlain: AC 4/2/205, 3 September 1914, Liddle: AIR 224: A.H. Morton, September 1914, IWM, Docs: West, Miss G.M.: 77/156/1, 20 September 1914, WRO: Ref 705:185: BA 8185: Parcel 2: Phillip A. Leicester, 2 September 1914, and NLS: Elizabeth S. Haldane: Mss 20243, 12 September 1914.

the women had already died of fright. He had also seen *children's* hands and feet cut off and exhibited.[65]

Belgian refugees also conveyed stories of German atrocities to the British population. In September a Wolverhampton man claimed to have met two Belgian refugee children in Hereford with their hands and ears chopped off.[66] On 23 September Mrs Johnson wrote: 'The Hartmanns have some French Frontier Refugees staying with them and there are some Belgians coming to Oddington. I believe their stories of German atrocities are almost incredible'.[67] Jack Whittacker's understanding of the war in Blackburn developed gradually. At first it seemed irrelevant as Belgium was such a long way from his home. But once the Belgian refugees arrived in Britain, some of whom could speak English, 'we could see that . . . Kaiser Wilhelm had given [the German troops] *ad lib* to do as they wanted'.[68] Children were not spared the gruesome content of the atrocity stories. Rose Kerrigan's schoolteachers at Garnert Hill School in Glasgow told her and her classmates about 'the German soldiers bayoneting babies'.[69] Hilda Moss, a schoolgirl in Birmingham, heard about German acts of brutality from adults discussing the issue around her.[70]

The nationwide belief in atrocity stories had a number of important consequences. First, it compounded the belief that the British people were fighting on the right side. People not only felt sympathy for the Belgians but were able to transpose these stories onto their own situation. R. W. M. Gibbs recorded in his diary:

The German army on Belgian soil, killed numberless people, including children, perhaps accidentally at first. Now picture if you can the feelings of a mother, or a father either for that matter, when her little baby child runs to her piteously moaning as only children can, with its little hand she loves so well, is it not in a sense a part of herself, hanging torn and bleeding from German shrapnel.[71]

On 15 September Laura Erwine, in Hendon, explained to Hanna Sheehy-Skeffington how despite war being 'a horrible and insensate thing' she was glad Britain was involved because:

this deliberate brutality on the part of the Germans is ghastly. There are lots of Belgian refugees here and their stories are hair-raising. Give me a good honest barbarian in preference. We women don't want German brutes raping our sisters and if we have to fight ourselves we'll do what we can to prevent it.[72]

This empathy increased support for the war effort. People now understood the 'realities' of war and realized that Germany was the enemy and had to be defeated.

---

[65] Liddle: GS 0861: Major General D.G. Johnson, 27 October 1914.
[66] *Midland Evening News*, 18 September 1914, 3.
[67] Liddle: GS 0861: Major General D.G. Johnson, 23 September 1914.
[68] NWSA: 1985.2365: Jack Whittacker (1985).
[69] IWM: 9903, Reel 1 (1987).
[70] City Sound Archive, Birmingham Museum: R76–77 (1981).
[71] MPP Bodleian: R.W.M. Gibbs: MS Eng misc c.159, 24 September 1914.
[72] NLI: Sheehy-Skeffington papers: Ms 22,667/1, 15 September 1914.

Harry Miller wrote on 18 September: 'When I try to picture to myself the terror of the people in France and Belgium . . . it is then that I understand about the reality of war.'[73] Consequently, atrocity stories encouraged recruitment and the theme was often integrated into PRC leaflets and recruitment posters.[74] German atrocities were repeatedly mentioned at recruiting meetings in 1914.[75] They all posed a similar question: would you let such horrors happen to your family? By extension, if Germany was not defeated owing to a lack of recruits, then this could happen on British soil.

These methods of recruiting appeared to be successful. For Donald Price of Caddishead, Greater Manchester, the stories of the German atrocities convinced him to enlist in 1914.[76] William Berry of Purley, Surrey did not want to enlist immediately at the outbreak of war, because, quite simply, he did not want to die. However, after seeing a newsreel in a Croydon cinema, he changed his mind. It depicted:

> a house in Belgium. There were the [German] soldiers with the butts of their rifles knocking in all the windows and other woodwork they could find. They then set it on fire because that particular house was in the way of the guns. I was very upset at this and sympathised; I was very angry and said, right, I am going to do something about it.[77]

On 24 October Phillip Leicester received his commission as Second Lieutenant. The following day he recorded that despite his father's objections 'there is one's duty to the country and also to the poor women and children of France and Belgium'.[78] In 1914, belief in rumours that German soldiers were cutting off the hands of Belgian babies, mutilating women, and crucifying their enemies was widespread amongst the British people. Doubters remained, naturally, and the 'fever' of atrocity stories dissipated around November. But it provided a potent image of the German enemy that paralleled and gave substance to British fears of a German landing on the east coast.

Many rumours spread amongst the home front populations of Britain, France, Germany, and Austria-Hungary in 1914, such as stories of poisoned water, the presence of enemy spies, and escaped POW.[79] However, not all rumours were negative. The story of the 'Angel of Mons'—a group of angels who protected British soldiers at the Battle of Mons—first appeared on the British domestic front as a short story by Arthur Machen on 29 September in the *Evening News* and was an example of an overtly positive rumour.[80] However, in 1914 this rumour

---

[73] IWM, Docs: Miller, H.: 02/38/1, 18 September 1914.

[74] For example, see PRC Leaflets Nos. 2, 6, 10, 18 and 19, seen at Flintshire Record Office: D/M/7074.

[75] Horne and Kramer, *German Atrocities, 1914: A History of Denial*, 185–6.

[76] IWM: 10168, Reel 1 (1988).

[77] IWM: 1, Reel 1 (1973).

[78] WRO, Ref 705.105. DA 8183: Parcel 2: Phillip A. Leicester, 24 October 1914.

[79] See Healy, *Vienna and the Fall of the Habsburg Empire: Total War and Everyday Life in World War One*, 143–8.

[80] It was later published in 1915, causing a flurry of similar accounts and a spread of wild rumours. See Harold Begbie, *On the Side of the Angels: A Reply to Arthur Machen* (London, 1915), Arthur Machen, *The Angel of Mons: The Bowmen and Other Legends of the War* (London, 1915).

remained within the press and did not appear in the diaries or letters of ordinary people on the home front.[81] Conversely, the positive, compensatory rumour of Russians with 'snow on their boots'—a counter-myth to protect Britain against invasion—is an example of a rumour that was sincerely believed by the British population in the opening months of the war. Emerging in late August, it spread across the United Kingdom, indiscriminate in age, gender, and class. This myth, that an army of Russian soldiers was travelling through Britain en route to France, provided a much-needed boost of morale to the British people at a time when their prized BEF were floundering on the Western Front and the German army was moving closer to the Channel coast.

VICTIMS OF WAR

For British civilians, the violence of war was not just confined to the imagination. It created victims on both the fighting and home fronts. On the morning of 16 December Britain's impenetrable island fortress was brutally violated. Scarborough, Hartlepool, and Whitby were subjected to a violent and terrifying sea bombardment by eight German enemy craft. The bombardment caused devastation, particularly in Hartlepool, where the assault lasted considerably longer than it did at the other two towns. The German ships pumped shell after shell into the towns, sending red-hot shrapnel in every direction, from tiny slivers of metal to forty-pound chunks of steel, prompting a mass exodus. In Hartlepool 9 soldiers, 97 civilian men and women, and 37 children were killed, and a further 466 wounded. As many as 600 houses were destroyed, leaving these people homeless. Scarborough and Whitby suffered less destruction with approximately 21 dead and 100 wounded.[82] According to Frank Lockwood, a Yorkshire resident, the Germans inflicted at least £200,000 worth of damage.[83]

Many accounts agree that the experience was terrifying. As a Scarborough resident wrote:

Heavy cannon firing. *Boom, boom, bang, shwish* as cannon after cannon and shells sounded. You *can't* imagine *what* it was like. It sounded like terrible thunder, but incessant and a thousand times worse. Everyone was in a panic. All the carts etc which had been going towards Scarboro' came flying back. I was all shaking and mother ditto . . . We . . . saw streams of men, women, children coming from Scarboro'. Many with no shoes on and not half dressed carrying babies etc. . . . People were *off their heads*. Some passing through here said 'Scarboro' is in flames'. Others said the Germans had landed . . . we . . . were afraid.[84]

---

[81] References to the 'Angel of Mons' do appear, from late August/early September 1914 onwards, in the diaries and letters of servicemen at the front. See, for example, John Terraine, *The Smoke and the Fire: Myths and Anti-Myths of War, 1861–1945* (London, 1992), 18.

[82] Richard Van Emden and Steve Humphries, *All Quiet on the Home Front: An Oral History of Life in Britain During the First World War* (London, 2004), 35–50.

[83] IWM, Docs: Lockwood F.T.: 96/52/1, 16 December 1914.

[84] Liddle: DF: Defence: Sea Bombardment of the East Coast: Whitby, Item 1, Letter 6, 16 December 1914.

Most people thought that the bombardment was the beginning of a German invasion. Mary Todd, who lived on William Street in Hartlepool in 1914, recalled a sudden outbreak of 'noise and banging and a soldier ran down the street shouting "run for your lives the Germans have landed"'.[85] Linking the fears of a German invasion with rumours of the 'enemy within' Lady Londonderry believed that the bombardment was the result of the Chairman of the Hartlepool Gas Company being German.[86]

Edith Rochester described 'men and women . . . running about in the street some of them still in there night attire'.[87] In their escape inland to West Hartlepool, the Watt family 'met droves of people evacuating . . . Panic was driving them on'.[88] Children were separated from their parents, schools and hospitals were attacked, and the wounded lay suffering in the streets. Chaos ensued as people frantically tried to escape the shelling. Sixty-three years later, Nancy Metcalfe, a nurse in Scarborough hospital in 1914, described how she felt: 'Well it was awful . . . All of us were shaking like leaves all the time the guns were firing and Scarborough itself was looking like a ball of fire . . . I am now nearly 79 but I would not like to go through all that again'.[89] Just over a week before Christmas, women ran through the streets of Hartlepool and Whitby, Christmas cakes in hand. Cora Tucker recalled her aunt arriving at her house: 'she had her baby in one hand and the Christmas cake in the other. She met a woman on the way over, and she was carrying candles in one hand and her Christmas cake in the other.'[90]

News of the bombardment quickly spread. T. H. Kirk, aged 15 in 1914, recalled his train being stopped in Stockton at 11 a.m. on 16 December: 'On the platform was my grandfather who put a jagged piece of metal in my hand and said "The Germans are in Hartlepool. Your train can go no further."'[91] News reached Great Leighs in Essex by four that afternoon.[92] Soldiers near Hartlepool conveyed details to their families as far away as the north of Scotland.[93] For Hilda Moss, a schoolgirl in Birmingham in 1914, news that Scarborough had been bombarded filled her with terror:

> I was terribly upset because I thought the Germans had landed . . . I'd get this fear and I remember that they'd bombed Brussels and they were in Brussels . . . and then I thought 'Oh well, they'll come here' . . . and we haven't got anywhere to go to . . . the Belgians came to us . . . and I thought all these things and I thought we can only go to America . . . and that's a long way and I shall not be able to take my toys.[94]

[85] Liddle: DF: Defence: Sea Bombardment of the East Coast: Hartlepool, Item 17 (1990).
[86] PRONI: Lady Londonderry papers: D/2846/2/18/66A and 66B, 17 and 21 December 1914.
[87] Liddle: DF: Defence: Sea Bombardment of the East Coast: Whitby, Item 1, Letter 3, 25 July 1977.
[88] Liddle: DF: Defence: Sea Bombardment of the East Coast: Hartlepool, Item 14 (1971).
[89] Liddle: DF: Defence: Sea Bombardment of the East Coast: Whitby, Item 1, Letter 4, 30 July 1977.
[90] Van Emden and Humphries, *All Quiet on the Home Front: An Oral History of Life in Britain During the First World War*, 48–9.
[91] Liddle: RNMN (Rec) 060: Dr T.H. Kirk (n.d.).
[92] Munson, ed., *Echoes of the Great War: The Diary of the Reverend Andrew Clark, 1914–1919*.
[93] IWM, Docs: Ferrie, Captain A.: 03/18/1, 16 and 18 December 1914.
[94] City Sound Archive, Birmingham Museum: R76-77 (1981).

Hilda recalled how surprised she was when her mother asked her to go to the local shops in Moseley later that day: 'I thought that if the Germans were coming we ought to be getting packed up or something... we went walking up to Moseley and I thought... there wouldn't be any Christmas.'[95]

The bombardment of the north-east coast cemented Britain's involvement in the war. It also placed the country on a more equal footing with other Allied victims, France and Belgium, since national territory had been attacked. According to H. W. Wharton, a Scarborough resident, 'We can now realise what the poor Belgians have suffered... we shall never feel safe till the war is over'.[96] Miss A. Logie Robertson concluded two days after the bombardment that:

> it only seems fair in a way that we should have a share of that sort of thing too, when Belgium and France have so much of it and in a much more brutal fashion. It's to be hoped that recruiting *will* be spurred on a bit.[97]

The French Ambassador, Paul Cambon, believed that it was this moment, four and half months into the war, which brought the reality home to the British people: 'The recent bombardment of three towns on the coast of the North Sea taught them more than any newspaper articles'.[98] He added that this act would not make the British yield: it served only to make them more defiant to defeat Germany. As William Watkins Davies recorded on 16 December: 'the war is now becoming alarmingly near, and people are getting excited. But it is too much for us to expect complete immunity from unpleasantness during a war of such magnitude!'[99] Britain had now been attacked on its own soil and the blood of its residents had been spilt, confirming that it was not invulnerable to attack. Balury Morton, serving in France with the Royal Field Artillery, told his fiancée, Iris Holt, in Lewes, Sussex on 18 December how he hoped that the bombardment would 'wake people up a bit' to the realities of war.[100] It also made the war visible to the British public. Not only did locals witness these attacks, but pictures immediately featured in the national press and were reprinted as postcards. Funerals of the victims of the bombardment were also publicized and attended by large crowds. Finally, it confirmed Britain's morality and Germany's brutality. On 17 December King George V recorded in his diary his anger at the damage and death inflicted on the east coast, bitterly concluding 'This is German "Kultur"'.[101] The most bitterness and anger was felt in the north-east as Cora Tucker remembers:

---

[95] City Sound Archive, Birmingham Museum: R76–77 (1981).

[96] NAS, GRH: Balfour of Whittingehame Papers: GD 433/2/251/4, 23 December 1914.

[97] Liddle: GS 1022: J.M. MaLachlan, 18 December 1914.

[98] 'Le bombardement récent de trois villes ouvertes sur la côte de la mer du Nord leur en a plus appris que tous les articles de journaux.' AMAE, Paris: Correspondence politique et commerciale 1897–1918: Nouvelle Série: GUERRE 14–8; Grande-Bretagne: Dossiers général: août – décembre 1914: Vol 534, ff. 205, 22 December 1914.

[99] NLW: W. Watkin Davies: 47, 16 December 1914.

[100] Liddle: AIR 224: A.H. Morton, 18 December 1914.

[101] Royal Archives, Windsor Castle: RA GV/PRIV/GVD/1914: 17 December.

It was a terrible thing to do, we were angry... Why had little children been killed
going to school? Why had babies been killed? Why had that lady in Thirlmere
Street... been killed?... I think that put a hatred of the Germans into us.[102]

The attacks were integrated into government propaganda almost immediately.
They featured in a number of recruitment posters including 'Remember Scarborough—Enlist Now' and 'Men of Britain—Will You Stand This?' In the former,
Britannia stands defiant, leading her citizen-army into battle, whilst Scarborough
burns in the background. In the latter, men are appealed to enlist to avenge the
death of innocent women and children, utilizing gender stereotypes in wartime.[103]
It would appear that the bombardment did motivate men to enlist. In fact, the
novelist Mrs Humphry Ward, had predicted as much in September 1914 when she
wrote, in frustration over young men still playing football rather than enlisting:
'One little raid on the East Coast—a village burnt, a few hundred men killed on
English soil—then indeed we should see an England in arms'.[104] One man from
Devon gave his reasons for enlisting as the attack hundreds of miles away, and the
realization that if such an attack could happen there, it could just as well happen in
his own coastal town.[105] Mr Watt, who lost one brother during the attack on
Hartlepool, remembered his mother forcing his surviving older brother to enlist the
day after the bombardment 'in spite of the fact that he had been wounded in the
finger'.[106] J. Herbert Lewis recorded on 17 December that 'the effect of yesterday's
bombardment has been to give a good stimulus to recruiting'.[107] In recruitment
terms the effect may only have been local. A total of 117,860 men enlisted in the
army or Territorials during that month, the lowest monthly enlistment rate for the
five months since the start of war.[108] However, the experience sent shock-waves
across the United Kingdom. The 'impenetrable fortress' had been violated.

Nine days after the bombardment—on Christmas Day 1914—a German Zeppelin was seen over Dover. With hindsight this was an ominous indicator of
Britain's vulnerability to future air attacks. At the time, sightings of the Zeppelin
were limited to the south-east. Those who did spot the Zeppelin attached little
significance to the event. Air warfare was not a real possibility: any attack would
more likely come from the sea. P. G. Heath, who was encamped at Belhus Park,
Aveley recalled the Zeppelin simply because it interrupted his Christmas dinner.[109]
Mr S. H. Ratcliff, from Westcliff-on-Sea, Essex, was 'only mildly interested and
certainly not alarmed' by the sighting.[110] For Florence Buckland from Gravesend

---

[102] Van Emden and Humphries, *All Quiet on the Home Front: An Oral History of Life in Britain
During the First World War*, 51.
[103] Both posters seen at the Liddle Collection, Leeds.
[104] Trevelyan, *The Life of Mrs Humphry Ward* (London, 1923), 266.
[105] Van Emden and Humphries, *All Quiet on the Home Front: An Oral History of Life in Britain
During the First World War*, 51.
[106] Liddle: DF: Defence. Sea Bombardment of the East Coast: Hartlepool, Item 14 (1971).
[107] NLW: J. Herbert Lewis: B28, 17 December 1914.
[108] HMSO, *Statistics of the Military Effort of the British Empire during the Great War, 1914–1920*
(London, 1922).
[109] Liddle: WF Recollections: P.G. Heath: File H 17 (n.d.).
[110] ERO: T/Z 25/618 (1966).

in Kent the 'sudden excitement' of the Zeppelin was 'quickly over'.[111] However, J. Herbert Lewis did realize the ominous significance of the sighting. On 28 December he wrote 'news of air raid on Cuxhaven on Christmas Day ... as time goes on these air attacks will become more frequent. What will be the future of this frightful new arm?'[112] Reasons as to why these sightings were not taken seriously can only be guessed at, but perhaps it was because some people's apprehensions could only stretch so far: their imaginations literally could not foresee an attack from the air.

Victims of the east-coast bombardment were outnumbered by the more visible and widespread Belgian victims of the violent German invasion. By December 1914, nine-tenths of Belgium was under German control and 27 per cent of its population had been made refugees.[113] By mid-June 1915 there were around 265,000 Belgian refugees (a quarter of the total number of Belgian refugees) in Great Britain.[114] Stories about the experiences of refugees in France and Belgium and their very presence on British soil heightened people's understanding of the brutality and reality of modern warfare. The refugees were eventually distributed all around the country, including Wales, Scotland, and Ireland in towns and small villages. Consequently, the majority of the British public were made unequivocally aware that this was a war in which civilians suffered as well as soldiers. Moreover, these civilians had suffered at the hands of Germans, cementing their reputation as a brutal enemy.

Ben Carbis, a Signaller with 1/4th South Lancashires stationed in Kent, described a Belgian family, billeted next door to his parents in Mersey on 9 October. He told of how well they were integrating; the children were going to school and the whole family were learning English. But he hinted at how much they had lost: a father, a fiancée, and their livelihood. With affection he described the children: 'You could not pity them enough if you saw them'.[115] The same month, Ursula Tyrwhitt, from Oxford, wrote to her friend, the artist Gwen John, in Paris about the latest consignment of refugees that had arrived at Charing Cross station in London:

> It was most pitiful—many looked quite numbed with despair, others seemed happy, these were mostly young ones glad to have escaped and having their life still before them. All carried little pathetic bundles done up in handkerchiefs, all they possessed. Fearful stories of cruelty ... were told. I won't tell you any, you will have read so many in the papers, they are true. Seeing these people one can't help but believe the worst.[116]

Violet Clutton also witnessed their arrival at Charing Cross. For her it made the 'terrible side of the war' seem 'far, far more real than ever before'.[117] People evidently compared notes about the refugees in their towns and villages. On 18

---

[111] ERO: T/Z 25/602 (1966).
[112] NLW: J. Herbert Lewis: B28, 28 December 1914.
[113] Schaepdrijver, 'Occupation, Propaganda and the Idea of Belgium', 269–70.
[114] David Bilton, *The Home Front in the Great War* (Barnsley, 2004), 217.
[115] LanRO: Letter from Ben Carbis: DDX/872/2/1, 9 October 1914.
[116] NLW: Gwen John: Mss 22311D, ff. 52, October 1914.
[117] DRO: Violet Clutton: 6258M/Box 1, Vol II, 10 October 1914.

October, Eleanor Peart wrote from North Shields to her friends, the Hills-Johnes in Dolaucothi: 'We have also got three families of Belgian refugees in the town. One says her husband burnt to death five weeks ago . . . Poor, poor thing!'[118]

However, despite people's best intentions there was a degree of 'voyeurism' to the arrival of Belgian refugees in Britain. R. Jeffrey Axton, a child in London 1914, recalled in 1992 how he was taken by his mother to visit some Belgian refugees. He described them as 'rough-looking peasants in ugly black or dark clothes . . . I remember comments that they were "a surly lot" and I have no recollection of any of them smiling. Perhaps we thought we were making rather an exhibition of them, like animals in a zoo, but it is certain that it was all well meant'.[119] Going to 'see' the Belgians became something of a family outing, as Constance Baldwin described on 18 December.[120] Similarly, Reverend Yonge, of Boreham in Essex recorded on 16 October the arrival of Belgian refugees 'at the big Hotel, many people looking on. They received many presents of tobacco, sweets, papers fastened on strings . . . Quite an excitement'.[121]

Aside from sympathy, horror, revulsion, and indignation, the main reaction amongst the British people to the arrival of refugees was to help them. On 22 October Dr James Maxwell, in Bromley, Kent, wrote to his son and daughter-in-law: 'Indeed the whole country is active on behalf of Belgium, everybody desiring to do something on their behalf'.[122] Mary Coules, from London, recorded how 'everyone was Belgian mad for a time'.[123] Help came in a variety of forms including the establishment of committees to shelter, feed, clothe, entertain, and eventually arrange employment for the refugees.[124] These committees were financially supported by the government, private donations, and various fund-raising events, such as concerts and flag days.

However, after the initial outpouring of universal altruism, reactions towards Belgian refugees became more selective. Class was an issue, as Ada McGuire illustrated on 11 October: 'Mr Malvern says a gentleman he knows offered to adopt two little Belgian girls but said he would like them to be of decent parentage. The authorities wrote and told him that there were two little girls, who judging by the fine quality of their underwear were of a refined upbringing.'[125] Between 15 and 16 October 340 refugees arrived in Birmingham. Elizabeth Cadbury, who was working for the refugee housing committee, described their arrival and 'distribution' on 20 October:

[118] NLW: Dolaucothi: Estate and family records of the Johnes and Hill-Johnes of Dolaucothi, Carmarthenshire: D L8699, 18 October 1914.

[119] Liddle: DF Recollections: Box A-C: R. Jeffrey Axton (1992).

[120] WRO: Ref 705:775: BA 8229L Parcel 11: Constance Baldwin diary 1914, 18 December 1914.

[121] ERO: Diary of Reverend Denys Yonge: D/DU 358/26, 16 October 1914.

[122] University of Birmingham, Special Collections: Dr James Laidlaw Maxwell: DA 26/2/1/6/45, 22 October 1914.

[123] IWM, Docs: Coules, Miss M.: 97/25/1, September/October 1914.

[124] For more detail see Peter Calahan, *Belgian Relief in England During the Great War* (New York, 1982).

[125] IWM, Docs: McGuire, Misses A. & R.: 96/31/1, 11 October 1914.

We wrestled with the huge number of people at Moseley Road, and the terribly trying people who came to try and help us. It is quite extraordinary how difficult and impossible some people are, and how little they seem to realise what an enormous work it is to house all these people. They prowl around picking and choosing amongst the refugees, as though they were so many prize cattle; it is quite uncomfortable.[126]

Miss G. West and her family, from Gloucestershire, decided on 24 September to take in two Belgian refugees and received six members of the Leughels family. By 20 November there were complaints: 'Belgians getting on pretty well though they are a bit exacting about their food and garment. Mrs [the Belgian mother] refused a charming little red coat because "red does not suit fair babies"'. She continued:

Other peoples' Belgians are not so amiable. Those in Woodchester do their own catering and run up huge bills, buying only the best joints and quantities of butter and eggs. The lady who looks after them says that the only thing that brings a passing smile to their faces is roast pork so although it is awfully dear she can't refuse it them. Most people agree that they are fat, lazy, greedy... and inclined to take all the benefits heaped on them as a matter of course. Our man has got a job as overseer at a little factory started for the refugees in Painswick. Before he got this, he would never do anything for us. When we asked him to help us dig the potatoes, Ernest being away, he always sighed and said "Will tomorrow do" and generally sneaked off or sent his little boy who is too young to be any use.[127]

By 30 November the Leughels had moved on from the West household after an incident where Monsieur Leughel arrived home at 1 a.m., 'drunk as a cork'.[128]

A common reaction to refugees, after the novelty of their arrival had worn off, was one of annoyance. Many people complained about them being ungrateful. Sybil Morrison, from London, attempted to excuse their 'nasty and sulky' behaviour by empathizing with the horror of their experiences. However, she felt she was in the minority as most people complained about them, arguing that they should have been more grateful.[129] Daisy Spickett from Pontypridd echoed these opinions: 'They were very difficult, many of them, because they were in a terrible condition, had lost everything... It was very pathetic but many of them were very, very difficult, expecting the earth.'[130] By late 1914 Mary Coules was less understanding:

The Belgians are not grateful. They won't do a stroke of work, and grumble at everything, and their morals...! It may be true enough that Belgium saved Europe, but... save us from the Belgians! As far as I am concerned Belgianitous has quite abated.[131]

There was also an increasing concern that German spies had infiltrated Britain disguised as Belgian refugees, which added to people's disillusion. Consequently, the welcome towards refugees became frostier. As Sidney Perkins from

---

[126] BCA: MS 466/432: Box 3: Cadbury Family Journal, 20 October 1914.
[127] IWM, Docs: West, Miss G.M.: 77/156/1, 20 November 1914.
[128] IWM, Docs: West, Miss G.M.: 77/156/1, 30 November 1914.
[129] IWM: 331, Reel 3 (n.d.).
[130] IWM: 514, Reel 1–2 (1974).
[131] IWM, Docs: Coules, Miss M.: 97/25/1, December 1914.

Tynewydd, recalled, such rumours meant that 'the refugees suffered grossly and unfairly'.[132] Clearly as time went on, Belgian refugees were no longer a novelty.

However, relief efforts did not cease for Belgian refugees arriving in Britain even if they were sometimes performed with less goodwill than before. The presence of Belgian refugees on British soil in 1914 confirmed for many people the reality and consequences of modern warfare. The British people had a choice: they could either be overwhelmed by these horrors and collapse, or put these negative energies into something practical, useful, and, moreover, distracting. Along with caring for the wounded, dealing with refugees—whether positively or reluctantly—became a part of the process of settling into war. Instead of lamenting the situation and discussing frightening horrors, people got on with the job at hand.

Combatants were obviously the primary victims of violent warfare. Despite the lack of reliable war news in the printed press, lists of casualties, the missing, and the wounded made the violence of the war horribly visible to the British population. Additionally, the arrival of Belgian refugees and wounded soldiers to Britain, and funerals of those who perished on British soil also provided visual evidence of the destruction and violence of modern warfare.

John Faulkner, as a civilian volunteer with the Red Cross in Chester, dealt with arrivals of wounded soldiers at Birkenhead station. He described some of the sights he witnessed in 1914:

> One man had nine shirts on . . . you couldn't tell who was who, or what was what cos they hadn't had a wash, they hadn't had a shave, and they were very grimy . . . there were some nasty cases . . . there was one fellow, his arm was black . . . I saw the doctor . . . he said . . . "we'll have to operate on this straightaway".[133]

This incident deeply disturbed Faulkner, despite being hardened to this kind of sight. Another gruesome aspect of Faulkner's job was to dispose of amputated limbs: 'there was one man, from the Warwicks . . . they gave me his leg . . . It was just like a leg of mutton'.[134] For Elizabeth Haldane, the sight of appalling injuries and the way the soldiers coped instilled in her a belief in the courage of the British soldier. After a nursing shift at Portsmouth Hospital on 17 October she commented: 'Our own men wonderful; a man with one foot off would not be commiserated, "One boot only to clean!"'[135] In Leicester, towards the end of 1914, 'concrete and unchallengeable proof came to hand' about the reality of modern warfare when 'men arrived at their homes . . . with shattered frames, armless, legless, and in a variety of ways broken, wounded and disabled'.[136]

[132] Carmarthenshire Archives Service, Carmarthen: 'Memories and Reflections' by Gunner S.P. Perkins DX/201/1 (1904).
[133] IWM: 560, Reel 1–2 (1975).
[134] Ibid.
[135] NLS: Elizabeth S. Haldane: Mss 20243, 17 October 1914.
[136] ROLLR: Leicester, Leicestershire and Rutland Prisoners of War Committee, Annual Reports: 14 D 35/24 (1915).

Lady Betty Balfour recorded her first casualty list in her diary on 25 August. She believed around 2,000 British soldiers had been killed or injured at Mons.[137] However, the following day she was sceptical of this statistic, believing it to be too low owing to over-zealous press censorship:

I think it is wholly unnecessary—for instance, saying that two of our line Regiments and one cavalry regiment had suffered heavily and not mentioning which they were ... The War Office expected 10,000 casualties from these first battles, compared with 2,000 seems small... Gerald at dinner spoke of the terrific losses that would be entailed in this war. Greater than in any previous battles.[138]

The comment—'2,000 seems small'—suggests that she was steeling herself for worse to come. The figure of 10,000 was repeated by Elizabeth Haldane on 4 September: 'so many wounded and killed, about 10,000 casualties out of 150,000 I suppose or near it'.[139] On this estimation 7 per cent of troops were killed. However, this percentage paled in comparison to the statistics Lawrence Colby received. Serving with the 1st Battalion Grenadier Guards, Colby told his father on 3 September that he had 'received a lot of news from wounded officers who have already returned, the 4th Guards Brigade had a very stirring encounter at a place called Landrecis... Only 30 men returned out of the 250 Coldstream company.'[140] At this rate 88 per cent of the company had perished during its encounter with German machine-gun fire. The same day Alice Henry, wife of the Irish botanist Augustine Henry, living in London, recorded in her diary that 82 per cent of the officers of the Cheshires were 'missing'. A Regular soldier she knew who was departing to Boulogne to join the Cheshires now had 'no regiment to join'.[141]

Some people attempted to predict the number of casualties. Annie Chamberlain told her husband Neville, on 3 September, about the casualty list published that day. Although she described it as 'terrible' she added that it was 'hardly as big as I expected'. Moreover, she added that 'the full list of missing cannot be true if yesterday's statement of 395 was correct'.[142] Perhaps she was bracing herself for a bigger list that correlated with her original estimation. By 5 December, Rudyard Kipling calculated that Britain had 'lost 50 per cent more than the full strength of the entire United States army'—about 50,000 men.[143] On 2 December *The Times* military correspondent estimated that the BEF had suffered about 84,000 casualties.[144] Yet, precise numbers did not matter—what did was their regularity and the ominous feeling that a telegram might arrive on the doorstep at

---

[137] Actually 1,600 British soldiers perished during the Battle of Mons.

[138] NAS, GRH: Balfour of Whittingehame Papers: Lady Betty Balfour: GD 433/2/348, 25 August 1914.

[139] NLS: Elizabeth S. Haldane: Mss 20243, 4 September 1914.

[140] NLW: Ffynnone2: Additional Material: 2422, 3 September 1914.

[141] NLI: Mrs Augustine Henry: Ms 7981–82, 3 September 1914.

[142] University of Birmingham, Special Collections: Personal Correspondence between Neville and Annie Chamberlain: NC 1/25/14, 3 September 1914.

[143] Pinney, ed., *The Letters of Rudyard Kipling*, 274. The US Army in 1914 had a strength of 98,000 men.

[144] *The Times*, 2 December 1914, 9.

any time. On 22 September, Elsie Russell, in Jedburgh in the Scottish Borders, described how much she hated the casualty lists and how her mother's hair was turning grey through worry.[145] Iris Holt, in Lewes, Sussex, wrote on 30 September how she lived in terror of the casualty lists. Her cousin Nell had been left a widow two months after her wedding.[146] M. M. Goodwin in Scotland described the month of December as 'grim. Casualty lists began coming in . . . so many days were like each other, but always the appalling casualty lists kept coming in'.[147] All classes were affected by loss. Paul Cambon described to Théophile Delcassé, the French Foreign Minister, on 18 September how British losses were so considerable that there was no family which was not in mourning.[148] On 8 November the King described to his son Bertie, the future George VI, how broken-hearted his friend Harry Legge was at the news of his son's death at the front.[149] Five days later he recorded in his diary how 'all the best Officers and our friends are going in this horrible war'.[150] According to Rudyard Kipling 'we are all hit in our degree': no one was able to escape the fear, anxiety, and grief wrought by war.[151]

However, more frightening were the huge lists of 'missing' published in September 1914. Rudyard Kipling believed this was a deliberate tactic on the part of Germany to increase the agony of relatives in Britain. On 5 October he recounted the experience of an old friend and neighbour whose son had been reported missing in early September. Over the course of the month she had been told that he was dead, imprisoned, wounded:

> . . . and so the horrible see-saw goes on; she dying daily and letters of condolence *and* congratulation crossing each other and harrowing her soul . . . And that is but one case of many, many hundreds. *Per Contra* one comes across cases of the reported missing miraculously restored and then one sees the envy in the eyes of other women.[152]

On the whole, people soon became aware that 'missing' probably meant dead or imprisoned. Wounded soldiers in Leicester spoke for the first time of 'Prisoners of War' in late 1914; from this point 'there began to be alarming anxiety in many Soldiers' [sic] homes'.[153] As Reverend Yonge recorded on 3 September, after reading the newspapers: 'the names of fallen officers. *RIP*. Sad indeed for relatives. More sad is the list of missing = frightful anxiety.'[154] According to Elizabeth Cadbury, who commented on 1 September, 'want of news about the men's whereabouts and destination is a terrible strain for all these poor women to bear'.[155]

---

145 Liddle: GS 0251: A.S.G. Butler, 22 September 1914.
146 Liddle: AIR 224: A.S. Morton, 30 September 1914.
147 ERO: T/Z 25/668 (1966).
148 AMAE, Paris: Papiers Delcassé: Lettres de Diplomates III: Paul Cambon, ff. 339, 18 September 1914.
149 Royal Archives, Windsor Castle: RA GV/AA59/318, 8 November 1914.
150 Royal Archives, Windsor Castle: RA GV/PRIV/GVD/1914: 13 November 1914
151 Pinney, ed., *The Letters of Rudyard Kipling*, 256.
152 Ibid. 256, 259–60.
153 ROLLR: Leicester, Leicestershire and Rutland Prisoners of War Committee, Annual Reports: 14 D 35/24 (1915).
154 ERO: Diary of Reverend Denys Yonge: D/DU 358/26, 3 September 1914.
155 BCA: MS 466/432: Box 3: Cadbury Family Journal, 1 September 1914.

Confirmation that a man was actually dead provided absolute proof of the destructive nature of war, for an individual, their family, and often their community. Marjorie Tamblyn, a schoolgirl in Edgbaston in 1914, recalled: 'My first realisation that war was something really terrible was when a friend of [my mother's] passed the window in widow's weeds...and mother was crying. I knew then that war was a disastrous thing.'[156] Ada McGuire recalled visiting a mother of a dead soldier in late November: 'Poor thing, she is quite brokenhearted and cannot speak of him without breaking down... My word, he was honoured in death!... It was the biggest funeral that there has been over here for some time, not that that is much consolation for her.'[157] For Olive Holt, the war proved too much for her. Although she was working in Chelsea in late 1914, the 'rumours of invasion and evacuation [in her home-town of Colchester]' and 'newspaper stories of French families broken up, as homes were evacuated, together with this news from home, and also tidings of the death in the trenches of a certain young man all proved too much for me, and I returned home suffering from "a nervous breakdown"'.[158]

Finally, funerals of dead soldiers were another opportunity to visualize the violence of war. Between October and December 1914, sixteen Belgian soldiers—who had died of wounds in Manchester and Salford hospitals—were buried locally in a public ceremony organized by the Belgian consul and the city authorities. It was advertised as an opportunity for local people to pay tribute to the bravery of Belgian soldiers. However, a cynic might interpret these lavish funerals as a way of reinforcing the message of Britain's just war in the name of Belgium. Some people were against these funerals in case they opened wounds amongst the ordinary population. In a response to such a complaint, the head of the Belgian funeral committee, J. H. Billinge, wrote on 12 November:

> The procession and ceremony were instituted to enable citizens to show their appreciation of what the gallant Belgians had done and certainly no intention of "opening any wounds". As regards the view which our Belgian guests took of the matter I can assure you that those who were present at the funeral were very deeply touched in-deed first by the enormous attendance of the public not only in the City itself but also at the Cemetery and also the respectful and reverential attitude of silence of the crowd.[159]

***

The British population were involved both directly and indirectly in this unprecedented violence. The enormous explosion of violence that commenced in August 1914 immediately and scathingly refuted all predictions that had been made in the preceding years.[160] Violence became part of the fabric of ordinary people's lives.[161]

---

[156] City Sound Archive, Birmingham Museum: R85 (1981).
[157] IWM, Docs: McGuire, Misses A. & R.: 96/31/1, 29 November 1914.
[158] ERO: T/Z 25/603 (1966).
[159] MALSL: Funerals and Enquiries regarding expatriate Belgian soldiers: M138 Box 29, File 1 and M138 Box 30, File 2.
[160] Audoin-Rouzeau and Becker, *1914–1918: Understanding the Great War*, 21.
[161] Healy, *Vienna and the Fall of the Habsburg Empire: Total War and Everyday Life in World War One*, 5.

Sometimes this violence was imagined. The German invasion of Belgium and the ensuing Battle of the Frontiers sparked fears amongst the British population, particular those living along the east coast, that the Germans could (and would) land on British soil. German atrocities in Belgium were, for the British, invasion by proxy. In an effort to diffuse heightening fears about the fate of the BEF in France, a compensatory myth, in the form of the Russian troops landing in Britain, spread nationwide and dissipated only when the BEF was known to be back on the offensive, halting a possible German invasion.

The British also experienced violence directly. Violence created victims, and in the case of the bombardment of Scarborough, Whitby, and Hartlepool on 16 December, these were British civilians. The consequences of violent warfare were also made visible to the British public in the form of the arrival of other victims: Belgian refugees and returning wounded soldiers, the ever-increasing lists of casualties and missing, and the funerals of those who succumbed to war wounds on British soil. People did their best to cope with these phenomena, but the pain and grief of losing a loved one literally brought the war home.

Military history indicates that Britain was not directly threatened by an invasion in 1914, but this is not how contemporaries perceived it. Statistics tell us that British casualties were far less than those of the French army, but for the British people, the impact of death was no less tragic. They were exposed to the anticipation, apprehension, and experience of war and the violence that characterized it in 1914. Moreover, although in 1914 the BEF was relatively small, its losses were high and this affected the home population intensely. By the end of the First Battle of Ypres, in mid-November, the original BEF had virtually been destroyed. The men dying between August and November 1914 were professional soldiers or Territorials who had been serving or recalled in August. The ranks had to be replenished, and the only method available to the British authorities in 1914 was via voluntary enlistment.

5

A Volunteer War

On 4 August 1914 Britain did not have an army capable of fighting a major war on the continent. The regular British army, not including reservists, consisted of only 247,432 officers and men, about one-third of whom were in India. The overwhelming bulk of military spending had concentrated on the navy, and compulsory military service—a staple of the other major European powers—had not been introduced. The small professional army was enough to send an expeditionary force of seven divisions to France to help stem the German invasion, the military plan for which had been elaborated since 1905. However, in the eyes of Lord Kitchener, who was appointed Secretary of State for War on 5 August, Britain was vulnerable to invasion and the reserve Territorial Army was inadequate for its defence. This led him to reduce the BEF to five divisions. Kitchener also believed that the war would be a protracted affair. Although no decision had been taken about a major military commitment to the continent, he felt that a large-scale expansion of the armed forces was vital both for home defence and for future eventualities.

Given the deeply ingrained British hostility to conscription, as the National Service Movement had found out in the years since the South African War, voluntary recruitment, as in that earlier conflict, was the only source from which an expansion of military numbers could come. In the event, the United Kingdom mobilized over 5 million men during the First World War, half of them by volunteering and half by compulsion, once conscription had reluctantly been introduced in Britain (but not Ireland) in the first half of 1916. Volunteering (as the regular means of recruitment to the armed forces) was a response open to contemporaries from the moment war loomed, and 4 August was marked by large numbers of men presenting themselves at recruiting offices. But it was Kitchener more than anyone who turned spontaneous volunteering into a concerted attempt to raise a mass, continental-style army by voluntary means, beginning with his declaration at the end of the first week of the war, on Friday, 7 August.[1]

This raises a series of important questions. What was the chronology of recruitment? Why did men volunteer? What factors encouraged or discouraged them? How did the experience of volunteering affect women, parents, and children? What was the geography of recruitment? These questions in turn can only be answered in

---

[1] Trevor Wilson, *The Myriad Faces of War: Britain and the Great War, 1914–1918* (Cambridge, 1986), 36–7. See also Simkins, *Kitchener's Army: The Raising of the New Armies 1914–1916* (Manchester, 1988).

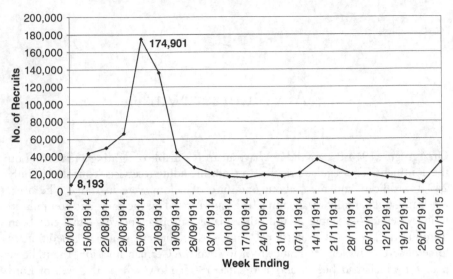

Fig. 5.1. The number of recruits per week to the regular army, 8 August 1914 to 2 January 1915

NA, Kew: CAB 21/107, 13 April 1916.

the light of the experiences of war already discussed—the national cause, the nature of the enemy, and the violence of war as imagined and encountered.

CHRONOLOGY

As discussed, no 'rush to the colours', took place in August owing, in part, to the dislocation and uncertainty caused by the outbreak of war. Figure 5.1 illustrates the number of recruits who enlisted per week to the regular army between the weeks ending 8 August 1914 and 2 January 1915. The highest and lowest weekly enlistment rates are marked by their data value.

This graph reconfirms that the highest monthly rate of enlistment during these five months occurred in September and not August 1914, despite Kitchener's published appeals on 7 and 28 August.[2] By the end of 1915, more than 2.5 million men had joined up; 32 per cent of them volunteered in 1914, and 16 per cent in September.[3] The highest peak for recruiting in Britain during the entire war was the week ending 5 September 1914. The PRC did not have its first meeting until 31 August, and was therefore inactive during the biggest surge in recruitment. Although local recruitment efforts were taking place in the first few weeks, these

---

[2] See *The Times*, 7 August 1914, 5 and 28 August 1914, 6.
[3] Silbey, *The British Working Class and Enthusiasm for War, 1914–1916* (London, 2005), 1. See also, NA, Kew: CAB 21/107, 13 April 1916.

were disorganized and often ineffective. So what happened in early September to affect enlistment rates so dramatically?

As seen, during the first three weeks of war Britain received little bad military news from official sources such as the press. However, by late August disturbing information about events in France and Belgium began to appear. On 25 August the government issued *The Belgian Official Report*, which summarized German actions in Belgium and recounted the wave of atrocities against civilians, shortly followed by the publication of the Mons Despatch in *The Times* on the same day. Arthur Moore of *The Times*, who was with the British forces, wrote a depressing account of the BEF in retreat:

> Our losses are very great. I have seen the broken bits of many regiments . . . To sum up, the first great German effort has succeeded. We have to face the fact that the BEF, which bore the great weight of the blow, has suffered terrible losses and requires immediate and immense reinforcement.[4]

It ended with a stark appeal for more men to join up.[5]

The Times' article had an instant effect.[6] Over the next four days more than 10,000 men enlisted. By 31 August, daily enlistment topped 20,000, and on 3 September 33,204 men joined the army, the highest enlistment for any day of the war. In the week between 30 August and 5 September, 174,901 men joined the colours.[7] The surge continued unabated in the week beginning 7 September when just over 136,000 men enlisted. The contrast in numbers volunteering before and after the article was published is striking. In London, for example, the daily average in the week before the article was 1,606; the day after it appeared (31 August), 4,001 men enlisted. Similar patterns of recruitment occurred outside the capital. In Liverpool the figures for the same dates were 220 and 725 respectively; in rural Hertford, 43 and 204.[8] As *The Times* was published in London, it is understandable that recruiting figures increased here first. The effect of the article then rippled outward to the rest of the UK. For the month of August, London supplied around 15 per cent of the country's total recruits. On 31 August alone, London supplied 19 per cent of the national total. The next day, as other local and regional papers reprinted the article, the London share of enlistees decreased to around 13 per cent and averaged 11 per cent for the following week.[9] Thus, far from signing up in an initial burst of enthusiasm, the largest single component of volunteers enlisted at *exactly* the moment that the war turned serious.[10]

Contemporaries were aware of the connection between the German advance, Allied defeats, and the need for more men. James Brady, from Rochdale,

---

[4] *The Times*, 30 August 1914, 1.

[5] Many criticized *The Times* for publishing the article. In self-defence, the paper revealed that not only had the article been passed by the appropriate government office, but that the Press Censor had added the final line demanding more soldiers. (Silbey, *The British Working Class and Enthusiasm for War, 1914–1916*, 24.)

[6] Gregory, 'British "War Enthusiasm"' in 1914: A Reassessment', in *Evidence, History and the Great War: Historians and the Impact of 1914–18*, ed. Gail Braybon (Oxford, 2003), 81.

[7] Simkins, *Kitchener's Army: The Raising of the New Armies 1914–1916*, 65.

[8] NA, Kew: NATS 1/398.

[9] Silbey, *The British Working Class and Enthusiasm for War, 1914–1916*, 24.

[10] Gregory, 'British "War Enthusiasm"' in 1914: A Reassessment', 81.

Lancashire, enlisted with the Royal Army Medical Corps in early September. He recalled: 'news of the Retreat [sic] spread like wildfire casting gloom and . . . despondency around the serried ranks of workers cottages in the town. But it had the effect of stimulating recruiting'.[11] In her diary on 3 September, Gladys Hutchinson, a London resident, noted:

> Germans pressing on to Paris all the time. Behaving shamefully!! Using Red flag then firing etc. More and more recruits required. People waking up more now. Lots of recruits at Richmond.[12]

E. T. John, Liberal MP for East Denbighshire, appealed to Asquith on 9 November to allow Allied defeats to be openly published as a way to encourage recruiting, arguing that 'as a matter of fact military misfortunes appear to have so far proved a most effective stimulus to recruiting'.[13] People could calculate that a demand for more men meant either insufficient numbers were originally sent out or that many had already been lost. Either way, it was understood that Britain was not doing well in September and that its 'quick victory' seemed increasingly remote.

The volunteer soldiers were therefore aware that they were needed to replace men who had been killed or wounded in late August/early September. Rifleman Henry Williamson, who departed for the front in September, 'had a feeling from having talked to chaps from Mons in the local hospital [in East Sussex] that it wasn't altogether going to be a picnic'.[14] Although some men accepted their duty with high spirits to boost morale, others were frightened. Phillip Leicester recorded in his diary how a soldier, concerned about what would confront him in France, had whispered to his mother to pray for him as the train pulled out of Worcester station.[15] In short, enlistment rates were at their peak in early September when people were becoming aware of the violence and horror of war. Wounded soldiers and Belgian refugees were conveying terrifying stories of German atrocities to the British people. Casualty lists were being printed and they, along with the frightening Mons Despatch, shocked Britons. Defeats encouraged many men to enlist. Alexander Thompson, a solicitor's clerk in Newcastle, warned his mother on 28 August that 'unless the Allied forces' prospects are better on Monday than they are at present . . . I will join Kitchener's Army'.[16] The retreat from Mons persuaded Andrew Buxton, an employee at the Westminster branch of Barclay's Bank, that he could no longer postpone his decision to enlist. 'I know you don't want me to enlist', he told his sister on 31 August, 'but I cannot help thinking it my duty from every point of view . . . to do so soon—say next week or the week following.'[17] Defeats continued to affect enlistment rates in Britain. Rates dropped after the Allied success on the Marne in September, and then improved again for a short

---

[11] IWM, Docs: Brady, J.: 01/36/1 (1980).
[12] Liddle: DF 068: Gladys Hutchinson, 3 September 1914.
[13] NLW: Edward Thomas John: ETJ 1252, 9 November 1914.
[14] Arthur, *Forgotten Voices of the Great War*, 48.
[15] WRO: Ref 705:185: BA 8185: Parcel 2: Phillip A. Leicester, August 1914.
[16] IWM, Docs: Thompson, Lt Alexander: 79/55/1, 28 August 1914.
[17] Edward S. Woods, ed., *Andrew R. Buxton: The Rifle Brigade, A Memoir* (London, 1918), 39.

Table 5.1. A comparison of recruits in proportion to male population in two neighbouring Scottish districts, August to September 1914*

Area	% of total recruitment, August to September 1914
Aberdeen, Forfar, and Inverness	2.71
Lanark and Ayr	56.54
Rest of Scotland	40.75

* NA, Kew: NATS 1/398 and census 1911.

period during the First Battle of Ypres in November, again when the BEF were doing badly.[18]

SOCIAL AND GEOGRAPHICAL COMMUNITIES

Men from urban communities were more likely to enlist than those from agricultural ones.[19] This can be explained in part by the impact the war had on industry and the unemployment that ensued in the opening months of the war. While Scotland contributed disproportionately to war production later in the conflict, there was a period of initial industrial dislocation and unemployment. In mid-August, the percentage of unemployment among workmen in insured trades—building, engineering, shipbuilding, and vehicle making—was 5 per cent, compared with 4 per cent at the end of the previous week and 3 per cent at the corresponding period of 1913.[20] Industrial unemployment was reflected in Scottish recruitment rates. By October 1914, of the thirty major industries surveyed for a Board of Trade Report on the State of Employment in Britain, twenty were shown to have produced a higher percentage of recruits than average in Scotland. These included the five main industries in Scotland: coal-mining, engineering, shipbuilding, iron and steel, and building. These were precisely the industries that had suffered a contraction in trade. For the first three months of war Scottish industry alone accounted for 109,714 recruits—13.5 per cent of the United Kingdom total and over 92 per cent of the total Scottish recruits up to this point. Commerce and agriculture therefore provided less than 8 per cent.[21] These conclusions are confirmed geographically in Table 5.1.

The three most agricultural areas in Scotland (Aberdeen, Forfar, and Inverness) provided only 2.71 per cent of the recruits in the September 'surge', while the two most industrial areas (Lanark and Ayr) provided 56.54 per cent. When the distribution of Scotland's male population is taken into account, the industrial

[18] Simkins, *Kitchener's Army: The Raising of the New Armies 1914–1916*, 171.

[19] Osborne, *The Voluntary Recruiting Movement in Britain, 1914–1916* (New York, 1982), 8.

[20] Derek Rutherford Young, 'Voluntary Recruitment in Scotland, 1914–1916' (PhD, University of Glasgow, 2001), 100–1.

[21] Board of Trade, *Report of the Board of Trade on the State of Employment in the United Kingdom in October 1914*, Cd. 7703, 38 cited in Ibid. 99.

counties of Lanark and Ayr (with over 36 per cent of Scotland's male population) were contributing a disproportionately high number of recruits due partly to the contraction in industry and the economic needs of its workforce.[22]

However, this is not to argue that enlistment was heaviest among those with insecure employment. Unemployment, as a motivating factor, only partly explains why some men enlisted in 1914. Whilst soldiering in peacetime may seem preferable to civilian unemployment, in wartime, the risk of death or injury would outweigh any material benefits.[23] Although regional differences between all occupied workers were slight, the lowest enlistment rates were registered in the East Midlands and Yorkshire, and among textile and clothing workers in particular, despite this industry being badly hit by the outbreak of war.[24] This could be explained by the make-up of employees in these trades, in which large numbers of married women were employed. The textile industry, like agriculture, tended to have an older cohort of workers. There were fewer labourers aged 20 to 44 in the textile industry than in mining or metalwork.[25] Recruitment was naturally greater amongst those occupations with a 'younger' age structure. Therefore, unemployment, or the threat of it, does not fully explain the 1914 pattern of enlistment.

The 'urban/rural' divide affected the whole of the United Kingdom, including Ireland, in 1914, and is perhaps more useful when trying to understand recruitment at the outbreak of war. On 13 October, the Director of Recruiting in Great Britain reported that as far as the regular army was concerned:

> Towns and mining localities give far the best results, probably because it is the easiest to get at people where the population is most dense. It follows that we should endeavour to work the country districts more thoroughly.[26]

Another official felt that the 'farming classes' were quite 'backward' in coming forward.[27] It is difficult to analyse the number of recruits from urban and rural areas as the authorities recorded where the recruits enlisted, not where they came from. However, this distortion can be partially overcome by analysing figures from counties with and without large urban centres. Cornwall, Cheshire, Devon, and towns from north Wales are representative of counties with no large urban centres and a high percentage of rural workers. For major urban counties I have selected London, Northumberland and Durham, Lancashire, Warwick, and Lanark (including Glasgow). Tables 5.2 and 5.3 show the proportion of males of military age who volunteered in these areas between August and November 1914:

[22] Young, 'Voluntary Recruitment in Scotland, 1914–1916', 151–2.
[23] David Fitzpatrick, 'The Logic of Collective Sacrifice: Ireland and the British Army, 1914–1918', *The Historical Journal* 38 (1995), 1028.
[24] J. M. Winter, *The Great War and the British People* (London, 1986), 33.
[25] P. E. Dewey, 'Military Recruiting and the British Labour Force During the First World War', *The Historical Journal* 27 (1984), 199–223.
[26] DRO: Devon Parliamentary Recruiting Committee: 1262M/L153, 13 October 1914.
[27] Silbey, *The British Working Class and Enthusiasm for War, 1914–1916*, 39.

Table 5.2. Recruiting in proportion to population in four predominantly rural areas*

Recruiting District	(A) Male pop. of military age (19–38)	Recruits Enlisted up to 12 November 1914	
		(B) Regulars	% of (B) to (A)
Cornwall	42,324	1,122	2.7
Cheshire	144,946	12,178	8.4
Devon	102,357	4,767	4.7
Rural North Wales (Flint, Denbigh, Merioneth, Caernarvon, Anglesey, Montgomery)	70,895	3,598	5.1
TOTAL for England, Wales, and Scotland	6,105,086	625,154	10.2

* NA, Kew: CAB 37/122/164.

Table 5.3. Recruiting in proportion to population in four predominantly urban areas*

Recruiting District	(A) Male pop of military age (19–38)	Recruits Enlisted up to 12 November 1914	
		(B) Regulars	% of (B) to (A)
London	747,072	106,943	14.3
Northumberland and Durham	319,071	35,101	11.0
Lancashire	738,720	89,498	12.1
Warwick	192,668	37,775	19.6
Lanark (including Glasgow)	231,679	41,903	18.1
TOTAL for England, Wales, and Scotland	6,105,086	625,154	10.2

* NA, Kew: CAB 37/122/164.

Table 5.2 indicates that those areas that were predominantly rural had lower levels of recruitment in proportion to their male population of military age. All four of the areas featured in Table 5.2 supplied lower levels of recruits than the national percentage of 10.2 per cent. Cornwall was the worst offender with only 2.7 per cent of its males of military age volunteering for the army by 8 November 1914. Conversely, all of the areas featured in Table 5.3 supplied recruits well above the national percentage, Warwick being the most successful owing to the inclusion of Birmingham in its statistics.

Was there a constraint on rural men to enlist? Some farmers told their labourers that their job on the farm was just as important as soldiering. On 11 December the *Devon and Exeter Gazette* reported how a farmer's son believed that he was carrying on the business of the nation by staying at home and working on the farm, rather than enlisting. Although he loved 'his King and Country . . . his father says if he enlists he will have to sell the cattle'. Surely, according to the paper, producing food for the nation was a patriotic act in itself?[28] But industrial workers were often being told the same thing. A restriction, unique to rural areas, was the harvest which slowed enlistment rates in August and September. Billy Dixon, a labourer in Norfolk, 'joined as soon as we had finished harvest'.[29] One Cornish farmer writing to the *Royal Cornwall Gazette* claimed that 'farmers' sons were well justified in staying at home keeping things together [as] these sons are the stay of the farm, and many people forget that if we want to reap next year, the work on the farm must be accomplished in the winter'.[30] However, the disparity between levels of recruitment in primarily urban and rural areas remained similar in the period before conscription, suggesting that the harvest was not the only factor holding men back.[31]

Were lower levels of recruitment in rural areas a symptom of opposition to the war? Authorities at both local and national level were concerned about Devon's recruitment returns.[32] Certain recruiting officials believed that low recruiting levels in rural Devon equated to opposition to the war. In late August, Lord Fortescue, the Lord Lieutenant, questioned the loyalty of men from Bideford, north Devon, believing that traditions in the area were 'all against war and anything connected with it'.[33] On 18 October Stanley Jackson, from Oakleigh, Torrington, informed the Lord Lieutenant that 'after nine weeks recruiting I am pleased to state that I have had about 147 recruits for the regular army and Territorials, but regret to state that there are hundreds still in this district that will not do their duty'.[34] The Chairman of the Barnstaple Recruiting Committee told his superiors on 9 November that recruiting levels were low in the area because 'there has been a want of appreciation of the true situation, due to ignorance, a lack of loyalty and patriotism, and a disposition not to recruit unless it pays them well'.[35] On 25 November Lieutenant-Colonel Alexander, from the Recruiting Office for North Devon, wrote a concerned letter to the Town Clerk of Okehampton about the difficulty of getting recruiting posters put up in the town. He reported: 'In some instances after they had been affixed they had been torn down.'[36] This action suggests that there was opposition to recruitment. In a speech made at a recruiting meeting in Tiverton on 1 December, a local dignitary felt the need to specifically address landlords and farmers to encourage the rural community in Devon to enlist. He made an emotive appeal—again using the example of the fate of Belgium—to farmers to let their sons and labourers enlist:

---

[28] *Devon and Exeter Gazette*, 11 December 1914, 13.
[29] Alun Howkins, *Poor Labouring Men: Rural Radicalism in Norfolk, 1870–1923* (London, 1985), 116.
[30] *Royal Cornwall Gazette*, 10 December 1914.
[31] Gilbey, *The British Working Class and Enthusiasm for War, 1914–1916*, 40.
[32] DRO: Devon Parliamentary Recruiting Committee: 1262M/L153, 1 December 1914.
[33] DRO: Lord Lieutenant's Papers: 1262M/L129, 31 August 1914.
[34] DRO: Lord Lieutenant's Papers: 1262M/L129, 18 October 1914.
[35] DRO: Devon Parliamentary Recruiting Committee: 1262M/L153, 9 November 1914.
[36] DRO: Okehampton Town Council Correspondence: 3248A/13/76, 25 November 1914.

My farmer friends can plead and plead with truth that they have already made sacrifices. In various cases their sons have gone, many of their men are gone, and many a soldier's wife is living rent free in the cottage which her husband occupied before he enlisted and which his employer still generously lets her have. I do not suppose there is a farmer in the County who has not subscribed according to his means to one or more of the War funds. Many a farmer too is taking his share of the extra public work imposed on most of us by the war, and they ask how if the land is to be cultivated, how if business is to go on as usual, can we spare more labour, whether it be that of our sons or our labourers. My answer is that life is more than meat. If we cannot get men without injury to business the business must be let go. Unless we find enough men and find them quickly we shall not win, and if we fail to win our fate will be as the fate of Belgium, business will disappear, there will be no farms to till and many a family now in comfortable circumstances will be wandering homeless and ruined, suppliant for food and shelter.[37]

Edrica de la Pole, in Tremar, Devon, tried to encourage local men to enlist. She recorded in her diary on 1 September how she had started with 'Mr Bully who was taking up barley'. Despite spending fifteen minutes trying to induce him and vowing to 'give 5/Bounty to every Kingston man who would join the army before the 7 Sept [sic]', she conceded that she 'could do nothing with him'. According to the local constable 'nothing short of conscription' would bring the men from Kingston forward. However, according to de la Pole it was not opposition that made men reluctant. It was ignorance and indifference: 'the people have not the remotest conception of what their War is or signifies'.[38]

Similar opinions were echoed in Cornwall: 'owing to the fact that [rural communities] are so far from the centre of things the people do not realise the tremendous issues at stake'.[39] Yet there were also occupational and regional specific reasons for lower enlistment rates in Cornwall.[40] Rates of volunteering were low, in particular, amongst Cornish clay miners. However, this was not an expression of opposition to the war: it was a reflection of their recent interactions with the 'establishment'. Resentment was still felt for the brutal suppression of their strike the previous year. They were certainly reluctant to join up and fight a war for the authorities now. The Reverend Booth Coventry, Primitive Methodist Minister, speaking at a recruitment meeting for clay miners in November 1914 was met with shouts of 'What about twelve months ago? We don't forget', whilst other recruiting officials were forced to admit that the clay miners were still 'nursing a major grievance due to the authorities bringing in corps from outside and prepared to used martial force to break the strike'.[41] Furthermore, it is misleading to focus entirely on enlistment to the army as a measure of commitment to the war effort, particularly in the Cornish case. Many men in the county stepped forward to answer the navy's demands for recruits, believing this route to be more acceptable than joining the

---

[37] DRO: Devon Parliamentary Recruiting Committee: 1262M/L153, 1 December 1914.
[38] PWDRO: Diary of Edrica de la Pole: Acc 1306/22, 1 September 1914.
[39] *West Briton*, 20 May 1915.
[40] Dalley, 'The Response in Cornwall to the Outbreak of the First World War,' *Cornish Studies* 11 (2003), 99–105.
[41] *Cornish Guardian*, 2 October and 14 November 1914.

Table 5.4. Recruiting in proportion to population in Essex and Devon*

		Recruits Enlisted up to 12 November 1914	
Recruiting District	(A) Male pop of military age (19–38)	(B) Regulars	% of (B) to (A)
Essex	149,482	5,763	3.9
Devon	102,357	4,767	4.7
TOTAL for England, Wales, and Scotland	6,105,086	625,154	10.2

* NA, Kew: CAB 37/122/164.

army. The *West Briton* wrote of 'places in the county . . . where calls for the army are unheeded by youths and young men who are really anxious to join the Navy'. Indeed, by mid-September many believed that Cornwall's contribution to the navy was 'surpassing that of any other county in the United Kingdom in proportion to its population'.[42]

Perhaps men from rural communities, far from any sense of coastal vulnerability, with news reaching them belatedly via the local press, were less inspired to join up owing to a sense of detachment, rather than opposition, to the war. On this reasoning, however, one would expect more rural men to enlist in Essex owing to closer proximity to the war. Yet a comparison of the proportion of recruits in the male population in Essex and Devon reveals similar—low—percentages in the two cases (see Table 5.4).

A comparison of the weekly enlistment rates for Exeter and Colchester between 4 August and 31 December also suggests that the pattern of enlistment was very similar, and followed the same national peaks and troughs.[43] It does not appear that men in Essex experienced an unusually high level of enlistment just at the point when fear amongst local people was at its height in the second and third weeks of November.

However, Essex saw men enlisting at higher than usual rates to the Special Constabulary, rather than the army, in November 1914.[44] This would tally with the belief that their homes needed defending from a German threat on British, rather than French, soil. Similarly, men in Kent were caught between a desire to get the harvest in and to protect their 'front line county' from invasion, fears of which stemmed back to a sense of vulnerability felt during the Napoleonic wars. In the north of the county—the more industrial zone—men enlisted at a quicker rate than those in the south.[45] Aware of the significance of the harvest, Lord Harris, Lord

[42] *West Briton*, 7 and 14 September 1914.
[43] NA, Kew: NATS 1/398.
[44] Peter Durr, 'The Governance of Essex Police, 1880–1920' (MA, Open University, 2003), 36.
[45] Mark Connelly, *Steady the Buffs! A Regiment, a Region, and the Great War* (Oxford, 2006), 10.

Lieutenant of the County, juxtaposed it against the threat of invasion in a speech to a Canterbury recruiting meeting in early September. He asked: 'Was there anything more terrible to imagine than all the peaceful occupation of harvest being carried on with interruption, and the smiling dales and hills that made Kent so beautiful, being tarnished by the horrors of invasion?'[46] The most attractive option for many men must have been the Territorial Force, which, in early September, was not obliged to serve abroad.[47] Under-strength in the summer of 1914, the two Kent Territorial battalions were suddenly swollen by an influx of recruits following the outbreak of war. The 4th Battalion stood 1,300 strong by early September. In the case of Essex, a high proportion of men also joined the Territorial Forces in 1914, 38 per cent compared to the 28 per cent nationally in 1914. Many men from the south-east of England might have regarded the Territorials as a compromise: a good way of combining their domestic work lives and farm commitments with honourable national service.[48] This would explain the low levels of volunteering to the regular army without dismissing the depth of fears felt about invasion in the area in 1914.

Men also enlisted because of a sense of commitment to their local community. The recruiting campaign was particularly successful amongst mining communities. According to one survey, 115,000 members of the Miners' Federation of Great Britain volunteered at the outbreak of war.[49] This represented 15 per cent of the membership of the Union.[50] The highest rates were in Glamorgan, Durham, Northumberland, and in some Scottish coalfields, where pre-war industrial militancy had been pronounced. Despite their recent turbulent history, large numbers of miners in South Wales enlisted. Miners formed the majority of the 1st and 2nd Rhondda Pals battalions of the Welsh Regiment and of the 1st and 2nd Gwent's of the South Wales Borderers.[51] Oliver Powell, a Tredegar miner, recalled how 'scores and scores' of his fellow miners enlisted because the Tredegar Company offered to pay a hefty separation allowance to their wives.[52] On 6 November the *Western Mail* reported:

> Recruits are pouring in at the rate of between 80 and 100 a day . . . close upon 300 miners have already been enrolled from the Rhymney Valley into the Rhondda Battalion, whilst it is estimated that up to date over 1,600 employees of the Powell Duffryn Colliery Co., have joined the colours.[53]

---

[46] *Kentish Gazette*, 5 September 1914.

[47] Ian Beckett, 'The Territorial Force', in *A Nation in Arms: A Social Study of the British Army in the First World War*, ed. I. F. W. Beckett and Keith Simpson (Manchester, 1985), 127–64.

[48] Connelly, *Steady the Buffs! A Regiment, a Region, and the Great War.* 10.

[49] Board of Trade, *Report of the Departmental Committee Appointed to Inquire into the Conditions Prevailing in the Coal-Mining Industry due to the War*, Session 1914–1916, Vol. XXVIII, Cd. 7939.

[50] R. Page Arnot, *The Miners: Years of Struggle, A History of the Miners' Federation of Great Britain (from 1910 onwards)* (London, 1953), 60.

[51] Mark David Price, 'The Labour Movement and Patriotism in the South Wales Coalfield during the First World War: The Case of Vernon Hartshorn, 1914–15' (MA, University of Wales, Aberystwyth, 1999), 16.

[52] SWML, HH: SWCC AUD/271: Len Jeffreys (1972). SWML: HH: SWCC AUD/316: Oliver Powell (1973).

[53] *Western Mail*, 6 November 1914.

According to Len Jeffreys, in Cross Keys, Newtown, there was a general acceptance among the miners in his village about the need to enlist: 'only individuals here and there' opposed the war.[54] Fred Morris, a Maerdy miner, joined up 'to get out of [mining] . . . mostly escapism . . . I wanted to be like the others, my brother was out there see.'[55] On 24 August *The Times* commented on how Welsh miners showed no hesitation in joining the forces.[56] Whilst unemployment and a desire to escape the mines contributed to the willingness of miners to enlist, sentiments about nation and empire, stemming from a sense of duty to their community, encouraged miners to volunteer.

One of the most striking features of enlistment in the first year of the war was 'the extent to which the recruiting drive tapped powerful sentiments of loyalty felt by men, whatever the occupation, to town, county, or community'.[57] Men volunteered with their friends, family, and colleagues to form the locally raised 'Pals' Battalions. General Henry Rawlinson, Director General of Recruiting, initially suggested that men would be more willing to join up if they could serve with people they already knew. Lord Derby was the first to test the idea when he announced at a recruiting meeting in Liverpool on 28 August that he would try to raise a battalion in Liverpool, comprised solely of local men. Within days, Liverpool had enlisted enough men to form four battalions. A number of 'Pals' battalions were composed mainly of middle-class men, originating from the schools they attended. But many were made up of working-class men. Other units were formed among men with common experiences and loyalties. In late November eleven members of the Heart of Midlothian football team volunteered for the army.[58] Edwin Yates, a solicitor in Darwen, Lancashire, established a 'Bantam' Battalion consisting of clerical men aged forty to forty-five who were under the regulation size of five feet three inches in height, but otherwise fit for service.[59] A sense of community was also inherent to the locally raised Territorial battalions, initially raised for home defence in the pre-war period. Members of the Liverpool Territorials shared 'a middle-class web of sociability' in which members not only frequently worked together and lived in the same districts of the city, but took part in communal leisure activities and often worshipped at the same churches.[60] The power of local identities was recognized by the War Office, both as a recruitment tool and as a means of maintaining troop morale at the front, and it attempted to preserve the regional identity of the British army as far as possible.

Community affiliation did not always result in enlistment. Despite optimistic reports in the press, between August and December the actual numbers of men responding was proportionally less in Welsh-speaking than in English-speaking

---

[54] SWML, HH: SWCC AUD/271: Len Jeffreys (1972).
[55] SWML, HH: SWCC AUD/192: Mr and Mrs Fred Morris (1973).
[56] *The Times*, 24 August 1914, 2.
[57] Winter, *The Great War and the British People*, 30.
[58] *Edinburgh Evening News*, 26 November 1914, 5.
[59] Liddle: DF 146: Edwin Yates, 29 August 1914.
[60] McCartney, *Citizen Soldiers: The Liverpool Territorials in the First World War* (Cambridge, 2005), 26.

parts of Wales.[61] By 31 August 7,612 men had volunteered in Wales; up to the same point 34,760 men had volunteered in London, 8,722 in Birmingham, and 8,003 in Manchester.[62] This proportionally lower figure was an early indication of a trend that was to continue throughout the first two years of the war.[63]

This is despite the fact that appeals for recruits were tailored towards regional audiences; in theory, Scottish and Welsh identities were accommodated within the boundaries of the United Kingdom. On 22 September, Lord Rosebery, Lord Lieutenant of Linlithgowshire, told potential volunteers residing in the parishes of Currie and Colinton, Midlothian, that if they fought against 'this wicked and dangerous foe' they would be welcomed home 'as were the heroes of Bannockburn', a reference to the fourteenth-century Scottish victory in the Wars of Scottish Independence.[64] The creation of the 38th (Welsh) Division attempted to entice Welsh volunteers by meeting their linguistic and religious needs.[65] On 19 September, Lloyd George had drawn on his Welsh roots in his speech to Welshmen at the Queen's Hall, London. He called for a:

Welsh Army in the Field. I should like to see the race who faced the Normans for hundreds of years in a struggle for freedom, the race that helped to win Crecy, the race that fought for a generation under Glendower, against the greatest captain in Europe— I should like to see that race go and give a taste of its quality in this great struggle in Europe. And they are going to do it.[66]

Drawing comparisons between Wales and Belgium, he proclaimed that the 'world owed much to the little five-foot-five nations'.[67] Ellis Griffith, Chairman of the Welsh Parliamentary Party and Parliamentary Secretary to the Home Office, told an Aberystwyth audience in October that 'they were fighting for Wales on the plains of France'.[68] In Welsh-speaking communities the campaign was delivered primarily in Welsh. Public meetings were conducted in Welsh, bilingual forms were issued for some administrative functions, and patriotic literature and posters were usually published in both languages. In addition, speakers referred to a Welsh military tradition. At times this could backfire. On one occasion the *Western Mail* published extracts of speeches by Welsh military leaders from earlier periods, not realizing they were with reference to a war against the English.[69] Yet the aim was clear. By playing upon the regional identities of potential recruits, the moral

---

[61] By 12 November 1914, 10.1 per cent of England's male population of military age had enlisted compared with 11.9 per cent of Scottish males and 8.9 per cent of Welsh males. See NA, Kew: CAB 37/122/164, 12 November 1914. See also Cyril Parry, 'Gwynedd and the Great War, 1914–1918', *Welsh History Review* 14 (1988), 88.

[62] NLW: Welsh Army Corps: WAC C12/30 and NA, Kew: NATS 1/398.

[63] Barlow, 'Some Aspects of the Experiences of Carmarthenshire in the Great War', 27.

[64] St Deiniol's Library, Hawarden: WW1 Pamphlet Collection: Box A: *War! 'A Fight to the Finish' A Martial Call to the Scots by Lord Rosebery* (1914).

[65] Morgan, '"Christ and the War": Some Aspects of the Welsh Experience, 1914–1918', *Journal of Welsh Religious History* 5 (1997), 75.

[66] *The Times*, 20 September 1914, 3.

[67] Ibid.

[68] Cited in Kenneth O Morgan, *Wales in British Politics, 1868–1922* (Cardiff, 1970), 275.

[69] Parry, 'Gwynedd and the Great War, 1914–1918', 86–7.

foundations of the war were made more accessible. Recounting earlier victories of local warriors, and promising a local identity on the fighting front, gave a sense of historical continuity and inarguable duty to the call to arms of 1914. However, despite speeches in both English and Welsh from local dignitaries and religious leaders, recruitment remained sluggish in Welsh-speaking areas.[70]

Lower recruiting figures in Carmarthenshire were a combination of a feeling of rural detachment from the war and inadequate machinery to deal with the recruits who were making themselves available. It was reported that in Llanelli, recruiting had been hampered because a recruiting officer did not arrive in the town until 10 August.[71] Recruiting was also low in Cardiganshire, and on 9 September the local MP, Vaughan Davies, attributed this to a general lack of enthusiasm to Kitchener's appeal for men. At first glance the war does appear to be at odds with the Nonconformist, pacifist values prevalent in much of Welsh society during the period. However, as mentioned earlier, prominent Nonconformists lent their support to the war effort and rallied for men to enlist from the pulpits and the recruiting platforms. Overall, English-speaking Welsh seem to have strongly supported the war. The more anglicized the individual in Wales was in culture and speech, the more readily he could identify with the war and endorse the government's policies.[72] But native Welsh-speakers found this more difficult, and as a result were more apathetic in their response to volunteering.[73] One author from rural Anglesey felt that 'soldiers and armies and all things military were distant and alien to us at the time, they belonged to the English and the making of war was England's work with us hearing of her achievements'.[74] This sense of detachment was reflected in recruitment statistics.

MOTIVATIONS AND REACTIONS

Recruitment in 1914 was more than simply the product of patriotism and naïve idealism.[75] A variety of complex and nuanced social, political, and economic factors encouraged men to enlist. This is not to deny that for many men part, or all, of their decision to enlist was due to a sense of patriotism and duty— whether that duty was to their country, their community, their religion, their friends, their womenfolk, or a combination. The men who volunteered were products of Edwardian society and believed that Britain was the best country in the world and needed defending. This is what they had been taught at school. Add to these values a widespread indignation at Germany's behaviour in France and

---

[70] See, for example, the experience in Aberystwyth: Roynon, ed., *Home Fires Burning: The Great War Diaries of Georgina Lee* (Stroud, 2006), 33.
[71] Bailow, 'Some Aspects of the Experiences of Carmarthenshire in the Great War', 27.
[72] Parry, 'Gwynedd and the Great War, 1914–1918', 80.
[73] *North Wales Observer and Express*, 4 September 1914.
[74] Ifan Gruffydd (1963) cited in Parry, 'Gwynedd and the Great War, 1914–1918', 80.
[75] Ferguson, *The Pity of War* (London, 1999), 198–211, Simkins, *Kitchener's Army: The Raising of the New Armies 1914–1916*, 167–75.

Belgium and many men were spurred on to enlist to restore the right order to the world, with Britain victorious and superior. Frank L. Watson volunteered because 'the Germans were in Belgium, their presence threatened England, and no one suggested any other way of getting them out except by force'.[76] In a letter to his father dated 31 August, Bruce Baily, in London, assured him that 'nothing would please me better than to die fighting for my country'.[77] Corporal Upton, encamped in Aldershot in December, believed that it was his Christian duty to enlist: 'I think it is the duty of every young man who has a spark of Christianity in him to take up arms against the Germans'.[78] Harry Wight, serving with the 2nd Battalion Border Regiment, told his fiancée Alice, as he was sailing from Southampton to France on 6 December, that he was 'very proud tonight because I am ready and I am proud to think you are willing to let me go . . . I am quite happy when I have you to look to and protect and love'.[79] Alfred Chater, a Territorial, tried to console his girlfriend, Joy, over his decision, in August, to serve abroad with the 28th Battalion London Regiment:

> Old girl, you probably know that I'm not one of those adventurous sportsmen who are always on for this kind of thing—but I am convinced now—though I was not until a few days ago—that it is the plain duty of each man who can to go out if called upon. It is true that one is asked to go beyond the conditions of one's service but there is no doubt that it is a case of absolute necessity.[80]

Robert Graves was outraged to read about the German atrocities in Belgium, and even though he discounted 'twenty percent', he enlisted and began training on 11 August.[81] The national cause, perceptions of the enemy, an awareness of the realities of war, and fears for Britain's survival all contributed to why men were willing to volunteer for the army.

However, men who did join up in 1914 did so for a variety of reasons inclusive, or exclusive, of patriotism. Some men enlisted in 1914 owing to pragmatic reasons, their friends, and the thrill of adventure and new experiences, amongst many other factors. Of course, the contemporary patriotism may have been edited out of the remembering over the years. Norman Ellison, from West Kirby, Cheshire, volunteered with the King's Liverpool Regiment on 10 August 'most certainly not "to guarantee the integrity of Belgium", nor ultra patriotic motives . . . it was the chance of adventure, of getting out of a rut'.[82] There was often an economic enticement to enlist. Jim Davies 'couldn't get in the army quick enough' because he was going 'to get a shilling a day'.[83] Alfred Woodcock recalled in 1982 how his friend Bill Rymel, from Birmingham, enlisted because 'he was out of work at the

[76] C. B. Purdon, ed., *Everyman at War: Sixty Personal Narratives of the War* (London, 1930), 55.
[77] IWM, Docs: Baily, Captain Bruce W. Seymour: 03/16/1, 31 August 1914.
[78] Liddle: DF 017: Mr and Mrs Cyrus Brady, 7 December 1914.
[79] Liddle: GS 1732: H.R. Wight, 6 December 1914.
[80] IWM, Docs: Chater, Captain A.D.: 87/56/1, August 1914.
[81] These comments also survived Graves' edited reprint that first appeared in 1957. See Robert Graves, *Goodbye To All That* (London, 2000), 60–2.
[82] IWM, Docs: Ellison, Norman F.: DS/MISC/49 (1958).
[83] IWM: 9750, Reel 2 (n.d.).

time and he'd got no home life'.[84] Victor Woolley, from Sutton Coldfield, decided to enlist along with three friends on 4 August because 'they were older and decided to go [so] I . . . decided to join them'.[85] James Bennett volunteered because he was attracted by romantic ideas about war and chivalry: 'the idea of mounting a horse and wielding a sword and winning all sorts of medals'.[86] Home pressures also encouraged men to volunteer. Men enlisted through fear of being labelled anti-patriotic or 'shirkers'. Harry Siepman enlisted in the Royal Field Artillery to avoid suspicion as he was the son of a German.[87] Malcolm Hancock felt 'very conspicu-ous' as a civilian and did not want to be labelled a 'scab'.[88] Alan Dorward, although eventually deemed unfit for active service, was keen to enlist because 'people may think me a "skulker" not to be fighting'.[89] When he was told that he could never serve he recorded in his diary: 'Others will have to do the fighting for me. I am only a weakling. It is humiliating'.[90] Being unable to enlist made him feel effeminate and less of a man.

The experience of volunteering involved all members of society regardless of gender, and also of class and age. Whilst some men enlisted out of a desire to protect their wives, mothers, sisters, and daughters, women were actively involved in encouraging men to enlist—or publicly humiliating them if they did not. Young women began distributing white feathers to 'young men found lolling on the beach and the promenades' at Deal, Kent, at the beginning of September.[91] When Edrica de la Pole heard that a local Devonshire shopkeeper had refused to allow her son to enlist, she closed her account and gave her work to 'a woman who has a son in one or other [regiment]'.[92] These women may have had no male relatives of military age and were emotionally distanced from the process of enlistment. Or perhaps these women had already sent men off, and felt that it was only fair that this sacrifice was shared equally. Enlistment of a man in a familial or social circle also reflected positively on a woman's commitment to the war effort.[93] Hallie Eustace Miles utilized her influence in London's catering industry to get the same song 'sung at different Restaurants by way of getting more "loafers" to enlist'.[94] Iris Holt wrote to her fiancé on 30 August, telling him how she had convinced two men to enlist because all her 'men friends have either gone or enlisted' and she felt it was her duty

[84] City Sound Archives, Birmingham Museum: R167-168 (1982).
[85] City Sound Archives, Birmingham Museum: R89 (1981).
[86] NWSA: 1985.0020: James Bennett (n.d.).
[87] Liddle: GS 1469: Harry A. Siepman (n.d.).
[88] IWM: 7396, Reel 1 (n.d.).
[89] University of Liverpool, Special Collections: Dorward Diaries, Diary 10: D446/10/10, 25–7 August 1914.
[90] University of Liverpool, Special Collections: Dorward Diaries, Diary 10: D446/10/10, 28–9 August 1914.
[91] *The Times*, 2 September 1914, 3, cited in Douglas, 'Voluntary Enlistment in the First World War and the Work of the Parliamentary Recruiting Committee', *Journal of Modern History* 42, no. 4 (1970), 569, Nicoletta F. Gullace, 'White Feathers and Wounded Men: Female Patriotism and the Memory of the Great War', *Journal of British Studies* 36 (1997).
[92] PWDRO: Diary of Edrica de la Pole: Acc 1306/22, 1 September 1914.
[93] Liddle: GS 0861: Major General D.G. Johnson, 16 September 1914.
[94] Miles, *Untold Tales of War-Time London: A Personal Diary* (London, 1930), 22.

to encourage them.[95] The following month she told him how proud she was that she did not have 'a single friend or relation eligible to serve who is not doing'.[96] On 6 November William Watkin Davies recorded in his diary how his sister Ceri was 'devoting herself with energy to the double task of knitting garments for those who have enlisted, and of making life unpleasant for those who have not'.[97]

These reasons are not exhaustive. Others include familial pressure because of other relatives already in the BEF, escape from the police, pressure from employers and social superiors, and, even, being drunk. Indeed 'the factors which impelled so many to enlist were as diverse as the recruits themselves. Probably only a small number had a single overriding motive for enlistment, most recruits being driven to join by a combination of external pressures and personal desires and loyalties'.[98] Allowance must be made for the fact that some men volunteered impulsively, with little thought of the consequences of their actions.[99]

Clearly, there is not one overriding reason why men joined the army in 1914. Consequently, it cannot be argued that men enlisted in a wave of naïve enthusiasm for war. Statements such as 'thousands joined up in a holiday spirit and with an entirely unfounded conviction that the war would end by Christmas' do not stand up against the evidence.[100] Positive 'pull' factors such as excitement, a sense of adventure, desire to be with friends, and pride in one's country worked in tandem with negative 'push' factors such as guilt and pressure from women and employers. Many of the latter reasons involved external forces, which perhaps removes the 'voluntary' component from the equation. Social and economic compulsion cancels some of the freedom of choice which symbolizes the true 'volunteer'.[101] However, it might be more accurate to suggest that in 1914 there was an 'internalized compulsion' which combined personal reasons and external pressures to conform in the only acceptable answer—volunteering—to a complicated and emotional decision.

For those men who enlisted because of patriotism, it should be noted that 'love of country' was not a form of national hysteria or jingoism. It was a considered, reflective sense of obligation. This is expressed in a letter from Robert Graves, stationed at Wrexham Barracks with the Royal Welch Fusiliers on 25 October. Having seen the latest 'awful' casualty list of his old school, Charterhouse, he began to question why he had enlisted: 'I can't imagine why I joined: not for sentiment or patriotism certainly . . . France is the only place for a gentleman now, principles or no principles'.[102] The bulk of Kitchener's volunteers were motivated by a sense of well-considered duty and necessity, not excitement and an impulsive desire to fight. Soon after applying for a commission on 10 August the poet Charles Sorley wrote

---

[95] Liddle: AIR 224: A.H. Morton, 30 August 1914.
[96] Liddle: AIR 224: A.H. Morton, September 1914.
[97] NLW: W. Watkin Davies: 47, 6 November 1914.
[98] Simkins, *Kitchener's Army: The Raising of the New Armies 1914–1916*, 185.
[99] Avner Offer, 'Going to War in 1914: A Matter of Honour?', *Politics and Society* 23 (1995), 232.
[100] Winter, *The Great War and the British People*, 29.
[101] Young, 'Voluntary Recruitment in Scotland, 1914–1916', 16–17.
[102] IWM, Docs: Robert Graves: Special Miscellaneous: Spec Misc M4, 25 October 1914.

from Cambridge: 'I could wager that out of twelve million eventual combatants there aren't twelve who really want it. And "serving one's country" is so unpicturesque and unheroic when it comes to the point'.[103] Sorley appeared to understand the realities of war: that millions of men would be required; that much of their hoped 'adventure' would be monotonous and hard; and that despite not really wanting war, they would go anyway. Volunteering for war in 1914 did not, therefore, equate to war enthusiasm.

If the evidence above suggests that the volunteers' motives were more complex than simple enthusiasm, then the reaction of parents, partners, children, and friends to the decision of 'their man' to enlist compounds this argument. No one was left untouched. For Queen Mary, even before war had been declared, the prospect of her 19-year-old son Bertie fighting with the 1st Battle Fleet of the Royal Navy 'was not an agreeable thought'.[104] Her anxiety was shared by her husband, the King. On 4 August he recorded in his diary 'Please God [the war] may be soon over and that he will protect dear Bertie's life'.[105] On 7 August Rudyard Kipling wrote to H. A. Gwynne telling him that his son John had enlisted with the Territorials. 'It's a bit of a wrench', Kipling wrote, 'but I don't see what else can be done'.[106] On 21 August Linster Tully, in Peckham, wrote to his mother to inform her that he had joined the army that morning and apologized for not seeking her consent beforehand. At the top of the letter, his mother wrote 'My heart is broken'.[107] Two days before war was officially declared, Dorothy Holman, a young woman in Teignmouth, Devon, reacted with dread to the announcement that England would require 'a million volunteer soldiers'; on those estimations the war would affect 'the nearest and dearest of everyone'. The next day both she and her mother burst into tears at the news that Tommy (Dorothy's brother), a pre-war soldier, would be going straight to the front.[108] Her reactions were not simply the result of tension leading up to the outbreak of war; when Dorothy heard the news that another male relative was off to France on 18 September, she cried 'off and on all the morning'.[109]

For many, the moment of departure was also distressing. Mr S. H. Ratcliff recalled the memory of seeing the wives of naval personnel returning from Sheerness Pier, Kent, after saying goodbye to their husbands on 6 August 1914:

> They were slowly returning to their homes. Mainly they were quiet, a few were crying and one or two talking in that artificially loud voice indicative of emotional strain; but most were walking in silence. These women wore tightly buttoned-up pale faces from which all blood and animation seemed to have been drained... This was my first personal experience of the human tragedies of war.[110]

[103] Wilson, ed., *The Collected Letters of Charles Hamilton Sorley* (London, 1990), 184–5.
[104] Royal Archives, Windsor Castle: RA QM/PRIV/CC26/95, 28 July 1914.
[105] Royal Archives, Windsor Castle: RA GV/PRIV/GVD/1914: 4 August 1914.
[106] Pinney, ed., *The Letters of Rudyard Kipling* (London, 1999), 251.
[107] Liddle: GS 1634: C.L. Tully, 21 August 1914.
[108] DRO: Dorothy Holman: 3830M/F9, 2–3 August 1914.
[109] DRO: Dorothy Holman: 3830M/F9, 18 September 1914.
[110] ERO: T/Z 25/618 (1966).

Fig. 5.2. Departure of British troops from Sutton Coldfield station, Birmingham, 1914
Birmingham City Archives ZZ/65b/348217, p. 48, Photo 45. Reproduced with the permission of Birmingham
Libraries and Archives.

Figure 5.2 depicts women and children waving goodbye to soldiers of the Royal
Warwickshire Regiment as they departed from Sutton Coldfield Station, Birmingham in 1914. Although it is difficult to determine individual reactions, there is little
evidence of celebration amongst the gathered crowd: no Union Jacks, military
bands, or local dignitaries appear in the picture. It would seem that although the
men are being waved off with a smile, the scene is not one of enthusiasm or
festivity.

On 5 and 6 August Reverend James Mackay comforted women and soldiers at
Newcastle-upon-Tyne railway station as they said their farewells:

> The sights are heartrending. Weeping women and children are everywhere. There is no
> cheering no great ovations no wild enthusiasm just a great stricken mass of humanity
> broken hearted as a mother who has lost her only child . . . There is an occasional cheer
> but for the most part things are very grave . . . [A] picture of deep sorrow.[111]

Noel Chavasse, the son of the Bishop of Liverpool, and encamped at Tunbridge
Wells awaiting his orders to depart for the front, described the scenes of departure
to his parents on 29 October:

---

[111] IWM, Docs: Mackay, Reverend James: Box 74/135/1, 5 and 6 August 1914.

They certainly bring before one pretty vividly the tragic side of war. Wherever I go I see little parties of [soldiers] and generally a huge kilted man. On one side of him a small mother, evidently on the verge of tears, and on the other side a stoutish middle-aged father puffing furiously at pipe or cigar and also evidently very much upset. One poor old man has hung about the empty house we live in for 3 days waiting for a chance to see his son . . . Every one of the parents is bearing up wonderfully and all seem quite satisfied that their sons should go but I think the sight of people bearing up well to be one of the most depressing I have yet struck.[112]

Other heart-rending scenes of departure were recorded in Essex, Huddersfield, Sunderland, Argyllshire, Monmouthshire, London, and Manchester.[113] On 10 December a woman died at Peebles North British Station in the Scottish Borders. She had desperately held onto her husband's hand (who was departing with the King's Own Scottish Borderers) as the train pulled out and had stumbled, been dragged five yards under the train, and killed.[114]

***

Without volunteers, Britain could not have fulfilled its military commitment to its allies and its own defence. The fundamental originality of the United Kingdom's war effort (unlike the continental powers or Britain in the Second World War) was that it consisted of a mass volunteer army for the first half of the war. The experience of volunteering did not only concern men. Women encouraged men to enlist, and sometimes sought to restrain them. They agonized over the decision of their husband, son, father, brother, fiancé, or lover to go to war and endured the pain of separation. Children, too, felt the loss of their adult menfolk, whether father, brother, or teacher. The motives of the volunteers cannot be summarized in the monolithic term 'enthusiasm' any more than they can be put down to economic constraint or opportunism. The reality was much more complex. It was grounded in the men's perceptions of the national cause, the nature of the enemy, and the necessities of modern warfare. It was also rooted in the geography and social make-up of the many communities from which they came.

Where did the volunteers go? Whilst Christmas 1914 is often associated with the 'truce' on the Western Front between some German and Allied soldiers, the experience that winter for the bulk of the new British army was life under canvas across the United Kingdom as it underwent training and conversion into a real fighting force before being sent overseas. Whilst the Germans were digging in on the Western Front, their future British opponents were still an army in waiting. They would encounter each other *en masse* only at the Battle of the Somme in 1916. But in 1914, no one's horizons extended that far.

---

[112] MPP Bodleian: Noel Chavasse Chavasse Dep 6, ll. 13–16, 29 October 1914.
[113] ERO: T/Z 25/675 (1966), Liddle: DF Recollections: Box J-M: Mrs E. Mann (1984), Liddle: DF Recollections: Box D-I: Margaret Grocock (n.d.), Liddle: DF Recollections: Box A-C: Dr A.M Campbell (n.d.), NLW: Idris Davies: Mss 22412, ff. 4–10 (n.d.), Miles, *Untold Tales of War-Time London: A Personal Diary*, 18., and IWM, Docs: Higson, Edward Jarman: 01/45/1 (2000).
[114] *Edinburgh Evening News*, 11 December 1914, 5.

6

John Bull's Other Island[1]

When the British government declared war on Germany, the Ulster unionist and Irish nationalist paramilitary organizations faced each other warily, while the British troops in Ireland had demonstrated that they were not prepared to enforce the wishes of their government.[2] Whilst in Britain the labour and suffragette movements had agreed to temporarily suspend their causes and rally behind the national effort for the duration of the war, such loyalty was not guaranteed in Ireland. If any group was going to cause trouble for the United Kingdom's entry into war, it would be nationalist Ireland, rather than the loyal and conformist Ulster unionists, and it is this group that receives most attention in this chapter. Would civil war still erupt? Would mobilized paramilitaries lay down their arms? Would Germany replace Britain as the enemy for nationalists? How would nationalist Ireland respond to Britain's rally-cry to unite behind the war effort? Ultimately, how unified was the United Kingdom of Britain and Ireland in the late summer and autumn of 1914?

---

[1] Bernard Shaw, *John Bull's other island; and Major Barbara; also How he lied to her husband* (London, 1907).

[2] A number of terms are used consistently throughout this chapter and are defined below:

- *Ulster Volunteers:* Created in January 1913, during the third Home Rule crisis, to coordinate the paramilitary activities of Ulster unionists.
- *Nationalists:* Irish nationalists of any faction or party.
- *Redmondite:* Exponents of a specific rhetoric, 'Redmondism', primarily used by the Irish party's leader, John Redmond, advocating support for the Empire and the war, and conciliation with unionists.
- *Irish National Volunteers:* The nationalist Volunteer movement of 1913–1914, prior to its split in September 1914.
- *National Volunteers:* Those who remained loyal to Redmond after the split.
- *Advanced nationalists:* Those nationalists who opposed Redmond's war policy. Many would have been supportive of Eoin MacNeill and the Irish Volunteers post-September 1914. Sometimes referred to as 'extreme' nationalists.
- *Irish Volunteers:* Those Volunteers who, following the split, supported Eoin MacNeill, opposing Redmond's war policy.

THE ONSET OF WAR

Unsurprisingly, European affairs were of even less prominence in Ireland than Britain, owing to the pre-war domestic situation. Although the assassination of Archduke Franz Ferdinand on 28 June was condemned as a 'foul deed' by the *Cork Examiner*, the majority of Irish newspapers considered it an internal Austro-Hungarian affair.[3] Very quickly the event was overshadowed by the machinations and ramifications of the Home Rule Bill. On 31 July news of the European situation was still less important than the news of the shootings on Bachelor's Walk.[4] Around this time the 1st Bedfordshire Regiment were moved from Armagh to Mullingar. Sheldon Gledstanes, serving in the Regiment, described to his father how 'the inhabitants here [Mullingar] refuse to believe there is any chance of war and think we have come back to keep them in order'.[5]

Reality began to sink in when military precautions were set in place and mobilization orders for naval and garrison reserves were sent out on 29 July. The following day the mass movement of troops began and the Admiralty took over Cork Harbour (Queenstown). These visible changes fuelled speculation over the war. According to Wesley Frost, the American Consul in Cork, at this moment 'the disquiet in connection with the Irish troubles...has suddenly been rendered inconspicuous by the international situation arising from the Austro-Servian War'.[6] As in Britain, opinion began to change noticeably over the Bank Holiday weekend. People were anxious and confused about what the future held. On 3 August in a letter to Joseph McGarrity, the Clann na nGael leader in America, Pádraig Pearse wrote: 'Heaven knows what the future holds if England is drawn into this European war.'[7] Kevin O'Sheil, in Dublin, recalled how 'by the first week of August, events that we had hardly noticed had plunged Germany, France, Russia, Austria, and Servia into war'.[8] No more than in Britain was there a desire for war. Dr Dowse, the Church of Ireland Bishop of Cork, said 'This war was not of our asking. It was thrust upon us.'[9] In early August, Captain George Berkeley, military instructor of a company of INV in Belfast, felt that with the threat of war the world had gone mad: 'Almost 10 million men shooting each other without having the slightest quarrel. Perfectly insane'.[10] Prior to the official declaration of war, the majority of Irish people hoped that it would be avoided.

[3] *Cork Examiner*, 30 June 1914.
[4] IWM, Docs: Kirkpatrick, Sir Ivone: 79/50/1, 31 July 1914.
[5] Liddle: GS 0633: Sheldon A. Gledstanes, early August 1914.
[6] National Archives of the United States, Maryland Campus: American Consulate, Cork: M367, Roll 12 (763.72/421), 31 July 1914.
[7] Séamas Ó Buachalla, ed., *The Letters of P. H. Pearse* (Gerrards Cross, 1980), 324.
[8] NA, Dublin: BMH Witness Statements: Kevin O'Sheil: WS 1,770 (n.d.).
[9] *Cork Constitution*, 13 August 1914.
[10] NLI: George Berkeley letters: Ms 13,266/1, 4 August 1914.

Across the United Kingdom 4 August was a momentous day and Ireland was no exception. Newspapers were devoured and many people were delighted by Sir Edward Grey's reference on 3 August to Ireland being the 'one bright spot' in the whole 'terrible situation'.[11] The outbreak of war came as a shock. According to Kevin O'Sheil 'the idea of such a war struck us as fantastic and, indeed, ludicrous . . . It was almost as incredible as though we had heard that man had reverted to cannibalism'.[12] Yet many people felt that the war was necessary. The veteran nationalist MP and infighter Timothy Healy, told his brother Maurice (independent nationalist MP for Cork City) on 4 August: 'I don't think the government have any option save to support France . . . if Germany were victorious, and they remained neutral now, they would be in a pretty pickle at the end of the war'.[13] There was, however, one distinctive feature of Irish responses: war abroad meant peace at home. It is one of the paradoxes of modern Irish history that the outbreak of war in Europe may have prevented civil war in Ireland in 1914.[14] In consequence, the war was greeted with a short-lived sense of relief. On 4 August George Berkeley confided in his diary that the outbreak of war 'meant *peace*'.[15] To his wife, on the same day, he added 'I feel far more at ease now' that the threat of fratricidal conflict had been defused.[16]

As in Britain, the Irish landscape changed immediately. One witness described 'bewildering changes . . . in rapid confusing succession' in his home town of Cappoquin, County Waterford.[17] In Cork, holidaymakers were warned to steer clear of fortifications being erected at the harbour. Soldiers were sent to guard coastal areas, and towns and bridges were put under police guard.[18] By 8 August the football and cricket fields and tennis courts in Newbridge, County Kildare, were all being utilized by the army for commandeered horses.[19] In Dublin, wireless telegraphy equipment was dismantled and shipowners were notified that their vessels could be commandeered at any moment.[20] There was an element of panic in some of these preparations. Three City of Cork Steam Packet Company's vessels had shots fired across their bows from Fort Camden as they entered Cork harbour.[21]

Between 30,000 and 40,000 British soldiers were stationed in Ireland in 1914, and by 22 August most had embarked from Irish ports for the continent or England. Special trains from all over Ireland transported men to the docks in Cork, Dublin, and Belfast where ships were earmarked to take the troops directly

[11] Great Britain, Parliamentary Debates, Commons, Fifth Series, Vol. LXV, 1914, 1809, 3 August 1914.
[12] NA, Dublin: BMH Witness Statements: Kevin O'Sheil: WS 1,770 (n.d.).
[13] Frank Callanan, *T. M. Healy* (Cork, 1996), 506.
[14] Timothy Bowman, 'Composing Divisions: The Recruitment of Ulster and National Volunteers into the British Army in 1914', *Causeway* 2 (1995), 26.
[15] NLI: George Berkeley diary: Ms 10,923, 4 August 1914.
[16] NLI: George Berkeley letters: Ms 13,266/1, 4 August 1914.
[17] NA, Dublin: BMH Witness Statements: Michael O'Donoghue: WS 1,741 (n.d.).
[18] *Cork Examiner*, 1 and 3 August 1914.
[19] Liddle: GS 0445: Walter Edward Denney, 8 August 1914.
[20] NLI: A Dubliner's Diary: MS 9,620, 5 August 1914.
[21] National Archives of the United States, Maryland Campus: American Consulate, Cork: M367, Roll 12 (763.72/421), 31 July 1914.

to France.[22] Changes were particularly noticeable, therefore, in areas where these men mobilized and departed. On 15 August, as ships departed down the Liffey River in Dublin, transporting troops to the front, Thomas King Moylan, a lunactic asylum clerk, recorded how 'the fog horns and sirens of every vessel were blown, making a most heart rending wail ... Last night the hooting was kept up almost continuously between 6 o'clock and 9.' He observed the irony that whilst the newspapers were trying to keep troop movements secret, the sounds of the departing ships gave the game away.[23] In Dublin 'tangible and unmistakable signs' of the war's 'ugly reality' were all around.[24] George Duggan, a civil servant in Dublin Castle in 1914, recalled, in early August, 'the Man-of-War Roads in Dublin Bay. There lay at anchor five or six transports shortly to sail with horse and troops from Ireland to France. War had already stretched out its hand this far.'[25] The roads, streets, and railways were crowded with soldiers and sailors on their way to barracks or to entrain at stations, and reservists on their way to rejoin the colours. Gearoid Ua h-Uallachain[26] was working at the Dublin Port and Docks Board Power Station. As soon as Britain declared war on Germany, the port became a hive of industry:

> It was stated at the time that Dublin was only second to Southampton in the facilities for the rapid dispatch of troops. There was a military guard placed on the power-station at once and nobody was allowed on the North Wall extension or Alexandra Wharf without a permit or for business reasons. Troops started to arrive from all parts of the country, horse, foot and artillery, and I was working almost continuously for the first week. I had to stand by in case the electric cranes would break down. I also fitted a telephone on the top of the 100-ton crane at the point of the North Wall, so that a watch could be kept for submarines ... The number of men who went away was colossal. You can judge the congestion of traffic when you think that men who left the Curragh Camp at six o'clock in the morning did not reach Dublin until evening [a distance of approximately forty miles], and did not sail until perhaps three o'clock the following morning. They were carried away in the mail boats and in liners escorted by destroyers. There would be troops packed everywhere, in the lifeboats, on the bridge, from stem to stern. All the other ships in the harbour would blow their sirens, while everybody sang *Rule Britannia, Britannia Rules the Waves* and *God Save the King* ... During this week the Army authorities went round the different firms in the city and commandeered the best horses available for war work. There was hardly a family in Dublin that was not affected, with the exception of the extreme Nationalists, and even these were affected in some cases.[27]

Eyewitness accounts of the type of send-off British troops received as they left Ireland during the first weeks of war counter post-war myths about negative Irish reactions to the outbreak of war. Cheering crowds were common. In Dundalk, County Louth, Thomas McCrave, a local member of the INV, watched as the local

[22] Henry Harris, *The Irish Regiments in the First World War* (Cork, 1968), 12.
[23] NLI: A Dubliner's Diary: MS 9,620, 15 August 1914.
[24] NA, Dublin: BMH Witness Statements: Kevin O'Sheil: WS 1,770, (n.d.).
[25] UCD, Archives: George Chester Duggan: LA24 (n.d.).
[26] Also known as Gary Holohan.
[27] NA, Dublin: BMH Witness Statements: Gearoid Ua h-Uallachain: WS 328 (n.d.).

British military garrison in Dundalk left the town for the front. 'They were conducted to the railway station by the Dundalk Emmet Band, and they got an enthusiastic send-off from the townspeople.'[28] In Dublin, the men of the King's Own Scottish Borderers, who only days previously had fired on a crowd of civilians killing three people, were given a 'rousing send-off' by local people as they marched to the docks to embark for the front.[29] On 6 August an estimated crowd of 50,000 people accompanied reservists to the North Wall at Dublin port and was 'most enthusiastic for England, singing and playing *God Save the King*, an unheard of thing hitherto among . . . nationalists'.[30] Charles Arnold, a Regular stationed in Ireland in 1914, left Dublin with his regiment on 13 August: 'What crowds there were to see us off! The Dublin people went mad, flags were flying, bands playing, in fact we got a right Royal send off (including a packet of fruit, cakes and cigarettes for each man).'[31] It is unlikely that Irish people were cheering simply because they were happy to see British soldiers leave Irish soil as Walter Denny's experience illustrates, a Regular who left Dublin with his regiment the following day:

This being Sunday, the civil population of the city turned out on a sight seeing expedition and cheered us on our way . . . Many songs were sung, the people on the quayside joining in the melody and finally amidst cheers and screeching of sirens we steamed out of the harbour . . . The people of Dublin presented us with a paper bag containing a bun, cigarettes, chocolates and matches and on the bags these words were printed "From Irish friends who are proud of you". This inspired us, as a week or so before they would have hung us if possible, as there was some trouble there between the military and the volunteers over the illegal landing of arms.[32]

Nor could these scenes be described as enthusiastic for war. When troops departed from Cork the *Cork Free Press* described 'a vast crowd filled the spacious station yard, and the scenes full of pathos, tinged at times with humour, have never been equalled in the memory of the oldest inhabitant'.[33] As in Britain, there was a sense of giving soldiers a good send-off in the knowledge of the hardships they were about to face abroad.

The economic impact of the war was felt immediately in Ireland. As in Britain, banks were closed until 7 August and food prices rose during the first weeks of war. In Dublin, by 6 August, 'coal has gone up 5/s a ton, and such things as meat, milk, and bread are also up' and, in Cork, prices of foodstuff had risen between 5 and 120 per cent, the latter figure applying to sugar 'of which the dearth is extreme'.[34] This led to protests in some areas. In Mallow, Cork, a crowd of local labourers gathered at the town-square to protest about the 'sudden and . . . unwarrantable increase in

[28] NA, Dublin: BMH Witness Statements: Thomas McCrave: WS 695 (1956).

[29] NA, Dublin: BMH Witness Statements Kevin O'Sheil: WS 1,770 (n.d.).

[30] NLI: A Dubliner's Diary: MS 9,620, 6 August 1914.

[31] Stephen Royle, ed., *From Mons to Messines and Beyond: The Great War Experiences of Sergeant Charles Arnold* (Studley, 1985), 15.

[32] Liddle: GS 0445: Walter Edward Denney, 16 August 1914.

[33] *Cork Free Press*, 6 August 1914.

[34] NLI: A Dubliner's Diary: MS 9,620, 6 August 1914 and National Archives of the United States, Maryland Campus: American Consulate, Cork: M367, Roll 13 (763.72/758), 6 August 1914.

the prices of provisions and coal, already dear enough'.[35] Others panicked and began to stock up on food and provisions, with some shopkeepers 'delighted to get a chance of increased profit'.[36] The *Western Nationalist* wrote of 'shivering' bank accounts and 'food traitors' increasing their prices.[37] The Irish tourist industry was badly hit. Thomas Moylan, who went on a three-week cycling holiday around Ireland starting on 7 September, observed:

> The effects of the war are very visible in the hotels, there having been only three people in the Adelphi Hotel, Waterford, a fairly large place; only three or four in the Hotel Metropole, Cork, which is also a large hotel, and when I got to Glengariffe I pulled up at a little hotel where there was no one staying, nor had there been anyone there for something like a month . . . There were two gun boats lying in the shelter of the islands opposite the Eccles hotel.[38]

In Ballingeary, County Cork, Piaras Béaslaí, a member of the Irish Republican Brotherhood (IRB), described to his father, in Cheshire, how the financial panic had spread to the most rural areas of Ireland. Within the first day or two of war, prices rose incredibly and banknotes were difficult to obtain. The war 'has . . . upset everything in the business line and the number of unemployment [sic] is very great'.[39]

Employment was affected just as quickly and severely as in Britain. Belfast shipbuilding, which was later to flourish in wartime conditions, suffered dislocation as reserve soldiers were called up and workers left for industrial districts in Britain. Employment in the city's engineering industry was badly affected by the loss of continental demand for textile machinery. Linen workers were put on short time in Belfast, Lurgan, Antrim, and Drogheda. 'Non-essential' trades felt the greatest impact. In Dublin unemployment was high amongst cabinetmakers and seamstresses. As in Britain, unemployment levels peaked in September.

SOLIDARITY

Responding to the outbreak of war, many Irishwomen quickly mobilized themselves to 'succour the brave men now fighting for our rights and liberties'.[40] Voluntary work in Ireland drew support from all classes, religious denominations, and political affiliations.[41] As in Britain, Irish suffragettes suspended their political campaign and set about supporting the war by knitting socks for soldiers and looking after Belgian refugees. Relief work for Britain's war was easily aligned with

[35] Claire Carroll et al., 'The Approach of War, July and August 1914', *Times Past* 7 (1990–91), 5.
[36] NLI: A Dubliner's Diary: MS 9,620, 6 August 1914.
[37] *Western Nationalist*, 15 August 1914.
[38] NLI: A Dubliner's Diary: MS 9,620, 8 October 1914.
[39] NLI: Piaras Béaslaí Papers: Ms 33,972/7, 6 August 1914.
[40] *Church of Ireland Gazette*, 21 August 1914.
[41] NA, Kew: CO 904/94, RIC County Inspector report, Cavan, September 1914. See also Margaret Downes, 'The Civilian Voluntary Aid Effort', in *Ireland and the First World War*, ed. David Fitzpatrick (Dublin, 1986), 27.

the political outlook of unionist organizations, such as the Ulster Women's Unionist Council, which converted unionist headquarters in Belfast into premises where the women's council, amongst many activities, sorted, packaged, and dispatched food and comforts, and assembled military dressings.[42]

Nationalists perhaps found voluntary work particularly conducive owing to the reservations many of them had about enlisting for military service. Volunteers across Ireland helped wounded soldiers by making clothes and bandages and providing respite care. Although some unionist papers tried to ridicule southern Irish relief efforts, a letter in the *Irish Times* dated 2 December, by one British—and unionist—soldier, addressed such accusations directly:

> In reference to the shameful calumnies noted in your paper [*Ulster Guardian*] of the 14 inst. from the Belfast Press in regard to the treatment of the wounded in Dublin, will you allow me, as one of the invalids landed there from Boulogne, to say that nothing could have exceeded the kindness accorded to us . . . Everything that care and skill and money could do was done for us . . . A strong Unionist—as are all members of my family—I feel impelled to speak of what I know.[43]

Soldiers fighting abroad were also cared for via fund-raising events, letter-writing, and sending comforts. Local businesses sponsored their work, such as the Cork Steam Packet Company which sent Red Cross goods free of charge.[44] In Ardagh, County Limerick, Mabel O'Brien, wife of the artist Dermod, knotted tobacco strings and made '15lbs of crab jelly' for the soldiers.[45] By 13 August Helen Duffin and her Aunt Charlotte, in Newcastle, County Down, were furiously knitting socks for the soldiers. Her sister Molly soon became overwhelmed by her altruism. On 26 August she complained that she was a member of so many relief organizations that she wished they would amalgamate to lessen her confusion.[46] In other areas, employers offered financial security to those who wanted to enlist by offering to keep their jobs open for when they returned. Soldiers' dependants were also looked after under the auspices of the Prince of Wales' National Relief Fund; in Cork alone, by 28 September, £2,610.18.10 had been raised.[47] Again relief efforts—both local, Irish, and across the United Kingdom—were deemed constructive for morale and morality, providing opportunities and 'centres where . . . women can gather for mutual comfort and help'.[48]

The intense feeling for Belgium and sympathy with its sufferings were manifested in a practical way when the refugees began to arrive in Ireland. Associations and organizations sprang up to help these 'victims of the monstrous barbarity of the

---

[42] See for example, PRONI: D/1098/2/5/1, D/1098/2/6/1, and D/2688/1/5-6. Diane Urquhart, '"The Female of the Species is More Deadlier Than the Male"? The Ulster Women's Unionist Council, 1911–1940', in *Coming into the Light: The Work, Politics and Religion of Women in Ulster*, ed. Janice Holmes and Diane Urquhart (Belfast, 1994), 104–5.
[43] *Irish Times*, 2 December 1914.
[44] *Cork Constitution*, 23 September 1914.
[45] NLI: Dermod O'Brien papers: Ms 36,702/3, 5 October 1914.
[46] PRONI: Duffin Family papers: D/2109/9/1, 26 August 1914.
[47] *Cork Examiner*, 28 September 1914.
[48] *Sláinte*, December 1914 (Vol. 5).

enemy', and as representatives of a Catholic nation, Irish people had to answer the call and look after them. In Cork, the first group of refugees arrived on 27 September followed by sixty-eight more on 16 October. Local people met them with demonstrations of sympathy, and monetary donations flooded in to help look after them.[49] As Kevin O'Sheil recalled 'the women-folk in my family, in common with most other families, whatever their religion or politics, busied themselves from morning to night on all manner of work for those new guests of the nation— knitting, sewing and making garments, and cooking and packing food for them'.[50] As in Britain, concerts and lectures were organized to raise vital funds. When Belgian refugees were entertained at the Palace Theatre in Cork the 'house was specially decorated for the occasion, prominently displayed being the Irish and Belgian flags entwined, and surmounted by the Union Jack', a striking visual demonstration of Ireland's support for a collaborative war with Britain to liberate Belgium.[51] However, this sense of affiliation with 'little Catholic Belgium' did not mean Irish people were immune to the frustrations experienced in Britain when the novelty of caring for the refugees wore off. The 1914 minutes of the Belgian Refugees Committee on Upper Mount Street, Dublin reveal how by 25 November complaints were being made about the 'inappropriate behaviour' of some Belgian refugees in Balrothery, and by early January 1915 rumours were circulating that refugees were German spies in disguise.[52]

As in Britain, striking the right moral tone for the home population in the momentous circumstances of the time was also a concern. This particularly concerned the war's impact on women. Vigilance committees, like those established in Britain, were set up in Ireland in army towns and major ports. On 6 September, Annie Brunton, in Foynes, County Limerick, castigated a local woman who had sold clothes she had received from her local Prince of Wales' National Relief Fund and made a considerable profit.[53] Unease regarding women's immorality and intemperance led to a public meeting in Dublin to establish an Irishwomen's League of Honour in November 1914. The Church of Ireland Primate, Archbishop Crozier, addressed the Dublin meeting and outlined the purpose of the League:

> It is proposed to band together women and girls with the object of upholding the standard of women's duty and honour during the time of war, to raise a strong force of public opinion and support amongst women and girls with which to combat some of the social and moral dangers emphasised by the war; to deepen amongst women and girls a sense of their responsibility for the honour of the nation, and by their influence to uplift manhood.[54]

[49] *Cork Examiner*, 25 September, 28 September, and 17 October 1914.
[50] NA, Dublin: BMH Witness Statements: Kevin O'Sheil: WS 1,770 (n.d.).
[51] *Cork Constitution*, 10 October 1914.
[52] UCD, Archives: Belgian Refugees Committee, Minute Book October 1914–June 1915.
[53] NLI: Diary of Annie Brunton: Ms 13,620/2, 6 September 1914.
[54] *Church of Ireland Gazette*, 27 November 1914.

The Dean of St Patrick's Cathedral also proposed that Irishwomen shun those who did not volunteer for service: 'Visit them with the severest disapproval, and when they expect a smile just look them straight in the face and turn away'.[55]

Overall, people in Ireland were willing to help and answer the call of the hour regardless of their political affiliation. For whatever reasons—political expediency, hope, fear, gratitude, affiliation with Catholic Belgium, economic benefit—the war absorbed their attention and support. Even those who were suspicious of the war helped in their own way. Rosamond Jacob, the Waterford playwright, was unwilling to offer financial support to her local Belgian relief fund, instead preferring to use her money for Irish people in distress because of the war.[56] Her support for the war was conditional and limited, but she was willing to support it nonetheless. Solidarity efforts allowed room for Irish and British identities to work together. As evidenced, at fund-raising events Union Jacks were used alongside Irish and Belgian flags. On 5 August Thomas B. Sweeney from Clonmel, County Tipperary, wrote to the American Ambassador in London asking for permission to display the American, Russian, French, and British flags from his house during the war. Although the Second Secretary of the Embassy replied that this was a matter for the local police, it indicates a desire in rural Ireland to show solidarity with neutral America and the major allies, including Great Britain.[57] The Prince of Wales' National Relief Fund, a symbol of the British monarchy, was utilized to positive effect in Ireland. On 7 December Mabel O'Brien described to her husband how, at the end of a charitable concert in Newcastle, County Down, '*God Save the King* was sung and the audience all rose to their feet. Think of that now!'[58]

IMAGINING AND EXPERIENCING WAR

During the first five months of war, although a minority of advanced nationalists believed that Britain was the enemy, on the whole, the population in Ireland, just as in Britain, felt that Germany was the enemy and that the cause against it was just. Some people, particularly those from academic, literary, or artistic backgrounds, tried to remain rational and placed responsibility for the war with the Kaiser and his government, rather than the entire German population.[59] But for many, stories of German atrocities in Belgium were so horrific that they cemented the belief that the Germans were in the wrong and needed to be beaten. People feared Germany's aggression, its tyrannical rule and, in Catholic Ireland, its Protestantism. On 5 September the *Roscommon Journal* stressed that if Ireland did not resist Germany, it would be 'Lutheranised'.[60] Although advanced nationalists believed that rumours

---

[55] *Irish Times*, 20 November 1914.
[56] NLI: Diary of Rosamond Jacob: Ms 32,582/27, 4 September 1914.
[57] National Archives of the United States, Maryland Campus: American Embassy, London: RG 84: Records of Foreign Service Posts: Diplomatic Posts: Great Britain: Vol 0608: 801.5, 5 August 1914.
[58] NLI: Dermod O'Brien papers: Ms 36,702/4, 7 December 1914.
[59] NLI: Dermod O'Brien papers: Ms 36,781/8, 16 November 1914.
[60] *Roscommon Journal*, 5 September 1914.

of German atrocities were a propaganda technique on the part of the British, many Irish people believed these stories as fact. On 9 August, Kathe Oldham, in Dublin, responded to the Irish suffragist and socialist Francis Sheehy-Skeffington's request for her to write a piece rehabilitating Germany in the Irish press. She asked: 'How can I *being a German* write in any Irish paper at present, even if I tried my best to try to put my opinions in an article for the *Irish Citizen*, the *public* would only jeer at and laugh that I am "blowing my own trumpet"—it would have no effect at all!' suggesting that pro-German opinions, on the whole, would not be tolerated by the Irish population in 1914.[61] Thomas Moylan recorded in his diary in October:

> Many tales of brutality of the Germans have been circulated . . . I have heard it said that a Civil Servant out of one of the Dublin offices, who joined the Army was invalided to Netley with his hands and ears cut off, and so otherwise mutilated that his doctors think it better for him to die. A little girl is said to have been in Dublin a week or so ago, a refugee from Belgium, whose hands were also cut off . . . Belgian girls have . . . have been outraged, their breasts cut off, and other indignities inflicted on them.[62]

Throughout the opening months of the war, the Sheehy-Skeffingtons felt that they were not only battling the war but also the 'tide of anti-German jingoism' that had swept across Ireland.[63] Clearly, exaggerated rumours of German brutality towards French and Belgian civilians was a UK-wide phenomenon in 1914.

Francis Sheehy-Skeffington's fears about this 'tide' were realized on 15 and 16 August when a wave of attacks on German pork butchers' shops occurred across Dublin. Led by a soldier who had recently enlisted and wanted to start fighting the 'barbarians' immediately, the most serious attacks were on the premises of Frederick Lang in Wexford Street and George Reitz at Leonard's Corner on South Circular Road, Portobello.[64] Another attack also occurred on Thomas Street. According to the *Freeman's Journal* the crowd were 'principally of youths' and 'completely wrecked the shop—threw all furniture, fixtures, and meat stocks out onto the street'. No reason for the attacks could be ascribed 'except that the proprietors of the premises were believed to be German'.[65] Further smaller attacks also occurred in Dublin following the destruction of Louvain on 25 August.[66] German atrocities and violations of Catholic landmarks in Belgium had stirred certain people into action. As in Britain, anti-German feeling became blurred with pre-war anti-Semitism. Leonard Abrahamson, from Newry, noted 'the virus of anti-Semitic feeling, born of ignorance and fostered by unrelenting prejudice, still courses in the veins of numerous'. His father, David, was subjected to anti-Semitic

---

[61] NLI: Sheehy-Skeffington papers: Ms 33,611/11, 9 August 1914.

[62] NLI: A Dubliner's Diary: Ms 9,620, 8 October 1914.

[63] NLI: Sheehy Skeffington papers: Ms 33,612/16, 9 August 1914.

[64] Manus O'Riordan, 'The Justification of James Connolly', in *James Connolly, Liberty Hall and The 1916 Rising*, ed. Francis Devine and Manus O'Riordan (Dublin, 2006), 25, and *Irish Independent*, 16–18 August 1914.

[65] *Freeman's Journal*, 17 August 1914, 6.

[66] NA, Dublin: BMH Witness Statements: Kevin O'Sheil: WS 1,770 (n.d.).

abuse and attacked by loyalists in Newry despite having no connection with Germany.[67]

Under orders from Westminster, officials in Dublin Castle immediately set in place defence measures, including the guarding of vulnerable points and the incarceration of enemy aliens. Ostensibly, the British authorities were implementing national policy. However, caution in Ireland was motivated by a fear that Germany would do its best to stir up trouble in Ireland, whether by political agitation through Irish-American organizations, or by direct military aid to Irish separatists. It was well known that Roger Casement, who had now sided openly with advanced nationalism, was seeking such assistance from the Germans.[68] Despite this, the bulk of security concerns related to the German enemy rather than dissident nationalists. George Duggan, a civil servant in the Castle, recalled that the impact of war was made evident on 5 August when:

> there arrived from the Home Office in London copies of the various Proclamations and Orders arising from a state of war. New problems arose for the Civil Service; Chief Secretary's office became the medium through which the Home Office handled the problem of aliens, enemy and neutral. I interviewed waiters cut off from the Fatherland—could they show that they were oppressed Czechs or Slavs, not arrogant Austrians or domineering Germans? Or should they follow others into internment?[69]

Around 41 per cent of registered correspondence to and from the Chief Secretary's Office in Dublin between 4 August and 31 December was concerned with enemy aliens and their incarceration, compared with only 10 per cent of correspondence discussing the activities of the Volunteer movements and 8 per cent concerned with dissent amongst advanced nationalists.[70]

As in Britain, with the lack of official news about the progress of the war, rumours about spies abounded. On 4 August, a gentleman of 'foreign appearance' and two ladies who accompanied him were arrested in Crosshaven, Cork, on charges of espionage. On his arrest, sketches and photos of the harbour were found in his possession.[71] Shortly after war broke out, leading Cork chess player F. U. Beamish, was arrested for suspicious behaviour after being seen 'studying a position on a pocket chess board' in a local park.[72] On 26 August, Molly Duffin, in Newcastle, County Down, described to her mother how rumours were circulating about a girl who had not heard the warnings of a sentry and been shot as a suspected spy in Orlock Point, County Down.[73] Two foreigners arrested in Tarmonbarry, County Longford, were said to be studying the village's bridge over the Shannon.[74] In Sligo, a

[67] Dermot Keogh, *Jews in Twentieth Century Ireland: Refugees, Anti-Semitism and the Holocaust* (Cork, 1998), 68.

[68] Eunan O'Halpin, *The Decline of the Union: British Government in Ireland 1892–1920* (Dublin, 1987), 107.

[69] UCD, Archives: George Chester Duggan: LA24 (n.d.).

[70] NA, Dublin: Index of Chief Secretary's Office Registered Papers, 1914, CSO CR 297–298.

[71] NA, Kew: CO 903/18, Intelligence Notes, 1914.

[72] *Cork Weekly News*, 22 August 1914.

[73] PRONI: Duffin Family papers: D/2109/9/1, 26 August 1914.

[74] *Leitrim Observer*, 29 August 1914.

spy scare led to all visitors to the town being watched.[75] Some people even believed that German spies in Ireland had caused the outbreak of the war: they were able to convey to the Kaiser the extent of domestic discontent within the country in July 1914, suggesting to the Germans that it was the optimum moment to start a war on the continent.[76]

As elsewhere in the United Kingdom, the vacuum of official news was filled by rumour and speculation. The rumour that the British army had been annihilated in France reached Dublin by late August. However, adding a local twist, it was also suggested that some Irish regiments had been wiped out as well.[77] Earlier chapters have linked the fear of enemy spies with the fear of a German invasion on the east coast of Britain in 1914. The prominence of domestic politics in Ireland compli-cated perceptions of the German 'enemy', and by extension those of a possible invasion. Certain advanced nationalists in Ireland wanted Germany to invade in order to provide additional weaponry and support against the British occupying force in Ireland. On 27 August, Francis Sheehy-Skeffington wrote, from Dublin: 'The Germans have no hostility to Ireland; if they do land here (as I hope they will) they will land as the enemies of England, and as such ought to be welcomed as the French were welcomed in'98.'[78] At a meeting of the IRB on 4 September—at which plans for what would become the Easter Rising were first mooted—Seán T. O'Kelly, Honorary Secretary of Sinn Féin, recalled that Arthur Griffith, founder of the party, and the other men present decided to accept an offer of German help if it was forthcoming, but to fight German troops if they landed without invitation.[79] On 7 November the *Irish Volunteer* published a fictional story from the near future telling of the first days of the German occupation of Ireland in 'The Coming of the Hun'. Germans occupying Dublin would fly the flags of the Irish Republic and the city of Dublin by order of the German Emperor and arrest any English soldiers.[80] This story is an interesting reworking of fictional tales in Britain of a German invasion.

However, this was a minority opinion. Matthew Nathan, the Under-Secretary for Ireland, wrote on 3 November from Dublin that 'an invasion of Ireland may appear practicable to the Germans but nothing seems less likely than that the Irish would rise in support of it. In fact it would I believe be a serious blow to the Sinn Féiners if it got to be believed in the country that their activities . . . were going to lead to a German invasion.'[81] Other Irish citizens were frightened by rumours of German spies and a possible invasion. On 15 August the *Sligo Champion* published a 'Call to Arms to the Manhood of Sligo', arguing that 'County Sligo as a coastline is liable at any time to be raided . . . It is the bounden duty of every man fit to bear

---

[75] *Sligo Independent*, 29 August 1914.
[76] Timothy Michael Healy, *Letters and Leaders of My Day*, vol. 2 (London, 1928), 546.
[77] NLI: A Dubliner's Diary: Ms 9,620, 26 August 1914.
[78] NLI: Sheehy-Skeffington papers: Ms 33,612/16, 27 August 1914.
[79] Ben Novick, 'The Advanced Nationalist Response to Atrocity Propaganda, 1914–1918', in *Images, Icons and the Irish Nationalist Imagination*, ed. Lawrence W. McBride (Dublin, 1999), 137.
[80] *Irish Volunteer*, 7 November 1914, 7.
[81] MPP Bodleian: Augustine Birrell: MS Eng c.7033, ff. 8–17, 3 November 1914.

arms... to protect his home and family from the foreign invader'.[82] The Royal Irish Constabulary (RIC) Inspector General believed that a 'general dread of a German invasion' had triggered arrests of suspicious foreigners.[83] The timing of arrests of suspected enemy aliens is linked to a fear of German invasion. Over 60 per cent of the arrests made in Ireland under the 1911 Official Secrets Act occurred between 3 and 9 August, whilst the remainder were made in October and November, when fears of invasion were at their height in Britain.[84] This is the same chronology as in Britain, where the outbreak of war caused immediate fears of invasion that subsided until renewed speculation over a German landing arose in November following the fall of Antwerp and the defeat of the BEF at the First Battle of Ypres.

Attempts were made to calm the population by the local press. On 10 September the *Midland Reporter* noted how chances of a German invasion were now remote.[85] Although by 19 September, A. Duffin in Cushendun, County Antrim, believed that the opportune moment for a German landing on Irish shores had passed, she still feared that they 'may try to set up a scare with Zeppelins'.[86] In October one Dublin resident observed how anti-invasion measures such as searchlights and restricted public lighting, in place in London, had not been replicated in Dublin, presumably because the city was 'too far for such a raid'.[87] However, by January 1915 plans to deal with a German invasion of Ireland, similar to those made in Essex, were being drawn up by the authorities in Ireland.[88]

Unlike the population in Scarborough, Hartlepool, and Whitby, Irish citizens did not experience the violence of a German bombardment in 1914. Arguably, it would not be until 7 May 1915, when the Cunard passenger liner, RMS *Lusitania*, was sunk by German U-boats off Kinsale, County Cork, killing 1,198 passengers and crew, that the Irish were forced to confront the horrors of modern warfare, although sinkings of commercial and military vessels had occurred off the Irish coast before this date. Nonetheless, in 1914 Irish people were exposed to the horrifying and upsetting ramifications of the war. From the outset the Irish press stressed the horror of war and the damage it would cause. For the *Roscommon Messenger* on 8 August, the conflict would be the most appalling in history.[89] For the *Leitrim Advertiser* it was 'the Armageddon', particularly powerful language in a religious country like Ireland.[90] High casualties reported in the British press at the end of August were widely circulated in Ireland along with Kerry-born Kitchener's prediction that the war would last for two to three years. The violence of war was also visible in Ireland. On 26 October a hospital ship arrived at

---

[82] *Sligo Champion*, 15 August 1914.
[83] NA, Kew: CO 904/94, RIC Inspector General report, August 1914.
[84] NA, Kew: CO 903/18, Intelligence Notes, 1914.
[85] *Midland Reporter*, 10 September 1914.
[86] PRONI: Duffin Family papers: D/2109/9/1, 19 September 1914.
[87] NLI: A Dubliner's Diary: Ms 9,620, 8 October 1914.
[88] See NA, Kew: CO 904/174/2, Instructions to RIC about the possible invasion of Ireland, January to April 1915.
[89] *Roscommon Messenger*, 8 August 1914.
[90] *Leitrim Advertiser*, 3 September 1914.

Queenstown, and a train brought the wounded to Cork. By the time the train reached the city 'an immense crowd had gathered in the precincts of the station, the Lower Glanmire Road being almost impassable'.[91] Around the same time, in Sligo a steamer was sunk by German mines drowning fourteen men.[92]

All Irishmen who enlisted left families behind. Parents, siblings, family, and friends were scared, worried, and anxious. Michael J. Moynihan, an Irish-born Regular with the British army, informed his mother on 4 August that he had been mobilized. The following day she wrote, from Tralee, County Kerry, how much his letter had alarmed her. Her friends and priest were consoling her: 'May God grant they are right. Take all the care possible of yourself and I have confidence in God's goodness you will be alright.' He was killed in action in June 1918.[93] People were also aware, from an early stage, that they might not see their loved ones again. According to Timothy Healy, low levels of recruitment amongst the farming classes were not due to 'pro-Germanism' but because 'the farmers don't want their sons to leave their work, and perhaps return cripples, or not at all'.[94] Farewells and separation had to be endured. On 7 August Thomas Moylan described an emotional scene he had witnessed in Dublin:

> Many moving sights are to be seen in and around the City these days . . . [I] saw an officer hurrying up the steps of a house in Mount street as if he were just rushing to say goodbye . . . The officer paused, then went down the steps slowly, wiping his eyes and walking with lagging steps. Then he braced himself up and set off at the same rapid pace at which he had arrived. Evidently he had come to say goodbye to some friend and found them out. These seem to [highlight] the grimness of this war.[95]

On 23 November Rosamond Stephen, in Belfast, described a woman whose husband had departed to the front: 'Poor little thing she was almost crying, and I told her the women were very often the real heroes, because they had all the hard part and none of the fun'.[96]

Death and grief did not discriminate politically or by class. Captain George Berkeley, in Belfast, first encountered death in the war on 2 September when he heard news of a fellow nationalist colleague killed in action.[97] In October Shane Leslie heard the ominous sound of the chapel bell tolling 'for whose death I knew not' at Glaslough, Monaghan. The following month Leslie visited an Irish friend whose son had been killed in the war. He 'kept me an hour talking of his dead boy. He read his letters aloud but broke down. At this rate everybody in a year will be mourning. I can think of half a dozen already.'[98] On 7 October Annie Brunton described in her diary a local woman in Foynes, County Limerick:

[91] *Cork Constitution*, 27 October 1914.
[92] *Sligo Independent*, 31 October 1914.
[93] UCD, Archives: Michael J. Moynihan: P57/50, 5 August 1914.
[94] Callanan, *T. M. Healy*, 511.
[95] NLI: A Dubliner's Diary: Ms 9,620, 7 August 1914.
[96] Oonagh Walsh, *An Englishwoman in Belfast: Rosamond Stephen's Record of the Great War* (Cork, 2000), 20.
[97] NLI: George Berkeley letters: Ms 13,266/1, 2 September 1914.
[98] NLI: Sir Shane Leslie: Ms 22,863, 12 November 1914.

She began to talk of the war. "Oh, it do be awful," she said, "all the fine young men going out there to be killed . . . the son of my sister is there and I not liking to ask her of them [sic]. Oh I would not be liking [sic] to hear of the war, that is the way I feel. I would not be hearing of the war" . . . The little excited old thing in a black shawl with her eyes full of tears.[99]

WARTIME: THE POLITICS OF DOMESTIC PEACE

Not all aspects of the war experience in 1914 were felt equally across the United Kingdom. The political situation in Ireland could not be conjured away or suspended at the outbreak of war. It had to find other expressions that made parts of the Irish experience unique in 1914. The politicization of the Great War as a symbol of the battle between unionism and nationalism was in place from the very beginning of the war, and continues to this day. The immensity of the conflict, the involvement of the United Kingdom, the issues for which it seemed to be fought, and the danger it seemed to present made it necessary for both nationalists and unionists to define their relationship to it. Responses to the outbreak of the war were, naturally, conditioned, among both nationalists and unionists, by pre-war politics and perceptions, and specifically by attitudes about the relationship between Great Britain and Ireland. The pre-war issue itself—Home Rule and partition—had to be reviewed by both parties in the new context. Redmond wanted Home Rule enacted while Carson wanted it dropped. The compromise passed in mid-September was that Home Rule would be put on the statute book but not activated until the end of the hostilities, and then special provision would be made for Ulster.

It is a myth that Ulster offered complete support to the war, while nationalists saw 'England's difficulty as Ireland's opportunity'. In reality, when war was declared both Carson and Redmond hoped their respective Volunteers would be recognized as integral parts of the British army and be used to defend Ireland from German attack. In effect, they were competing with each other to provide the most troops; 'the war was, quite literally, the continuation of politics by other means'.[100] Both parties made certain demands, jockeyed for position, and attempted to extract every ounce of political advantage from the new situation created by war.[101]

Within two weeks, the war had changed the political mood of Ireland. Police reports from June 1914 recorded the deep levels of distrust and hatred that existed between Protestants and Catholics in Ulster; two months later they reported that the UVF and the INV were turning out together with their bands to escort the troops leaving for the front.[102] On 5 August, Charles D'Arcy, Protestant Bishop of

---

[99] NLI: Diary of Annie Brunton: Ms 13,620/2, 7 October 1914.

[100] David Howie and Josephine Howie, 'Irish Recruiting and the Home Rule Crisis of August-September 1914', in *Strategy and Intelligence: British Policy during the First World War*, ed. Michael Dockrill and David French (London, 1996), 22.

[101] Bowman, 'Composing Divisions: The Recruitment of Ulster and National Volunteers into the British Army in 1914', 26–7.

[102] NA, Dublin: BMH Witness Statements: Kevin O'Sheil: WS 1,770 (n.d.).

Down, Connor, and Dromore, wrote 'Amazing change in Irish feeling—all united in support of Great Britain'.[103] By the end of August, local police reports were unequivocal that popular opinion had taken England's side in the war.[104] Almost all papers expressed genuine sympathy for the Allies and hostility to Germany. The *Longford Leader* made it clear that Ireland could not exchange English for German rule, 'the most autocratic, bureaucratic and tyrannical in the world'.[105] For the nearby *Roscommon Journal*, Ireland would have to bear every sacrifice rather than bow down to the 'Moloch of German iniquity'.[106] Desmond Fitzgerald, an advanced nationalist, recalled that his immediate reaction to the outbreak of war, one of rejoicing at England's difficulty, soon gave way to despair as Germany became the popular enemy, and Ireland's martial spirit was 'canalised' for the defence of England: 'our castle of dreams toppled about us with a crash'.[107] In a sense, therefore, August 1914 saw an Irish *Burgfrieden*: the outbreak of war had created civic peace. Support for the war—albeit for opposed reasons—outweighed dissent. This support may have been superficial and the political gulf too wide to be securely bridged, but there was a genuine desire to close the gap between the two sides at the initial outbreak of war.

In his celebrated intervention in the House of Commons on 3 August, John Redmond pledged Ireland's support for the Allies in the coming conflict and urged the government to leave the defence of the Irish shores to the Irish National and Ulster Volunteers. Although Redmond was encouraged by Margot Asquith, the Prime Minister's wife, to say something along these lines, the spontaneity he expressed on behalf of nationalists was notable. Redmond made the speech without consultation with his senior colleagues and it soon turned into a major political liability.[108] However, at the time his statement reflected the feelings of the vast majority of nationalists of 'all schools and sects'. Even some advanced nationalists were 'delighted with it and acclaimed him for making it'.[109] Newspapers claimed that Redmond's speech 'wrought a miracle' in changing Irish attitudes and local support for his policy was quickly forthcoming.[110] The Irish Catholic Church (representing 74 per cent of the population) also pledged their support for Redmond's position, and priests took their places on the recruiting platforms, alongside politicians, denouncing Germany as a ruthless barbaric destroyer of civilization and liberty.[111] The Bishop of Kildare and Leighlin, Patrick Foley, summarized Irish

[103] Charles Frederick D'Arcy, *The Adventures of a Bishop: A Phase of Irish Life: A Personal and Historical Narrative* (London, 1934), 195.
[104] NA, Kew: CO 904/94, RIC County Inspector report, Dublin, August 1914; NA, Kew: CO 904/94, R.I.C. County Inspector reports, Leitrim, Roscommon, Sligo, Westmeath, August 1914.
[105] *Longford Leader*, 8 August 1914.
[106] *Roscommon Journal*, 5 September 1914.
[107] Desmond Fitzgerald, *Desmond's Rising: Memoirs, 1913 to Easter 1916* (London, 2006), 58.
[108] F. S. L. Lyons, 'The Revolution in Train, 1914–1916', in *Ireland Under the Union, II: 1870–1921*, ed. W. E Vaughan (Oxford, 1996), 189.
[109] NA, Dublin: BMH Witness Statements: Kevin O'Sheil: WS 1,770 (n.d.).
[110] *Munster Express*, 8 August 1914.
[111] Jerome Aan de Wiel, *The Catholic Church in Ireland 1914–1918: War and Politics* (Dublin, 2003), 1–41.

Catholic opinion about the conflict in an open letter published in the *Irish Times* on 16 August:

> It becomes the duty of us as faithful Christians and loyal citizens of the great God, on whom all Nations and Empires, as well as individuals, absolutely depend, to come to the aid of the armies which are fighting on the side of justice and right; and to enable them through the might of His power to triumph over their adversaries.[112]

Inspired by Redmond's lead, nationalist sympathies were almost wholly on the side of the Franco-British alliance. Apart from the events of the war itself, there had always been feelings of friendship towards France in the country, stemming from Irish sympathy for France during the Franco-Prussian War of 1870–1871.[113] However, just as in Britain, the event that stirred public feeling most deeply was the German invasion of Belgium on 4 August. On 27 August, Redmond summarized Irish nationalist camaraderie with Belgium:

> The spectacle of a small nation making these heroic sacrifices in defence of their independence and honour against overwhelming odds appeals in a very special way to the sentiments and the feelings of Ireland ... the people of Ireland are in sympathy with Belgium ... and ... they are willing to do what rests with them to assist her in the maintenance of her independence.[114]

The invasion, and the resulting atrocities, outraged the Irish public. In particular the burning of cathedrals and churches, and the destruction of the library of the Catholic University of Louvain and the church of St Pierre, enraged Catholic Irish opinion and rallied support for 'little Catholic Belgium'. Patrick Joseph Paul, a Redmondite from East Waterford, accepted 'unquestioningly ... the catch-cries raised at the time by the Irish Party in support of this recruiting campaign—"the fight for small nations" and "by fighting in France we were fighting for Ireland"', and he enlisted in the Royal Irish Regiment in 1915.[115] Even the O'Brienite publication, the *Cork Free Press*, believed that the war was 'against military despotism and in defence of the integrity of small nations. "Louvain" and "Rheims" alone are cries which would stir the blood of a Catholic Irishman'.[116] Many people understood the war as a conflict between ideals, and whatever doubts people had about Britain, they believed that in comparison to Prussian militarism, Britain was fighting to uphold peaceful civilization. Belgium was a small nation trying to protect itself against a more powerful aggressor and nationalist opinion could relate to this. But it was also understood that alone, Ireland could not protect Belgium. It had to stand with Britain and France.[117]

---

[112] *Irish Times*, 16 August 1914.
[113] NA, Dublin: BMH Witness Statements: Kevin O'Sheil: WS 1,770 (n.d.). Ironically support for that war was fuelled by British and unionist support of Germany.
[114] Cited in J. B. Lyons, *The Enigma of Tom Kettle: Irish Patriot, Essayist, Poet, British Soldier 1880–1916* (Dublin, 1983), 254.
[115] NA, Dublin: BMH Witness Statements: Patrick Joseph Paul: WS 877 (1953).
[116] *Cork Free Press*, 23 September 1914.
[117] *Cork Constitution*, 10 October 1914.

The nationalist decision to support the Franco-British alliance in 1914 was also pragmatic. If Germany won the war there would be no Home Rule. Many nationalists understood support for the war as a precondition to securing their aims for a Dublin parliament. On 21 September William O'Brien, independent nationalist MP for Cork City, stated: 'Whether Home Rule is to have a future will depend upon the extent to which Nationalists, in combination with Ulster Volunteers, do their part in the firing line on the fields of France.'[118] If nationalists failed to support the war, this would add fuel to the fire of unionists' arguments that Home Rule was a menace and a danger to England. Redmond also recognized the part that British public opinion would play in the achievement of Home Rule and that a refusal by nationalists to support the war would turn opinion against their cause.

For the nationalists, the war was also a chance to claim autonomy on the same basis as the white Dominions: Canada, Newfoundland, South Africa, and Australia. Redmond did not want the nationalists to be outdone by the unionists in their sacrifice to the Empire. He explained that 'the basic theory of the whole constitutional movement for the last century in Ireland . . . has been that we in this country claim to be an autonomous nation within the circle of Empire'. If Ireland wanted to enjoy the advantages that flowed from its connection to the Empire then it had to 'manfully and honestly bear her share of the burdens'.[119] As a result, war, according to Redmond, offered Ireland a new 'international place' defending such virtues as 'Honour, Justice, Freedom, Pity'. The war provided Ireland with its greatest opportunity yet to prove its national character. The country, for the first time, could put a national army in the field and, as a result, the spillage of Irish blood on the battlefield would fertilize an Irish nation and Irish national identity.[120] There was a desire that Irishmen, from north and south, would fight side by side as equals for an Irish nation. Tom Kettle, the poet, lawyer and former Irish Parliamentary Party (IPP) MP for East Tyrone, hoped that the 'tragedy of Europe' would reconcile 'Protestant Ulster with Ireland, and . . . Ireland with Great Britain'.[121]

Support shown at the beginning of the war obscured the nuances that divided unionist and nationalist opinion on the war's importance, which, ultimately, pushed nationalists and unionists further apart.[122] Although public expressions of sympathy for Britain remained the norm for most of 1914, the new-found mood of Irish unity was already unravelling before the end of August. Central to this unrest was the delay over the final decision about Home Rule, postponed since the outbreak of war. The gap between Redmond's speech on 3 August and the passing of the Home Rule Bill into law on 18 September allowed anxiety and intra-nationalist tensions to foment. In Ulster, intelligence notes recorded that

---

[118] Joseph V. O'Brien, *William O'Brien and the Course of Irish Politics, 1881–1918* (London, 1976), 215.
[119] *Freeman's Journal*, 19 October 1914.
[120] John Redmond, introduction to Michael MacDonagh, *The Irish at the Front* (London, 1916).
[121] Thomas M. Kettle, *The Ways of War* (London, 1917), 71.
[122] Thomas Hennessey, *Dividing Ireland: World War One and Partition* (London, 1998).

'considerable unrest prevailed alike in the unionist and nationalist ranks as to the action the government would take with regard to the Home Rule Bill'.[123]

Uncertainty regarding the Home Rule Bill was beginning to affect recruitment in Ulster. Although the Ulster Volunteers were 'ready and anxious to rally the flag in defence of the country' they wanted assurance that when they returned from the war 'the flag for which they have fought and the country which they have helped to defend will still be theirs'.[124] Ultimately, there was very little the unionists could do in this situation having lost the upper-hand—the threat of civil war in Ulster. As James Craig told Carson on 20 August 'however much we curse and damn the P.M.—we must say that we will do our best under the circumstances for the Army and the country'.[125] Unionists could not leave themselves open to accusations that they were putting politics before patriotism.

In the weeks following the outbreak of war, nationalists also experienced high levels of anxiety fearing that Home Rule was permanently off the agenda before it had been properly ratified by royal assent. Redmond had warned Asquith of the dangers of postponing the Home Rule Bill on 4 August. At the end of August the RIC Inspector General noted that 'a feeling of mistrust set in pending the disposal of the Home Rule Bill', whilst the *Longford Leader* described Ireland as 'almost bereft of patience'.[126] Additionally, nationalists began to feel that the British government was spurning Redmond's 3 August offer, with the INV receiving no official support from the War Office. Although, outside Sinn Féin and advanced labour circles, public feeling was still 'strongly anti-German', outright opposition from advanced nationalists became more vocal. They were still only localized and isolated, but these instances set the tone for future dissent.[127] The mood in early September was summed up by John Dillon, deputy leader of the Irish party and MP for East Mayo, in a letter to T. P. O'Connor, IPP MP for Liverpool. For Dillon the situation in Ireland was 'a good deal worse' than he had supposed, caused by government indecisiveness over Home Rule over the past three weeks: 'Now the country is seething with suspicion and disappointment . . . You can see how the Sinn Féiners are preparing the ground . . . Our friends are disheartened and bewildered.'[128]

Although the Home Rule Bill received the royal assent, the accompanying Suspensory Act effectively delayed its implementation indefinitely during the war, and amending legislation concerning Ulster's exclusion was promised. It was a package of measures best summed up as a 'post dated cheque for a limited freedom'.[129] Asquith's compromise was greeted by unionists with the 'cry of

---

[123] Breandán Mac Giolla Choille, ed., *Intelligence Notes, 1913–1916* (Dublin, 1966), 101.

[124] *Northern Whig*, 10 August 1914.

[125] Ian Colvin, *The Life of Lord Carson* (London, 1934), 30.

[126] NA, Kew: CO 904/94, RIC Inspector General report, August 1914 and *Longford Leader*, 29 August 1914.

[127] NA, Kew: CO 904/94, RIC County Inspector reports, Belfast City, Cavan, and Dublin, September 1914. See also Michael Wheatley, *Nationalism and the Irish Party: Provincial Ireland 1910–1916* (Oxford, 2005), 204.

[128] TCD, Manuscripts: Dillon Papers: Ms 6740-4/225, 5 September 1914.

[129] Stephen Gwynn, *The Irish Situation* (London, 1921), 34.

broken pledge'. Across Ulster there were protests against the King. Pictures of George V were booed and members of congregations in some Protestant churches walked out when the national anthem was played.[130] However, unionists realized that to continue urging their cause, at the expense of supporting the war effort, would have no effect except to set the British electorate against them, including many who would otherwise have been friendly.[131]

In the short term, the passage of Home Rule over its last hurdle relaxed feelings amongst nationalists.[132] On 17 September, a day before its passage, Redmond issued a statement extending the commitment of Irish nationalists in the war beyond Ireland.[133] Three days later, the sentiment of this speech was most famously repeated to a crowd of INV at Woodenbridge, County Wicklow.[134] It is unclear why Redmond changed his mind. It may have been the fact that developments on the Western Front made it clear that the decisive battles were going to be fought in Flanders and northern France; it may have been a desire to compete with Carson who was eager for Ulstermen to fight overseas; it may have been a sudden urge of gratitude for Home Rule having finally been placed on the statute book; it may have been a desire to force a showdown with the militant section of the Volunteers. It 'reflected both a genuine, principled support for the war effort and an array of political calculations'.[135] Irish nationalists may have felt a moral duty to participate in the war, but this was accompanied by a rational assessment that turning their back on Britain in the middle of a terrible war would do nothing to help their Home Rule situation afterwards.

For Redmond and his supporters, the period following Woodenbridge was superficially peaceful and was spent galvanizing support for the recruiting campaign on behalf of the 16th (Irish) Division. The new campaign claimed an 'extraordinary manifestation of popular regard' for Redmond and enjoyed a high political profile in its early stages, similar to that of the 36th (Ulster) Division.[136] On 24 October, Redmond addressed the Belfast regiment of the National Volunteers. He reminded them of the Irish reputation as a 'fighting race' and encouraged them to enlist for overseas service, to 'strike a blow for Ireland where the real fighting is going on', and that 'the proper place to guard Ireland is on the battlefields of France'.[137] That day Union Jacks hung from prominent buildings like the Catholic Boys Hall and Celtic Park, indicative of the amelioration in relations between nationalist Ireland and Britain, now that Home Rule was on the statute book. In the words of James Connolly's daughter, Nora, 'you would not believe you were living on the Falls Rd

---

[130] *Ulster Guardian*, 3 October 1914. See also Geoffrey Lewis, *Carson: The Man Who Divided Ireland* (London, 2005), 168–9.

[131] *Belfast Newsletter*, 4 September 1914.

[132] F. S. L. Lyons, *John Dillon: A Biography* (London, 1968), 360.

[133] *The Times*, 17 September 1914, 10.

[134] F. X. Martin, *The Irish Volunteers, 1913–1915: Recollections and Documents* (Dublin, 1963), 148.

[135] Wheatley, *Nationalism and the Irish Party: Provincial Ireland 1910–1916*, 207.

[136] *Westmeath Examiner*, 24 October 1914.

[137] *Irish News*, 26 October 1914 and Stephen Gwynn, *John Redmond's Last Years* (London, 1919), 179.

[sic]. You'd think some magician had taken your house and set it down on the Shankhill Road. Never was there so many Union Jacks hung out to honour Sir Edward Carson as there were . . . in honour of J.E. [Redmond]'.[138]

Redmond was, on the whole, supported in his position on the war. Redmond's three chief parliamentary supporters, T. P. O'Connor, Joseph Devlin, and John Dillon, all backed his campaign.[139] Others went further and showed their support to England by enlisting, including some of Redmond's friends, family (his brother and son), and political colleagues such as Tom Kettle.[140] However, the situation was different amongst advanced nationalists. If Redmond's 3 August speech was interpreted as 'madness or treachery' by many advanced nationalists, then Redmond's Woodenbridge speech was blasphemous.[141] Unpremeditated as it was, it produced a crisis within the Volunteer movement. The Volunteer organization split into two sections, the larger of which (between 150,000 and 170,000 men) stayed with Redmond to form the National Volunteers and contribute to a steady stream of recruits to the British army. The minority, consisting of between 9,700 and 11,000 of the more extreme members, broke away to form their own force, retaining the name of Irish Volunteers, led by Eoin MacNeill.[142] Although this number only made up around 6 per cent of the pre-split Volunteers, many of the 'deserters' were the most active members. Whilst, in the short term, the split freed Redmond from his critics, in the long term it would have serious ramifications. A revolutionary conspiracy began to take shape to which the whole concept of Home Rule was irrelevant.

Advanced nationalists could not temporarily suspend their political beliefs and support the war. Redmondite nationalists, like Kettle, could reconcile Irish independence within a framework of Great Britain and the British Empire. Participation in the war could help Ireland attain dominion status—a virtually self-governing state of the British Empire. As a dominion, Ireland could attain the status of 'nationhood' and political independence from the United Kingdom, whilst still enjoying the benefits of Empire. Advanced nationalists, along with the anti-war, anti-imperialist members of the Irish labour movement, did not want Ireland to be any part of the British Empire and wanted absolute and unambiguous independence from Westminster. In their opinion 'Ireland cannot, with honour and safety, take part in foreign quarrels otherwise than through the free actions of a national government of her own', and denied 'the claim of any man to offer up the blood and lives of the sons of Irishmen and Irish women to the services of the British Empire'.[143] For

---

[138] Nora Connolly-O'Brien, *Portrait of a Rebel Father* (London, 1935), 201.

[139] *Freeman's Journal*, 6 October 1914.

[140] William 'Willie' Redmond, John's younger brother, enlisted in 1914 with the Royal Irish Regiment and died at the Battle of Messines, Belgium in June 1917. William Archer Redmond, John's son, survived the war. Five IPP MPs volunteered for the war: Stephen Gwynn, J. L. Esmonde, Tom Kettle, Willie Redmond, and Daniel D. Sheehan.

[141] Ó Buachalla, ed., *The Letters of P. H. Pearse*, 326.

[142] Fergus Campbell, *Land and Revolution: Nationalist Politics in the West of Ireland, 1891–1921* (Oxford, 2005), 196.

[143] Martin, *The Irish Volunteers, 1913–1915: Recollections and Documents*, 154.

them Ireland was, and always would be, their first priority. For advanced nationalists, their enemy was England, and Ireland needed its men to protect Irish shores from the British imperialist threat. As a result, speeches by Redmond and his comrades were condemned, arguing that these leaders, in their support of Britain's war, had abandoned Ireland. On 19 September, the day after the royal assent, Tom Scanlan MP, visited Sligo to celebrate the glory of Home Rule achieved. Speaking from the upper window of the Imperial Hotel he declared 'The statute which was enacted makes Ireland free but this same statute binds Ireland indissolubly to the British Empire.' This statement provoked a certain amount of disorder: people shouted insults and 'To Hell with the Empire', and several members of the crowd in the street below engaged in a 'spirited bout of fisticuffs and the proceedings terminated abruptly'.[144] James Connolly opposed Redmond's concept of empire. For the Irish socialist leader, such an imperialist war was a total abomination:

> the most fearful crime of the centuries. In it, the working class are to be sacrificed so that a small clique of rulers and armament makers may sate their lust for power and their greed for wealth. Nations are to be obliterated, progress stopped, and international hatreds erected into deities to be worshipped.[145]

By widening responsibility for the war, animosity towards Germany was diluted. According to Arthur Griffith 'Germany is nothing to us in herself, but she is not our enemy.'[146] Francis Sheehy-Skeffington believed that 'our enemy is not German militarism, but English militarism—Kitchenerism [sic]'.[147] James Connolly preferred a German victory over a British one, and at the outbreak of war began negotiations to prepare a military insurrection in Ireland with German aid. In October he hung a banner 'We Serve Neither King Nor Kaiser But Ireland' from Liberty Hall, Dublin, and used it as a masthead of the *Irish Worker*. He felt it was absurd to be fighting for another country whilst Ireland was still enslaved. Others went further and saw an opportunity for Ireland to fight back against its occupier whilst it was distracted on the continent. Pádraig Pearse, who would be executed by the British government for his role in the Easter Rising of 1916, prophetically wrote on 3 August that with Britain and its army absorbed by the war 'Ireland falls to the Volunteers, and then—well then we must rise to the occasion'.[148]

The language utilized by advanced nationalists is the key to understanding their dissent in 1914. They opposed 'England' rather than Great Britain. Scotland and Wales were not part of their argument: their quarrel was with England—and more specifically, Westminster. Anti-English sentiment manifested itself in an anti-recruitment campaign. Just as a minority of British and Irish suffragettes questioned why women should support a government in war who had refused them equal participation in peace, certain Irishmen questioned why they should volunteer to die for a country that did not offer them citizenship or equal rights. Such

[144] *Sligo Independent*, 20 September 1914.
[145] *Forward*, 15 August 1914.
[146] *Sinn Féin*, 8 August 1914.
[147] NLI: Sheehy-Skeffington papers: Ms 33,612/17, 3 September 1914.
[148] Ó Buachalla, ed., *The Letters of P.H. Pearse*, 324.

campaigns against the British army—'mercenaries' of the Westminster government—were not new in Ireland and became the primary tactic of advanced nationalists in 1914.[149] The content of this material played heavily on the fact that Home Rule was still an expectation and not a fact. Ultimately the anti-recruitment movement wanted to 'prevent . . . one single Irishman from selling himself body and soul to the only enemy Ireland has in the world—ENGLAND'.[150] Anti-recruitment activity began in early September, when the British government were deliberating whether the Home Rule Bill would receive the royal assent, and reached its peak in October.

Although most Irish newspapers supported Redmond's position on the war, an underground press began to pour out anti-recruiting propaganda, particularly in Dublin. Following the DORA regulations of 28 November, the authorities began to take on seditious newspapers. Out of the seven papers of doubtful loyalty (*Irish Freedom, Ireland, Fianna Fail, Sinn Féin, The Leader*, the *Irish Volunteer*, and the *Irish Worker*), three stopped publication of their own accord, two remained in order and did not warrant seizure, and two were closed down (*Irish Freedom* and the *Irish Worker*). Outside Dublin only two papers caused the authorities concern: the *Kerryman* and the *Cork Celt*. Under the DORA, the former came into line and the latter ceased publication.[151] Very rapidly, the sale and circulation of advanced nationalist newspapers in Belfast had 'noticeably diminished'.[152]

Anti-war meetings, organized by Francis and Hanna Sheehy-Skeffington and their supporters, were held mainly in Dublin.[153] Another anti-recruitment technique was to interrupt recruitment meetings. John Hosty, from Castlegar, County Galway, recalled a recruiting meeting held in the Town Hall, Galway, by Stephen Gwynn and other Redmondite supporters in 1914, where the police turned away likely hecklers. A local priest, Father Connolly, of St Joseph's, Garbally, Ballinasloe, was refused admittance. However, undeterred:

> He came away. Directly opposite the Town Hall lies the Convent of Mercy Schools with a six-foot wall around it. Fr. Connolly mounted the wall, and addressed the overflow. In case of interference with him he was immediately surrounded by a fairly hefty crowd of young men. He finished what he had to say without interference and got as good a reception—an enthusiastic one at that—as the gentlemen inside closed doors had from their own supporters.[154]

At other recruiting meetings officers were often asked probing and awkward questions about the freedom of Ireland when they spoke about defending 'poor little Belgium'.

As evidenced above, some Catholic priests contributed to the anti-recruitment campaign. The Archbishop of Dublin, William Walsh, was disgusted by Redmond's

---

[149] Terence Denman, '"The Red Livery of Shame": The Campaign Against Army Recruitment in Ireland, 1899–1914', *Irish Historical Studies* 29 (1994).
[150] NLI: Piaras Béaslaí Papers: Ms 33,912/1 (1914).
[151] NA, Kew: CO 903/18, Intelligence Notes, 1914.
[152] NA, Kew: CO 904/95, RIC County Inspector report, Belfast City, November 1914.
[153] NLI: Sheehy-Skeffington papers: Ms 33,612/16, 16 August 1914.
[154] NA, Dublin: BMH, Witness Statements: John Hosty: WS 373 (n.d.).

support of the war and felt that the Irish party was no longer serving Ireland but their masters, the English Liberals. He demonstrated his discontent by refusing to take part in any recruitment drives, a significant loss as he was the most important member of the Catholic hierarchy and head of the largest diocese in Ireland.[155] Dublin Castle kept a close eye on clergymen who used seditious or anti-recruitment language in their sermons. Between August and October, nineteen occasions of clergymen using seditious or anti-recruiting language were reported to Dublin Castle from across the country. In these cases, recruitment to the British army was discouraged, friendship with Germany was encouraged, and England's maltreatment of the Irish was emphasized.

It is difficult to assess the extent and impact of the anti-recruitment campaign. A fine line existed between suppression of dissent and alienation of Irish public opinion. Repressive measures against extremist bodies could alienate Redmondite nationalists and lessen support for the war. The authorities were persuaded by Redmondites like Dillon that stamping down heavily on Sinn Féin anti-recruiting propaganda would backfire.[156] His views were supported by Joseph Devlin, who told Nathan that 'the Sinn Féiners except in Dublin . . . are a small minority . . . Irishmen are not affected by the stuff that appears in the seditious press and that it would be playing into their hands to make martyrs of them'.[157]

On the whole, people felt that police surveillance remained relatively unobtrusive. On 4 October, Rosamond Jacob distributed some anti-recruitment leaflets in Ballybricken, Waterford City. She noticed that 'there were some peelers [police] but they did not interfere with us and we did not court their notice'.[158] The authorities were undoubtedly following Redmondite advice not to make martyrs of the dissidents. Also shutting down the papers was fruitless as they tended to reappear a few days later under different titles. More generally, the United Kingdom in 1914 allowed room for controlled dissent as the example of labour dissidence in Glasgow showed. But this was only the case provided the broad population could be counted on to limit anti-war and especially anti-recruitment feeling. All the available evidence at the end of 1914 showed that this was still so in Ireland.

The best indication of this was that large numbers of Irishmen did enlist in the British army from both north and south, as discussed below. Despite anti-enlistment posters all over Sligo on the evening of 29 October, the *Sligo Independent* noted, on 7 November, 'a very marked enlistment spirit'.[159] Ironically, the Irish Transport and General Workers' Union—one of the largest opponents of recruiting—had contributed 2,700 former members to the British army by May 1915.[160]

[155] Jerome Aan de Wiel, 'Archbishop Walsh and Mgr. Curran's opposition to the British war effort in Dublin, 1914–1918,' *The Irish Sword* 22 (2000), 193–5.
[156] Lyons, *John Dillon: A Biography*, 362.
[157] MPP Bodleian. Augustine Birrell: MS Eng c.7033, ff. 22–4, 10 November 1914.
[158] NLI: Diary of Rosamond Jacob: Ms 32,582/27, 4 October 1914.
[159] *Sligo Independent*, 7 November 1914.
[160] Tim Bowman, 'The Irish Recruiting Campaign and Anti-Recruiting Campaigns, 1914–1918', in *Propaganda: Political Rhetoric and Identity 1300–2000*, ed. Bertrand Taithe and Tim Thornton (Stroud, 1999), 234.

Francis Ledwidge, who had supported MacNeill in the split in the Meath Volunteers and had been accused of being pro-German by his local Board of Guardians, enlisted with the Royal Inniskilling Fusiliers on 24 October 1914. While this may seem contradictory, given his rejection of Redmond's policies, Ledwidge himself saw no inconsistency in his actions. He felt the best way to combat the Germans was at the front, not 'by passing resolutions at home'.[161] He was killed in Flanders on 31 July 1917. A letter from Florence Pielou, the landscape painter, described to Francis Sheehy-Skeffington on 15 August the difficulties she was encountering trying to sell the radical labour paper, *Irish Citizen*, in Dublin:

> On Thursday last I spent an hour on the steps of the Mansion House doing my best to sell the *Citizen* to the people going to the meeting but all in vain! I could not even get rid of one—and during the time a lady asked me if I were not ashamed of this week's number... I have noticed a great decrease in sales.[162]

In late September the *Freeman's Journal* described the negative reaction of the crowds at one of Francis Sheehy-Skeffington's anti-recruitment meetings in Dublin. According to the journalist, he was 'jeered and hooted by the crowd' and arrested for his own 'protection'.[163] Parents of schoolboys attending St Enda's College—the bilingual school set up by Pearse in Rathfarnham, County Dublin in 1908—showed their distrust of Pearse's political opinions by withdrawing their sons from the school in autumn 1914.[164] Thomas Hynes, a MacNeillite Volunteer in Galway, recalled how 'we tried to break up recruiting meetings but we generally got beaten up ourselves as at least eighty per cent of the population were hostile to Sinn Féin, for a number of their husbands and sons were in the English army and navy'.[165]

By early November the battle to control the Volunteers was largely over, with the Irish party victorious. On 25 November Colonel Maurice Moore, the Inspector-General of the Irish Volunteers, found that 'opinion is changing in Ireland and recruits are coming in. W. Redmond and I went to Cork on Sunday and found the feeling very good'.[166] Three days later Dillon wrote to Matthew Nathan: 'I do *not* believe that the Sinn Féiners and pro-Germans are making any headway against us in Ireland'.[167] By November only four complaints of anti-English sermons by Catholic clergymen were made to Dublin Castle, and the following month only one. A memorandum on the publication and circulation of seditious newspapers in Ireland published in early January 1915 highlighted how their threat had, for the time being, dissipated.[168]

[161] Oliver Coogan, *Politics and War in Meath, 1913–1923* (Dublin, 1983), 65.
[162] NLI: Sheehy-Skeffington papers: Ms 33,611/11, 15 August 1914.
[163] *Freeman's Journal*, 26 September 1914.
[164] Ó Buachalla, ed., *The Letters of P. H. Pearse*, 330.
[165] NA, Dublin: BMH Witness Statements: Thomas Hynes: WS 714 (1952).
[166] NLI: Maurice Moore papers: Ms 10,561/24, 25 November 1914.
[167] Lyons, *John Dillon: A Biography*, 361.
[168] NLI: Joseph Brennan papers: Ms 26,161 (1914) and Ms 26,159, 22 January 1915.

Following the split, Volunteer activity, amongst both Redmondites and Mac-Neillites, tapered off and had slumped to derisory levels by December. This was not necessarily due to a lack of support for the nationalist cause. The movement had been weakened by the number of army reservists who had been called up at the beginning of the war who had previously provided the Volunteers with military skills and drill instruction. Furthermore, the constant threat that Britain was going to impose conscription on Ireland dissuaded Volunteers from parading openly. Men feared that if they publicly took part in Volunteering then they would be called up to the army.[169] During late September and October there was heightened expectation, emanating from Sinn Féin papers in Dublin, that the government would bring into operation the Militia Ballot Act, dating from 1882. The story was fuelled by ambiguous comments made by Redmond in Waterford on 11 October when he suggested that a victorious Germany would introduce conscription in defeated states. His opponents twisted this to make it appear that Redmond was predicting conscription should the Allies suffer substantial defeats. On 16 October the *Irish Independent* claimed that reactivation of the Act was imminent and the story was carried in several local papers the next day.[170] Nationalist opinion was outraged. In a letter to his father Desmond Ryan, at St Enda's College in Dublin, wrote 'There are here people fired up, jumping out of their skins about a note in the *Independent* saying that it was settled by the government to enact the Military Ballot. There will be a very big fuss if such a thing is done'.[171] This story triggered a full-scale conscription scare and young men began to emigrate from southern Ireland in their hundreds. In October, the Inspector General recognized that the membership of the Volunteers was 'now steadily on the decline' because the members 'dread of being called on for military service in the war'.[172] The police estimated that 600 Volunteers, aged between 18 and 30, sailed from Queenstown to America on 21 to 22 October alone.[173] The scare was short lived owing to unequivocal denials from both Redmond and the government, and some of the emigrants did return.[174] However, it demonstrates the paradox in Irish nationalist support for the war: while most nationalists endorsed Redmond's support for England's war, they were not necessarily willing to fight in it.

By the end of 1914 politics had quietened significantly in comparison to late July. On the whole, the Irish party still led the large majority of nationalists, and popular opinion was on Britain's side in the war. Opposition to the war was limited and extreme opinions were held by only a minority of people. Year-end police reports displayed a common pattern: interest in the war, sympathy for the Allies, dormant Volunteers, no drilling, no public political meetings, and little recruiting. In November, Augustine Birrell, Chief Secretary of Ireland, wrote 'The Irish have

[169] Wheatley, *Nationalism and the Irish Party: Provincial Ireland 1910–1916*, 214–15.
[170] *Irish Independent*, 16 October 1914.
[171] UCD, Archives: William Patrick Ryan papers: LA11/E/190/33, 17 October 1914 (Translated from the original Irish by Thérèse Sullivan, 2007).
[172] NA, Kew: CO 904/95, RIC Inspector General report, October 1914.
[173] NA, Kew: CO 904/120/5, RIC Crime Special Branch report, October 1914.
[174] Wheatley, *Nationalism and the Irish Party: Provincial Ireland 1910–1916*, 221–2.

changed, and their attitude today, north, south, east and west towards England in her tremendous struggle with Germany and Austria is, speaking of Ireland as a whole, one of great friendliness.' There was still a 'disloyal minority', but the 'Fenian strain' was worn 'very thin indeed'. This change of opinion, he concluded, was 'unprecedented and calls for notice'.[175]

However, recruitment suggested a growing distance between nationalists and their leader. A friend of Rosamond Jacob told her that nationalists in Limerick 'mostly say sure they must support Redmond, but they don't seem to have any intention whatever of enlisting'.[176] On 10 December, Timothy Healy, in Dublin, wrote to his brother Maurice that advanced nationalists 'are not pro-German', but that enlistment was a 'price too high for the kind of Home Rule that has been "granted"'.[177] At the end of December, the Roscommon County Inspector summed up the limitations of nationalist support for the war and for Redmond's wartime policy: 'So far as the Volunteers in this county are concerned the recruiting for the army is nil. They hope that Germany will be defeated, but it rests there.'[178] More worryingly, Redmond's recruitment campaign had created a new opposition identified by many as 'Sinn Féiners' or advanced nationalists, who, in the coming eighteen months, would destabilize Anglo-Irish relations beyond repair.

RECRUITMENT

Recruitment, thus, took on even more significance in the Irish case, for nationalists had more reason than most to question their sense of duty and loyalty to the British war effort. Yet, in the first five months of war, nowhere was the competition for 'loyalty' more evident than in recruitment. Both unionists and Redmondite nationalists jockeyed for the position of providing the most Irishmen for the British army, even down-playing the contribution of their opponents. When discussing the factors which influenced recruiting in Ireland two common mistakes are made. First, just as the surge of recruitment in England, Wales, and Scotland in 1914 is used as evidence of 'war enthusiasm', lower rates of enlistment in Ireland are used as evidence of anti-war sentiment. Second, by simply equating Protestant with unionist, the large numbers of Protestants in Ulster who joined the army is explained by their attachment to the British Crown, and by default, used to demonstrate the lack of support for the war amongst Irish Catholics.

Belfast, in particular, holds a sacred place in unionist folk memory of the war as a source of willing recruits without equal in Ireland. Unionists in Belfast argued that by 1916 the city had provided proportionately the most recruits of any city in the United Kingdom owing to 'the loyal traditions of the men of Ulster' which motivated them to rally 'promptly and spontaneously to the call . . . of their King

---

[175] NA, Kew: CAB 37/122/171.
[176] NLI: Diary of Rosamond Jacob: Ms 32,582/27, 10 October 1914.
[177] Healy, *Letters and Leaders of My Day*, 552.
[178] NA, Kew: CO 904/95, RIC County Inspector report, Roscommon, December 1914.

and country'.[179] In contrast to their absolute loyalty, they argued that inferior returns generated in the south stood testimony to the inherent disloyalty of Irish Catholics and nationalists. The reality was a good deal more complex.

Recruiters in Ireland in 1914 used similar methods to those employed in Britain. Major newspapers as well as prominent politicians and individuals attempted to persuade Irishmen, from north and south, to enlist. The *Freeman's Journal*, the oldest nationalist newspaper, took a pro-recruiting stance and individual MPs called for recruits. Prior to the establishment of the Central Council for the Organization of Recruiting in Ireland early in 1915, recruitment posters and advertisements circulating in Ireland were the same as British posters—appealing mainly to loyalty to the Empire—and tended to be void of any Irish sentiment.[180] William King, in Galway, recalled the 'big display of placards outside the RIC barrack. They were mostly recruiting posters with headings such as "Recruits Wanted" and "Your King and Country Need You"'.[181] On 11 September, Francis Sheehy-Skeffington observed how the famous Kitchener poster was displayed all around Dublin, but that some had been vandalized with graffiti.[182]

As in Wales and Scotland, recruiting rhetoric was made specific to local audiences. At a recruiting meeting in Collooney, County Sligo, in September, the local priest, Reverend Father Doyle, urged the audience to contemplate what the consequences would be for Ireland if Germany won:

> The Germans have cherished the ambition for the past thirty years of planting their surplus population on the fair fields of Ireland and of relegating the ancient Celts once more in the bogs and the mountains. The old age pension would disappear and land reform would cease because it would have no meaning.[183]

Making reference to Ireland's bitter history of land agitation, Tom Kettle urged men to help Belgium, 'the latest and greatest of evicted tenants'.[184] Attention was also drawn to the potential of invasion: an attack on the east of England could easily be transformed into an attack on the east of Ireland. Recruits were needed to stop the Germans reaching Calais and beyond. By December 1914, around 50,000 Irishmen had been recruited to the British army. Although the lowest result in the United Kingdom, by 12 November 5.7 per cent of the Irish male population had volunteered.[185]

By 31 December although Dublin was performing worst, Belfast was not the leading city for recruitment. Cardiff, Birmingham, and Glasgow had 'out-enlisted' Belfast.[186] An analysis of the recruitment levels of National and Ulster Volunteers

---

[179] Eric Mercer, 'For King, Country and a Shilling a Day: Recruitment in Belfast during the Great War, 1914–1918' (MA, Queen's University, Belfast, 1998).

[180] Mark Tierney, Paul Bowen, and David Fitzpatrick, 'Recruiting Posters', in *Ireland and the First World War*, ed. David Fitzpatrick (Dublin, 1986), 47–58.

[181] NA, Dublin: BMH Witness Statements: William King: WS 1,381 (1956).

[182] NLI: Sheehy-Skeffington papers: Ms 33,612/17, 11 September 1914.

[183] Michael Farry, *Sligo 1914–1921: A Chronicle of a Conflict* (Trim, 1992), 42.

[184] Lyons, *The Enigma of Tom Kettle: Irish Patriot, Essayist, Poet, British Soldier 1880–1916*, 273–4.

[185] NA, Kew: CAB 37/122/164.

[186] NA, Kew: NATS 1/398.

allows conclusions to be made about the relationship between political affiliation and loyalty to the British army. In September 1914 membership to the UVF in Belfast stood at around 30,700, compared with around 3,250 in the National Volunteers.[187] Based on police records and figures published in the press, almost 9,000 men of the Belfast UVF and over 1,200 of the city's National Volunteer force had enlisted as voluntary recruits by mid-December. Therefore whilst almost 30 per cent of the Belfast UVF had enlisted, 37 per cent of the city's National Volunteers had also enlisted: hardly any difference between the two.[188] Despite Belfast being the most polarized Irish city politically, similar levels of volunteering occurred on both sides.

According to official British statistics the total number of recruits who had enlisted within the United Kingdom by 15 September 1914 stood at 501,580. Expressed as a proportion of males of military age, Ireland stood out as the weakest contributor to the war effort, providing only 2.6 per cent of males of military age (compared with 6.2 per cent for England and Wales and 7.6 per cent for Scotland).[189] Southern Irish 'recalcitrance was widely ascribed to . . . incurable disloyalty'.[190] However, wartime recruitment in nationalist southern Ireland has been revised and rehabilitated, the sources of lower recruitment being identified as occupational status rather than political or religious beliefs.[191]

The reason for lower rates of enlistment in nationalist southern Ireland in 1914 can be best explained by the rural/urban, agricultural/industrial divide. The difference between Irish and British volunteering rates can largely be explained 'by the scarcity of urban adult males who constituted the most likely material for the army'.[192] The family farm remained dominant in the organization of Irish labour in 1914. Evidence suggests that men from farming families were discouraged from enlisting owing to the negative impact this would have on the communal family income.[193] As the majority of Irish males of military age (57.4 per cent) were employed in agricultural rather than industrial occupations, and as recruits were more likely to volunteer from industrial rather than agricultural communities, the proportion of male recruits contributed by Ireland increases, as follows:

---

[187] Mac Giolla Choille, ed., *Intelligence Notes, 1913–1916*, 73–4.

[188] NLI: Redmond papers: MS 15,259 and Fitzpatrick, 'The Logic of Collective Sacrifice: Ireland and the British Army, 1914–1918,' 1028.

[189] NA, Kew: NATS 1/398.

[190] David Fitzpatrick, '"The Overflow of the Deluge": Anglo-Irish Relationships, 1914–1922', in *Ireland and Irish Australia: Studies in Cultural and Political History*, ed. O. MacDonagh and W. F. Mandle (London, 1986), 83.

[191] See Patrick Callan, 'Recruiting for the British Army in Ireland during the First World War', *The Irish Sword* 17 (1987), Fitzpatrick, 'The Logic of Collective Sacrifice: Ireland and the British Army, 1914–1918', Martin Staunton, 'Kilrush, Co. Clare and the Royal Munster Fusiliers: The Experience of an Irish Town in the First World War,' *The Irish Sword* 16 (1986).

[192] Fitzpatrick, '"The Overflow of the Deluge": Anglo-Irish Relationships, 1914–1922', 83.

[193] Fitzpatrick, 'The Logic of Collective Sacrifice: Ireland and the British Army, 1914–1918', 1028.

Table 6.1. Proportion of available male industrial population of military age enlisted*

Area	No. of Recruits (by 15 September)	% of males aged 20–45 (occupations not taken into account)	% of males of military age working in Industrial Occupations
England and Wales	416,717	6.2%	7.1%
Scotland	64,444	7.6%	8.9%
Ireland	20,419	2.6%	6.1%

* NLI: Redmond papers: MS 15,259, 30 September 1914.

The recruitment rate in Ireland should therefore be understood as much closer to that of Britain. Levels of recruitment in urbanized Ireland were quite impressive when put in a United Kingdom context:

Table 6.2. Recruits per 10,000 of the population by 4 November 1914 in the UK*

Area	Recruits per 10,000 of the population
Southern Scotland	237
Midlands	196
Lancashire	178
London/Home Counties	170
Yorkshire, Northumberland, Durham	150
Ireland (Ulster, Dublin, Wicklow, Kildare)	127
Western England	88
East Anglia	80
Southern Ireland (agricultural districts)	32

* Keith Jeffery, 'The Irish Military Tradition and the British Empire', in *'An Irish Empire'? Aspects of Ireland and the British Empire*, ed. Keith Jeffery (Manchester, 1996), 98, Simkins, *Kitchener's Army: The Raising of the New Armies 1914–1916*, 112.

As in Britain, the bulk of the rural population supported the war but believed their loyalty was better expressed through increased agricultural output than by enlistment to the army. For example, in rural Wexford, a Protestant farmer was less inclined to enlist than a Catholic urban labourer, whatever the intensity of his political loyalty. Even if religion can be seen as an indicator of possible political loyalty, which is not necessarily the case, then occupation affected recruitment to a much greater degree than loyalty or lack of it.[194] Although statistically Ulster did provide the majority of Irish recruits in 1914, this cannot be explained by their religious beliefs and political loyalty. It was more likely due to the influence of Belfast and its urban population, who would have been inclined to join the army regardless of their politics. Ulster's contribution was to do with proletarianism as

[194] Pauline Codd, 'Recruiting and Responses to the War in Wexford', in *Ireland and the First World War*, ed. David Fitzpatrick (Dublin, 1986), 18, 23–5.

much as Protestantism. Recruitment levels in rural Ulster, like those in south-western Ireland, did not peak until 1915.[195]

Other factors slowed recruitment in Ireland in 1914. Recruitment statistics are not enlistment statistics. Medical rejection rates in Ireland were as high as 74 per cent, which leaves open the possibility that many more men were willing to enlist than were accepted.[196] Perhaps one of the biggest disincentives was the impact of Kitchener's deep-seated hostility of the Irish and opposition to the creation of new army divisions with political overtones. Despite being born in Ireland, he was inflexible to any suggestions of separate badges, flags, and bands that would harness the emotions of traditional nationalism to the needs of the British war machine. This perceived discrimination was exacerbated by the acceptance of Craig's proposal that the Ulster Volunteers should form the nucleus of the 36th (Ulster) Division; a similar proposal for the creation of a territorial force incorporating the National Volunteers was refused. On 24 December John Dillon could not over-emphasize to T. P. O'Connor the negative impression the War Office had made on Irish recruiting. By the end of 1914 he had become so disillusioned that he resolved to speak on no more recruiting platforms.[197] The goodwill channelled into the 16th (Irish) Division was not nourished or built upon. A crucial atmosphere of trust was missing between the authorities and potential nationalist volunteers.

Despite this perceived lack of support from the British authorities, by the autumn of 1914 it was possible to give the title 'Irish' to no less than three divisions in the first of Kitchener's new armies, a considerable achievement, particularly in the light of Anglo-Irish relations only days before the outbreak of war.[198] Augustine Birrell believed that 'Ireland as an island had done at least as well as any historically-minded person has any right to expect', and that Ireland had sent more soldiers to the war under the voluntary recruiting system than the purely agricultural districts of England.[199] Redmond had persuaded thousands of nationalist Irishmen to join an army which, only a short time before, had been killing Irishmen on the streets of Dublin. Those men who did enlist from Ireland did so for very similar reasons given by British recruits.

As discussed, enlistment could not be explained as simply economic rationality. For both British and Irishmen, the risk of death or injury would have far out-weighed any economic incentive. Men below the poverty line did not always enlist, and men who had stable and steady jobs, like doctors and businessmen, also enlisted. Furthermore, 'recruiting levels . . . were of the extent that economic

---

[195] Fitzpatrick, *Politics and Irish Life, 1913–1921: Provincial Experience of War and Revolution*, 110–11.

[196] Bowman, 'The Irish Recruiting Campaign and Anti-Recruiting Campaigns, 1914–1918', 234.

[197] TCD, Manuscripts: Dillon papers: Ms 6740-4/229, 24 December 1914 and Lyons, *John Dillon: A Biography*, 362.

[198] Granted that only one third of these divisions—the 36th (Ulster)—could be said to have been thoroughly homogenous, being composed, as it mainly was of Carson's Ulster Volunteers (Lyons, 'The Revolution in Train, 1914–1916', in *Ireland Under the Union, II: 1870–1921*, ed. W. E Vaughan (Oxford, 1996), 190.)

[199] Augustine Birrell, *Things Past Redress* (London, 1937), 218.

motives could not account solely for enlistment'.[200] As in Britain, Irish individuals, regardless of political affiliation, volunteered for a variety of reasons. For some it was a combination of an opportunity for adventure and/or a sense of duty. Many identified with Ireland's ideological support of the war. According to George Berkeley, nationalists in Belfast were keen to enlist as soon as war was declared because they wanted 'to do anything in the way of guarding Ireland for the Empire; many of them—the unmarried—would serve abroad—*soon*'.[201] Nationalist sympathies were always about what was best for Ireland. In 1914 most nationalists believed that supporting Britain in a war to defend Belgium and France was the best prospect to secure an independent future. Thus it was not contradictory for those who supported the war in 1914 to also support the Irish insurrection in Dublin in Easter 1916. As Thomas McCrave, from Dundalk, highlighted, nationalists in his town 'were absolutely anti-German' but simultaneously 'they could not be described as pro-British'.[202] Support for Belgium was a significant motivating factor. According to Kevin O'Sheil, recruiting for the British army was very brisk after the German invasion. He recalled meeting an advanced nationalist in Dublin who had enlisted in the British army. Although 'still quite anti-English' he 'was quite frank as to his motive in joining up—"poor little Belgium", and his yearning to "get a belt at those bloody bastards and swines, the Huns"'.[203] As has been explored elsewhere, a strong tradition existed of Irishmen enlisting in the British army, both before and after the First World War.[204] Some men were simply following a family tradition of soldiering, entering into a respectable career. Others followed the example of their fathers and grandfathers who had fought in South Africa and the Crimea. Group loyalties were, as in the British case, significant in motivating men to enlist: 'The readiness of individuals to join the colours was largely determined by the attitudes and behaviour of comrades—kinsmen, neighbours, and fellow-members of organisations and fraternities.' Whilst some collective influences were negative, such as amongst farming families, the influence of Ireland's political militias was generally positive—for both the Ulster and National Volunteers alike.[205]

***

Placing Ireland in an all-UK context, rather than projecting back onto 1914 the divergence of response that occurred after the Easter Rising two years later, has demonstrated that many aspects of the Irish responses to war in 1914 were akin to those in Britain. The immediate outbreak of war caused similar feelings of anxiety, shock, and concern, and comparable levels of dislocation and change. Irish people, on the whole and regardless of political affiliation, rallied in support of charitable

---

[200] Staunton, 'Kilrush, Co. Clare and the Royal Munster Fusiliers: The Experience of an Irish Town in the First World War', 75–86.

[201] NLI, George Berkeley letters: Ms 15,266/1, 4 August 1914.

[202] NA, Dublin: BMH Witness Statements: Thomas McCrave: WS 695 (1956).

[203] NA, Dublin: BMH Witness Statements: Kevin O'Sheil: WS 1,770 (n.d.).

[204] Jeffery, 'The Irish Military Tradition and the British Empire', in *'An Irish Empire'? Aspects of Ireland and the British Empire*, ed. Keith Jeffery (Manchester, 1996).

[205] Fitzpatrick, 'The Logic of Collective Sacrifice: Ireland and the British Army, 1914–1918', 1028.

relief efforts and felt anger and suspicion towards the German enemy both within and without. The enemy for the majority of Irish people in 1914 was Germany—not unionists or nationalists. Just as in Britain, Irish people experienced the violence of war with the arrival of refugees and wounded soldiers, and fears of invasion. Rumours widespread in Britain did not leave Ireland untouched. Moreover, a large number of Irishmen volunteered for the British army and the peaks and troughs of recruitment followed a UK-wide pattern. A lower level of recruitment in Ireland cannot be attributed to political or religions affiliation, or a sense of anti-Englishness. Instead it was connected with the smaller pool of industrialized workers in Ireland available to volunteer in 1914. Overall, Ireland contributed substantially to the British war effort as well as sharing much of the experience.

The major difference between the British and Irish experience in 1914 was the complicated political situation. Politics, which had in some degree been suspended in Britain, was intensified in Ireland. This made it more difficult for both unionists and nationalists to rally unquestioningly around the cause. Both parties used their support for the war as a means to achieve their political goals. Although unionists saw the war, not as an end in itself, but rather a means to a political end, they also understood that the war was the central question facing Ireland and the rest of the United Kingdom. As part of the British Empire they sought the application of English law in Ireland. They were Irishmen with political loyalty to Westminster. Like Englishmen, they felt their existence directly threatened. A German victory would spell the end of British supremacy in the world. German imperialism was the antithesis of what the British Empire stood for. The unionists' future was bound up in their support for the war and they had to see it through to the end. For them there was only one nation in the United Kingdom and that was the British nation. The war encouraged unionists to reject their Irishness in favour of being British.[206]

Nationalists, while acknowledging that the war was just resulting from German aggression, saw the fate of the Home Rule Bill as their primary concern. Their identity was firmly Irish: they would do all that was necessary for Ireland. Support for the war was always going to be conditional. Two cartoons published in *The Lepracaun* in October 1914 depict the war as a 'trading card' for self-determination, by which Irish support for the war had earned nationalists 'credit' to be cashed in at the end of the conflict.[207] In this sense, Irish nationalists felt affiliation with their Polish counterparts, who, like the Irish, were fighting on behalf of imperial armies under the promise of the establishment of an independent Poland after the war. It was always going to be more difficult for nationalist Ireland to embrace the British cause. The dominance of the internal pre-war political situation framed the nationalist reaction to war and Ireland's involvement in it. Ireland's national question remained unanswered, and the war, and any involvement Ireland was to have in it, was framed by this issue. How could a population view itself as a positive collective unit when its borders were in flux and it was governed from abroad? How

---

[206] Hennessey, *Dividing Ireland: World War One and Partition*. (London, 1979), 79.
[207] *The Lepracaun*, October 1914, 69, 72.

Fig. 6.1. 'Pax in Bellum; or, United Kingdomers'.
The Lepracaun, August 1914, 39. Reproduced with the permission of The Board of Trinity College, Dublin.

could the nation be mobilized for war, when national self-determination was still being debated? How could men volunteer to fight for a country that had not provided them with equal citizenship? There was far more at stake for Ireland in the war. Its involvement in it would determine whether or not its national aims were achieved. Irish entry into the war was therefore a much more cautious, calculated, negotiated, and gradual process.

However, nationalist Ireland *did* enter the war in 1914 and believed that by supporting the war and the aims that Britain stood for—honour, freedom, and the liberty of small nations—Ireland would benefit as a result. Nationalist Ireland did contribute on an almost equal level with volunteers, charity, and underwent parallel experiences of fear, rumour, anticipation, and emotion. British fears of dissident nationalist reactions were vastly exaggerated. As the following cartoon from *The Lepracaun* illustrates, the relationship between unionist and nationalists could be renegotiated within the national identity of being 'United Kingdomers'. Rather than being a looming dark cloud, war is now a ray of light that shines over John

Redmond and Edward Carson shaking hands, marking a new atmosphere of cooperation.

This may have been wishful thinking. But a short war, ending in 1915, would have left the configuration of Irish politics and the relationship between Britain and Ireland in a very different, and more positive, state to that of 1916. The Redmondite strategy might well have governed the nationalist policy and Redmond retained the leadership. The Kingdom of Great Britain and Ireland was much more united in 1914 than has previously been appreciated.

7

Settling Into War

> I regret to say one got the bad news last night that poor Jack Hamilton had
> been killed on the 9th [November] while leading his men in an attack and was
> shot through the head and lungs. [After breakfast] We shot at Castle Rising . . .
> there were quite a nice lot of partridges. Our bag was 320 pheasants, 250
> partridges, 45 hares, and 5 woodcock. It was a perfect day.[1]
>
> King George V, diary entry, 21 November 1914

According to Vera Brittain 'by the time . . . that we started believing in Russians,
England had become almost accustomed to the War'.[2] After the jolt of the food
panic and a brief financial scare 'the vast inertia of everyday life in England asserted
itself'.[3] How did British and Irish people settle into the war, once the initial shock
and chaos of the opening six weeks had died down? What socio-economic changes
occurred in these months? Who and where was most affected? How long did people
believe they would have to live in these new circumstances?

The phrase 'business as usual' has become synonymous with the opening phase
of the war in the United Kingdom. Frequent references exist in the post-war
literature describing how the British and Irish people, once the shock of war had
worn off, brushed themselves down and carried on as normal as if nothing had
changed. The phrase has its origins in the business world of 1914—businessmen
were well aware that their best interests were served by a continuance of normal
trading habits—and was officially endorsed by the government in the first war
budget, introduced by the Chancellor of the Exchequer on 16 November.

But what the government did in reality made nonsense of the slogan. They
intervened in the insurance and financial markets on a large scale. Between mid-
August and late 1914 they pledged their own credit behind almost the entire
financial system in order to re-establish confidence and restart foreign trade. On
18 August the Cabinet launched what they hoped would be a concerted trade war
on Germany's overseas markets. To assist them the Board of Trade organized a
number of trade exhibitions and suspended patents taken out by German companies in Britain. The phrase, therefore, was more an expression of hope than a
description of the reality of wartime society. Trying to go on as if there was no war

---

[1] Royal Archives, Windsor Castle: RA GV/PRIV/GVD/1914: 21 November 1914.
[2] Brittain, *Testament of Youth* (London, 1933), 97.
[3] Wells, *Mr Britling Sees It Through* (Leeds, 1916, 1969), 202.

at all was a way of demonstrating 'the truest form of patriotism'.[4] However, whilst people attempted to continue as normal, it could never be 'business as usual'. Too many socio-economic changes occurred in 1914 for anyone to carry on as if the war was not happening. Moreover, business could not carry on as 'usual' if the higher demands of sacrifice—across all sections of society—were to be met. Tension manifested itself where people attempted to continue as if the war was not happening, thereby making the term 'business as usual' redundant. Whilst people aspired to carry on as normal, the best they could achieve in these unprecedented circumstances was a gradual acceptance of the new situation and a 'settling down' to life in wartime. Paradoxically, this meant that whilst economically things levelled off, emotionally, by October/November, people became gloomier and more depressed as they received the news from the front, compounded by regular lists of casualties published in the press, leading up to the final halting of the Germans (and their potential invasion) at the First Battle of Ypres in November.

DISLOCATION OF THE ECONOMY

Overall, by September the economic situation had become clearer and the impact of the war on the economy had levelled out. In a few trades, employees were dismissed after being on temporary short time, but in the majority of cases factories had resumed normal working hours. Although the total number of men employed in industry fell by 10.2 per cent, this was counterbalanced by the rate of enlistment, which reduced total male unemployment to 1.4 per cent. However, 8.4 per cent female unemployment indicated a more severe industrial depression than the male unemployment figures suggest. By October the situation had much improved in all but one or two trades. Although short-time figures were still abnormal and considerable unemployment existed amongst women, an increase in export activity plus large war contracts from the government and Britain's allies aided a steady recovery of business confidence in the United Kingdom. By December, recruitment almost offset the reduction of male employment due to the war, while female unemployment improved to 3.2 per cent.[5] Trade Union returns on unemployment in this period illustrate the 'settling down' of the economy in 1914 (see Figure 7.1 below).

Surviving War Relief Committee records reflect a similar pattern. The total number of civilian applications made per week to the Leicester War Relief Committee between 5 September and 26 December corroborate the figures on unemployment. Most applications were made between early September and mid-October. By the end of October, and for the remainder of the year, applications

---

[4] Ibid., 203.

[5] Session 1914–1916, Vol. XXI, Cd. 7703: *Report of the Board of Trade on the State of Employment in the United Kingdom in October 1914* and Session 1914–1916, Vol. XXI, Cd. 7755: *Report of the Board of Trade on the State of Employment in the United Kingdom in December 1914*.

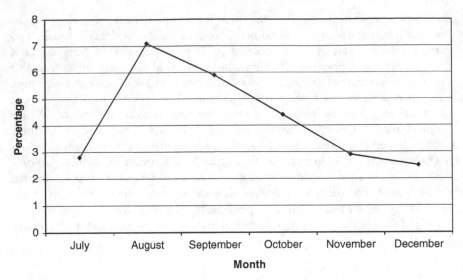

Fig. 7.1. The percentage of unemployed as returned by trade unions, July to December 1914

Kenneth D. Brown, *Labour and Unemployment, 1900–1914* (Newton Abbot, 1971), 190.

decreased, averaging thirty per week for the last five weeks of 1914.[6] In Birmingham, Elizabeth Cadbury also noticed a significant decrease in relief applications to the local Unemployment Committee in mid-November.[7] Similarly, in Ireland, unemployment began to level out after September, and by December the situation had significantly improved.[8]

The economic impact of the war confirms that local circumstances shaped popular reactions to the conflict. Certain regions suffered more than others. Manufacturing districts, particularly of textiles, were hit by the disruption to overseas markets. Hallie Eustace Miles recorded in late September how the Nottingham lace-makers had 'all their lace thrown back on their hands as the huge orders from abroad have been cancelled in consequence of the War'.[9] Unemployment amongst women was high, mainly because of the impact of the war on Lancashire's cotton trade.[10] Although the cotton trade was already depressed in July, the outbreak of war 'threatened complete paralysis' in Lancashire. The Bolton and District Operative Cotton Spinners' Provincial Association gave out more unemployment benefit between August and December 1914 than in 'any previous

[6] ROLLR: 14 D 35/27/ii: Leicester War Relief Committee, Report 24 August–26 December 1914.
[7] BCA: MS 466/432ı Box 3. Cadbury Family Journal, 10 November 1914.
[8] Session 1914–1916, Vol. XXI, Cd. 7703: *Report of the Board of Trade on the State of Employment in the United Kingdom in October 1914.*
[9] Miles, *Untold Tales of War-Time London: A Personal Diary* (London, 1930), 16.
[10] *Liverpool Courier*, 30 September 1914 and Session 1914–1916, Vol. XXI, Cd. 7755: *Report of the Board of Trade on the State of Employment in the United Kingdom in December 1914.*

full year in the Society's history'.[11] Mrs D. Bowes, whose father was a dyer and finisher in Shipley, West Yorkshire, in 1914, recalled in 1991 the anxiety felt by her family as the best dyes were German. Whilst she had no close relatives at the front, her family were fearful in 1914 of the economic repercussions of war.[12] In a letter to his cousin dated 18 September, J. Wallace, from Chorley, Lancashire, informed him that most of the mills in the area were 'working less than half time, and nearly everyone is suffering more or less from the effects of the war'.[13] However, by November the situation was improving and:

> practically the whole trade was employed, either full time or varying degrees of short time. The situation at the end of the year is still a grave one, but is much better than anyone could reasonably have expected under the extraordinary circumstances.[14]

It was not only large industries that faltered. Small businesses paid a heavy price. Resort towns, such as Scarborough, found their summer season ruined, with hotel and boarding-house keepers suffering heavily. In Cambridge, less than half the usual number of undergraduates enrolled, withdrawing much of the business that the town survived on. Again it was the lodging-house keepers who suffered the most.[15] Charles Bell recalled how his father's fruit importing business in Liverpool suffered because of the suspension of international trade in 1914. A consignment of lemons from Hamburg, ordered before the outbreak of war, were the family's first 'war casualty'.[16] The self-employed were also hit. Thomas Batty, leader of a London society-band in 1914, told his sisters on 16 November that the war meant his prospects were:

> very black; there is no prospect of any engagements in my particular line this winter and although I have tried to get work in other orchestras I have only had two weeks [sic] work since the first week in Sept [sic]. I am in for a very bad time so I must sit tight and see it through.[17]

However, despite his personal privation, Thomas acknowledged that the overall economic situation was much improved: 'Lloyd George and his men have done wonders with the financial situation and saved a panic which would have resulted in the ruin of thousands and the loss of millions of money as well as entailing an appalling amount of distress through unemployment. The manager of a city financial firm . . . can now find no praise too high'.[18]

---

[11] Bolton Archives and Local Studies Centre, Bolton: Bolton and District Operative Cotton Spinners' Provincial Association, Annual Report 1914: FT/21/9.

[12] Liddle: DF 016: Mrs D. Bowes (1991).

[13] Bolton Archives and Local Studies Centre, Bolton: Walt Whitman Collection: ZWN/6/20, 18 September 1914.

[14] Bolton Archives and Local Studies Centre, Bolton: Bolton and District Operative Cotton Spinners' Provincial Association, Annual Report 1914: FT/21/9.

[15] *Cambridge Daily News*, 31 December 1914.

[16] IWM, Docs: Bell, Lt C.G.H.: 92/13/1 (n.d.).

[17] IWM, Docs: Batty, T.: 91/5/1, 16 November 1914.

[18] Ibid.

Local organizations and authorities sought to stem unemployment. In Barnstaple, North Devon, the Town Council accelerated the building of a new drill hall for the Territorial Force Association in order to employ the men left short of work owing to the war.[19] In Oldham, Lancashire, the local Committee for the Care of Mothers and Children, in coordination with the Local Representative Committee, set up the Regent's Street Workroom in October. This employed around forty women aged 16 and over, whom the war had made unemployed, to mend and make garments.[20] In October, staff at the Glasgow and West of Scotland College of Domestic Science were called upon to give advice regarding cheap menus suitable for working-class households in wartime, and students were instructed in this branch of work.[21] There was huge concern, particularly amongst the Labour movement, that the working classes would suffer the most in wartime. The War Emergency Workers' National Committee was a joint Labour organization established at the very beginning of the war to protect the interests of the working classes on matters such as employment, wages, and conditions of service, and supply of essential commodities in the wartime situation.[22] As well as supporting the vulnerable poor, it was another symbol of the unity within Britain amongst groups who had previously been anti-government before the war. Materially, the working classes did suffer at the outbreak of the war. For example, the cheapest cuts of meat increased in price more than expensive cuts between July and October. Moreover, the working classes were less able to meet the rising prices with a shift in diet or to cheaper food. During the first few months of war the biggest increase in the cost of food fell upon the class least able to bear it.[23] Out of desperation, a minority of people resorted to crime. Edith Morgan of Coedpenmaen, Pontypridd, appeared in court on 5 September on charges of stealing items worth £9, including a coat and a watch. Her excuse was that she was financially embarrassed because her husband was at the front.[24]

Government action curbed the early panic on the supply side by ensuring sufficient quantities of basic foodstuffs were available. By 23 August, Christina Lawson, in Anstruther, Fife, confirmed that 'food prices are back to normal again'.[25] On 3 September Lydia Middleton, in London, informed her son that food prices, which had rocketed in August, were 'going down so fast that it is actually cheaper than usual just now'.[26] Only fresh eggs continued to rise in price

---

[19] NDRO: Borough of Barnstaple Town Council Minutes, 1913–14: 2654A/1/4, 18 September 1914.

[20] Oldham Local Studies and Archives, Oldham: Lees Family papers: D/LEE/119, October 1914.

[21] Now the Glasgow Caledonian University. From the personal research notes of Carole MaCallum, Glasgow Caledonian University.

[22] See R. Harrison, 'The War Emergency Worker's National Committee, 1914–1920', in *Essays in Labour History 1886–1923*, ed. A. Briggs and J. Saville (London, 1971), Horne, *Labour At War: France and Britain, 1914–1918* (Oxford, 1991), J. M. Winter, *Socialism and the Challenge of War: Ideas and Politics in Britain, 1912–1918* (London, 1974).

[23] Frances Wood, 'The Increase in the Cost of Food for Different Classes of Society Since the Outbreak of the War,' *Journal of the Royal Historical Society* LXXIX (1916).

[24] *Pontypridd Observer*, 5 September 1914.

[25] University of Glasgow, Special Collections: Christina Hunter Lawson papers: Ms Gen 525/18, 23 August 1914.

[26] Liddle: DF 091: Mrs Lydia Middleton, 3 September 1914.

after October, while all other food products gradually levelled off after the initial surge in prices in August.[27] In contemporary testaments, sugar (which was mainly imported from the Caribbean) was the product people missed most.[28]

Across the United Kingdom, people were immediately encouraged to be economical with their food supplies. The middle and upper classes were warned that in wartime they 'must not live to eat and drink' but 'eat and drink just sufficiently to enable [them] to live'.[29] Violet Clutton was encouraged by the King's example who had 'done away with all grand dinners at the Palace and will only have what is absolutely necessary'.[30] Organizations, such as the Vegetarian Society, published recipes and pamphlets with guidance on economical living in wartime.[31] The situation was eased by the arrival of supplies of flour from September provided by British Dominions such as Canada. This not only helped economically but added to a sense of unity and alliance with the empire. This new sense of economy made many people especially grateful in the harvest thanksgiving ceremonies in late September.[32] Yet, despite the levelling out of food prices, some people continued to be cautious about their food supplies. On 8 November Arnold Bennett noticed how, at an auction in Frinton, Essex, 'young housewives hesitated to buy astounding bargains in fruit etc'.[33] In the long run, voluntary economizing was not enough to deal with overall shortages, and, as in other areas such as military service, compulsion had to be introduced in the form of extended price controls and, eventually, rationing.

In Britain and Ireland in 1914 there was a sense of simplification amongst the population. People were aware that in wartime it was appropriate to do without certain 'luxury' items. Whether these sacrifices were large or small depended on a person's pre-war situation. In Essex, Mrs A. Purbrook and her family 'agreed to do without sugar' in their tea.[34] Reverend Clark recorded in his diary the sacrifices the local Manor House in Great Leighs had agreed to make including 'either butter or jam, not both' and 'no cake at tea'.[35] Brighouse, one of the major European centres for the silk trade, felt the lash of war on a 'luxury' industry. 'Nobody wants silk today, for luxuries are banned' bemoaned the *Brighouse Echo* on 18 September.[36] Dolly Shepherd recalled how her aunt's feather business was ruined by the war because it was 'a luxurious trade' that had no place in wartime society.[37] London's furniture trade also suffered for the same reason.

[27] NA, Kew: MAF 60/562.
[28] Liddle: DF 040: Miss H.W. Davison (1981).
[29] MacDonagh, *In London During the Great War* (London, 1935), 43.
[30] DRO: Violet Clutton: 6258M/Box 1, Vol. I.
[31] GMRO: G24/1/1/9: Vegetarian Society Minute Book, May 1912–December 1914.
[32] Munson, ed., *Echoes of the Great War: The Diary of the Reverend Andrew Clark, 1914–1919* (Oxford, 1985), 13.
[33] Bennett, *The Journals* (Middlesex, 1932, 1971), 380.
[34] IWM, Docs: Purbrook, Mrs A.: 97/3/1.
[35] Munson, ed., *Echoes of the Great War: The Diary of the Reverend Andrew Clark, 1914–1919*, 12.
[36] *Brighouse Echo*, 18 September 1914.
[37] IWM: 579, Reel 5 (1975).

People in rural areas were materially less affected than those in urban areas. A schoolboy in Corwen, North Wales, recalled how his family was never short of food as local farmers would provide butter, eggs, and vegetables.[38] Michael MacDonagh observed the abundant and varied food supplied to the soldiers billeted in rural Abbots Langley, Hertfordshire.[39] Phillip Leicester, on holiday in rural Norfolk in early September, felt the countryside was undisturbed by the war.[40] The Roscommon RIC County Inspector reported at the end of 1914 how 'farmers are well pleased with themselves' because of the profits that had been made on cattle exports and the increased price of food that had risen within the United Kingdom between 15 and 17 per cent by 1 December.[41]

Towns that relied on industries vital to the war effort benefited from the new situation. As early as 8 August the *Barrow News* appealed to townspeople to assist in housing the workmen who were flooding in to work at the Vickers naval and munitions works.[42] Henry Dotchin was an apprentice riveter on a dockyard in Middlesbrough in August 1914. Although he did not celebrate the outbreak of war, he welcomed the fact that he had guaranteed employment for its duration.[43] From September onwards the woollen and worsted trades 'were relieved more than any other industry by government contracts'.[44] Demand for khaki in Huddersfield was unprecedented. On 29 September, Frank Lockwood, a lithographic artist from Linthwaite, Yorkshire, noticed how busy the mills in Huddersfield were 'working overtime . . . Khaki, French Grey and Blanketing are causing the rush'. The 'great boom in the Huddersfield and Colne Valley textile trade' continued throughout November and December owing to Allied contracts. By 1 December the town was producing 300 miles of khaki per week. The war increased Lockwood's own workload. Increased prices meant that food labels had to be reprinted. Public interest in the war also created work for publishers and printers. By December the lithographers were 'very busy with another edition of . . . Jane's *Fighting Ships*', the third new edition in twelve months.[45] Other businesses were flexible enough to adapt to the new economic situation. The Huddersfield firm Messrs. Benjamin Crook and Sons supplied sporting goods, such as footballs, before the war. As the debates raged over the appropriateness of playing sport in wartime, their leather factory changed to producing haversacks for the French army.[46] As Gearoid Ua h-Uallachain noted, the war gave Ireland a chance to recover economically, in

[38] ERO: T/Z 25/680 (1966).
[39] MacDonagh, *In London During the Great War*, 30.
[40] WRO: Ref 705:185: BA 8185: Parcel 2: Phillip A. Leicester, 10 September 1914.
[41] *Leitrim Advertiser*, 31 December 1914.
[42] *Barrow News*, 8 August 1914.
[43] IWM: 8846, Reel 4 (1985).
[44] Session 1914–1916, Vol. XXI, Cd. 7755: *Report of the Board of Trade on the State of Employment in the United Kingdom in December 1914*, 31.
[45] IWM, Docs: Lockwood F.T.: 96/52/1, 29 September, 9 October, 1 December, and 13 December 1914.
[46] *Huddersfield Examiner*, 2 November 1914.

particular after the effects of the 1913 lock-out and strike in Dublin. For many, therefore, the war was economically 'a God-send'.[47] However, those making profits from the war—whilst men were giving their lives for their country—were open to severe criticism.

The distress anticipated by many at the outbreak of the war, by and large, never eventuated. But significant changes did occur to the economy. Combined with increased government intervention, the economic situation in the United Kingdom following the outbreak of war could not be 'business as usual'. Although the situation calmed down after September, it did not return to pre-war levels.

CHANGING LANDSCAPES

People's lives and landscapes began to change, in varying degrees, in the weeks and months after war was declared. These changes were not just material and economic: people's world's looked and felt different. As the writer, Thomas Hardy, in Dorchester, told his friend Edward Clodd in late September, 'We are continually getting evidences of the war, if we go outside our gate, and even if we don't'.[48]

Visual changes were manifest. London soon discovered what was to become a hallmark of twentieth-century war: blackouts, searchlights, and the fear of enemy attack from the air. Basil H. Ryder, in training with the Royal Field Artillery, cut short his visit to London in September 1914 because it was too depressing:

> They have brown paper over all the lamps that are alight and that's only half of them and search lights at Hyde Park Corner and Marble Arch, and on top of Charing X [sic] station. London is full of uniforms, more officers and Belgian soldiers than Tommies... All the bridges and tube stations are guarded by two soldiers with fixed bayonets. I felt quite frightened when I walked up a tube platform and the sentries spring to attest and present arms.[49]

By mid-September anti-Zeppelin searchlights were blazing across London. On 15 September Violet Clutton commented on them in her diary concluding that 'soon we will take them as a matter of course'.[50] On 9 October she noted how houses in Oxford Circus and Piccadilly were draped in the Allied flags and believed that this was done in an effort to keep London 'as bright and as cheerful as possible during this terrible time'.[51] By October clocks, including Big Ben, 'the mighty heart of London', had been silenced and their night dials dulled. Michael MacDonagh felt that it was at night-time that Londoners fully noticed the changes caused by the war. London was blacked out, and instead people looked fearfully to the skies for any sign of an impending air raid.[52]

---

[47] NA, Dublin: BMH Witness Statements: Gearoid Ua h-Uallachain: WS 328 (n.d.).
[48] BL: Ashley Volume B VI, ff. 62, late September 1914.
[49] Liddle: GS 1408: Lt B.H. Ryder, 1914.
[50] DRO: Violet Clutton: 6258M/Box 1, Vol I, 15 September 1914.
[51] DRO: Violet Clutton: 6258M/Box 1, Vol II, 9 October 1914.
[52] MacDonagh, *In London During the Great War*, 39, 47–8.

Such changes not only made London look and sound different, but Londoners acted differently to greater and lesser degrees. By October, Hallie Eustace Miles and her husband stopped accepting evening engagements because the city was so dark and felt too 'weird...and so dangerous'.[53] Similarly, Elizabeth Haldane also noticed how wartime London was dark and 'eerie'; combined with the constant rumours of defeats and possible Zeppelin raids she concluded that London was 'not a good place at a time like this, too jumpy'.[54] For Michael MacDonagh, the lowering of the lights in his train carriage simply meant he could no longer read his evening paper.[55]

Similar changes were taking place across the United Kingdom. A friend in Belfast wrote to Hanna Sheehy-Skeffington, in Dublin, on 18 November describing how:

> the war is more than even our daily food, and it seems to be coming to our doors. There is talk of a German submarine near the Lough, of mysterious ships on the Island, and the City Hall and Albert Memorial are darkened in the evenings and a generally cheerless air in the streets prevails. On Saturday last, the shops were not allowed to display their usual outside lights.[56]

Gardens of upper-class households lost their formally immaculate appearance as workers were called up.[57] In areas where self-sufficiency was encouraged different crops began to grow. Lawns were turned over to potatoes, and Hilda Moss, in Birmingham, recalled how flowers were removed to make room for edible crops.[58] Not only were people's outfits changed by the war—for example more khaki and fewer luxurious accessories such as feathers and jewellery—but the war even changed people's physical appearances. Hilda Davison, in Sunderland, recalled how adulterated flour brought some people out in a rash: 'I can remember one of my cousins covering her cheeks with her hands and saying—"oh, don't look at our war bread faces"'.[59] A common observation was the number of recruiting posters, appearing on 'every taxicab, on every carrier van, on every blank wall'.[60] Other home defence precautions, such as the digging of trenches, physically altered the scenery that people were used to. The picture in Figure 7.2, depicting trenches being dug along the Folkestone cliffs, was taken by a cousin of Mary Coules—an act for which he nearly got arrested as a German spy. Evidence of earlier invasion fears appear in the background, in the form of a Martello Tower. It is striking how inexperienced the forces building them were, as the trenches are straight, without dog-toothing to prevent enfilade fire.

By late 1914 the results of mass recruiting were visible everywhere. Almost every major centre had become a garrison town swarming with soldiers in the making,

[53] Miles, *Untold Tales of War-Time London: A Personal Diary*, 26.
[54] NLS: Elizabeth S. Haldane: Mss 20243, 17 October 1914.
[55] MacDonagh, *In London During the Great War*, 22.
[56] NLI: Sheehy-Skeffington papers: Ms 33,604/6, 18 November 1914.
[57] Horn, *Rural Life in England in the First World War* (Dublin, 1984), 40.
[58] City Sound Archives, Birmingham Museum: R76–7 (1981).
[59] Liddle: DF 040: Miss H.W. Davison (1981).
[60] IWM, Docs: Tower, Miss W.L.B.: P472, 15 October 1914.

Fig. 7.2. Trench-digging on Folkestone cliffs, September 1914

with a constant stream of trains to and from the ports on the south coast taking troops, weapons, stores, and bringing back wounded and men on leave. Army camps sprouted, disrupting life in the surrounding area with the noise and bustle of military activity. Rudyard Kipling, in Burwash, Sussex, described the changes to the landscape to Theodore Roosevelt on 4 December:

> I don't say all England is yet an armed camp because there are gaps where you can go for ten miles without seeing troops, but so far as my wanderings have led me there is no road where you can go twenty miles without running into them in blocks. The second million will be coming as soon as we can get accommodation for them.[61]

People regularly commented on the number of men in uniform that were appearing in towns and villages. By mid-August, the streets of Dublin were swarming with soldiers.[62] By 2 September London looked 'quite different', owing to the men drilling in every square-inch of open space in the city.[63] The populations of small towns and villages, unaccustomed to large numbers of people, mushroomed as men were put up across the United Kingdom. Around 1,600 men were billeted in the small market town of Tring in Hertfordshire, with another thousand or so in nearby villages.[64] L. D. Jarvis recalled in 1990 how his village—Stock in Essex—

---

[61] Pinney, ed., *The Letters of Rudyard Kipling* (London, 1999), 271–2.
[62] NLI: A Dubliner's Diary: Ms 9,620, 12 August 1914.
[63] DRO: Violet Clutton: 6258M/Box 1, Vol I, 2 September 1914 and NAS, GRH: George Hope papers: GD 364/1/Bundle 22, 8 November 1914.
[64] Horn, *Rural Life in England in the First World War*, 33.

increased from 1,000 to 2,000 people overnight when the 7th Battalion Warwickshire Regiment arrived at the end of August.[65] In September Iris Holt told her fiancé how her home town of Lewes, Sussex, 'had her population doubled at a days notice'. In October she added that she had no idea that that many men existed in the country.[66] The war literally created a 'New Aldershot', as the local press termed it, 'with barracks crowded and teeming with life, such as no year in its history has witnessed'.[67] A Kensington resident was so concerned about the number of men billeted in and around London that she feared the possibility of an outbreak of serious illness, such as scarlet fever, owing to the drainage systems being overtaxed.[68] Entire buildings, including schools, were handed over to the military authorities for billeting, hospitals, drilling, recruiting, and other requirements.

There was a landscape of sound which was also changed by the war. With the influx of Belgian and French refugees, and foreign soldiers, foreign accents were further evidence of the changes the war was bringing, along with the dialects from across the United Kingdom. For Hallie Eustace Miles, by September there were so many French accents in London she felt 'as if one is in France'.[69] In December, a friend of Arthur Butler, injured in hospital, described to him how London was 'swarming with foreigners', particularly Belgians, and how they dressed and sounded very different.[70] James Lewis recalled how the streets of Liverpool 're-sounded with the sounds of military bands accompanying the various route marches, 5,000 troops at a time and at night the skies were lit up by the searchlights at Brooke Vale'.[71] Mrs E. Shead in Widford, Essex, also recalled the sound of 'heavy nailed boots' as characteristic of the opening months of war.[72] The auditory landscape was changed by the singing of wartime songs and Allied anthems. Hallie Eustace Miles recorded in early August the 'small and subtle changes' in wartime London: 'people in the streets are now whistling the "*Marseillaise*", and "*God Save the King*", and "*Rule Britannia*"; the children are marching instead of walking, and are carrying bits of stick as bayonets and using old pieces of tin pails as drums'.[73] On 23 August Annie Brunton, in London, awoke to the sound of 'wild shrieks' of a crowd 'cheering or rather squealing at a regiment going off to Vauxhall'. The soldiers were 'singing and then . . . whistling' as they marched.[74] Many people recorded the sound of newsboys shouting to advertise the latest war news on the streets—often to the point of making complaints to the police.[75]

[65] ERO: SA 13/598/1 (n.d.).

[66] Liddle: AIR 224: A.H. Morton, September 1914.

[67] *Aldershot News*, 21 August 1914.

[68] IWM, Docs: Diary of a London lady (anonymous): Misc 29 (522), 4 September 1914.

[69] Miles, *Untold Tales of War-Time London: A Personal Diary*, 21.

[70] Liddle: GS 0251: A.S.G. Butler, Letter A15, December 1914.

[71] NWSA: 2001.1016. James Richard Lewis (2001).

[72] ERO: T/Z 619 (1966).

[73] Miles, *Untold Tales of War-Time London: A Personal Diary*, 14.

[74] NLI: Diary of Annie Brunton: Ms 13,620/2, 23 August 1914.

[75] Glamorgan Record Office (GRO): Chief Constable of Swansea, Reports to Watch Committee: D/D Cons/S 2/3/3, 29 September 1914.

The requisitioning of horses, a chief requirement for the army in the first two weeks of war, had a significant impact on both urban and rural livelihoods. In Morecambe, it resulted in the tram-car service (pulled by horses) being suspended.[76] In other urban areas such as Birmingham, Bristol, and Manchester, the loss of horses in business was keenly felt and work was made especially difficult for bakers and milkmen.[77] In rural areas, the requisitioning of horses affected the speed with which the harvest was gathered in and efforts to get the land ready for winter sowing.[78] Many farmers almost came to blows with requisitioning officers who sought their workhorses.[79] Horses were often bought 'in the shafts', the owner only able to complete his journey if he promised to hand over the animal as soon as he reached home. This policy was adopted because of the number of farmers who were conveniently 'absent' when the army called for their horses, suggesting that a minority of British and Irish people were not always compliant with the government's wartime policies. Requisitioning also had an emotional impact. Dorothy Owen recalled in 1963 how devastated she was to see the horses she used to enjoy feeding as a girl being taken away by the army.[80]

Other aspects of the British and Irish landscape changed during the latter months of 1914. Public houses closed at 10 p.m. A change in traditional rituals also marked a separation between life before and after the outbreak of war. Guy Fawkes' night was celebrated on 5 November without the usual fireworks and bonfires owing to the threat of invasion and aerial bombardment.[81] The Lord Mayor's Show, held in London on 9 November, was revised out of sensitivity to the moral order of wartime. The traditional pageantry accompanying the opening of Parliament on 11 November was dimmed.[82] German-owned shop-fronts were anglicized, as were names. For those in contact with wounded soldiers, sights and smells changed. William Gover was a medical student at Oxford University in 1914. The Examination School became a large military hospital and he recalled the experience of visiting such wards: 'The smell in the wards was not easily forgotten: a mixture of infected wounds and iodoform, a pungent antiseptic, and eusol, a then newly discovered chlorine preparation'.[83] Civilians, unfamiliar with hospitals, who visited wounded soldiers, were doubtless shocked by the sights and smells of a society at war.

---

[76] Macdonald, *1914—The Days of Hope* (London, 1987), 59.
[77] R. H. Brazier and E. Sandford, *Birmingham and the Great War, 1914–1919* (Birmingham, 1921), 48, *Bristol Times and Mirror*, 6 August 1914, 6, *The Times*, 13 August 1914, 3.
[78] Munson, ed., *Echoes of the Great War: The Diary of the Reverend Andrew Clark, 1914–1919*, 21.
[79] Macdonald, *1914—The Days of Hope*, 59.
[80] IWM: 4190, Reel 1 (1963).
[81] IWM, Docs: Miller, H.: 02/38/1, 5 November 1914.
[82] MacDonagh, *In London During the Great War*, 37, 40.
[83] Liddle: RNMN Gover: Dr W. Gover (n.d.).

SEPARATIONS

Whilst for some people the state of war was marked by an increase in uniformed men around them, for others it signalled their absence. This was also true of the everyday framework of civilian society. With mass enlistment, men were regularly noticed as 'missing' from their accustomed place. The Annual Report for the University of Liverpool, published in December 1914, commented on the decrease in male students and staff as an impact of war.[84] Hallie Eustace Miles, who co-owned a restaurant in London, noticed the lack of men at the tables by September.[85] On 1 September Elizabeth Cadbury recorded in her diary how surprised she was to see so many more women than men in a local Birmingham tearoom. The same day she responded to a friends' letter commenting how '[Doncaster] must seem like a strange town, with such an enormous number of soldiers about'.[86] Birmingham, in 1914, was the fourth biggest city in the United Kingdom; for Elizabeth Cadbury to comment in this way highlights how an absence of men was becoming part of the norm of wartime society in certain parts of Britain and Ireland.

The departure of men was felt deeply by those loved ones who had to endure an extended and indefinite period of separation. Separation was happening in early autumn as Regulars were sent abroad and volunteers trained. In 1911 the population of Great Britain was grouped into 8,954,000 families, and the average size of a family was 4.35 persons.[87] With a million volunteers, few, if any, households were left unaffected by the experience of separation. Bertram Neyland, a Post Office clerk in Port Talbot, South Wales, in 1914, recalled how 'every family had a son or a husband or an uncle, everybody was connected with the war in that some male relative was away somewhere'.[88] On 23 August Nellie Barry, in Mortimer, Berkshire, told her cousin Rose, in America, about the 'dreadful happenings' of the last few weeks. 'One hears nothing but sudden parting with husbands, sons and mothers and then the awful silence swallows everything up, for no word must reach home of *where* they are or what they are doing, lest the enemy . . . gets to know the places of England'.[89] On 13 September, Christina Lawson wrote from Edinburgh how 'every family has someone off'.[90] One mother recalled how she lay awake 'through the long, unhappy nights' listening to the sound of trains en route to Southampton, enduring the separation from her husband.[91] In late September

[84] University of Liverpool, Special Collections: Annual Reports of the University, 1908–1914: R/ LF 371 A1, December 1914.
[85] Miles, *Untold Tales of War-Time London: A Personal Diary*, 20.
[86] BCA: MS 466/432: Box 3: Cadbury Family Journal, 1 September 1914.
[87] Mark Abrams, *The Condition of the British People, 1911–1945* (Bath, 1970) 39 41
[88] IWM. 318, Reel 1 (1974).
[89] Liddle: DF 009: Jessica Barry, 23 August 1914.
[90] University of Glasgow, Special Collections: Christina Hunter Lawson papers: MS Gen 525/17, 23 September 1914.
[91] Peel, *How We Lived Then, 1914–1918: A Sketch of Social and Domestic Life in England During the War* (London, 1929), 21.

Thomas Laidlaw, encamped with the 5th Battalion Cameron Highlanders in Aldershot, comforted his wife Bertha, in Glasgow, over their separation. He told her: 'it has made me so happy to hear that you are taking the French meaning of "Grass Widow". I know you are a brave wee girl and I want you to keep like that, you may have to in the future'.[92] According to Rudyard Kipling '*every* young man, with *one* exception . . . with whom Elsie [Kipling's daughter] danced at the beginning of the season is at the War'. Her mother wrote how Elsie 'had been so upset by the war and went away [to stay with a family friend in Perthshire] sad for a loss of another friend news of whose death was in the morning paper. Killed in action. She says very soon she won't know any man *who is alive*'.[93] In early September Clara Mason was charged with being drunk and disorderly on St Andrews Plain in Norwich. She had been abusive to a passer-by who had asked her to stop singing *God Save the King*. In her defence Mrs Mason said: 'I have been worrying this past month about my Husband and lost my head a bit . . . He is at the front and I have not been right since. I cannot eat anything. A friend of mine gave me a drink and it got hold of me'.[94] On 8 October, in a letter to her husband serving in China, Mrs Johnson, in Daylesford, expressed her feelings on the issue: 'I think England is asking a little too much of her women just now, for it isn't only one's best and dearest but everyone else too'.[95] In some cases there was more than one man leaving a single home. Although newspapers celebrated the sacrifices made by British and Irish mothers who had more than one child at the front, this must have multiplied the anxieties of parents.

The experience of separation was not exclusive to women: fathers, sons, brothers, and male colleagues shared the sense of anxiety and potential devastation. Rudyard Kipling wrote on 5 October how 'almost all the men I used to know are gone—some past recall: and the staple of conversation when one meets is as to the whereabouts of such and such a one, son or husband or father of so and so. It is the uncertainty that kills'.[96] Soldiers also experienced the ordeal of separation. William Scott, attached to the Shropshire Yeomanry in 1914, recorded in his diary the anxiety he felt at being away from his family: 'I have not felt very cheerful today—cannot help thinking of dear Kathleen [his wife] and the children . . . our separation looks like being a long one and it hits me very hard'.[97]

Leave, or the absence of it, compounded the agony of separation. Many letters exist between loved ones desperately trying to arrange visits whilst the soldier was in training on British soil. Often it was too difficult, or permission was cancelled at the last minute. This was common during December 1914. At a time when people

---

[92] A term which connotes a woman temporarily separated from her husband, usually on business. IWM, Docs: Laidlaw, Thomas Douglas: 66/81/1, late September 1914.

[93] Pinney, ed., *The Letters of Rudyard Kipling*, 258–9.

[94] *Eastern Daily Press*, 2 September 1914, cited in Gregory, 'British "War Enthusiasm" in 1914: A Reassessment', in *Evidence, History and the Great War: Historians and the Impact of 1914–18*, ed. Gail Braybon. Oxford, 2003), 82.

[95] Liddle: GS 0861: Major General D.G. Johnson, 8 October 1914.

[96] Pinney, ed., *The Letters of Rudyard Kipling*, 259.

[97] IWM, Docs. Scott, Major W.S.: 99/12/1, 5 September 1914.

particularly wanted to be reunited with their families, the threats of a potential German raid cancelled Christmas leave for many men.[98] Despite the obvious pleasures of being reunited, for some this was perhaps a blessing in disguise as the men would always have to return at some point, and the leave was always too short to satisfy. Hallie Eustace Miles described the pain of 'second partings' where men were leaving for the second time in as many months.[99]

Children also experienced the distress of separation with the departure of their fathers, uncles, friends, and brothers and were unsettled by the distress displayed by their mothers at their parting. For James Whittaker, a schoolboy in Bonahaven, West Scotland, his awareness of being at war 'was intensified by the gradual departure of the men' in particular his friends. When he returned to school he discovered with a shock that 'Malcolm was missing, and Peter, and Donald, and Alec. Jimmy had gone, Johnny had gone, so had Colin, Angus, Neil, George, Dugal—they had all gone'.[100] Others felt that the children of serving soldiers needed special attention. By late August 1914, Ada Macguire preferred to concentrate her relief efforts on the children of departed men, rather than soldiers or refugees, who she believed were suffering in silence.[101]

Children's lives and landscapes changed in 1914 for similar reasons as their parents' did. They would have been aware of certain traditions, like Guy Fawkes' night, not being celebrated as usual. Belgian refugees were integrated into local schools, teachers enlisted, lessons were adapted for the war, and children were heavily involved in relief efforts, such as Belgian Flag Days, knitting, and local concerts. On 17 August, King George V wrote to his son George Edward, aged 12, asking if his teacher, Mr Hansell, was teaching him about the war: 'He should read the accounts in the papers to you every day, as you ought to know what is going on'.[102] Children were also educated about the war from friends, overhearing adult conversations, and through literature aimed at their age group. The trade journal *Games and Toys* reflected how the war was integrated into children's toys: war-themed toys were the most popular sellers from September 1914 onwards.[103] Dorothy Owen recalled how, following the announcement of war, her grandmother took away all her German-made toys 'amongst them a camel of which I was very fond'.[104] On 18 August Violet Clutton visited friends in Potters Bar, Hertfordshire, where 'the younger members of the family were spending their time hunting for German spies and begging the [older] boys to come out with their guns to shoot a spy they had found who afterwards turned out to be the milkman!'[105] On the evening of 14 September she heard, from her house in London:

[98] IWM, Docs: Butlin, Lt James H.: 67/52/1, 27 December 1914.
[99] Miles, *Untold Tales of War-Time London: A Personal Diary*, 29.
[100] James Whittaker, *I, James Whittaker* (London, 1934), 87.
[101] IWM, Docs: McGuire, Misses A. & R.: 96/31/1, 28 August 1914.
[102] Royal Archives, Windsor Castle: RA GV/PRIV/AA59/293: 17 August 1914.
[103] *Games and Toys*, July to December 1914 seen at the Museum of Childhood, Bethnal Green.
[104] IWM: 4190, Reel 1 (1963).
[105] DRO: Violet Clutton: 6258M/Box 1, Vol I, 18 August 1914.

Fig. 7.3. Young schoolgirl, Kathleen, saluting in an over-sized army uniform

Liddle: DF Items, Education, Children and Students, 1914. Reproduced with the permission of Leeds University Library.

a great commotion outside and saw 'Kitchener's Army' marching past. This consists of about twenty to thirty small boys armed with toy rifles and carrying flags, and accompanied by a number of little girls wearing large red crosses. They pass here nearly every day and the first time we saw them Mother asked one of them who they were and received for answer "Why K o'K's army of course!"[106]

Playing at soldiers was not exclusively a male pursuit, as the picture of Kathleen, a young schoolgirl in 1914, illustrates (see Figure 7.3). The subject is photographed wearing a grown-up's uniform—possibly belonging to her father or brother—but clearly not a child's replica. Girls also emulated their female role-models by playing at being nurses. Jennie Lee in Cowdenbeath, Fife, recalled playing a number of war games including 'hospitals'. She and her friends collected broken dolls, especially those with missing limbs, dressed up as nurses, and attended to their 'wounded'.[107] Children were integrated fully into the national war effort. A number of cartoons published in *Punch* between August and December 1914 show children talking about, re-enacting, or being subjects of various aspects of the

[106] DRO: Violet Clutton: 6258M/Box 1, Vol I, 14 September 1914.
[107] Lee, *To-Morrow is a New Day* (London, 1939), 37.

war.[108] What is of interest is less the images of children themselves than how they were portrayed. These cartoons suggest that the war changed every level of society, touching everyone and everything. If the issues of wartime had infiltrated even the most innocent and protected members of society, then nowhere was immune. Such images of children and childhood within the context of war were used to educate and convince. The images demanded their audience to question: what kind of a world would these children live in, if their elders failed to fulfil their national duty? By using the technique of a child's standpoint, 'adult' war issues, such as volunteering, duty, shirking, greed, and espionage, were made explicit through the frank exchanges between children. The adult audience were left in no doubt as to what was expected of them during this national crisis.

The shift in understanding and experience from a pre-war society to a society at war did not happen for everyone at the same time. Experience was individual, and people understood the impact of war in a variety of ways, such as a lack of certain food items, the loss of their horse, the military presence in their towns and villages, and/or the sweeping of searchlights in the sky. For many people the understanding that they were at war came when they suffered personally. This was most often when a member of their family departed for training or the front, and did not necessarily happen in 1914. But for many, autumn 1914 was that moment. George Ewart Evans only felt 'the bite of the war' when his friends and co-workers enlisted from the mining village of Abercynon, Glamorgan, in September.[109] For James Lewis, a schoolboy in Waterloo, Liverpool, the war became a reality when his teacher left to join the army and returned to visit his school in his officer's uniform.[110] Other people were aware of the realities of war when they suffered a change in circumstance or experienced privation. For example, Miss G. West in Gloucestershire, was left to 'clean the stables, sift the cinders, dig potatoes and clean the boots, not to mention half a hundred other horrid unexpected little jobs' when her family's garden-boy, Ernest Rigsby, enlisted in 1914. It was at this point that war became a reality for her.[111] Many people came to terms with what modern warfare involved through the sufferings of others. Michael MacDonagh felt that the first 'shock of war' was the arrival of a batch of wounded soldiers on 30 August.[112] Ernest Cooper did not realize 'what war really meant' until 15 October when hundreds of Belgian refugees arrived in the town. It forced him and other residents to contemplate what their fate might be if Germany's advance continued.[113] A large number of people were 'shocked' into wartime society in October 1914 by the fall of Belgium, which added fuel to the rumours of German spies in Britain and Ireland.

---

[108] See for example, *Punch*, 30 September 1914, 280, 21 October 1914, 345, 16 and 18 November 1914, 413, 16 December 1914, 493.

[109] Evans, *The Strength of the Hills: An Autobiography* (London, 1983), 13.

[110] NWSA: 2001.1016: James Richard Lewis (2001).

[111] IWM, Docs: West, Miss G.M.: 77/156/1, 19 and 20 August 1914.

[112] MacDonagh, *In London During the Great War*, 19.

[113] IWM, Docs: Cooper, Ernest Read: P121, 15 October 1914.

Regardless of when change was noticed, it marked a rupture, the beginning of a different period, the start of a new era. According to George Rose, by 14 September 'the war [was] changing everything'.[114] Sir Alfred Dale believed that by 23 October British national life was undergoing change, and that 'men and women who were cynical have become serious'. If this mood lasted it would signify, he believed, 'the opening of a new chapter in the experience of the nation'.[115] What does this periodization mean? Why is it significant that people were aware of this shift? Does this suggest that August 1914 was, as Eric Hobsbawm has argued, the beginning of the short twentieth century?[116]

INSIDE THE WAR

For all the sense of personal rupture, the war generated its own sense of collective normality. It created its own temporal horizons, within which British and Irish people had to dwell. After rupture, came acceptance; the process of entering into war eventually led people 'inside the war'. People experienced what Rudyard Kipling described as 'settling down to the business of war' in various ways.[117] By late August, early September, public opinion appeared to be calming down. This assessment was supported by the public's behaviour which was often described as orderly, cool, and with 'quiet restraint'.[118] This acceptance of the new situation was also reflected in recruitment statistics. Once the shock of war had worn off, men flocked to volunteer in the first week of September. On 19 September Reverend Denys Yonge, Vicar of Boreham, Essex, recorded in his diary how 'quiet reigns supreme after a month of excitement'.[119] Mrs C. S. Peel acknowledged this change in mood: 'From the moment that war was declared the nation set its mind to win the war, at first with excited enthusiasm, afterwards with grim and dreary obstinacy'.[120] Phillip Leicester recognized a change in atmosphere in Worcester between the early days of war and the mood in late August. After heady days of excitement and anxiety, the town was now calm and quiet as people were busy occupying themselves with relief work.[121] On 1 September Thomas Moylan, in Dublin, observed that 'now the first shock of [war] is over we are settling down . . . and there is little to indicate that masses of troops are wiping out one another some four hours journey from London'.[122] Rudyard Kipling, on 5 October, described 'how quietly—for our note is ever quietude—the English have taken to the grim business

---

[114] ERO: Diaries of George H. Rose: D/DU 418/15, 14 September 1914.

[115] University of Liverpool, Special Collections: Letter Book of Vice-Chancellor Sir Alfred Dale: S 2341: Letter 475–6, 23 October 1914.

[116] Eric J. Hobsbawm, *Age of Extremes: The Short Twentieth Century, 1914–1991* (London, 1994).

[117] Pinney, ed., *The Letters of Rudyard Kipling*, 253.

[118] *Liverpool Post and Mercury*, 21 August 1914.

[119] ERO: Diary of Reverend Denys Yonge: D/DU 358/26, 19 September 1914.

[120] Peel, *How We Lived Then, 1914–1918: A Sketch of Social and Domestic Life in England During the War*, 20.

[121] WRO: Ref 705:185: BA 8185: Parcel 2: Phillip A. Leicester, 29 August 1914.

[122] NLI: A Dubliner's Diary: Ms 9,620, 1 September 1914.

of arms and how well the afflicted bear their sorrow'.[123] Less than twelve months later Rudyard himself would become one of the 'afflicted' with the loss of his son, John, at the Battle of Loos on 27 September 1915.

Despite the upheaval that he knew the war would cause, Alan Dorward, in Cambridge, believed that by late August/early September people had 'settled down to accepting the inevitable' and 'already discounted all the loss that must come . . . It is now a question of saving what we can from the ruin'.[124] For all the visual changes taking place in London in September, Macleod Yearsley felt that the inhabitants were 'carrying on quietly' despite alarmist rumours about the progress of the war. Moreover, the 'spirit of the people was being slowly trained' to meet the hardships of wartime.[125] The writer, Walter Dixon Scott, also sensed a 'settling into war' amongst the population in Manchester on 24 September:

> Don't you discover already a new sincerity and grit about? The gravity and dignity of the public isn't just leader writer's flummery. There's a splendid display of earnestness and intelligence all round. And of kindliness, tolerance, humanity . . . We see the silliness of rancour, and the contemptibility, the comic contemptibility, of squabbling jealousies. England has never seemed to me so sane and civilised as now.[126]

Emrys Hughes, at teacher-training college in Leeds, noticed how the excitement of the first month of war had been replaced by a serious and subdued atmosphere, a comment reiterated by other witnesses around the United Kingdom.[127] The same change was experienced in Dover. After the men had departed, Mabel Rudkin described how the town faced up to the 'unparalleled situation' quietly and calmly.[128] Two months into the war, R. W. M. Gibbs commented from Oxford on the change in atmosphere compared to the heady excitement of the opening fortnight of the war. For Gibbs, Britain was a different country. 'A wonderful change' had taken place and there was a new-found sobriety in people's responses to the war.[129] By 23 November Mrs Humphry Ward dreaded opening *The Times* in case the casualty lists featured any of her five nephews at the front. But in the same letter she added 'yet how quickly one accustoms oneself to it, and to all the other accompaniments of war!'[130] This sense of good spirit and self-sacrifice on the home front appeared to last until the end of 1914. Elizabeth Haldane recorded in her diary on 3 December: 'What is fine is the way people are acting, and people one thought quite frivolous are coming out so wonderfully and showing self-sacrificing spirit. The women's vote and the prospect of immensely increased taxation is hardly noticed, and the War Loan is said to be subscribing twice over'.[131]

---

[123] Pinney, ed., *The Letters of Rudyard Kipling*, 259.
[124] University of Liverpool, Special Collections: Dorward Diaries, Diary 10: D446/10/10, 29 August 1914.
[125] IWM, Docs: Yearsley, P. Macleod, DS/MISC/17 (n.d.).
[126] MALSL. Walter Dixon Scott: MISC/391, 24 September 1914.
[127] NLS: Emrys Hughes: Dep 176/Box 7 (n.d.).
[128] Rudkin, *Inside Dover, 1914–18: A Woman's Impression* (London, 1933), 40.
[129] MPP Bodleian: R. W. M. Gibbs: MS Eng misc c.159, 27 September 1914.
[130] Trevelyan, *The Life of Mrs Humphry Ward* (London, 1923), 266–7.
[131] NLS: Elizabeth S. Haldane: Mss 20243, 3 December 1914.

This quietness could descend into depression, compounded by the change of season into a dark and gloomy winter.[132] Percy Webb recalled in 1975 how the atmosphere in Ferndown, Dorset, became gloomy and despondent once the men had departed. People were depressed because they realized the war would affect them for some time to come.[133] In a letter to her son on 3 September, Lydia Middleton wrote: 'the heavy cloud that lies over all people. It is *dreadful,* a dark oppression, a nerve-maddening excitement. It is *quite different from the S. African War* [sic]'.[134] On 4 October H. Rider Haggard recorded in his diary the atmosphere in London: 'the town looks melancholy, and so are its inhabitants . . . there is a gloom in the air'.[135] At the same time, Violet Clutton, also in London, could not help:

> feeling gloomy. Antwerp has fallen. The Germans will soon be at Ostend and then what then? In all probability an invasion—terrible—dreadful! Today it is pelting with rain, the weather is gloomy, we are gloomy, everything is gloomy. Everyone feels in a bad temper and out [of] sorts. I never felt so utterly cross and miserable in my life. Mother says it reminds her of the "black week" in the S. African War [sic], when each day the news seemed worse and worse, everybody's spirits sank to zero and cold, rain and fog made all seem more gloomy than ever.[136]

On 18 November Charlotte Despard, in London, recorded in her diary: 'These are sad days. We hear of all sorts of miseries and the war does not seem to move. Germans and allies still face one another, little advantage from day to day. *When* is this awful war to end?'[137] However, despite pockets of depression, on the whole morale remained positive as both the American and French Ambassadors reported to their home governments in November.[138]

How did the war affect the first Christmas of the conflict? Events in December rocked any sense of normality that people had been able to establish. The bombardment of Scarborough, Whitby, and Hartlepool on 16 December and the sighting of a German aeroplane over Dover on Christmas Day literally brought the war closer to home. Many people felt unable to celebrate Christmas as usual, particularly if their loved one was absent. Louisa Harris, in Yeovil, Somerset, recorded in her diary how Christmas 1914 was like no other: 'terribly sad . . . and very quiet'. The atmosphere was so depressing that she told her sister Bessie not to bother spending Christmas Day with her in Yeovil.[139] Macleod Yearsley observed a change in atmosphere in London: 'the streets and shops were full, but less so than usual, and the crowds were well sprinkled with khaki' owing to the men who had

---

[132] IWM, Docs: Miller, H.: 02/38/1, November and December 1914.
[133] IWM: 578, Reel 1 (n.d.).
[134] Liddle: DF 091: Mrs Lydia Middleton, 3 September 1914.
[135] D. S. Higgins, ed., *The Private Diaries of Sir H. Rider Haggard, 1914–1925* (London, 1980), 9.
[136] DRO: Violet Clutton: 6258M/Box 1, Vol II, 13 October 1914.
[137] PRONI: Charlotte Despard: D/2479/2, 18 November 1914.
[138] National Archives of the United States, Maryland Campus: American Embassy, London: M367, Roll 271 (763.72/119/36), 18 November 1914 and AMAE, Paris: Papiers Delcassé: Lettres de Diplomates III: Paul Cambon, ff. 342, 15 November 1914.
[139] Liddle: DF 062: Louisa Harris, 25 December 1914.

received short-leave during December.[140] Michael MacDonagh, however, felt the festive season had remained unchanged. People bought gifts, supplies were plentiful, prices were only a little higher and money was no issue. People exchanged season's greetings with 'heartier vigour' but overall the changes were minimal.[141] In contrast to MacDonagh's optimism, a number of people ended their diaries for 1914 on a negative note. Louis Casartelli, Bishop of Salford, wrote on 31 December: 'Surely the most terrible and deplorable year of all our lives—perhaps in History [sic]! May God send us during this New Year at last Peace!!'[142] Reverend Hugh Cernyw Williams, Baptist Minister at Corwen and Cynwyd, concluded that 1914 had been 'a year of darkness and sorrow. The war clouds have caused rivers of woe to flow'.[143] Lawrence Parsons ended his diary with 'And so sadly ends 1914. A terrible war still raging indecisively with awful losses'.[144]

Overall, from September 1914 onwards, or whenever individuals realized personally that they were at war, there appears to be a sense of settling down, and getting used to the changes and disruption. People also developed a sense of resolve that they would accept the changes war brought and see it through to the end. Once the men had departed, Bertram Neyland, in Port Talbot, South Wales, recalled how the cheering and excitement of the first few weeks gave way to a hardening of feeling that developed into a resolve that Britain had to win the war.[145] On 11 September, Walter Hines Page, the American Ambassador in London, described how the British people felt 'a silent, grim determination to make an end forever' of the German military system.[146] On 16 October the *Brighouse Echo* reported that 'the people are characterised by quiet determination to see the thing through rather than an exuberant enthusiasm'.[147]

People slowly began to accept the conditions imposed on them by the war. The *Keighley News*, in an article headed 'Settling Down' published on 22 August 1914, believed that:

> The first unsettlement caused by the war . . . having been got over, people have begun to view things not merely in a philosophical but in a genuinely practical and businesslike spirit. Even those who were most flustered at the outset have come to realise that the bottom has not altogether dropped out of the world. Things have not come to a complete standstill.[148]

The London Letter of the *Cambridge Daily News* reported in early September how 'there are no more crowds in the Mall and no more cheering in the Palace'. Khaki-clad soldiers were no longer unfamiliar sights in the streets and people 'no longer

[140] IWM, Docs: Yearsley, P. Macleod: DS/MISC/17 (n.d.).
[141] MacDonagh, *In London During the Great War*, 45.
[142] Salford Diocesan Archives, Burnley: 1914 Diary of Bishop L. C. Casartelli, 31 December 1914.
[143] NLW: Reverend Hugh Cernyw Williams: Mss 22608A, 31 December 1914
[144] NLI: Lawrence Parsons' Diary: Ms 21,524, 31 December 1914.
[145] IWM: 318, Reel 1 (1974).
[146] National Archives of the United States, Maryland Campus: American Embassy, London: M367, Roll 14 (763.72/838), 11 September 1914.
[147] *Brighouse Echo*, 16 October 1914.
[148] *Keighley News*, 22 August 1914 cited in Good, 'England Goes To War, 1914–15', 53.

buy every edition of the evening papers'.[149] On 1 November R. W. M. Gibbs recorded in his diary how people's 'feelings are gradually becoming blunted to horrors'.[150] As time went on, were people becoming hardened to such horrors as casualty lists, atrocity stories, wounded soldiers, and the realities of modern warfare?

In some ways there was a sense of monotony and 'banality' about the war as it became part of everyday life, similar to experiences in France.[151] But this should not suggest that people were no longer interested in the war or were immune to its impact. Instead, it had infiltrated every aspect of their lives and become a subconscious part of it. On 31 October, Hallie Eustace Miles, in London, could 'hardly remember what it was to think ever of anything but the War. Or ever to read anything but the papers.'[152] Dr John Johnston, a GP in Bolton, recorded in his diary on 15 November: 'And what a monopoly does [the war] claim upon our minds and hearts today! How it bulks up and towers over every other subject! We seem to be able to talk and think of nothing else. Every conversation revolves around it; and nothing else seems of any consequence'.[153] On 3 December Elizabeth Haldane wrote in her diary 'no conversation gets off war at present, and no wonder'.[154] Thomas Batty, in London, apologized to his sisters in his letter dated 16 November for writing so much about the war, but he could 'read or think of little else'.[155] His apology suggests that perhaps he felt he was boring them with his constant talk of war.

Some people failed to emerge from Lloyd George's 'sheltered valley' and remained indifferent to the war.[156] H. A. Gwynne wrote to Lady Bathurst, proprietor of the *Morning Post*, on 26 August:

> It is not that men will not serve, but you cannot bring it home to [the public] that we are fighting for our existence. They will persist in thinking it is a Continental war and not one in which England is most intimately involved.[157]

Rural areas were often accused of indifference and apathy, indicated by low levels of recruitment. Edrica de la Pole became increasingly frustrated with the level of indifference she witnessed amongst local people in Tremar, Devon. On 4 September she noted in her diary: 'In the face of such utter indifference as people here show it is hard to believe there *is* such a thing as a War going on anywhere.'[158] A recruiting speaker from the West Riding declared in October that 'what had struck

---

[149] *Cambridge Daily News*, 2 September 1914.

[150] MPP Bodleian: R.W.M. Gibbs: MS Eng misc c.161, 1 November 1914.

[151] Jean-Jacques Becker, *The Great War and the French People* (Oxford, 1985).

[152] Miles, *Untold Tales of War-Time London: A Personal Diary*, 22.

[153] Bolton Archives and Local Studies Centre, Bolton: Diaries of Dr John Johnston: ZJO/1/36, 15 November 1914.

[154] NLS: Elizabeth S. Haldane: Mss 20243, 3 December 1914.

[155] IWM, Docs: Batty, T.: 91/5/1, 16 November 1914.

[156] From Lloyd George's speech made in the Queen's Hall, London on 19 September 1914, that gave support to Britain's entry into the war and introduced the idea of the formation of a Welsh Army Corps. Cited in MacDonagh, *In London During the Great War*, 27–9.

[157] Wilson, ed., *The Rasp of War: The Letters of H.A. Gwynne to The Countess Bathurst, 1914–1918* (London, 1988), 25.

[158] PWDRO: Diary of Edrica de la Pole: Acc 1306/22, 4 September 1914.

him since he returned to Huddersfield was the indifference of the youth of the town'. Everything was going on 'as usual and the consequence was that they were not alive to the situation'.[159] On 13 December, the Archbishop of Canterbury pinpointed rural areas in Yorkshire and Northumbria for demonstrating 'a great deal of utter apathy about the War, and even some hostility to recruiting'.[160]

Although people attempted to carry on as normal in 1914—such as attending or continuing to play in football matches—a new wartime society, and the rules of moral conduct that came with it, meant there was a continual tension between the rally-cry of 'business as usual' and respecting the soldiers' sacrifice. These decisions were difficult to make. When was it appropriate to 'carry on as normal' and where did changes in behaviour have to be made?

Newspapers in August 1914 were full of adverts encouraging people to continue 'as normal' with their holiday plans and to visit British seaside resorts as part of the war effort. If people spent money in these resorts they would be contributing to Britain's cause by keeping people in business. However, those that did follow instructions were often severely chastised for enjoying themselves in a time of national crisis. People were in a double-bind. Cecil Harper recalled how frustrated he became with a university friend who still insisted on their annual holiday to Guernsey in August, despite the fact that Cecil had enlisted. 'He seemed incapable of understanding why I called it off'. Whilst Cecil's friend insisted that the Channel Islands were perfectly safe, he failed to grasp that the holiday was cancelled because of Cecil's commitment to the war effort. 'This was perhaps the first time that I came face to face with the wide difference in values and priorities.'[161] It would appear that most people chose to ignore official advice because holiday resorts did suffer at the outbreak of war. On 7 October, John Evans, Deputy Town Clerk for Aberystwyth, pleaded with the secretary of the Welsh Army Corps to billet a few thousands troops in the town during the winter months because the town, which depended on its summer trade, had suffered because of the lack of visitors owing to the war. Without the soldiers the outlook was 'a gloomy one', with many Boarding and Lodging House Keepers 'facing the winter with very little resources to fall back upon'.[162] People had chosen to cancel their annual holiday, either because they were deterred by the disruption of the transport system, or felt that holidaying when others were fighting a war was deemed inappropriate moral behaviour.

Iris Holt, writing from Hove on 10 September, told her fiancé how she felt continuing as 'normal' in wartime was wicked and callous in contrast to his life as a combatant. 'We loathe ourselves for being so helpless and useless and to go more or less pleasure seeking as usual and yet there is no alternative . . . The hardest thing is to have to be left behind and to go on living as usual'. In October she attempted to bring some normality back into her life by organizing hockey games for local girls,

[159] *Huddersfield Examiner*, 29 October 1914.
[160] Lambeth Palace: Davidson Papers: British Conduct of the War: Volume 13 [Private papers], ff. 14–27.
[161] IWM, Docs: Harper, Lt C.G.: 98/2/1 (1998).
[162] NLW: Welsh Army Corps: AA/19, 7 October 1914.

something she had been actively involved in before the war. People were at first against the idea and it was not until mid-November that Iris found girls comfortable with the idea of playing sport in wartime.[163] Those who did attempt to continue with 'business as usual' were open to criticism. On 24 November Louisa Harris, in Yeovil, Somerset, refused to attend the annual local fair because the war had cast such a gloom over her mood. She was left wondering 'how some can be so pleasure-seeking at such a grave crisis in our history and knowing what numbers of our brave countrymen are sacrificing their lives'.[164]

'Settling into war' was an ambiguous process. It could suggest that the excitement of August was only transitory, and that the public had slipped back into their old ways as the months passed. Yet in reality it was impossible for people to return to their old ways. Too much had changed. Instead, the phrase suggests a nation accepting the situation and steeled for conflict. Pre-war normality was anathema, and even accepting the new normality of war involved considerable tensions over appropriate behaviour. Acrimony existed throughout the war: soldiers accused civilians, middle class accused working class, and the working class pointed to profiteers. In some ways it is possible to suggest that the British and Irish population in 1914 were using normality as a form of resistance against the Germany enemy in a similar sense to the French population occupied in the Second World War. Normality may not have existed, but it was a good way for non-combatants to stand up to the enemy in their own way.

WAR WITHOUT END

The 'tragic underestimation' that the British and Irish people believed a war in Europe would be swift, decisive, and 'over by Christmas' is embedded in historiography.[165] In reality, contemporaries frequently speculated over the length of the war; there was a variety of opinions as to the duration of the war in 1914 rather than any sort of consensus, let alone around a short war.[166] Macleod Yearsley recalled that amongst his friends 'the favourite topic was the probable duration of the war'.[167] In particular, correspondence with soldiers, in training or abroad, highlights how curious and concerned people were with this issue. Iris Holt became increasingly frustrated with the lack of information regarding the length of the war. She interrogated her fiancé over the issue. On 11 October she wrote: 'Have you any idea how long this is going to last . . . I would love to know . . . I would know what to do then. I'm afraid there are hundreds of people in the same position'.[168] As with

[163] Liddle: AIR 224: A.H. Morton, 10 September 1914 and November 1914.
[164] Liddle: DF 062: Louisa Harris, 24 November 1914.
[165] John Turner, *British Politics and the Great War: Coalition and Conflict, 1915–1918* (London, 1992), 4.
[166] Stuart Halifax, '"Over by Christmas": British Popular Opinion and the Short War in 1914,' *First World War Studies*, Issue 1, no. 2 (2010), 104.
[167] IWM, Docs: Yearsley, P. Macleod: DS/MISC/17 (n.d.).
[168] Liddle: AIR 224: A.H. Morton, 11 October 1914.

other aspects of the war, people attempted to piece together accurate information from the printed press, word of mouth, and returning soldiers. People adjusted their predictions as they discussed it further. Some people even placed wagers; Frederick Spencer, in training in Britain in August, placed 'large sums of money' on the war being over within the year.[169] Barclay Buxton, a mathematics student at Trinity College, Cambridge, had it down to the exact day; he believed that 'Germany would be defeated by the 7th October' in time for the start of the new academic year.[170] Estimates about the length of the war varied from a few weeks, to four years. People did not know how long the war would last, and definitive answers were impossible. Dorothy Holman, in Chudleigh, Devon, recorded on 7 August how a family friend had enlisted concluding 'he may be back in a day or a year'.[171] Shane Leslie even went so far as to consult a fortune-teller in Castleshane, County Monaghan, in order to approximate how long he would be separated from his wife if he was to enlist.[172]

However, the idea of the war being over by Christmas—and the specific use of that phrase—was not widespread amongst contemporaries. In fact, Christmas 1914 is remarkable for its *scarcity* among contemporary accounts, whether public or private.[173] By November, people had readjusted their temporal horizons to expect a long and drawn-out struggle for victory. The first recruiting appeal that appeared on 7 August stated that the terms of service would be for a 'period of three years, or until the war is concluded'.[174] A week later, in an analysis of the current situation, the editorial of *The Times* concluded that 'in such conditions the war may be long, very long'.[175] Georgina Lee commented on 15 August: 'Our illusions as to the short duration of the war are rapidly vanishing. Today we are being prepared for the possibility of its lasting two years, perhaps more.'[176] On 25 August, in his first appearance in parliament as Secretary of State for War, Kitchener repeated his prediction that the war would last at least three years; his statement was widely publicized in the local and national press the following day. People trusted Kitchener and believed what he was telling them.[177] Ralph Verney informed his wife, Nita, that Kitchener was correct to act as if the war would be a long one.[178] The day after Kitchener's maiden speech, Violet Clutton recorded her respect for Lord Kitchener's decision to prepare for a three-year war. Although she hoped he was being over-cautious, she felt he was 'quite right to act in such a manner' and declared her faith in his leadership.[179] Kitchener's statement was substantiated by

---

[169] Liddle: GS 1513: Lt-Col Frederick Albert Spencer, August 1914.

[170] IWM: 299, Reel 1 (1974).

[171] DRO: Dorothy Holman: 3830M/F9, 7 August 1914.

[172] NLI: Sir Shane Leslie: Ms 22,863: 7 October 1914.

[173] Gregory, 'British "War Enthusiasm" in 1914: A Reassessment', 85.

[174] Marwick, *The Deluge: British Society and the First World War*, (London, 1965), 35.

[175] *The Times*, 15 August 1914, 7.

[176] Roynon, ed., *Home Fires Burning: The Great War Diaries of Georgina Lee* (Stroud, 2006), 13, 23.

[177] MacDonagh, *In London During the Great War*, 19.

[178] Verney, ed., *The Joyous Patriot: The Correspondence of Ralph Verney, 1900–1916* (London, 1989), 140.

[179] DRO: Violet Clutton: 6258M/Box 1, Vol I, 26 August 1914.

his call for another 500,000 volunteers. People were able to infer from the sheer quantities of men being called upon—and who would require at least six months' training—that this war would not be over quickly. People were also able to infer that the war would not be over quickly by the immense and immediate mobilization of relief and fundraising efforts to support British troops and their families. The national charitable campaign launched by Princess Mary to send Christmas gift boxes to all serving men at the front and at sea was launched on 15 October. By mid-November the public had responded so generously that the scheme was expanded to include all British, Colonial, and Indian troops serving outside the British Isles. By 22 December the Fund had raised over £151,000. The contributors to this scheme, and other local gift funds, clearly did not expect the troops to be home by Christmas. Regional papers echoed this sentiment throughout the autumn; although no predications could be made, it was best to assume that the struggle was 'bound to be a long one'.[180] On 29 October *The Scotsman* believed that 'those who still adhere to the view that the present war will be over by Christmas are now an insignificant minority'.[181]

The language used to describe the war in the printed press also indicated that the war would not be over quickly. In his foreword to the first edition of *The War Illustrated* published on 22 August, H. G. Wells described the war as 'the vastest ... [and] greatest armed conflict in human history'.[182] Both *The Times* and the *Manchester Guardian* started publishing 'instant histories' of the war in 1914. This language permeated the minds' of ordinary people. A. H. D. Acland, in Felixstowe, believed on 5 August that the war was 'the greatest event of my life time for this country that we should be in this gigantic European War'.[183] For Beatrice Trefusis, the war was a momentous occasion for her generation. On 12 September she recorded her feelings in her diary: the war was 'going to be the biggest thing in our lives . . . We are up against something bigger than any of us in this generation have ever known.' By 7 October she described it as 'the greatest war ever known—and the longest battle-front and the greatest number of troops engaged ever known'.[184] Across all sectors of society the war was described as 'great', 'significant', 'unprecedented', 'a moment in history': language that does not suggest something short and compact, over in a couple of months. The fact that a number of people started diaries on 4 August 1914 solely to record the events of the war indicates that people believed this to be a life-changing, momentous occasion.

Local histories of the war, published after 1918, argue that people paid little or no attention to Kitchener's comments about a long war of attrition.[185] Contemporary evidence does not support this conclusion. On 6 August, in a letter to his mother, Lionel Sotheby, in London, told her that he believed the war would last at

---

[180] *The Times*, 18 September 1914, 8.
[181] *The Scotsman*, 29 October 1914 cited in Halifax, '"Over by Christmas": British popular opinion and the short war in 1914', 106.
[182] *War Illustrated*, 22 August 1914, 2.
[183] DRO: Journal of A.H.D. Acland: 1148M, add 23/F29b, 5 August 1914.
[184] Liddle: DF 129: B.M. Trefusis, 12 September 1914 and 7 October 1914.
[185] Brazier and Sandford, *Birmingham and the Great War, 1914–1919*, 24.

least four years and that the loss of life would 'number into millions'.[186] Charles Aston, serving in India, warned his mother, in Greater Manchester, on 9 August that the war would be 'a tough and long business'.[187] On 1 September, H. A. Gwynne wrote to Lady Bathurst that 'we are in for a long and desperate war'.[188] Two days later, the American Ambassador in London observed that:

> The dominant English opinion is that if [the Kaiser] be let off then the war will have been in vain. The resolve is to give a death blow to the Germans at any cost in time, men and money. The English are preparing for a long war and, as I read in their mood and character, they will not stop till they have succeeded.[189]

In a letter dated 8 October, Lydia Middleton reassured her son, serving in India, about not getting to the war in time as it looked 'as if it might go on forever'.[190] Philip Kerr, in London, told his mother on 28 October that 'nobody seems to think that the end of the war is in sight yet'.[191] On 13 December the Archbishop of Canterbury recorded in a memorandum that 'one does not meet many people who think that War is soon going to be over. There were many such in the early weeks, and I still meet such a person now and then, but they are rare'.[192] In a letter to his son dated 25 November Dr James Maxwell, in Bromley, Kent, described how 'the war drags its slow length along'.[193] In November, Shane Leslie was selected to serve as an interpreter with the British Ambulance Corps. On 25 November he was fitted with his uniform and commented on his 'British Red Cross identity disk numbered 1934 which I guess will be the final date for the War'.[194]

Where references to a short war are found they are often readjusted as the war progressed. This is understandable: people in 1914 could only speculate about the length of the war and opinions were open to change. For example, Reverend Andrew Clark, in Great Leighs, first ruminated on the length of the war in his diary on 15 September. According to a soldier invalided home, the war would not run into 1915. However, by 9 November, when the Allies were doing badly, Clark acknowledged that further German victories would mean 'an end to all hopes of ending the war soon'.[195] Montie Carlisle, an officer in the Northumberland Fusiliers, was at first concerned that the war would be over within six months, before he had got to the front. By November his opinion had changed after hearing

[186] Liddle: GS 1507: Lionel F.S. Sotheby, 6 August 1914.
[187] IWM, Docs: Aston, Lt-Col C.C.: Con Shelf, 9 August 1914.
[188] Wilson, ed., *The Rasp of War: The Letters of H. A. Gwynne to The Countess Bathurst, 1914–1918*, 27.
[189] National Archives of the United States, Maryland Campus: American Embassy, London: M367, Roll 371 (763.721119/19), 3 September 1914.
[190] Liddle: DF 091: Mrs Lydia Middleton, 8 October 1914.
[191] NAS, GRH: Philip Kerr papers: GD 40/17/464/48, 28 October 1914.
[192] Lambeth Palace: Davidson Papers: British Conduct of the War: Volume 13 [Private papers], ff. 14 27.
[193] University of Birmingham, Special Collections: Dr James Laidlaw Maxwell: DA 26/2/1/6/49, 25 November 1914.
[194] NLI: Sir Shane Leslie: Ms 22,863, 25 November 1914.
[195] Munson, ed., *Echoes of the Great War: The Diary of the Reverend Andrew Clark, 1914–1919*, 18, 30.

from other soldiers that the war would last for a long time.[196] Nita Verney also changed her opinion about the length of the war between August and November. In a letter to her husband, Ralph, on 26 November she informed him that despite recent military successes 'people seem to have resigned themselves to a long and indefinite struggle'.[197] Interestingly, towards the close of 1914, those who still believed in the possibility of a short war tended to be pessimists who thought it would end with the annihilation of the Allies in a swift German victory, not by British and French troops marching victoriously into Berlin in time for Christmas. On 28 December Alexander MacCallum Scott, Liberal MP for the Bridgeton constituency of Glasgow, recorded in his diary: 'An early end to the war can only be favourable to Germany. To do the work we have got to do will mean a long long war.'[198]

As Christmas approached, speculation over the length of the war was accompanied by a realization that the very nature of warfare had changed. On 11 November H. Rider Haggard recorded in his diary how:

> This war lacks the grandeur and picturesqueness [sic] of those of old time. There are no great battles, only one long hideous slaughter in the trenches. In the same way, where now is the majesty of Nelson's battles on the sea? In the place of them we have mines and sneaking submarines.[199]

On 13 December James Thursfield, the journalist and naval historian, wrote to Lady Londonderry describing his fear that the war would 'be long and terrible'.[200] On 30 December W. S. Armour wrote to his father, Reverend Armour in Balleymoney, County Antrim, reflecting on the degree to which 'warfare has changed even since the Boer business'.[201]

The belief, amongst Britons, in a swift, victorious war has been greatly exaggerated since 1918. The idea that the war would be 'over by Christmas' was not used by contemporaries. The phrase appears in post-war accounts, especially oral records of survivors of both the First and Second World Wars.[202] So where does the 'short war illusion' come from? Why does it continue to have such resonance? It is difficult to pinpoint exactly where the phrase originated. Suggestions include that it was used in the American Civil War, or that it is connected to the alleged Christmas Truce of December 1914, where the war did 'end', if only for a day.[203] The idea of a war being 'over by Christmas' was not without precedent. At the start

---

[196] Christopher Carlisle, ed., *My Own Darling: Letters from Montie to Kitty Carlisle* (London, 1989), 11.

[197] Verney, ed., *The Joyous Patriot: The Correspondence of Ralph Verney, 1900–1916*, 164.

[198] University of Glasgow, Special Collections: Alexander MacCallum Scott Political Diary: Ms Gen 1465/5, 28 December 1914.

[199] Higgins, ed., *The Private Diaries of Sir H. Rider Haggard, 1914–1925* (London, 1980), 14.

[200] PRONI: Lady Londonderry papers: D/2846/2/23/97A, 13 December 1914.

[201] PRONI: Papers of Reverend J.B. Armour: D/1792/A3/5/39, 30 December 1914.

[202] Many examples exist within the IWM, including 8280, Reel 1 (n.d.), 95, Reel 1 (1973), 330, Reel 1 (1974), and 9903, Reel 1 (1987).

[203] My thanks to Dr Adrian Gregory for these observations.

of the South African War in October 1899 it was anticipated that hostilities would have ceased by the end of the year.[204]

Perhaps the 'short war illusion' manifested in the post-war(s) period(s) because in retrospect, with the knowledge that the war lasted for fifty-four rather than five months and amassed millions of casualties, people wished to express a feeling of regret that the war did not end in December 1914. It may suggest a feeling that there is a difference or cut-off point between the war of August to December 1914, and the war that evolved from January 1915 onwards; a war characterized by trench warfare, stalemate, and innumerable casualties. The point is not that the British and Irish people were naïve and ignorant about the realities of war in 1914; the evidence above shows they were aware that the war could last a long time with horrific consequences. Any hopes for a short war says more about human nature than anything else. Whilst people were aware the war could last years rather than months, they still hoped it would be over sooner rather than later. 'Wishful thinking in the face of adversity is one of the mechanisms by which people cope', but as the war continued, reality set in.[205] In the early months of the war many volunteers expressed concerns that the war would be over before they reached the front. But this tended to be more as a reassurance to their parents that, although they had enlisted, they would not be in danger because the war would be over so soon. The longer the war went on, the more people realized how much devastation and suffering it might bring. Encamped in Aldershot with the 6th Battalion Cameron Highlanders, Francis MacCunn, an assistant in the Department of History at Glasgow University before he enlisted, expressed such concerns to his mother, in a letter dated 6 December: 'We are convinced that, unless the war is much shorter than is generally supposed, we are not likely to get through un-scathed.'[206] He was killed in the Battle of Loos on 26 September 1915. By Christmas 1914, the war was just getting into its stride.

---

[204] Smith, *The Origins of the South African War, 1899–1902* (London, 1996), 2.

[205] Hew Strachan, 'Economic Mobilization: Money, Munitions and Machines', in *The Oxford Illustrated History of the First World War*, ed. Hew Strachan (Oxford, 2000), 134.

[206] University of Glasgow, Special Collections: Francis John MacCunn correspondence: Ms Gen 532/8, 6 December 1914.

Conclusion

This book has demonstrated that describing the reactions of over 40 million British and Irish people to the outbreak of war in 1914 as either enthusiastic in the British case or disengaged in the Irish is over-simplified and inadequate. A society as complex as the United Kingdom in the Edwardian era did not have a single, uniform reaction to such a major event as the outbreak of war in Europe.

Emotional reactions to the war were ambiguous and complex, and changed over time. War was understood to be necessary, but people also appreciated that it would bring misery. Non-combatants of both genders understood their men's desire to do their duty, but simultaneously felt deep distress and anxiety about their departure. People tried to balance confidence and determination in the BEF's performance with the irrefutable evidence in front of them—in the form of wounded soldiers, Belgian refugees, and ever-increasing casualty lists—that victory was not going to be easy. People simultaneously hoped that business would carry on as normal, whilst berating anyone who acted as if the war was not happening. Communities unified around charitable causes but were ruthless in their identification of those who did not conform to the new moral order. People believed in the superiority and righteousness of the British cause, but at the same time were terrified by rumours of German spies and a potential German landing. Some initially expressed hope that the war would be over by Christmas, but most came to terms with a very different reality. Expressions of excitement often masked more complex reactions. Scenes of departure at railway stations were often described as enthusiastic, but many people were simply trying to give the soldiers a good send-off. Cheering crowds on 4 August were more likely to be a release of tension after weeks of ambiguity. The British population greeted the outbreak of war with a multitude of reactions, including anxiety, excitement, fear, enthusiasm, panic, uncertainty, and criticism. It is difficult to separate out the chronology of feelings. Often they were felt at the same time, or, at the very least, within hours, days, or weeks of each other. Within a fortnight, Dorothy Holman, from Teignmouth, Devon, went from feeling shock and dread (1 August), grief (3 August), excitement (5 August), uncertainty and anxiety (9–13 August), fear (14 August), and relief (19 August), to depression (25 August).[1]

Like the work of Jean-Jacques Becker and Jeffrey Verhey, this book has shown that the idea of collective 'war enthusiasm' was a simplification of popular feelings

---

[1] DRO: Dorothy Holman: 3830M/F9, 1–25 August 1914.

and attitudes in a time of grave danger. The populations in France and Germany, like Britain and Ireland, experienced a mixture of various attitudes: excitement, curiosity, escape from routine, and adventure, in conjunction with suspicion, insecurity, depression, and fear. Like French and German responses, enthusiastic responses in Britain and Ireland are not so much repudiated as circumscribed; some people were enthusiastic at some moments, but most of the people most of the time were not. Differences in popular perception in Britain and Ireland, as in Germany and France, were often related to geographical, occupational, political, class, and gender differences. As in France, the British and Irish people failed to realize the gravity of developments in Europe in mid- to late July 1914. The rapidity of its development took many by surprise. Just as Madame Caillaux's trial dominated French press headlines as late as 29 July, the newspapers in Britain and Ireland gave more prominence to domestic affairs, in particular the shootings on Bachelor's Walk, Dublin, on 26 July. Just as mobilization was accepted but not welcomed in France, the British and Irish people accepted the seriousness of the situation, on the whole, without celebration or jingoism. French, German, British, and Irish people experienced similar anxieties over the 'enemy within', including fears of enemy spies on home soil and the poisoning of water supplies. Rumours were a common feature of the entry into war for all the belligerent countries.

Across the United Kingdom, people shared experiences characteristic of the French and German entry into war: the uncertainty before the announcement of war, the mobilization and departure of troops, mobilizing for charitable causes, seeing refugees and wounded soldiers, combating the 'enemy within', and coming to terms with the realities of modern warfare. In the United Kingdom there were, of course, differences between regions, cities, towns, villages, communities, and individuals. Along the east coast, stretching from Scotland to Dover, communities experienced the threat of a German landing and made preparations, believing the threat to be a real possibility. In Whitby, Hartlepool, and Scarborough, their fears were realized when, on 16 December, a German bombardment killed over 150 civilians. Although the entire nation was outraged by this act, the communities directly involved had a unique and localized introduction to the violence of modern warfare. Regional differences manifested themselves most obviously in differing recruitment levels. This was particularly apparent in rural as opposed to urban areas across the United Kingdom.

Overall, there were more similarities than differences in how different parts of the United Kingdom entered the war in 1914. Ireland, and Wales to some extent, have been labelled as unenthusiastic in their responses to war and dismissed as atypical peripheries of the United Kingdom. However, the response to the outbreak of war at the undisputed centre of the United Kingdom and Empire—London— was also less overwhelmingly enthusiastic than is generally assumed. In terms of a sense of unity, the threat from Germany provoked a shift in national symbols and rites, and people became 'United Kingdomers'. English, Scottish, Welsh, and Irish identities were forced to give way to more inclusive terms. Threats inspired unity and, as evidenced, men from England, Scotland, Wales, and Ireland united behind the British war effort and enlisted in droves.

Two major differences exist between the French, German, and British cases. First, volunteerism takes a more prominent place in the British and Irish experience of 'entry into war'. The most obvious aspect of this experience was the raising of a 'nation in arms', the biggest volunteer army in history. This experience was unique to Britain; conscription had been in place in France and Germany since the nineteenth century. Within a matter of months Britain went from having a small professional army to over 2.5 million men either in training or fighting in France and Belgium. But, as evidenced, beyond the needs of the army, volunteerism touched everyone and appeared in all parts of British and Irish society at war. Voluntary participation in the war was immediate, and essential, in Britain and Ireland from 4 August onwards. As in other countries, intellectuals, artists, academics, politicians, organizations, and agencies came forward to support the war. Ordinary people rallied around the cause and united as a national community in crisis.

The image of rampant jingoism greeting the outbreak of war has been replaced by a more complex picture of a process of engagement in the war by the British and Irish people based on pre-existing sentiments of national community in what was largely believed to be a war of national defence. People were not brainwashed into supporting the war. They made their own decisions, assessed newspaper reports critically, absorbed and processed information, sought updates where news was lacking, and, more often than not, self-mobilized to support the war. As discussed, the high diction speeches of 1914 found echoes in people's minds. This evidence further destabilizes the already problematic term 'propaganda'. In 1914 the British and Irish people did not need persuading that the war was one of defence and survival. If the majority opinion had been pacifist *then* a propaganda effort would have been necessary. However, this was not the case, and it is fair to conclude that British and Irish people would have acted in very similar ways in 1914 with minimal propaganda.

The second difference between Britain, France, and Germany is that of domestic politics, and more specifically Ireland. Whilst domestic politics in Britain were suspended, just as in France and Germany, war became part of the politics of domestic peace in Ireland. The war, and Ireland's commitment to it, was negotiable, particularly in terms of the relationship between recruitment and political entitlement. Why should Irishmen lay down their lives for a nation or an empire that did not treat them equally? The domestic political situation in Britain and Ireland was more complex than that of France and Germany. The potential for dissidence was high amongst Irish nationalists, and was a concern that neither France nor Germany had to contend with. However, following the outbreak of war, dissidence in Ireland was constrained by the degree of support for the war demonstrated by nationalist Ireland. Any dissent amongst advanced nationalists was limited. Therefore, despite the fragility of the relationship between Britain and Ireland, the Kingdom was united in 1914.

Many of the features of British entry into war were replicated in Ireland and across the main geographical regions examined in this book. What was seen to be at stake in the war—national honour, liberty, the rights of small nations—

immediately overwhelmed almost everyone in Britain and Ireland. The British army was fighting against a despotic and barbaric enemy who threatened the very values that Britain and Ireland were founded upon. The war embodied a moral crusade where the cost of defeat was a price too heavy to bear. The cause that Britain and Ireland was fighting for became absolute in some moral sense and was echoed not only in official discourse, such as pamphlets, recruiting speeches, and editorials, but was restated in layman's terms—in Music Hall songs, imagery, conversation, diaries, and letters. The war also generated a new moral order. In order to uphold justice, civilization, and liberty, ordinary people were expected to rally around the national cause and contribute in whatever way they could. For non-combatants this was via solidarity and relief efforts: helping families of soldiers, supporting Belgian refugees, behaving appropriately, and berating those who failed to support the war effort. For those who could fight, the obvious expression of commitment to the campaign was by volunteering for the British army. A mass volunteer army, made up mainly of ordinary citizens, was the only way a country like Britain, wary of conscription, could match the sacrifice and military commitment of its Allies on the battlefield.

Just as Britons were able to build a picture of what they were fighting for, they simultaneously constructed images of the enemy that they were fighting against. This foe was both external and internal. For the majority of people across the United Kingdom, Germany was the absolute enemy and the more wrongs it committed, the more righteous Britain and Ireland's cause became. Those expressing sympathy with Germany as a country were in the minority. It was understood to be a barbaric, ruthless, and despotic adversary. Constructing the external enemy in such absolute terms meant negotiated peace was impossible. An absolute enemy had to be defeated absolutely. Fear and hatred of the external nemesis made it necessary to find—and invent where they did not exist—scapegoats, so that such feelings could be discharged. Hence there was the imaginary formulation of the enemy within—as in every other belligerent society. This took two forms—the enemy alien and the spy—both of which possessed deep pre-war roots. When anxiety over the performance of the BEF increased, particularly as the Germans moved away from the Marne towards the Channel coast in October, fear and hatred manifested itself, in certain pockets of the United Kingdom, in violence against the perceived enemy within.

Just as the population of the United Kingdom were coming to terms with what the war was about, and were mobilizing in various ways behind the national cause and against the enemy, the actual violence of war was unfolding. This was both imagined and experienced. The German retreat from the Battle of the Marne— precisely the event that allowed the French population to momentarily catch its breath in relief—marked, for the British population, the point when they began to come to terms with the prospect of a German invasion. This fear was at its highest pitch along the eastern coast of England and Scotland. However, atrocity stories, transmitted by the press, word of mouth, soldiers, and refugees became the British experience of invasion by proxy. It was understood, across Britain and Ireland, that if the Germans were to land on British soil, the population would be submitted to similar horrors to those inflicted on Belgian and French civilians in August 1914.

The violence of war was not just confined to the realms of people's imaginations. The British people also experienced it directly in 1914. The arrival of almost 250,000 Belgian refugees by mid-1915 meant that most people had seen, if not interacted with, the primary victims of the German invasion in August 1914. These refugees transmitted stories of brutal atrocities committed by the German troops and were used as evidence to boost the national cause in a fight against an immoral and barbaric enemy. Wounded soldiers, funerals of those who succumbed to their injuries on British soil, and casualty lists, all compounded people's understandings of what modern industrial warfare entailed. The peak of this understanding in 1914 for the British people was on 16 December when German submarines bombarded the coastal towns of Scarborough, Hartlepool, and Whitby, killing over 150 people and injuring hundreds of others.

Entry into war was a process or a journey that eventually reached its destination. By September 1914 most people in Britain and Ireland were 'inside the war'. After the rupture and chaos of the outbreak of war, as pre-war understandings clashed with the realities of modern industrial warfare, the British and Irish reached a level of acceptance and understanding. By September 1914 the war had become a central feature of everyone's lives. The conflict had impacted on jobs and employment; it defined what leisure pursuits were acceptable or not; it prescribed appropriate behaviour; it changed what people could wear and the language people used; it altered landscapes and sounds; food scarcities and increased prices changed the way people ate; children's playtime evolved; families were dislocated; and by December over a million men were under canvas across the United Kingdom. The British and Irish people found themselves in the midst of a war to which they could see no end.

In 1914 no one knew what the war would produce, where it would go, or how it would conclude. However, there was one certainty—things could never be the same again, and the longer the war went on, the greater the change was likely to be. With millions of men volunteering en masse and the nation engaged against a common enemy, political and moral relations within society and between the component parts of the United Kingdom could not remain the same. But what direction would they go in? In the post-war period, in the light of three-quarters of a million British military deaths, the gap between the anticipations of 1914 and the reality of 1918 created a vacuum that became filled with new demands and expectations.[2] Civilians began to reassess their relationship to the state and nation that had taken them to war. Civilian investment in war, from the start, was based on the acceptance of sacrifice. But what would the reciprocal demands be when the war was over? Were claims for expanded suffrage and enlarged welfare partly rooted in 1914? The question was even more acute and immediate regarding the relationship between Britain and Ireland. In 1914, Irish people, whether unionist or nationalist, on the whole opted to support the war, but did so in the name of

---

[2] Winter, *The Great War and the British People* (London, 1986), 71.

diametrically opposed goals. In the end, that opposition and the eruption of the Easter Rising resulted in partition and set nationalist Ireland on the path to independence. But had the conflict ended sooner, nationalist support for the war might have led either to a different outcome or to a similar outcome by different means. The Kingdom united in 1914 did not stay united, but paths of division were strongly influenced by the length and nature of the war, matters that were still shrouded in mystery in 1914, and were by no means foreordained.

APPENDIX I

Dramatis Personae

NB: The following details persons whose private papers, published diaries/memoirs/journals, or oral recollections were consulted for this book. Not all names mentioned in the book are included in this list, for example, if it was a name mentioned in a newspaper article. Not all biographical detail is given for each subject; only sufficient to indicate their position and situation in 1914. The amount of detail varies between ordinary and elite figures for obvious reasons. Information for the former comes from the sources relating to them as indicated in the relevant footnotes. Information for the latter has been gathered mainly from the Oxford Dictionary of National Biography.[1]

A–B

Abrahamson, Leonard
Russian-born but brought up in Newry. Leonard's father, David, was subjected to 'anti-German' attacks in Newry and Bessbrook, Co. Armagh, during the First World War.

Acland, A. H. D. (1847–1926)
Liberal MP for Rotherham, 1885–99, and for the Chiltern Hundreds, 1899–1919; created 13th Baronet in 1919. Member of a wealthy family from Broadclyst, East Devon. The family left their home in Felixstowe for London on 5 August, to allow for the encampment of troops.

Addis, Sir Charles (1861–1945)
Banker and government advisor. Born in Edinburgh, he advanced rapidly to the top ranks of international banking and government counsel and was knighted in 1913. With the outbreak of the First World War, Addis's financial expertise attracted the attention of government leaders.

Addison, Christopher (1869–1951)
British doctor and politician. Born in Hogsthorpe, Lincolnshire. In 1907 was adopted as the Liberal Candidate for Hoxton, in East London. He entered the Commons in January 1910 and, with the outbreak of war, became Parliamentary Secretary to the Board of Education.

Ainsworth, Mrs Martha
An elderly woman, Mrs Martha Ainsworth, from Loughborough, was celebrated in the Leicestershire press in September 1914 for having six sons fighting at the front. Her seventh son had already been killed in action.

[1] H. C. G. Matthew et al., eds., *Oxford Dictionary of National Biography* (Oxford, 2004).

Allan, Fred
A Glasgow resident who protested to the Scottish authorities over the publication of the Scottish Socialist weekly, *Forward.*

Allcott, A. W.
A. W. Allcott enlisted in the Oxford and Bucks Light Infantry on 1 September 1914 at the Town Hall, Birmingham. On 6 September he was drafted to 10th Worcester at Tidworth. On 17 September he was transferred to 9th Worcester. He left for the Dardanelles in March 1915. He survived the war and was demobilized on 22 February 1919.

Angell, Norman (1872–1967)
An English lecturer, writer and MP for the Labour Party. Born in Holbeach, Lincolnshire, he was the author of the anti-war tract *The Great Illusion,* first published in 1909. He argued that the integration of the economies of European countries had grown to such a degree that war between them would be entirely futile, making militarism obsolete. Angell was one of the principal founders of the UDC, established soon after the outbreak of war in 1914.

Anthoine, L. T.
Born in Jersey, he served as an officer with 2nd Battalion (East) Jersey Militia on Jersey, 1914–1918.

Armour, Reverend J. B. (1860–1930)
Presbyterian minister and supporter of Home Rule. Lived in Ballymoney, Co. Antrim. His letters written between July and December 1914 are mostly to his son **W. S. Armour**, sometimes from the residence of his other son, Max, living in South Shields, Tyne and Wear.

Arnold, Sergeant Charles Prior (1893–1941)
A Regular soldier since 1909, he was stationed in Ireland at the outbreak of war. Over the course of the First World War he saw active service with 1st East Surrey Regiment in France, Belgium, and Egypt. In 1914 he fought at Mons and Le Cateau, where he was shot in the foot and badly wounded in the abdomen.

Ashe-Lincoln, F.
Schoolboy in Plymouth in 1914.

Asquith, H. H. (1853–1928)
Herbert Henry Asquith served as the Liberal Prime Minister from 1908 to 1916.

Asquith, Margot (1864–1945)
Born in Peeblesshire, Scotland, Margot Tennant married H. H. Asquith in 1894.

Aston, Sir George (1861–1938)
Joined the Royal Marine Artillery in 1879. Saw active service in Sudan (1884) and the South African War (1899–1900). Attached to Special Service, Admiralty War Staff 1913–1914. Chairman of the Committee on Defence of Admiralty Oil Reserves, 1914, and commanded expeditions to Ostend and Dunkirk.

Aston, Charles Cuthbert
Born in 1893. He was reading chemistry at Exeter College, Oxford in the summer of 1914. He joined the 4th Battalion of the Bedfordshire Regiment at Dovercourt within a month of the outbreak of war.

Axton, R. Jeffrey
Schoolboy in London in 1914.

Bagnall-Bury, John
Captain serving with the 4th Battalion of the Royal Welsh Fusiliers on the Western Front, 1914.

Baily, Bruce
Bruce Willis Seymour Stiles Baily, from Plymouth, was the son of the editor of the *Western Morning News*. After the outbreak of war he enlisted in the 5th Battalion Wiltshire Regiment and was commissioned in November 1914. Prior to the war he was training to be an architect.

Baker, Thomas Henry
Born 26th January 1896. Lived in Aston Clinton, Buckinghamshire. Worked as a gardener in 1914. Served with Chatham Battalion, Royal Naval Division in Britain and Gallipoli, 1914–15. Worked as driver for Army Canteen Committee in Britain, 1917–1919.

Baldwin, Constance
Elderly relative of Louise Baldwin, mother of the future Prime Minister Stanley Baldwin. Wealthy family based at their country residence—Astley Hall—near Stourbridge in the summer of 1914.

Balfour, Arthur (1848–1930)
Born in Whittingehame, East Lothian in Scotland. British Conservative politician and statesman, and the Prime Minister from 1902 to 1905. Succeeded as leader of the party in 1911 by **Andrew Bonar Law.**

Balfour, Lady Betty (1867–1942)
Born in London, Elizabeth Edith 'Betty' Bulwer-Lytton married Gerald William Balfour, younger brother of **Arthur** (above), in 1887.

Barbier, Madame Lucie (1875–1963)
French singer and pianist trained in Paris and closely involved with La Société des Concerts Français between 1907 and 1916. She moved to Aberystwyth in 1909 and proceeded to set up a Musical Club at the University College Wales, Aberystwyth. Aberystwyth in turn became a prime venue for French music and musicians. She used her influence to organize fund-raising concerts for Belgian refugees throughout 1914.

Barnes, George Nicoll (1859–1940)
Trade unionist and politician, born at Lochee, Forfarshire. Elected ILP MP for Glasgow Blackfriars (later Gorbals) at the 1906 general election. He continued to hold the seat largely on the basis of the Irish nationalist vote until his retirement in 1922.

Barry, Nellie M.
Resident in Mortimer, Berkshire in 1914.

Bartholemew, Harold W.
A Regular soldier living in Earls Colne, Essex, in August 1914. Called up to 8th Essex Cyclist Battalion at the outbreak of war and commenced home defence service along the south-east coast.

Barthorpe, Mabel
London resident who volunteered with the Soldiers' and Sailors' Families Association in 1914. She had lived through the South African War. Friend and correspondent of **Charlotte Fursdon**, in Shorwenton, Exeter.

Battenberg, Prince Louis of (1854–1921)
Louis Alexander Mountbatten was a minor German Prince who married a granddaughter of Queen Victoria and pursued a career in the Royal Navy, becoming a protégé of the future King, Edward VII. He served as First Sea Lord, the senior uniformed officer in the Royal Navy, from 1912 until he was forced to resign on 27 October 1914 owing to anti-German feeling.

Batty, Thomas
Living in Clapham, London, in 1914, he was working as the leader of a well-known society band before the war.

Béaslaí, Piaras (1881–1965)
(Percy F. Beazley) was born in Liverpool where his father, Patrick Langford Beazley, a native of Co. Kerry, was editor of the *Catholic Times*. Piaras worked as a freelance journalist in London and moved to Dublin in 1906 where he began to use the Irish spelling of his name. He gave summer lectures in Irish at the Munster College in Ballingeary and was actively involved in the Gaelic League. When the INV was formed in 1913 he was one of the sixteen IRB men on the Provisional Committee.

Bell, Charles
Charles Gowenlock Hopton Bell. Born 1898 at Liscard, Cheshire. At the start of the war he was aged 16 and working as an office boy in is father's business (fruit importer, Liverpool). Enlisted in Royal Naval Volunteer Reserve Service in Liverpool in 1916 (aged 18).

Bennett, Arnold (1867–1931)
British novelist born in Hanley in the Potteries district of Staffordshire. For much of 1914 he was based in Thorpe-le-Soken, Essex. During the First World War he became Director of Propaganda at the War Ministry.

Bennett, James
Born 1898 in Leeds. Volunteered for the British Army in 1916 when he turned 18.

Benson, Edward Frederick (1867–1940)
English novelist, biographer, memoirist, and short-story writer, known professionally as E. F. Benson. He was born in Berkshire.

Bentham, K.
Pre-school girl in Leicester in 1914.

Beresford, Lord Charles (1846–1919)
Joined the Royal Navy in 1859. From January 1910 he was Conservative MP for Portsmouth. Following the outbreak of war he was an avid 'anti-alien' campaigner and agitated for the removal of Prince Louis of Battenberg from the Royal Navy in October 1914.

Berkeley, George
A British-born Nationalist Volunteer who was involved in many campaigns against the separation of Ireland under the Home Rule Bill. He left Ireland once Home Rule was placed on the Statute books on 18 September 1914, seeing his work for Ireland and getting it an independent place in the empire as being complete. He returned to England and from December 1914 onwards worked as a Bisley Musketry Officer to eight or nine different Brigades, and spent the last thirteen months of the war in France and Italy.

Berry, William S.
British stores clerk in Purley, London, 1914–1915, working with the export department of an American trading company.

Billinge, J. H.
Honorary Secretary of the Belgian Consul in Manchester in 1914.

Bing, Dorothy L.
Born in 1900 to a pacifist family, she was a schoolgirl in London in 1914. Younger sister of conscientious objector, **Harold Frederick Bing** who was imprisoned in 1916 following the enactment of conscription.

Bird, Stanley Parker
Born 1895. Living in Colchester, Essex, in 1914. When war broke out he was encamped with the 1st Colchester troupe of Boy Scouts at Walton-on-the-Naze. He went on to become a non-commissioned officer and served with 16th Sanitary Section Royal Army Medical Corps in Britain, Egypt, Gallipoli, Sudan, and on the Western Front, 1914–1918.

Birrell, Augustine (1850–1933)
English Liberal politician, he was Chief Secretary of Ireland from 1908 to 1916.

Blades, D. P.
Editor of the University of Edinburgh's student publication *The Student.*

Blatchford, Robert (1851–1943)
British socialist campaigner and author born in Maidstone, Kent. He joined the Army at an early age and left in 1878 to become a journalist. He launched a weekly newspaper *The Clarion*, in 1891, and supported the ILP. However, as a supporter of the British government during both the South African War and the First World War, his socialism waned, and he moved to support the Conservative Party in 1924.

Blundell, F. N.
Cavalry Officer in England, France, and Ireland, 1914–1918. Blundell enlisted in the Lancs. Hussars on 24 August 1914. On 24 October the regiment left Knowsley for Canterbury.

Blunt, Wilfred Scawen (1840–1922)
British poet and writer. He was born in Sussex and, along with his wife, Lady Anne Noel, founded the Crabbet Arabian Stud. Blunt opposed British imperialism and his support for Irish causes led to his imprisonment in 1888.

Bonar Law, Andrew (1858–1923)
Conservative MP for Bootle since 1911, he took over the Party leadership from **Arthur Balfour** the same year. He furiously opposed the Liberals' plans to coerce the Ulster Protestants into a Home Rule Ireland; at a time when the latter were moving towards armed resistance, Bonar Law said that 'there were no lengths' to which Ulster could go and not receive his support.

Bowes, Mrs D.
Born in Huddersfield in 1902. The family moved to Shipley, West Yorkshire, in 1907, where she was attending school at the outbreak of war. Her father worked in a dyeworks in the town.

Brady, James
Born in Rochdale, Lancashire, in 1898, he worked as a bobbin-carrier in the warping shed of a local cotton mill before the war. Aged almost 17, Brady joined the Royal Army Medical Corps (RAMC) in September 1914 and served as a stretcher bearer from August 1915 to December 1918.

Braby, Mrs Cyrus
Lived in Sutton, Surrey, in 1914. Mother of F. C. Braby, Second Lieutenant, 6th Battalion, Lancashire Fusiliers, serving on the Western Front. Involved in local charity work, in particular providing blankets and knitted gloves for soldiers.

Brittain, Vera (1893–1970)
English writer, feminist, and pacifist best remembered as author of the best-selling 1933 memoir *Testament of Youth*, recounting her experiences during the First World War. Born in Newcastle-under-Lyme, Brittain was the daughter of a well-to-do family. She grew up on a farm in what is now the East Riding of Yorkshire. In the summer of 1914 she was about to start studying Classics at Somerville College, Oxford.

Broadbent, Mrs M.
Born in 1891 in Sunderland, her two brothers volunteered for war in 1914.

Brooke, Rupert (1887–1915)
English poet known for his *War Sonnets* written during the First World War. Born in Rugby, Warwickshire, Brooke was commissioned into the Navy shortly after his twenty-seventh birthday and took part in the Royal Naval Division's Antwerp expedition in October 1914. He sailed with the British Mediterranean Expeditionary Force on 28 February 1915, but developed septic pneumonia from an infected mosquito bite. He died on 23 April 1915 on his way to battle at Gallipoli.

Brunton, Anne (Annie) Stopford Agnes
Born in 1888 she was living in London at the outbreak of war but moved to Mount Trenchard Foynes, Co. Limerick in early September 1914. She was the younger sister of **Alice Helen Henry** (see below). In 1916 she changed her name by deed-poll to Anne Stopford Agnes Brunton-Lauder. In 1928 her married name became Kruming.

Buckland, Florence
Born in 1897 in Gravesend, Kent. Worked in the town in 1914.

Burns, John (1858–1943)
Prominent trade unionist, socialist, and politician, born in Lambeth, London. ILP MP for Battersea, he was fervently opposed to the South African War. In 1914, Burns was appointed President of the Board of Trade, but resigned from the government in protest at the outbreak of the First World War.

Butler, Arthur S. G.
Born in 1888 into an academic family. His father was Professor of Natural Philosophy at St Andrew's University. In 1914 he was in hospital recovering from a non-war related injury. On his recovery he enlisted.

Butlin, James H.
Soldier stationed in Weymouth on home defence duty, August to December 1914.

Buxton, Andrew R. (1879–1917)
Born in London to a Quaker family, Buxton graduated with a degree in zoology from Trinity College, Cambridge. A practising Christian, in 1909 he was appointed local director

of the Westminster branch of Barclay's Bank. At the outbreak of the war he enlisted and served with the Rifle Brigade on the Western Front until his death in action near Messines Ridge in 1917.

Buxton, Barclay Godfrey
Born 1895. In 1914 he had completed his first year studying mathematics at Trinity College, Cambridge. He was associated with the Cambridge Inter-Collegiate Christian Union and in early August had taken a party of children to the seaside on the Isle of Wight. He went on to become an officer serving with the 6th Battalion Duke of Wellington's Regiment on the Western Front, 1915–1919.

C–D

Cadbury, Elizabeth Mary (1858–1951)
English social reformer and philanthropist, née Taylor. Wife of George Cadbury, cocoa and chocolate manufacturer and social reformer. He moved the works to Bournville in Birmingham in 1879 and the family set up home in Northfield Manor. The family were practising Quakers and keen Liberals. During the war Elizabeth became involved in many philanthropic activities with various relief organizations.

Cain, Arthur C.
Living in Manchester in 1914, he lied about his age in order to enlist. He was billeted in Southport from November 1914 to May 1915.

Cambon, Paul (1843–1924)
Served as France's Ambassador to Britain between 1898 and 1920.

Campbell, Dr A. M.
Aged 13 in 1914 he was a schoolboy on the island of Islay, Argyllshire. His father was Captain of the Territorial Army, commanding the Islay Company of the County Battalion.

Carbis, Ben
Originally from Newton-le-Willows, St Helens, Merseyside, Signaller Ben and his brother, Corporal Tom Carbis, served with the 1/4th South Lancashire Regiment during the First World War. They were pre-war Territorials who volunteered for overseas service on the outbreak of war. In October 1914 Ben was stationed at Appledore, near Dungeness, Kent.

Carlisle, Montie
Born in 1889 he was working at the Baltic Exchange in London in 1914. He volunteered very early in the war and was given a Temporary Commission in the 8th (Service) Battalion, the Northumberland Fusiliers. After training in England, Montie joined his unit and landed at Suvla Bay on Gallipoli in August 1915.

Carrington, Charles Edmund (1897–1990)
Served as a British officer and wrote a noted memoir, *A Subaltern's War,* under the pseudonym Charles Edmonds in 1929. He volunteered for active service in September 1914 and served with the 1st/5th Battalion, Royal Warwickshire Regiment, and the 9th Battalion, Yorkshire Regiment, on the Western Front. He survived the war and went on to become a university professor.

Carson, Edward (1854–1935)
Leader of the Irish Unionists.

Casartelli, Louis (1852–1925)
Appointed Bishop of Salford in 1903, a position he retained until his death.

Casement, Roger (1864–1916)
Irish-born British diplomat, he was famous for his activities against human rights abuses in the Congo and Peru, prior to the outbreak of the First World War. His witnessing of atrocities in the Congo inspired his anti-imperialist and ultimately Irish Republican political opinions. By 1914 he was an Irish patriot, who had dealings with Germany prior to the Easter Rising in 1916.

Chamberlain, Annie (1883–1967)
Wife of politician **Neville Chamberlain** (see below) since 1911. In 1914 they were resident in Kings Norton, Birmingham with their two young children.

Chamberlain, [Joseph] Austen (1863–1937)
British statesman and politician and member of the Birmingham political dynasty. His father was Joseph Chamberlain (the British politician who died only a month before the outbreak of war) and his half-brother **Neville Chamberlain** (see below). In 1914 he was Conservative MP for Birmingham West and a strong supporter of the Unionist cause in Ireland. His stepmother was **Mary Chamberlain** who was the third wife of his father.

Chamberlain, [Arthur] Neville (1869–1940)
Younger half-brother of **Austen Chamberlain** and married to **Annie Chamberlain** (see above). In 1914 he was Chairman of Birmingham City Council's Town Planning Committee but he would rise through the political ranks to serve as Conservative Prime Minister from 1937 to 1940. His stepmother was **Mary Chamberlain.**

Chapman, Una
Una, her husband, and her two children (aged 3 and 9 years) had been living in Leyton, London since 1904.

Chater, Alfred D.
Alfred 'Micky' Chater was born in 1890 and had been serving with the Artists Rifles (28th London Regiment) since 1909. After training in the UK they departed for the Western Front in late October 1914. He was severely wounded in 1915 and did not serve again for the remainder of the war.

Chavasse, Noel Godfrey (1884–1917)
A British medic and soldier, he was the son of Francis James Chavasse, Bishop of Liverpool and founder of St Peter's College, Oxford. During the First World War, Chavasse was captain with the RAMC attached to the 1/10th (Scottish) Battalion of the King's Liverpool Regiment. He was awarded the Victoria Cross twice—once in August 1916 and again in August 1917. He died of the wounds he incurred during this second act of heroism.

Childers, R. Erskine (1870–1922)
Born in London to a Protestant Irish family, Childers was raised in Co. Wicklow, Ireland. He served in the South African War as an officer in the City Imperial Volunteers. On his return he wrote the novel *The Riddle of the Sands* published in 1903. He became increasingly attracted to Irish nationalism and was an advocate of Home Rule. In July 1914 he and his wife, Mollie, took part in the landing of arms at Howth, Co. Dublin. With the start of war,

Childers joined the Royal Navy as an Intelligence Officer and was active in the North Sea and the Dardanelles. However the violent suppression of the Easter Rising angered Childers, and after the war he moved to Dublin to become fully involved in the struggle against British rule. He joined Sinn Féin and was executed by the authorities of the newly independent Irish Free State during the Irish Civil War.

Churchill, Winston L.S. (1873–1965)
British politician who served as Prime Minister from 1940 to 1945 and again from 1951 to 1955. In 1911 he was made First Lord of the Admiralty, a post he held into the First World War.

Clark, Reverend Andrew
Rector of the village of Great Leighs in rural Essex. On 2 August 1914 he began to keep a diary and day by day, for over five years, he jotted down and pasted into a series of exercise books everything—news, views, gossip, letters, circulars—that had a bearing on the war.

Clodd, Edward (1840–1930)
Born in Margate, Kent, he was an English banker, writer. and anthropologist. He worked for the London Joint Stock Bank from 1872 to 1915 and had residences in Aldeburgh, Suffolk and London. He had a wide circle of literary and scientific friends, including **Thomas Hardy** (see below).

Cockhill, Miss D. L.
A 10-year-old schoolgirl in 1914 from Dovercourt, Essex.

Cokayne, Brien Ibrican (1864–1932)
British businessman and banker. In 1914 he was a partner in the firm of Anthony Gibbs and Sons, merchants and bankers. He went on to serve as Deputy Governor from 1915 to 1918, and Governor from 1918 to 1920 of the Bank of England.

Colby, Lawrence R. V. (1880–1914)
Born in 1880 in Ffyonne, Pembrokeshire. Educated at Eton he joined the 1st Battalion Grenadier Guards in 1899 and took part in the South African War. He left Southampton for the front on 4 October and was killed in action twenty days later at Gheluvelt, Belgium.

Coldrick, Will
Miner in Abersychan, South Wales, in 1914.

Connolly, James (1868–1916)
Irish socialist worker born in Edinburgh, Scotland, to Irish immigrant parents. He was shot by firing squad for his involvement in the Easter Rising of 1916.

Conway, Michael
Born in 1895 at Ballybronogue, Patrickswell, Co. Limerick. Left school at 14 to work on his father's farm. When the Irish National Volunteers were formed in Patrickswell in 1913 he joined immediately.

Cooper, Ernest Read
A solicitor from Southwold, Suffolk.

Cooper, Bryan
A southern Irish unionist who joined the Connaught Rangers in August 1914.

Coppard, George (1898–1984)
A British soldier who, aged 16, lied about his age to join the 6th Battalion Royal West Surrey Regiment on 27 August 1914. Having completed training in Guildford, the Battalion was posted to France in 1915. He survived the war and published his memoirs in 1969, prompting contemporaries to do the same with their wartime accounts.

Cordal, Miss N.
Working as a domestic servant in a big house between Lowestoft and Oulton Broad. She lost her job as a result of the outbreak of war as her employers tried to economize.

Coules, Mary
Daughter of a news editor at Reuters Press Agency in London.

Courtney, Lady [Catherine] Kate (1847–1929)
Social worker and internationalist born in Herefordshire. She married Leonard Henry Courtney, 1st Baron Courtney of Penwith, in 1883. Both she and her husband were Quakers and committed to international peace. When the First World War broke out Kate Courtney (who, on her husband's elevation to the peerage in 1906, had become Lady Courtney of Penwith) persisted in her pacifism. She helped to found an emergency committee to relieve destitute German civilians who had been stranded in Britain at the outbreak of the war; she visited German prisoners of war in prison ships; she publicized the work of her German counterparts in Berlin who were overseeing the welfare of British civilians and prisoners; she tried to intercede with the Home Office on behalf of German civilians threatened with deportation; she supported the American progressive Jane Addams's frustrated attempts in 1915 to organize a negotiated end to the war brokered by neutral nations; and finally, in 1918, she sought a way for British Quakers to go over to defeated Germany and take relief supplies to the starving over there. The first meeting of the Fight the Famine Committee was held at Kate Courtney's Chelsea home, 15 Cheyne Walk, in January 1919, when she was 71, and out of that committee developed the Save the Children Fund.

Cowell, Mrs G. M.
Aged 17 in 1914, she was on holiday at Frensham, Sussex, the weekend before war broke out. She immediately returned home to Walthamstow, London, and witnessed King George V and Queen Mary stepping out onto the balcony of Buckingham Palace on 4 August 1914.

Cracknell, Sonny
Born in 1906 he was a schoolboy in Colchester, Essex, in 1914.

Craig, James (1871–1940)
A prominent Irish unionist politician, leader of the Ulster Unionist Party and the first Prime Minister of Northern Ireland.

Crowe, Eyre (1864–1925)
German-born British diplomat, he entered the Foreign Office in 1885. He served in the Contraband Department during the First World War but was often subjected to criticism for being an enemy alien.

Crozier, Brigadier-General F. P.
An officer with the Royal Irish Fusiliers during the war.

Cubitt, D. D.
Under-Secretary of State for Scotland in 1914.

Dale, Sir Alfred W. W.
Vice-Chancellor of the University of Liverpool from 1903 to 1919.

D'Arcy, Charles Frederick (1859–1938)
Protestant Bishop of Down, Connor and Dromore, 1911–1919.

Davidson, T. Randall (1848–1930)
Archbishop of Canterbury, 1903–1928.

Davies, Bessie
Living with her family in Caerphilly in 1914, she had witnessed the explosion at Senghen-
nydd colliery in October 1914. Following the outbreak of war she worked at the Royal
Ordnance Works in Coventry, 1914–1919.

Davies, Dai Dan
South Wales coalminer in 1914.

Davies, Jim
Born in Windsor in 1896, he was performing in a West End theatre on the night that war
was declared. He was part of 4 August crowds along the Mall and outside Buckingham
Palace. He enlisted later in 1914 at Fulham.

Davison, Hilda
Aged 21 in 1914 she was living at home with her family in Sunderland. Her father worked as
a Chief Engineer on ships.

de la Pole, Edrica (1856–1946)
Fifth daughter of Sir William de la Pole, 9th Baronet of Shute House, Shute, East Devon.
On her father's death in 1895 she moved to Pound, near Hawkchurch, Devon, and thence
to Tremar, Kingston, where a residence was built for her and her sister Geraldine in 1900.
She was an experienced farmer and dog-breeder, and kept a small stud until her death in
1946.

Delcassé, Théophile (1852–1923)
French Minster of Foreign Affairs, 1914–1915.

Denny, Walter E.
A pre-war soldier, he served with the 120th Battalion, Royal Field Artillery on the Western
Front 1914–1916.

Derby, Lord (1865–1948)
Edward George Villiers Stanley became the 17th Earl of Derby in 1908. He played a major
part in raising volunteers, especially for the King's (Liverpool) Regiment, before being
appointed Director-General of Recruiting in October 1915.

Despard, Charlotte (1884–1939)
Born in Kent to an Irish-born father, she was a suffragette, novelist, and Sinn Féin activist.
She spent a lot of time in Frenchpark, Co. Roscommon, where she formed the Irish
Women's Franchise League.

Devlin, Joseph (1872–1934)
Irish nationalist politician and Irish Party MP for Belfast West, 1906–1918. At the outbreak
of war, Devlin supported **John Redmond** in his decision to encourage Irishmen to help
defend the British Empire.

Dillon, John (1851–1927)
Irish Party MP for Mayo East in 1914.

Dolden, A. Stuart
A solicitor's clerk in London in 1914, he was forced by his employers to wait until November before joining up. He eventually enlisted, serving as an infantryman on the Western Front.

Donaldson, William
A constituent in Stirling, represented by Liberal MP Arthur Ponsonby.

Dorward, Alan (1889–1956)
Professor Alan Dorward was Chair of Philosophy at the University of Liverpool between 1928 and 1954. In 1914 he was a scholar at Trinity College, Cambridge.

Dotchin, Henry E.
Born in Yorkshire in 1898, he worked as an apprentice riveter on a shipyard in Middlesbrough during the war.

Douglas, Mrs G.
Born in Sunderland in 1884.

Duffin, A.
A relative of **Helen**, **Terence**, and **Molly Duffin**, based in Cushendun, Co. Antrim.

Duffin, Helen
Based in Newcastle, Co. Down, Helen and her sister **Molly Duffin** corresponded with their mother in Belfast and their brother, **Terence Duffin,** in training with the British Army at Ballykinlar camp, Co. Down.

Duggan, George Chester
Originally from Killiney he worked as a civil servant in the Chief Secretary's Office, Dublin from 1912 to 1921.

Durning Holt, Richard (1868–1941)
Liberal MP for Hexham, Northumberland from 1907 to 1918. During the First World War he was a member of the Advisory Committee of the Ministry of Shipping. In 1914 his family were based in Liverpool.

E–G

Eaves, W.
Resident in Plymouth in 1914.

Eden, [Robert] Anthony (1897–1977)
Born in West Auckland, Durham, Eden served in the First World War and reached the rank of captain, receiving a Military Cross at the age of 21. His younger brother, Nicholas, was killed when the HMS *Indefatigable* was sunk at the Battle of Jutland in 1916. After the war he entered politics and became a Conservative MP and Prime Minister from 1955 to 1957.

Edwards, Norman
Born in Sutton Coldfield in 1894, he enlisted on 2 September 1914.

Eggeling, Professor Hans Julius (1842–1918)
Professor and Chair of Sanskrit and Comparative Philology at the University of Edinburgh from 1875 to 1914, second holder of its Regius Chair of Sanskrit, and Secretary of the Royal Asiatic Society, London. In August 1914 he left for a vacation in his native Germany. Whilst he was away he was forced to retire from the university owing to his nationality. He was unable to return before his death in 1918.

Ellison, Norman F.
From West Kirby in Cheshire, he volunteered for war in 1914 and served as a rifleman in the Liverpool Rifles, 1st/6th Battalion, the King's Liverpool Regiment.

Emmott, Lord (1872–1938)
William Lygon succeeded his father as Earl Beauchamp in 1891. He joined the Liberal Party in 1900 and served in the Liberal government as First Commissioner of Works from 1910 to 1914, and then as Lord President of the Council, 1914 to 1915. He was made Lord Lieutenant of Gloucestershire in 1911. His daughter Gwen was married to **Captain Hume Peel** (see below).

Erwine, Laura H.
Living in Hendon, London in 1914 she corresponded with **Hanna Sheehy-Skeffington** (see below).

Evans, Alfred W.
Living in Southall, he had worked as a piano tuner's apprentice since 1912 in a factory based in Hayes, Middlesex. He was immediately against the war and was eventually imprisoned in Harwich Redoubt as a conscientious objector in 1916.

Evans, George Ewart (1909–1988)
Welsh writer. Born in the mining town of Abercynon, South Wales, he was aged 5 in 1914.

Evans, John
Deputy Town Clerk for Aberystwyth in 1914.

Ewart, Wilfrid H. G. (1892–1922)
Author and journalist who served in the First World War.

Faulkner, John P.
Born in 1883 in Manchester, he moved to Chester in 1905. He worked at a flour mill but volunteered with the Red Cross Chester Division in his spare time from 1912 to 1916. He then served as a medical orderly with 29th Stationary Hospital, Royal Army Medical Corps in Salonika and Italy, 1916 to 1918.

Fewell, Mrs E.
She worked as a domestic servant in Essex in 1914.

Fitzgerald, [Thomas Joseph] Desmond (1888–1947)
Irish politician born in London to Irish parents. Tommy adopted the romantic name Desmond (the name of the rulers of the Munster of his ancestors) in his late teens when he had become a member of the imagist group of young London poets. On leaving school, he took a job as a clerk and began to learn Irish. In February 1913 he moved to Ireland, with his wife Mabel, alerted to the nationalist stirrings. They took up residence in Irish-speaking Co. Kerry. Desmond joined the newly formed Irish Volunteers in November 1913. He sided with **Eoin MacNeill** when the movement split on the outbreak of the First

World War. He was expelled from Co. Kerry in January 1915 on suspicion of signalling to German submarines.

Foakes-Jackson, Reverend Canon F. J. (1855–1941)
English theologian and church historian. A fellow of Jesus College, Cambridge from 1886, he was lecturer there from 1882 and Dean from 1895 to 1916.

Forester, Cecil G.W. (1899–1977)
Later 7th Baron Forester of Willey Park, Shropshire. He enlisted when he was 18 in September 1917 and served with the Household Cavalry 3rd Battalion. Before then he had left school because of ill health and was being home-schooled in Barrow.

Fortescue, Lord Hugh (1854–1932)
British peer and Lord Lieutenant of Devon from 1904 to 1928.

Frazer, J. G. (1854–1941)
Born and educated in Glasgow he is best known as a pioneer of social anthropology and comparative ethnography, and author of *The Golden Bough* (1890). He was knighted in 1914.

Frost, Wesley
In 1914 he was appointed US Consul to Queenstown, Cork, Ireland. Situated above a public bar, the consulate initially carried routine duties. The escalation of the war saw a corresponding rise in consular activities—including the collection and forwarding of wages and possessions of Germans interned in camps at Tipperary and Oldcastle.

Fursdon, Charlotte
Living in Shorwenton in Exeter in 1914 she was active in various relief organizations, including the Soldiers' and Sailors' Families Association. She corresponded with **Mabel Barthorpe** (see above).

Gallacher, William (1881–1965)
Scottish trade unionist, activist and communist, he was leader of the British Socialist Party along with **John McLean** (see below). Gallacher was opposed to Britain becoming involved in the First World War and was president of the Clyde Workers' Committee, an organization formed in 1915 to campaign against the Munitions Act, which forbade engineers from leaving the works where they were employed.

Gardner, Alan
Brigadier, later Second Lieutenant, Royal Field Artillery, serving on the Western Front and in India, 1914–1918.

King George V (1865–1936)
King of the United Kingdom and British Dominions and Emperor of India from 1910 until his death in 1936. King of the Irish Free State from 1922. He married Mary 'May' of Teck (**Queen Mary**) in 1883 and they had six children: **Edward** (1894–1972), **Prince Albert** (1895–1952), **Princess Mary** (1897–1965), **Prince Henry** (1900–1974), **Prince George** (1902–1942), and **Prince John** (1905–1919). The elder royals were active during the war. **Edward,** the Prince of Wales in 1914, had joined the Grenadier Guards in June 1914 but Lord Kitchener refused to allow him to serve on the front lines, much to Edward's disappointment. **Albert,** known to his family as 'Bertie' was commissioned as a midshipman in September 1913 and began his service in 1914. He saw action at the Battle of Jutland in 1916. **Princess Mary** visited hospitals and welfare organizations with her mother, assisting with projects to give comfort to British servicemen and assistance to their families. One of

these projects was Princess Mary's Christmas Gift Fund which raised funds to buy presents for servicemen. **Henry** was studying at Eton in 1914, whilst **Prince George** was in his final year at St Peter's Court Preparatory School at Broadstairs, in Kent. In 1917 George V relinquished all German titles and styles on behalf of his relatives who were British subjects, and changed the name of the royal house from Saxe-Coburg-Gotha to Windsor.

George, David Lloyd (1863–1945)
Welsh Liberal politician who was Chancellor of the Exchequer in 1914 under Asquith's leadership. In 1916 he replaced Asquith as Prime Minister and led the country for the remainder of the war.

George, William
A solicitor in Criccieth, Gwynedd, he was the brother of **David Lloyd George**.

Gibbs, R. W. M.
A mathematician later based at the University of Oxford.

Gledstanes, Sheldon A.
A pre-war soldier he was based in Ireland at the outbreak of war. He served with the 1st Battalion, Bedfordshire Regiment, on the Western Front and was killed in action in 1915.

Goodwin, Miss M. M.
A young woman living in a small town on the Firth of Clyde in 1914.

Gosse, Edmund W. (1849–1928)
English poet, author, and critic. He was working as librarian of the House of Lords in 1914.

Gover, William
Medical student at the University of Oxford in 1914.

Graves, Robert (1895–1985)
English poet, scholar, and novelist. Born in Wimbledon, he won a scholarship to St John's College, Oxford. At the outbreak of the war he enlisted, taking a commission with the Royal Welch Fusiliers.

Gray, Frank
Born in 1895 at Limby, near Nottingham. He was a medical student at the University of Cambridge in 1914. He enlisted in the Royal Navy as Surgeon Practitioner in 1916 and served on ships in British waters.

Green, Charles Albert
Born in 1907 in Leicester, he was a schoolboy when war broke out.

Greville, Lord Francis R. C. G. (1853–1924)
Born in Middlesex, he was a Conservative MP for East Somerset (1879–1885) and Colchester (1888–1893). He succeeded to the title of 5th Earl of Warwick in 1893. He was the Lord Lieutenant of Essex from 1901 to 1919.

Grey, Sir Edward (1862–1933)
British Liberal MP and Foreign Secretary in 1914.

Griffith, Ellis (1860–1926)
Born in Birmingham, he grew up in Brynsiencyn, Anglesey. He was a barrister and MP, elected Liberal MP for Anglesey in 1895. In 1912 he became chairman of the Welsh Parliamentary Party and was Parliamentary Secretary to the Home Office, 1912 to 1915.

Griffith, Arthur (1871–1922)
Irish nationalist, and founder and third leader of Sinn Féin.

Grover, John M. L.
Born in 1897 he trained at Sandhurst between June and December 1914. He left for France in May 1915 and served with 2nd and 1st Battalions, King's Shropshire Light Infantry on the Western Front, 1915–1919.

Gulliver, H.
A contributor to the charities supporting Belgian refugees in Glasgow in 1914.

Gwynn, Stephen L. (1864–1950)
Irish journalist, author, biographer, and nationalist politician. He entered Irish politics in 1904 and won a seat for Galway city in 1906 as a member of the Irish Party. On the outbreak of war Gwynn strongly supported John Redmond's encouragement of Irish nationalists and the INV to support the Allied war effort, especially as a means to ensure the implementation of the suspended Home Rule Act. Aged over 50, he enlisted in January 1915 with the 7th Leinsters in the 16th (Irish) Division. He served on the Western Front.

Gwynne, H. A. (1865–1950)
Born at Kilvey, near Swansea. Author and editor of the *London Morning Post* since 1911. He answered to the owner, the Countess of Bathurst, a.k.a. Lady Bathurst, control of the paper having passed to her in 1908.

H–L

Haggard, H. Rider (1856–1925)
Sir Henry Rider Haggard was born in Norfolk, England, and was a Victorian writer of adventure novels, perhaps most famously *King Solomon's Mines* (1885). He corresponded with **Rudyard Kipling** throughout 1914.

Haig, Douglas (1861–1928)
Scottish-born British soldier and senior commander (Field Marshal) during the First World War. Between 1912 and 1914 he was General Officer Commanding Aldershot. Upon the outbreak of war Haig had command of half of the BEF as his Aldershot command was formed into I Corps.

Haldane, Elizabeth (1862–1937)
Social-welfare worker, author, and sister of **Richard Haldane** (see below). She was the first female Justice of the Peace in Scotland.

Haldane, Richard Burdon (1856–1928)
Liberal and Labour politician and lawyer, and brother of the author **Elizabeth Haldane**. Liberal MP for Haddingtonshire since 1885, he was appointed Secretary of State for War in 1905 and undertook major army reforms including the creation of the BEF. His tenure also saw the creation of the Imperial General Staff, the Territorial Army, the Officer Training Corps, and the Special Reserve. In 1912 he was appointed Lord Chancellor but was forced to resign in 1915 after being accused of pro-German sympathies.

Hancock, Malcolm
He had just finished school, aged 17, in August 1914 and was spending his summer in his home town of Newquay in Cornwall. He eventually enlisted in the British Army.

Hankey, Maurice P. A., later Lord (1877–1963)
British civil servant. Appointed Naval Assistant Secretary to the CID in 1908 and became Secretary to the Committee in 1912, a position he held for 26 years. In November 1914 he took on the additional duty of Secretary of the War Council.

Hardie, [James] Keir (1856–1915)
Scottish socialist and labour leader. In 1900 he was elected Labour Party MP for the dual constituency of Merthyr Tydfil and Aberdare in the South Wales Valleys, which he would represent for the remainder of his life.

Hardy, Thomas (1840–1928)
English novelist and poet living in Dorchester in 1914.

Harmsworth, Alfred C. W. (1865–1922)
Also known as **Lord Northcliffe**. Powerful newspaper and publishing magnate, his media empire included *The Evening News,* the *Edinburgh Daily Record,* the *Daily Mail,* the *Daily Mirror, The Observer, The Times,* and the *Sunday Times.* In 1905 he was given the title Baron Northcliffe, and in 1918 advanced to Viscount Northcliffe.

Harper, Lieutenant Cecil G.
Served as a subaltern in the 10th Battalion Gordon Highlanders, July 1914–1915.

Harris, Louisa Charlotte
Young woman in Yeovil, Somerset in 1914.

Hawkins, J. B.
Chairman of the Local Emergency Committee for the Thorpe District, Essex in 1914.

Healy, Timothy Michael (1855–1931)
Irish nationalist politician and IPP MP for North East Cork since 1911. At the outbreak of war, he supported the war, along with his brother **Maurice Healy** (IPP MP for Cork City since 1911). Timothy's eldest son, Joe, fought at Gallipoli.

Heath, P.G.
Soldier in training at Belhus Park, Aveley in 1914.

Heath, Lieutenant C. Phil
Born at Portsmouth in 1893, he attended the Royal Military Academy, Woolwich. In 1914 he was in training in Plymouth. He served as Lieutenant Colonel with the 59th and 135th Siege Battery, Royal Garrison Artillery on the Western Front, 1915–1918.

Henry, Alice Helen (1881–1956)
Born in London (née Brunton) she was sister to **Annie Brunton** and married Augustine Henry, the Irish botanist, in 1908. In 1914 she divided her time between London and Dublin.

Hewitt, Leonard J.
Born in 1899 in Leicester. A British private, he served with 8th and 7th Battalions Leicestershire Regiment on the Western Front in 1918.

Hines Page, Walter (1855–1918)
American Ambassador to the United Kingdom during the First World War.

Hobhouse, Charles E. H. (1862–1941)
Liberal politician. He was MP for Bristol East from 1900 to 1918. In 1914 he was appointed Postmaster-General, a position he held until 1915.

Hobson, J. A. (1858–1940)
English economist and imperial critic, widely popular as a lecturer and writer. Hobson's opposition to the First World War led him to join the UDC in 1914.

Holman, Dorothy (1888–1983)
The Holman family lived at Holcombe Down, Teignmouth, and various addresses in London between 1904 and 1939. Dorothy served as a Voluntary Aid Detachment (VAD) nurse from 1915 to 1918 at the Anglo-French-American Hospital in Paris. Her brother, Tommy, enlisted in 1914.

Holt, Cecil
Brother of **Iris Holt** (see below), he was serving with the 6th Cyclists Battalion Royal Sussex Regiment in Norfolk on home defence duty in 1914.

Holt, Iris
Living in Lewes, Sussex, she was engaged to **Alan Handfield 'Balury' Morton** serving with the 40th Brigade of the Royal Field Artillery in France in 1914. Sister of **Cecil Holt**.

Holt, Olive
A teenager in 1914 living in Chelsea, London.

Hope, Lieutenant George
Originally from East Lothian, George was serving with the 1st Battalion Grenadier Guards on the Western Front in 1914.

Hosty, John
A member of the Castlegar, Co. Galway branch of the INV.

Howell, Annie Mary
Born in 1902, she was a small child in Bermondsey in 1914.

Hughes, Emrys (1894–1969)
Born in Tonypandy in Wales, he was at Leeds Training College in 1914, training to become a teacher. In 1924 he married Nan Hardie, the daughter of Keir Hardie.

Hulse, Edward H. W. (1889–1915)
Born in Westminster, he graduated from Balliol College, Oxford in 1912. After a period of training with the Coldstream Guards he was given his commission in the 1st Battalion Scots Guards in March 1913. He fought at Mons in August 1914. In November 1914 he transferred to the 2nd Battalion Scots Guards. He was killed at Neuve Chapelle on 12 March 1915.

Hunt, F. H.
Born in 1896 he was a private with the 2/5th Battalion Lincolnshire Regiment. He enlisted in October 1914 and sailed to France in August 1915.

Hutchinson, Gladys
Lived at the Manor House, Catterick, Yorkshire, during the First World War.

Hynes, Thomas
An Irish nationalist from Galway who sided with **Eoin MacNeill** after the INV split.

Jackman, Cecil
A businessman in London in 1914.

Jacob, Rosamond (1888–1960)
Irish playwright and Quaker. Born in 1888 she was living in Waterford, Co. Waterford in 1914.

Jameson, Margaret Storm (1891–1986)
Novelist, essayist, journalist, literary critic, and political activist, she was born in the Yorkshire harbour town of Whitby. After reading English Language and Literature at Leeds University, she was granted a research scholarship to University College, London in 1912. She transferred to King's College and completed her thesis on modern European drama in 1914.

Jarvis, L. D.
Born in 1904, he was a schoolboy helping out on his father's farm in the Essex village of Stock in 1914.

Jeffreys, Len
South Wales coalminer. Born in Newtown, Cross Keys, in 1899, he was working at Risca pit in 1914.

John, Augustus (1878–1961)
Welsh painter originally from west Pembrokeshire. At the outbreak of the war he was living in London. At the beginning of the First World War Augustus was an officer in the Canadian Army, and was given permission to paint on the Western Front. However, during this time it would seem that he managed very little actual painting, and after just two months, his involvement in a brawl led to him being sent home 'in disgrace'. He was the younger brother of **Gwen John** and romantically linked with **Doriela McNeill**.

John, Edward Thomas (1857–1931)
Ironmaster and Welsh nationalist, born at Pontypridd. He was a Welsh-speaking Calvinistic Methodist. In 1910 he became Liberal MP for East Denbighshire. During the First World War, John emerged as a critic of the government and was one of four Welsh Liberal MPs to oppose conscription in 1916.

John, Gwen (1876–1939)
Welsh artist and older sister of **Augustus John**. She was living in Paris in 1914 where she had modelled for the sculptor Auguste Rodin.

Johnson, Miss Louie
Born in 1888, she had just finished her nursing training in Hull and become a sister at the Hull Royal Infirmary when war broke out. She served with the Red Cross and Territorial Force Nursing Service in Leeds, 1914–1918.

Johnson, Mrs D. C.
Living in Daylesford, Gloucestershire in 1914, her husband Captain D. C. Johnson, was serving with the 2nd Battalion, South Wales Borderers in China (Tsing Tau) in 1914. He later served at Gallipoli and on the Western Front. Her brother-in-law, Jack Johnson, was killed in action in France in 1914. Mrs Johnson and her husband had a baby son, Peter.

Johnson, William W.
Residing in London in 1914.

Johnston, Dr John
Born in Dumfriesshire, Scotland, in 1852. A trained doctor, during the early years of the First World War he worked as a Civilian Medical Practitioner at Queen Mary's Military Hospital, Whalley, despite his natural objection to war as a Christian and socialist. He was a member of the Bolton Whitman Fellowship, a group of local men and women dedicated to the study and appreciation of Walt Whitman, the American poet.

Jones, William
Born in 1888 in Erdington, West Midlands, he was working as a clerk in the Gas Department of Birmingham Corporation in 1914.

Kavanagh, Matthew
Born in Arklow, Co. Wicklow, Kavanagh joined the INV in Arklow in 1914, aged around 19. He sided with **Eoin MacNeill** after the split.

Kell, Vernon G. W. (1873–1942)
Founder and first Director General of the British Security Service, MI5.

Kerr, Philip Henry (1882–1940)
British politician and diplomat. Born in London he was a member of the influential Scottish family, his father being Lord Ralph Drury Kerr. In 1930 Philip became 11th Marquis of Lothian. In 1914 he was living in London. He became private secretary to **David Lloyd George** in 1916.

Kerrigan, Rose
Born 1903, she was attending the Jewish Hebrew School in Hillhead, Glasgow in 1914. She would later become involved in the Scottish rent strike and anti-war movement during the war.

Kettle, [Thomas Michael] 'Tom' (1880–1916)
Irish nationalist and supporter of Home Rule, he was IPP MP for East Tyrone. He was also a poet, barrister, journalist, and economist. He was on an arms-gathering mission for the INV in 1914 when war broke out. He served with the 9th Battalion of the Royal Dublin Fusiliers on the Western Front. He was killed at the Battle of the Somme in September 1916.

King, William
Born at Drummin, Westport in Co. Mayo in 1903. He joined the INV in November 1917.

Kipling, Rudyard (1865–1936)
English author and poet best known today for his children's books, including *The Jungle Book* (1894) and *Just So Stories* (1895). Kipling sympathized with the anti-Home Rule stance of Irish Unionists and was friendly with **Edward Carson**. His only son, John, died in 1915 at the Battle of Loos. His daughter, **Elsie Kipling**, aged 18 in 1914, was devastated by the loss of her male contemporaries in the war.

Kirk, T. H.
Aged 15 in 1914, in August he was at the Rugeley Officers Training Corps annual camp. He lived in Norton-on-Tees, Durham with his family.

Kirkpatrick, Ivone E. S. (1899–1975)
Also attended the Officers Training Corps annual camp in Rugeley in August 1914, Ivone was a pupil at Shrewsbury School, Shropshire, until 1917 when he joined the Royal Flying Corps.

Kitchener, Horatio Herbert, Earl Kitchener of Khartoum (1850–1916)
Irish-born British Field Marshal, diplomat, and statesman. At the outbreak of war **Lord Kitchener** was appointed Secretary of State for War. He correctly predicted a long war that would last at least three years and require huge numbers of men. He was therefore at the centre of a massive voluntary recruitment campaign (1914–1916), which, amongst other tactics, featured the distinctive poster of himself designed by the artist Alfred Leetes.

Laidlaw, Thomas Douglas
Aged 30 in 1914 he was married to Bertha and they had two young children. In 1914 he was working for a stockbroker in Glasgow as their exchange dealer. Within twenty-four hours of war being declared he volunteered with the 5th Battalion Cameroon Highlanders and was sent down to Aldershot.

Larner, Herbert
A schoolboy in Leeds in 1914. At the outbreak of war he joined the local Defence Volunteers and Rifle Club.

Lawrence, D. H. (1885–1930)
Born in the coal-mining town of Eastwood, Nottinghamshire, Lawrence was a controversial and prolific English novelist, poet, dramatist, artist, and literary critic. In July 1914 he married his German lover, Frieda von Richthofen. Her German parentage and Lawrence's pacifism meant they were viewed with suspicion in wartime Britain. Later in the war they were accused of spying and signalling to German submarines off the coast of Cornwall. In late 1917, after constant harassment by the military authorities, Lawrence was forced to leave Cornwall at three days' notice under the terms of the DORA.

Lawson, Christina Hunter
A schoolteacher in Edinburgh in 1914.

Le Queux, William Tufnell (1864–1927)
British journalist and writer. He wrote mystery and espionage thrillers, particularly in the years leading up to the outbreak of war, perhaps his most famous being *The Invasion of 1910* (1906) and *Spies of the Kaiser* (1909), which described the invasion of Britain by German troops and spies. The former was serialized in the *Daily Mail* in 1905 and was promoted by actors dressed as German soldiers walking along Regent Street, London. At the outbreak of war he was living in Shepperton-on-Thames, Surrey, and was convinced that he was under threat from German enemies within. He therefore hounded the Metropolitan Police for personal protection.

Ledwidge, Francis (1887–1917)
An Irish poet from Slane, Co. Meath. A member of the Slane INV he originally sided with **Eoin MacNeill** after the split in September 1914. However, his opinion changed and he decided that he could not stand aside whilst others fought for Ireland's freedom. He joined the Royal Inniskilling Fusiliers and was killed in Flanders on 31 July 1917.

Lee, Elizabeth
Born in 1892 she was living in Sutton, Kent, in 1914. During the war she worked as a Red Cross driver in London and Kent and later at Sopwith's aeroplane factory in Sussex.

Lee, Georgina (c.1871–1965)
Eldest daughter of the English pastoral painter Henry William Banks Davis, she had married her solicitor husband aged 41 and had her only child, Harry, aged 43 or 44. It is to her baby

son that her Great War diaries are addressed. During the war, Harry was sent to live with family in Wales whilst Georgina and her husband remained in London. She was clearly torn between her longing to be with him and what she saw as her duty to stay with her husband, whose health was not good. She had two brothers-in-law in the Army. In 1914 she busied herself with various relief efforts including the Belgian Red Cross in London.

Lee, Jennie (1904–1988)
British socialist and Labour MP. Born in Lochgelly, Fife, her father, James, was chairman of the local branch of the ILP and she accompanied him to these meetings. Like most members, he was opposed to Britain's entry into the First World War. She was a schoolgirl in 1914.

Lees, Mary
Born in 1894, she was 17 when war broke out and had just come home to Devon that July. During the war she served with the Women's National Land Service Corps and Women's Land Army, 1915–1917, and the Air Ministry in London, 1917–1918.

Leicester, Phillip A.
Living in Worcester he was aged 27 in 1914. He was Honorary Secretary of the Worcester Rifle Club.

Leslie, Sir [John Randolph] Shane (1885–1971)
Irish-born diplomatic aide and writer. Living in London in 1914, during the war he was in a British Ambulance Corps, until invalided out; he was then sent to Washington, DC to help the British Ambassador, Sir Cecil Spring Rice, soften Irish-American hostility towards England and obtain American intervention in the war in the aftermath of the 1916 Easter Rising in Dublin.

Levi, Lillian
A 7-year-old schoolgirl at Newcastle Church High School in Glasgow in 1914.

Lewis, Sir John Herbert (1858–1933)
Liberal MP for Flintshire, 1906–1918.

Lewis, James Richard
Born in 1901 he was a schoolboy in Waterloo, Liverpool, in 1914.

Limerick, Angela Olivia
Born in 1897, she was a schoolgirl in Kent in 1914. She later served as a nurse with the VAD Red Cross in London and Surrey, 1915–1919.

Lockwood, Frank Taylor
Born in 1885 in Linthwaite, near Huddersfield in Yorkshire, he was working as an apprentice lithographic artist at Netherwood Dalton in Huddersfield in 1914. Between 1917 and 1919 he served with the Northumberland Fusiliers and then with the Royal Flying Corps.

Lody, Carl Hans (1877–1914)
Born in Berlin, he was executed as a German spy by firing squad in the Tower of London on 6 November 1914.

Londonderry, Lady Theresa (1856–1919)
Supporter of the Ulster Unionists. Wife of Charles Vane-Tempest-Stewart, 6th Marquess of Londonderry, a British Conservative and Unionist politician.

Lord, Martha
Born in 1904 in Whitchurch, Shropshire, her family moved to Cornholme, near Todmorden in around 1910 or 1911. They were living there when the war broke out.

Lorimer, Duncan
Called up as a Naval Reservist in August 1914 and served on board the *Cressy* and then the minesweeper *Bacchante* in 1914.

Lowes Dickinson, Goldsworthy (1862–1932)
English historian and politician activist. He led most of his life at Cambridge. He was closely tied with the Bloomsbury Group and was a noted pacifist who protested against Britain's involvement in the First World War.

M–P

MacCallum Scott, Alexander (1874–1928)
Secretary of the League of Liberals against Aggression and Militarism, and Secretary of the New Reform Club before becoming Liberal MP for the Bridgeton constituency of Glasgow in 1910. During the First World War he was Parliamentary Secretary to Winston Churchill.

MacColl, Dugald Sutherland (1859–1948)
British impressionist painter and critic. He served as the keeper of the Tate Gallery from 1906 to 1911 and the Wallace Collection from 1911 to 1924.

MacCunn, Francis John
An Oxford graduate, Francis was working as an assistant in the Department of History, University of Glasgow from 1912 to 1914. Author of *The Contemporary English View of Napoleon* (1914). As a member of the Officers Training Corps he enlisted in the Army in 1914 and served as a captain in the 6th Battalion Cameron Highlanders. He was killed at the Battle of Loos in 1915 exactly one year to the day after he joined the regiment.

Macaulay, Rose (1881–1958)
Born in Rugby, Warwickshire, she was an English novelist. She studied modern history at Somerville College, Oxford and during the First World War worked in the British Propaganda Department, after some time as a nurse and then as a civil servant in the War Office.

MacDonagh, Michael (1860–1946)
Irish-born journalist working for *The Times* in 1914.

MacKay, Reverend James
Born at Stemster, near Thurso, Caithness in 1889, he was a Methodist minister for most of his life. In 1914 he was working in Newcastle-upon-Tyne.

MacKenzie Brown, George (1869–1946)
Canadian-born Scottish publisher. In 1914 he was director of Thomas Nelson and Son, Ltd, an Edinburgh-based publishing house, in partnership with the Scottish novelist John Buchan.

Maclean, John (1879–1923)
Scottish left-wing politician born in Glasgow. As a schoolteacher he joined the Social Democratic Federation and remained in the organization as it formed the BSP. He heavily

opposed the war, as he felt it was a war of imperialism that divided workers against one another. He became a leading figure in of the Red Clydeside era.

Macleod, John Dunning
Born in 1894, he enlisted with the Army in 1914 and went on to become a captain with the 2nd Battalion Cameron Highlanders, serving on the Western Front and in Salonika.

Macmillan, Thomas
An office clerk in Glasgow in 1914. He tossed a coin with his brother to decide which one should volunteer. He lost the bet and enlisted in November 1914, joining the Benbow Battalion Royal Naval Division in the UK.

MacNeill, Eoin (1867–1945)
Irish nationalist and revolutionary born in Glenarm, Co. Antrim. In 1893 he founded the Gaelic League along with Douglas Hyde. In 1908 he was appointed Professor of Early Irish history at University College Dublin. In 1913 MacNeill became chairman of the council that formed the INV and he later became its chief of staff. However, he vehemently disagreed with IPP leader **John Redmond** over the party's support for Britain in the First World War and, in particular, the idea that Irish men should enlist for foreign service with the British Army. The INV movement split in September 1914, MacNeill leading the minority of advanced nationalists opposed to Redmond's policy.

Mann, Mrs E.
Schoolgirl in Brighouse in Yorkshire in 1914. Her father enlisted in November 1914.

Marshall, A. J. H.
Headmaster of a Church of England school in Freemantle, Southampton in 1914.

Maxwell, Dr James Laidlaw (1836–1921)
Born in Scotland, he studied there to become a doctor. He worked in London at the Brompton Hospital and in Birmingham at the Birmingham General Hospital. He was also an elder at Broad Street Presbyterian Church. He later became the pioneer medical missionary for the English Presbyterian Missionary Society and worked in Taiwan and China. He retired to London, still working with missionary societies.

Maxwell, Peniton
Editor of *Nash's Magazine* (1911–1914), a monthly London-based publication that merged with *The Pall Mall Magazine* in 1914.

May, Nellie
Working in the textile industry in Caterham, Surrey in 1914. She employed a number of 'girls' whose futures she feared for after the outbreak of war owing to the contraction of trade.

McCann, Beatrice
A teenager in 1914 living in a village eight miles outside of Hungerford, Berkshire.

McCarthy, James
Catholic Bishop of Galloway, based at St Benedict's, Maxwelltown, Dumfries, in 1914.

McCrave, Thomas
Member of the INV in Dundalk, Co. Louth since early 1914.

McDonald, [James] Ramsay (1866–1937)
British politician and twice Prime Minister of the UK. In 1906 he was elected as ILP MP for Leicester, a seat he held until 1918. In 1911 he became leader of the party but resigned the Chairmanship when the party voted to support the Liberal government in the war. He was replaced by Arthur Henderson.

McGuire, Ada
Schoolteacher at Somerville School, Liverpool, in 1914.

McIndoe, Thomas
A private who enlisted with the 12th Battalion Middlesex Regiment in 1914.

McIvor, William
Aged 12 in 1914, he was living in Birkenhead, Cheshire. He assisted his father in the transportation of wounded soldiers from Birkenhead Woodside station to local hospitals.

McKenna, Reginald (1863–1943)
Liberal MP for Monmouthshire (1895–1918) he was Home Secretary in Asquith's government from 1911 to 1915.

McKinnon-Wood, Thomas (1855–1927)
Liberal MP for Glasgow St Rollox (1906–1918) and Secretary of State for Scotland, 1912–1916.

McLachlan, Captain J. M.
Born 1888 in Edinburgh, Scotland, he trained as a dentist and then as a doctor. Before joining the Army he spent some time as a locum in various places around the UK. He was engaged to **Miss A. Logie Robertson** (see below), and in 1914 he enlisted with the Royal Army Medical Corps and served on the Western Front and in Salonika and Palestine. They married in August 1916 when he was home on leave.

McNeill, [Dorothy] Doriela (1881–1969)
Mistress, muse, and later second wife of the Welsh artist **Augustus John** with whom she had two children. She was also a friend of his sister, **Gwen John**.

Metcalfe, Nancy
Aged 16 in 1914 she was training to be a nurse at Scarborough Hospital. She experienced the bombardment of the town on 16 December 1914.

Middleton, Mrs Lydia
Married to Sir Thomas Middleton, working at the Board of Agriculture in 1914 (and later Deputy Director-General of the Food Production Department established in 1917), and living in Ealing, London. Her son, Alexander Allardyce Middleton, was serving as a Lieutenant with the Royal Horse Artillery in Madras, India, in 1914.

Miles, [Dorothy Beatrice] Hallie Eustace
Born in London, she married Eustace Hamilton Miles (1868–1948), sportsman, writer, and food reformer, in 1906. Over the next thirty years she collaborated closely with her husband in the health-food shop and vegetarian restaurant, with associated enterprises for physical, mental, and spiritual self-training, which began operation the same year from premises at 40–42 Chandos Street, Charing Cross. Within a few years Eustace Miles's Restaurant, which he promoted as a 'restaurant with ideals', had established a distinctive reputation, and it was wryly celebrated in E. M. Forster's *Howards End* (1910). Their business operations continued to expand after the First World War.

Miller, Harry
Born in 1900 to Jewish émigrés from Russia, he was a schoolboy in Grimsby, Lincolnshire, in 1914. He lived with his mother, maternal grandparents, two aunts, and three siblings. His father had gone to the United States in 1910 to make his fortune, but was unsuccessful and the family in Grimsby had very little to live off. He went on to work in advertising in London and Cheshire, and for the Ministry of Information from 1938 to 1945.

Milner, Lord Alfred (1854–1925)
German-born British statesman, Conservative politician, and businessman.

Molyneux, Lady Helena Mary (1875–1947)
She married Osbert Cecil Molyneux in 1898, who would become the 6th Earl of Sefton. They had three children including a son, Cecil Richard, who died in the Battle of Jutland in 1916 aged only 16. Their family seat was at Croxteth Hall in Croxteth Park, West Derby. Their London residence was at Sefton House in Belgrave Square. In Liverpool they owned a house on Lord Street.

Monkhouse, Allan Noble (1858–1936)
Playwright, novelist, and newspaper critic. Born at Barnard Castle in County Durham, he moved to Manchester and joined the cotton trade after he left school. He was to remain in the north-west of England for the rest of his life, ultimately settling in Disley, Cheshire. In 1902 he left the cotton business to join the editorial staff of the *Manchester Guardian*, a position he held until 1932.

Moore, Maurice George (1854–1939)
Born in Moore Hall in Co. Mayo, Maurice served with the Connacht Rangers in the South African War. He is credited by many as the founder of the INV, and in 1914 he was their Inspector-General. He was the younger brother of the Irish poet, dramatist, and novelist, George Augustus Moore (1852–1933).

Morel, E. D. (1873–1924)
British journalist, author, and socialist politician. He led the campaign against slavery in the Congo Free State in collaboration with **Roger Casement**, the Congo Reform Association and others. He played a large role in the British pacifist movement during the First World War, participating in the foundation and becoming secretary of the UDC. On this occasion he broke with the Liberal Party, of which he was previously a member, and after the war joined the ILP.

Morley, Lord John (1838–1923)
Born in Blackburn, Lancashire, he was a British Liberal politician and newspaper editor. From 1910 he had been Lord President of the Council but resigned in protest at the outbreak of the First World War along with **Charles Trevelyan** and **John Burns**. He was replaced by the Earl of Beauchamp, William Lygon.

Morris, Fred
Coalminer from Maerdy, South Wales. He volunteered in 1914 along with his brother.

Morrison, Sybil
Born in 1893 in London, she joined the WSPU in 1911 aged 18. She volunteered during the war as an ambulance driver.

Morton, Alex
Owner of Morton Sundour Fabrics, Ltd a textile factory in Dentonhill, Carlisle, Cumbria.

Morton, Lieutenant Alan Handsfield 'Balury'
Born in Wandsworth, South London, in 1890 he served with the 40th Brigade of the Royal Field Artillery between August and December 1914. He was engaged to **Iris Holt** (see above).

Moss, Hilda
Born in 1905 she was being home-schooled in Birmingham by her governess and aunt in 1914.

Moylan, Thomas King
Born in Co. Clare, Moylan was aged 28 and working as a Lunatic Asylum Clerk in Dublin in 1914. His father was a retired civil servant.

Moynihan, Michael J. (1891–1918)
A graduate of University College Dublin, he was working at the Inland Revenue offices at Croydon, London in 1914. In March 1914 he joined the Civil Service Rifles, a unit of the Territorials. When war broke out, he remained with this unit and did not return to the civil service. In 1916 Moynihan decided to sign up for foreign service despite his mother's opposition and he went to France at the end of June 1916 as a private in the London Regiment. He was killed on 3 June 1918 and is buried in Doullens cemetery, just north of Amiens.

Muirsmith, Mr W.
Managing Director of A. B. Fleming & Co, Ltd, an ink manufacturers and printing works which had headquarters in London and a printing works in Edinburgh.

Murray, Albert Victor
Born at Choppington, Northumberland, in 1914 he was studying at Magdalen College, Oxford where he was Secretary to the Students' Christian Movement. A pacifist, he opposed the war and was a conscientious objector, exempted from military service on health grounds.

Murray, James
Born in Maybole, Ayrshire, in 1895, he was working as a credit agent in Glasgow when war broke out. In 1914 he tried to enlist several times but was rejected on account of his poor eyesight. He finally got accepted in 1915. From November 1914 to October 1915 he worked as a riveter at the Fairfield Shipyard in Glasgow.

Murray, Lord Arthur Cecil (1879–1962)
Liberal MP for Kincardineshire from 1908 to 1918. He was Parliamentary Private Secretary to the Foreign Secretary, Sir Edward Grey, from 1910 to 1914. In mid-August 1914 he left his post and served with the 2nd King Edward's Horse in France until 1916. He was then Assistant Military Attaché in Washington from 1917 to 1918.

Napier, Lady Mabel
Living in Northumberland in 1914 her sons, Joseph and Charles, were at Neuchatel, Switzerland, at the outbreak of war, from where she was trying to get them safely back to England.

Nash, Alice
Born in Sunderland in 1898, in August 1914 she had been left in charge of her younger brothers and sisters whilst her mother was away visiting her husband in Hull as his ship had come in.

Nathan, Matthew (1862–1939)
Under-Secretary of State for Ireland from 1914 to 1916.

Nesbit, E. (1858–1924)
English author and poet who was known best for her fiction for children. She was politically active and co-founded the Fabian Society, a precursor to the Labour Party.

New, Miss Gladys Dolby
Born in Birkenhead in 1896, she had just left school when war broke out. In October she went to study at Liverpool University and was arrested for sketching the Mersey estuary.

Neyland, Bertram
Born in 1897, he was living in Port Talbot in 1914, training with the Post Office. He enlisted with the Army and served as a signaller in the Royal Engineers in Britain, the Western Front, and Ireland from 1916 to 1919.

Nisbet, Captain H. Ulric S.
A former student of Marlborough College, he served as a Second Lieutenant with the 3rd Battalion Queen's Own (Royal West Kent) Regiment in south-east England, August 1914 to July 1916.

Northcliffe, Lord
See **Alfred Harmsworth** above.

O–R

O'Brien, [William] Dermod (1865–1945)
Irish painter, who had studied in France, Italy, and Belgium before settling in Dublin in 1901. Grandson of Young Ireland leader William Smith O'Brien. He married **Mabel** (née Smyly) in 1902. On his father's death in 1909 he inherited the family estate in Cahirmoyle, Co. Limerick where they lived until 1919.

O'Brien, William (1852–1928)
Irish nationalist, journalist, and politician. Born in Mallow, Co. Cork, he was an independent nationalist MP for Cork City from 1910 to 1918. O'Brien saw the outbreak of war as an opportunity to unite Green and Orange in a common cause, declaring himself on the side of Britain's war effort. He spoke out in favour of the formation of an Irish Brigade and stood on recruiting platforms encouraging voluntary enlistment in the Royal Munster Fusiliers.

O'Connor, T. P. (1848–1929)
Irish nationalist, journalist, and IPP MP for Liverpool (Scotland Road) from 1885 to 1929. Born in Athlone, Co. Westmeath, he moved to London in 1870 where he was appointed a sub-editor on the *Daily Telegraph*.

O'Donoghue, Michael V.
Born in Portumna, Co. Galway in 1900, his family moved to Dungarven, Co. Waterford in 1909. In 1913 Michael was sent to Curraheen, Thurles, to help his uncle with farm work. In 1914 he was at school (Fourth Grade) at Lismore Christian Brothers' School, and living in Cappoquin.

O'Leary, Jeremiah Joseph
Born in 1889 in Colchester, Essex, he moved to London when he was fairly young. His father was from Wexford and his mother from Cork. He joined the Gaelic League in London in 1905 and the IRB in 1908. In early 1914 he was asked to start a South London company of INV who met in a German Gymnasium at Highbury.

Orelbar, Richard A. B.
Serving with the 2nd and 3rd Bedfordshire Regiment, attached to the Royal Irish Fusiliers, on the south-east coast in 1914 and then the Western Front and Salonika in 1915.

O'Rourke, Sean
Irish Nationalist Volunteer in Banbridge, Co. Down.

O'Sheil, Kevin R.
Irish Nationalist Volunteer who worked with the Irish Land Commission in post-civil war Ireland.

Owen, Dorothy M.
Born in 1907, she was a schoolgirl living in Britain in 1914.

Pankhurst, [Estelle] Sylvia (1882–1960)
British suffrage campaigner and left-wing activist. Born in Manchester, her mother was **Emmeline Pankhurst**, member of the ILP and suffrage campaigner. Sylvia's sister **Christabel**, would also become an activist for women's rights. In 1906 Sylvia started to work full-time with the WSPU with her sister and her mother. In contrast to them she retained her interest in the labour movement. In 1914 she broke with the WSPU over the group's promotion of arson attacks. Sylvia set up the East London Federation of Suffragettes. Unlike her mother and sister, Sylvia did not support the British war effort in 1914 and criticized the government's call for women's war service, given that the government still refused women full citizenship.

Parker, Robert
Born in 1894, he worked at Eastchurch Airfield between 1910 and 1914. He volunteered with the Army and served as a driver with the 68th Motor Transport Company Army Service Corps in Britain and on the Western Front between 1914 and 1915.

Parker, Mrs
A schoolgirl from Essex who spent the summer of 1914 with her aunt in Ramsgate, east Kent.

Parr, W. J.
A vicar in Lechlade, Gloustershire. His son, Jackie, volunteered in 1914 against his father's wishes and served with the 5th Highland Light Infantry in Egypt and on the Western Front, before being taken prisoner.

Parsons, Lawrence
Commander of the 16th (Irish) Division from September 1914 onwards.

Paul, Patrick Joseph
Born in 1896 in Waterford City, Ireland, to a nationalist, Irish-speaking family. The family were against the English because they had been responsible in previous years for the loss of property and land and therefore the family fortunes. Paul was Officer Commanding of the East Waterford Brigade of the INV, 1919 to 1921.

Pearse, Pàdraig (1879–1916)
Teacher, barrister, writer, Irish nationalist, and political activist. He believed that language was intrinsic to the identity of a nation. To this end he opened St Enda's bilingual school in Ranelagh, Co. Dublin in 1908. In 1910 the school moved to Rathfarnham. In early 1914 Pearse became a member of the IRB whilst also remaining a member of the INV. He became the INV Director of Military Organization and was the highest ranking Volunteer in the IRB membership. By 1915 he was on the IRB's Supreme Council, and its secret Military Council, the core group that planned for a rising in Ireland during the First World War.

Peart, Eleanor
Living in North Shields, near Tyne and Wear in 1914, she volunteered with a number of relief organizations, particularly those assisting Belgian refugees.

Peel, Mrs C. S. (1868–1934)
Constance Dorothy Evelyn Peel (née Bayliff) was a British journalist and writer on household management and domestic history, who wrote under her married name of Mrs Charles Steers Peel. Born at Ganarew, Herefordshire, by 1913 both her children were at school and she returned to her life as a journalist. She took up the post of editor of the household department of *The Queen*, a position she held for seventeen years, as well as working for *Hearth and Home* and *The Lady*. Her books such as *Marriage on Small Means* (1914) and *The Labour Saving House* (1917) instructed women in modern methods and technologies of household management. During the First World War, Constance Peel organized a Soldiers' and Sailors' Wives Club in Lambeth, and was a speaker for the United Workers' Association and the National War Savings Association. She worked as co-director of women's service for the Ministry of Food during the period of voluntary food rationing, March 1917–March 1918. She travelled round the country and delivered 176 addresses promoting the economical use of food. She was appointed OBE in 1919.

Peel, Captain Hume
Hume Peel entered the India Office in 1906 and joined the Army in September 1914 (1/8th Battalion, London Regiment, Post Office Rifles which fought in France as part of the 4th London Brigade). He was married to Gwen Lygon, daughter of **Lord Emmott** (see above). Peel was killed in action on 24 March 1918.

Perkins, Sidney
Aged 15 in 1914 he was living on a farm in Tynewydd, Mid Glamorgan. He eventually enlisted and served as a Gunner with the 325 Siege Battery, Royal Garrison Artillery.

Pielou, Florence
Landscape painter, and friend and political associate of the Sheehy-Skeffingtons in Dublin in 1914. She supported the Irish Women's Franchise League and distributed the organization's organ, the *Irish Citizen*.

Pilditch, P. H.
Aged 24 at the outbreak of war. Educated at Winchester and Cambridge University, he had joined the Territorials as a member of the London Brigade of the Royal Field Artillery. He served in this unit for two years prior to the outbreak of war. He then served with this regiment on the Western Front, 1915–1918.

Playne, Caroline E. (1857–1948)
Pacifist and historian born in Avening, Gloucestershire. She was elected an associate member of the University of London Women's Club in 1908 by which time she had

published two novels. Unusually among her contemporaries, Caroline Playne was one of the few women, such as **Lady Kate Courtney** (see above), who were alert, before 1914, to the danger of an imminent, cataclysmic European war. Already by about 1904 she had become a founder member of Britain's National Peace Council supporting the recently founded international court at The Hague, and in 1908 she attended the International Peace Congress in London also attended by Bertha von Suttner, whose biographer she later became. When the First World War finally broke out, Caroline Playne was devastated. She immediately joined the Emergency Committee for the Relief of Distressed Enemy Aliens (Germans trapped in Britain); she joined the UDC; she worked for the Nailsworth Peace Association and the National Peace Council; she collected suppressed pacifist pamphlets; and she also kept private notes of the constant war propaganda in the British press and a private diary of the war years. In the inter-war period she published her pioneering work in cultural history and social psychology. Her aim was to demonstrate and analyse the preconditions for irrational, righteous mass slaughter, hoping that she might thereby inoculate German, French, and British readers against being quite so vulnerable to mass media propaganda again.

Plunkett, Horace Curzon (1854–1932)
Anglo-Irish unionist and later Irish nationalist, agricultural reformer, and politician. A supporter of Irish Home Rule he founded the Irish Dominion League in 1914.

Ponsonby, Arthur (1871–1946)
British politician, writer, and social activist. In 1908 he was elected Liberal MP for Stirling Burghs. He opposed Britain's involvement in the First World War and joined with other opponents, such as **Ramsay MacDonald** and **E. D. Morel** to form the UDC in 1914.

Powell, Oliver
A miner from Tredegar, South Wales, who volunteered for the Army in 1914. His employer promised to pay ten shillings per week to every wife of a miner who volunteered, but failed to do so. In the 1920s Powell fought and won a compensation case against his former employer.

Pratt, James Davidson
Born in 1891 he was a pre-war soldier, serving with University Company 4th Battalion Gordon Highlanders from 1908 to 1916. He served with them on the Western Front from 1914 to 1915.

Price, Donald
Born in 1898 in Barry, South Wales, his family moved to Caddishead when he was 8 or 9 years old. He worked as an apprentice in the fur trade in Manchester from 1913 to 1914, after his father had died. He volunteered with the Army in 1914 and served with 20th and 13th Battalions Royal Fusiliers in Britain and the Western Front, 1914–1918.

Purbrook, Mrs A.
A housewife from Hornchurch, Essex, during the First World War.

Rafter, Charles
Chief Constable of Birmingham City Police in 1914.

Ratcliffe, Mr S. H.
A young man from Sheerness, Kent, he worked as an engine fitter in 1914.

Redmond, John Edward (1856–1918)
Irish nationalist and leader of the IPP from 1900 to 1918. He was also MP for Waterford City from 1891 to 1918. He was a moderate and constitutional politician who wished to achieve self-government for Ireland through legal rather than revolutionary measures. His elder brother, Willie Redmond, fought and died in the First World War. His son, William Archer Redmond, joined up and served on the Western Front with the Royal Dublin Fusiliers and then the Irish Guards. He survived the war.

Reece, Ada E. M. P. (1867–1968)
Born at Camberwell, south London, her maiden name was Perkins. She lived in London during the First World War.

Remington, Alice Christabel
Born in 1895, she was living in North Lancashire in 1914. In September 1914 she volunteered with relief efforts and learnt how to drive and simple mechanics at a local garage. She went on to be a driver and canteen worker with Angela Forbes' canteens in France in 1915. She later served as an ambulance driver with the Red Cross VAD in France, 1915–1918.

Riddey, John R.
Working in Deptford, London, in 1914 he volunteered for the Army and served with the 3rd Battalion Honourable Artillery Company. He was killed in action in 1917 on the Western Front.

Roberts, Eleanor
An American girl born to English emigrants in 1885, she travelled to England on 2 July 1914 to see her 'home' country and meet relatives. She stayed in London and Harrow, eventually departing on 2 September 1914 from Liverpool.

Roberts, Frederick, Earl (1832–1914)
Distinguished Anglo-Irish soldier and one of the most successful army commanders of the Victorian era. In the pre-war period he was a keen advocate of introducing conscription to Britain in order to prepare for a great European War. He was one of the leaders of the National Service League founded in 1901. He died of pneumonia at St Omer, France, while visiting troops on the Western Front in November 1914.

Roberts, Robert (1905–1974)
Teacher and writer, he was born in Salford, Lancashire, where he spent his youth. He attended Christ Church School, Hope Street, Salford, until the age of 14.

Robertson, Miss A. Logie
Living in Edinburgh she was engaged to Captain J. M. McLachlan (see above), serving with the Royal Army Medical Corps on the Western Front. They had met in 1911 and were married in August 1916 when he was home on leave.

Robinson, F. A.
Resident in Cobham, Surrey, in 1914 where he kept a daily diary from 22 July 1914 to 11 November 1918.

Rochester, Edith
A 7-year-old schoolgirl in Whitby on the east coast, she experienced the bombardment of her town on 16 December 1914. On that day she attended her school on Cliff Street when, during her first lesson, she heard the start of the bombardment.

Rooke, Louis
A soap-broker in Liverpool in 1914, his son, Leonard, was a regular soldier and departed for active service to Egypt with the King's Own Scottish Borderers on 6 August 1914.

Roome, J.
Aged 16 when war broke out in 1914, he was living in Walthamstow, London. He enlisted in 1916.

Rose, George H. (1882–1956)
Born in Chipping Ongar, Essex, Rose was a talented artist, working chiefly in watercolours. In late 1914 he went to work in the office of the Gas Company at Dalston, London, and later went to live in lodgings in London.

Rosebery, Lord (1847–1929)
Archibald Philip Primrose, 5th Earl of Rosebery since 1868, was a British Liberal statesman and prime minister (1894–1895). In 1914 he was Lord Lieutenant of Linlithgowshire but had generally retired from public politics. He sponsored a 'Bantam Battalion' in 1915. His son, Neil, was killed in action in Palestine in November 1917. His younger brother enlisted in November 1914.

Ross, Roderick
Chief Constable of Edinburgh City Police in 1914.

Rothenstein, William (1872–1945)
English painter, draughtsman, and writer. He was born into a Jewish family in Bradford and studied at the Slade School of Art and in Paris. He was an official war artist in both the First and Second World Wars.

Rothschild, Nathan Mayer, Baron (1840–1915)
British banker and politician from the international Rothschild financial dynasty, 1st Baron Rothschild since 1885 following the death of his uncle. He was the first Jewish member of the House of Lords and Lord Lieutenant of Buckinghamshire from 1889 to 1915.

Roy, James Stewart
A lecturer in English at St Andrews University. His father (a Presbyterian Minister) had recently died and his mother had moved down from Kirriemuir to live with him in St Andrews. Following the outbreak of war he was offered the position of Lecturer in German at the university because Dr Schaaf (the original lecturer) was interned in England as an enemy alien. He accepted with a contract until 31 December 1914 so he could decide if he wanted to enlist. He eventually served as an Intelligence Officer from 1914 to 1919.

Royden, A. Maude
A Christian pacifist living in London in 1914. Corresponded with **A. V. Murray** (see above).

Royle, Cyril
Born in 1901 he was aged 13 in 1914 and a schoolboy at Manchester Grammar School.

Rudkin, Mabel
Resident in Dover in 1914 with her husband, Erasmus.

Russell, Bertrand (1872–1970)
British philosopher, logician, mathematician, and advocate for social reform. He was a prominent anti-war activist and, during the First World War, Russell engaged in pacifist activities. In 1916 he was dismissed from Trinity College, Cambridge, following his

conviction under the DORA. A later conviction resulted in six months' imprisonment in Brixton prison for counselling men against conscription.

Russell, Elsie
Young woman living in Glen Douglas, Jedburgh on the Scottish Borders in 1914. She corresponded with **Arthur S. G. Butler** (see above).

Ryan, Desmond (1893–1964)
Son of W. P. Ryan, the Irish left-wing journalist, Desmond was born in London but moved back to Dublin with his family in 1905 when his father was appointed editor at *The Peasant.* He was educated at Westland Row Christian Brothers' School and at **Pàdraig Pearse**'s school, St Enda's (see above). He continued his association with Pearse while studying at University College Dublin, living in St Enda's, teaching some classes and acting as Pearse's secretary. He fought in the General Post Office, Dublin during Easter Week 1916, was imprisoned, and after his release began his career in journalism with the *Freeman's Journal.*

Ryder, Basil H.
A student at Bromsgrove School, Worcester, he enlisted in 1914 at the outbreak of war, and served first in the Royal Field Artillery. He was then attached to the Royal Flying Corps and, after training in England, crossed to France in March 1915.

S–Y

Sandhurst, Viscount (1855–1921)
British statesman, William Mansfield became 2nd Baron Sandhurst upon the death of his father in 1876. He was Lord Chamberlain from 1912 to 1921.

Saunders, Robert
Headmaster of the local national school in the small Sussex village of Fletching in 1914.

Schuster, Florence
Along with her family, she was in Constantinople (Istanbul), en route for the Crimea, at the outbreak of the First World War. The family returned to Manchester, where her father was a professor at the university, in September 1914. On their return her family were accused of being German spies owing to their Germanic surname. She later served at an Army Remount Centre and then as a postal van driver.

Scott, C. P. (1846–1932)
British journalist, publisher, and politician. Born in Bath, Somerset, he was editor of the *Manchester Guardian* from 1872 until 1929 and its owner from 1907 until his death.

Scott, Walter Dixon (1899–1915)
Literary critic, contributor to the *Manchester Guardian* and a friend of **Allan Monkhouse** (see above). He died of dysentery on the troop-ship *Aquintania* near the Dardanelles, three weeks after landing on 23 October 1915.

Scott, Dr William S. (1877–1952)
Born at Selkirk, he studied medicine at the University of Edinburgh where he qualified in 1900. In 1912 he acquired his own practice in Ellesmere, Shropshire. He was attached to the Shropshire Yeomanry before the war, and in 1914 served with the RAMC.

Shaw, George Bernard (1856–1950)
Irish dramatist, literary critic, and socialist. Author of the anti-war pamphlet *Common Sense About The War*, which appeared on 14 November 1914 as a supplement to the *New Statesman*. It sold more than 75,000 copies before the end of the year and made him internationally notorious. It resulted in his writings and speeches being banned from some newspapers and he was ejected from the Dramatists' Club, although he was its most distinguished member.

Shead, Mrs E.
Young woman living in Essex in 1914.

Sheehy-Skeffington, Francis (1878–1916)
Irish suffragist, pacifist, and writer. In 1903 he married **Hanna Sheehy**, whose surname he adopted as part of his name. He was a member of the Irish Women's Suffrage and Local Government Association, and the Young Ireland Branch of the United Irish League. He also supported the WSPU. Francis became joint editor in 1912 of a paper he co-founded, the *Irish Citizen,* issued by the Irish Women's Franchise League. He campaigned against recruitment on the outbreak of the First World War and was later jailed for six months.

Sheehy-Skeffington, Hanna (1877–1946)
Irish feminist, suffragist, pacifist, and writer. Along with her husband, she co-founded the Irish Women's Franchise League in 1908 with the aim of obtaining women's voting rights. She was also a founding member of the Irish Women's Workers' Union. Along with her husband, she was deeply opposed to British imperialism in Ireland.

Shepherd, Dolly
Born in 1886 in London, she was a balloonist and parachutist with Auguste Gaudron's display team (1904–1912). At the outbreak of war she volunteered with the Women's Emergency Corps and the Women's Volunteer Reserve in London. From 1917 to 1919 she served as a driver with the Women's Army Auxiliary Corps on the Western Front.

Sheppard, J. J.
Born in Brighton, Sussex, in 1893, he was working in an insurance company in London when war broke out. He volunteered in 1914 with 1st/19th Battalion London Regiment.

Siepman, Harry A.
Born in 1899, he was son of a German-born schoolmaster teaching at Clifton College, Bristol. An Oxford graduate, Harry had joined the Treasury in 1912. In 1914 he enlisted in the Army and served as a captain with the Royal Field Artillery serving on the Western Front, Italy, and Egypt. He assisted J. M. Keynes at the Versailles peace conference in 1919.

Singles, George (1895–1915)
George had joined the Royal Field Artillery in 1912. During the war he served with the 3rd Battalion Coldstream Guards in the 4th Guards Brigade on the Western Front. He was killed in action in 1915.

Snelling, Percy
Born in 1889 he had been a trooper in the Army since 1906. He served with 12th Royal Lancers in Britain, South Africa, and on the Western Front, 1910–1914. When war was declared Snelling was serving in the 'C' Squadron 12th Royal Lancers at Weedon. They then mobilized and joined the other two squadrons at Norwich.

Snow, Annie
Born in 1885 in Hinckley, Leicestershire, she was working as a button-sewer in Leicester in 1914. He husband enlisted in the Army.

Sorley, Charles Hamilton (1895–1915)
British war poet. Born in Aberdeen, he was educated at Marlborough College. At the outbreak of war, Sorley was studying in Schwerin, Germany, and after a brief detention in Trier, returned to England and volunteered for military service, joining the Suffolk Regiment. He arrived in France as a lieutenant in May 1915. He was killed in action five months later.

Spencer, Wilbert B. P. (1867–1915)
A pre-war soldier, he had joined the Wiltshire Regiment aged 16. In 1914 he was based at the Royal Military College, Sandhurst, in Surrey. During the war he served as a lieutenant with the Wiltshire Regiment, on the Western Front. He was killed in action on 10 March 1915.

Spencer, Frederick A.
Born in 1888, in Ireland, he served with the Machine Gun Corps during the war after mobilizing from Aldershot in August 1914. He corresponded with his only sister, Ruth Maurice, who was married to Henry Maurice, Fisheries Secretary, Board of Agriculture and Fisheries, 1913–1938.

Spender, [Edward] Harold (1864–1926)
Liberal political journalist and author. His family were based in Sheringham on the Norfolk coast in 1914, whilst Harold worked from London.

Spickett, Daisy C.
Born in 1882, she was living in the colliery valleys of Pontypridd, near Cardiff, in 1914. She volunteered as a nurse with the VAD during the war.

Spurrell, Hugh
Originally from Carmarthen, Hugh was a student at Clare College, Cambridge, in 1914. In July he was attending the annual Officers Training Corps camp at Aldershot. Soon after the outbreak of war he worked at the Guildhall in the office of the Territorials. On 4 September he enrolled and was ordered to fall in on 24 September from where they left to Ashtead for encampment and training.

Stamfordham, Lord (1849–1931)
Arthur John Bigge, 1st Baron Stamfordham since 1911, was Private Secretary to King George V from 1910 to 1931. His only son, John Neville Bigge, was killed in action in 1915.

Stanton, C. B.
Pre-war Welsh labour activist and political agitator.

Stephen, Rosamond (1868–1951)
An Englishwoman who spent most of her life unsuccessfully trying to reconcile Protestants and Catholics in Ireland. Her published wartime letters to her sisters records her unique approach to philanthropy, her fervent support for the war effort, and her growing disgust with the British administration of Ireland.

Stevens, G. S.
Resident of Morton Road, Exmouth, who, in November 1914, believed he was living next door to German spies.

Stevenson, D. M.
Lord Provost of Glasgow City Council in 1914.

Stopford Green, Alice (1847–1929)
Historian and Irish nationalist born at Kells, Co. Meath. The death of her father in 1874 forced the family to move to England, and they settled in Chester in 1875. She moved to London in 1903. From 1900 on, Stopford Green became increasingly interested in Irish issues. A constitutional nationalist, she was greatly enthused by the Home Rule Bill of 1912 and dismayed by Ulster Unionist threats to resist its implementation. She consequently endorsed the foundation of the INV. At the outbreak of war she supported the decision of Irish party leader John Redmond to pledge Irish support to the British war effort.

Sturt, George (1863–1927)
Author, born at Farnham, Surrey. Upon his father's death in 1884 he took over the family wheelwright's shop, despite his ambitions to be a teacher.

Swanwick, Helena (1864–1939)
British feminist and pacifist who opposed the war in 1914. In 1906 she joined the NUWSS in preference to the WSPU because of her belief in non-violence. On the outbreak of war, she began campaigning for a negotiated peace and was active in the UDC.

Sweny, Laurence
A schoolboy in Essex in 1914.

Tamblyn, Marjorie
Born in 1907 she was a 7-year-old school-girl in 1914 living in Edgbaston, Birmingham.

Tennant, Harold John (1865–1935)
Scottish Liberal politician. He was MP for Berwickshire from 1894 to 1918. He served as Under Secretary of State for War from 1912 to 1916.

Thomas, Bryn
Born in Ffairfach, Carmarthenshire, he was working as a miner and living in Llandybie, Carmarthenshire, in 1914.

Thomas, Sydney
A pre-war soldier at annual camp near Salisbury in early August 1914. He feared for the safety of his family (living at Wescliffe-on-Sea, Essex) in case of a German invasion. He made arrangements for them to seek refuge in Maidenhead.

Thomas, William
Former student of a Church of England school in Freemantle, Southampton, whose headmaster was **A. J. H. Marshall** (see above), who volunteered for the Army on 4 October 1914.

Thompson, Alexander
Originally from Mindrum, Northumberland, he was working as a solicitor's clerk in Newcastle at the outbreak of war. He enlisted in August 1914 with the 9th Battalion Northumberland Fusiliers (52nd Brigade, 17th Division) and trained in the United Kingdom until his departure to the Western Front in May 1915.

Thomson, Sir Basil Home (1861–1939)
Intelligence officer and colonial administrator, born in Oxford. In 1913 Thomson was appointed assistant commissioner of the Metropolitan Police and head of the Criminal Investigation Department at New Scotland Yard. When war broke out in 1914 this department became the enforcement arm of the War Office and Admiralty in intelligence matters. A secret service bureau had only been established in 1910 and had no machinery to arrest spies at the outbreak of war. It therefore fell to the Metropolitan Police, and especially the head of the Criminal Investigation Department, Thomson, to carry out the arrests of these suspects.

Thomson, William
New York manager of the publishing house, Thomas Nelson and Sons Ltd in 1914. See **George MacKenzie Brown** (above).

Thorpe-Tracey, R.
Working in London as an optical assistant in a manufacturing optical company in 1914, when war was declared he was at camp with his troupe of Scouts in Worthing. He volunteered with the Army immediately and served with 1/6th Battalion London Regiment on the Western Front, 1915–1916.

Thursfield, Sir James Richard (1840–1923)
Naval historian and journalist, born at Kidderminster. An Oxford graduate, he was appointed leader writer of *The Times* in 1881 and was based in Golders Green, London, in 1914. He corresponded frequently with **Lady Theresa Londonderry** (see above).

Todd, Mary
A pre-school age girl living on William Street, Hartlepool when the town was bombarded on 16 December 1914. Mary suffered injuries to her legs and her younger sister was almost killed. Mary's aunt (who lived next door) had her legs shattered and required artificial limbs and Mary's two cousins were killed.

Tomlinson, Mr
A young man living in Southport, Merseyside, in 1914. He tried to volunteer for the Army in August 1914 but was turned away owing to strict height restrictions. He eventually enlisted in early 1915.

Tower, Miss Winifred
Aged 20 in 1914, she was living with her parents in Cowes on the Isle of Wight from July to September 1914, and then in London from October 1914.

Travis, Eve
A 14-year-old schoolgirl living in Liverpool in 1914.

Trefusis, Beatrice Morwenna
An articulate woman of the upper classes, well connected in London society, and much influenced by a finishing-school education in Germany, with an admiration of German literature, culture, and music, maintained through contact with English friends still living there in wartime. She lived in London during 1914 and kept a day-by-day diary of the war.

Trevelyan, Sir Charles Philips (1870–1958)
Liberal politician and MP for Elland, in the West Riding of Yorkshire, 1899–1918. He resigned from the government on 4 August 1914 in protest at the outbreak of war. Along with other anti-war Liberals he helped to found the UDC and became the union's principal advocate in the Commons.

Tully. C. Linster
A young man living in Peckham, London in 1914, he joined the Army on 21 August 1914 along with some friends from Brixton. He served with the 2nd Battalion, Royal Fusiliers at Gallipoli and on the Western Front.

Tuohy, Ferdinand
Freelance journalist and later war correspondent, based in London in 1914.

Turvey, Ellen
A young woman living in Stratford, London, in 1914.

Tyrwhitt, Ursula (1878–1966)
British artist and intimate of **Augustus** and **Gwen John** (see above). She was based at Orchard House, Iffley Road, Oxford, in 1914.

Ua h-Uallachain, Gearoid
Also known as Gary Holohan. An Irish nationalist and INV, he was living in Glasnevin, Dublin in 1914, working at the Dublin Port and Docks Board Power Station, North Wall extension. He would later be in charge of the Four Courts command during the Easter Rising of 1916.

Upton, Corporal A.
In training with the British Army in St Albans, Hertforshire, in December 1914.

Vaizey, Brigadier
A young man living and working on his father's estate at Tilbury Hall, Tilbury-Juxta-Clare, Essex.

Verney, Ralph
Born in 1879, Florence Nightingale was his godmother owing to a close friendship with his grandfather. In 1900 he joined the Rifle Brigade and served as an officer in the South African War and the First World War. He was married to **Nita Verney** who resided in London. His father was Liberal MP for North Buckinghamshire. Ralph became Military Secretary to Lord Chelmsford from 1916 to 1921.

Walker, Reverend A. C.
A schoolboy in the south of England in 1914.

Wallace, J. W.
A draughtsman at a Bolton architectural firm, Bradshaw Gass, he was living in Adlington in 1914. He was the central figure of the Bolton Whitman Fellowship, of which **Dr John Johnston** (see above) was also a member. He was a supporter of left-wing anti-war politics, represented by people such as **Ramsay MacDonald**, and subscribed to the *Labour Leader*.

Ward, Mrs E.
Aged 16 in 1914, she lived with her family in a cottage near the River Orwell in Ipswich. She worked in a baker's shop on St Helen's Street.

Ward, Mrs [Mary Augustus] Humphry (1851–1920)
British novelist who wrote under her married name as Mrs Humphry Ward. One of the founders of the Women's National Anti-Suffrage League in 1908. During the First World War she was asked by Theodore Roosevelt to write a series of articles to explain to Americans what was happening in Britain during the war. She had five nephews fighting at the front.

Waring, Walter (1876–1930)
British Liberal politician, MP for Banffshire from 1907 to 1918. He served in the Yeomanry during the First World War in France and Macedonia, 1915–1917, and in the Naval Intelligence Division during 1918.

Watkin Davies, William (1895–1973)
Welsh historian, political scientist, and writer. Born in Criccieth he was educated at Barmouth, University College Wales, Aberystwyth, and St John's College, Oxford where he studied modern history.

Watson, Frank L.
A young man who volunteered for the army in 1914.

Watt, Mr
Living with his family in Hartlepool he experienced the bombardment of the town on 16 December 1914. His brother, Ralph, aged 11, lost his left arm, and his friend, Norman Edmondson, lost his foot. His aunt, Mrs Sarah Hodgson, was killed at her kitchen sink. His older brother was wounded in the finger trying to get the injured to hospital.

Webb, [Martha] Beatrice (1858–1943)
British socialist, economist, and reformer, born in Gloucester. In 1892 she married **Sidney Webb**, and they were active partners in political and professional activities including the organization of the Fabian Society and the establishment of the London School of Economics in 1895. During the war she served on several government committees.

Webb, Percy
Born in 1893, he was living in Ferndown, Dorset, in 1914, working in his father's business. He volunteered in December 1915 and served as a machine gunner with 7th Battalion Dorsetshire Regiment in Britain from 1915 to 1916, and 6th Battalion Dorsetshire Regiment on the Western Front, 1917–1918.

Wedgwood, Josiah C. (1872–1943)
British Liberal, Labour, and radical politician born in Staffordshire. He was the great-great-grandson of the famous potter Josiah Wedgwood. He was MP for Newcastle-under-Lyme from 1906 to 1942. Following the outbreak of war he volunteered for service with the Royal Naval Volunteer Reserve, holding the rank of Lieutenant-Commander. He served in France in 1914 with the Royal Naval Air Service and was wounded at Gallipoli in 1915.

Wells, H. G. (1886–1946)
English writer, best known for his science-fiction novels, such as *The Time Machine* (1895), *War of the Worlds* (1896), and *The Island of Doctor Moreau* (1898). He was an increasingly passionate and influential journalist, especially during the war years. *The War that will End War* (1914) set out his case for supporting the allies. In 1918 he was recruited by **Lord Northcliffe**'s ministry of propaganda at Crewe House, where his task was to work on a statement of war aims, chief among which was the setting up of the League of Nations.

West, Miss G.
A young woman who lived with her family, including her sister **Joan West** in Selsey, Gloucestershire. She worked as a VAD cook in Red Cross hospitals in the UK from 1914 to 1916, at Farnborough Aircraft Factory from January 1916, and then as a woman police officer in munitions factories until the end of the war.

Wharton, H. W.
Resident in Scarborough during the bombardment on 16 December 1914.

White, Ernest G.
Born in 1889, he was a pre-war soldier who had trained at Fulford Barracks, York, from 1906 to 1907. In August 1914 he was mobilized at Tidworth with the 18th Hussars and departed from Southampton for France that month.

Whitehouse, Percy
Born in 1893, he served as a Signaller with the 8th (Howitzer) Brigade Royal Field Artillery (5th Division) on the Western Front. A pre-war soldier, he was called-up whilst on service in Ireland. After some training at Kildare, near Dublin, he sailed to Le Havre in August 1914 and marched across the border into Belgium where he first encountered the Germans (23 August). He was demobilized in 1919.

Whitham, Grace
Born 1902, in Hexham, Northumberland, her family moved to Worsall, North Yorkshire when she was 8 years old. In 1914 she was working in the mill in the centre of the village.

Whiting, Alfred Edward
Born in Walthamstow in 1901, he was orphaned at the age of 3 when his parents were killed at Liverpool Street Station. Along with his brother, he lived in a series of children's homes and with foster families. During the First World War he was attending school near Wanstead.

Whittacker, Jack
Young man living in Blackburn, Lancashire, in 1914.

Whittaker, James
A schoolboy in Bonahaven, West Scotland, in 1914.

Wight, Harry R.
Served with the 2nd Battalion, Border Regiment on the Western Front from December 1914 to February 1915, and then at Gallipoli where he was wounded.

Williams, Reverend Hugh Cernyw (1843–1937)
Writer, poet, and Baptist minister at Corwen and Cynwyd, Denbighshire, from 1868 to 1918.

Williamson, A. R.
Second Lieutenant with the Royal Naval Reserve. Serving on SS *Santaren* off Cardiff and London at the outbreak of war, he served on HMS *Crescent* from January 1915 onwards.

Wilson, L.
Living in Hull in 1914, he enlisted with the Army against his mother's wishes. He left Hull for training at Cramlington Camp, near Newcastle. He trained with the 1/4th Battalion East Yorkshire Regiment (York and Durham Brigade, Northumbrian Division) and then transferred to the 1/5th Battalion Border Regiment (East Lancashire Division) where he served as a private in Belgium and France until a serious head wound received at the Battle of the Somme in 1916 left him unfit for overseas duty.

Wingfield-Stratford, Esmé
A young man living in Kent before the war, he was a keen cricketer and thought of little else before war was officially declared.

Wolsey-Smith, Mrs G. M.
In 1914 she was aged 23, living with her family in King's Lynn, Norfolk, and working as a teacher at St Margaret's Boys' School.

Woodcock, Alfred
Born in 1891 at Wednesbury, West Midlands, he was working in Walsall at a brewery in 1914.

Woodhouse, Percy
Vice-Chairman of the Manchester Conservative and Unionist Association in 1914.

Woodman, Norah
A nurse, in 1914 she was appointed Assistant Matron at St Giles' Home, London, which provided residential care for the destitute families of enemy aliens.

Woolf, Virginia (1882–1941)
English novelist, essayist, and publisher, she was a significant figure in London literary society and a member of the Bloomsbury Group. From 1911 onwards, although based in London, she had started renting small houses near Lewes in Sussex, particularly Asheham House. She was there when war broke out, recuperating from a series of mental breakdowns that had begun in 1895 following the death of her mother, half-sister, and father.

Yates, Edwin
Born in 1871, he was a solicitor at Lloyd's Bank Chambers in Darwen, Lancashire. In his spare time he was also secretary of the National United Service Club, and, during the war, specialized in encouraging enlistment to Bantam units.

Yearsley, P. Macleod
Resident in London during the First World War.

Yonge, Reverend Denys (1836–1920)
Vicar of Boreham, Essex from 1885 to 1918.

APPENDIX II

Statistical Breakdown of 441 Witnesses Featured in Dramatis Personae (see Appendix I for detail)

1. GENDER AND AGE IN 1914

Males	324	*Adult*	403
Females	117	*Child (Fourteen or under)*	38
TOTAL	441	TOTAL	441

2. PRE-WAR OCCUPATION

Occupation	Numbers	Occupation	Numbers
Actor	2	Military/Naval	30
Architectural Draughtsman	1	Mill Worker	2
Artist	7	Miner	7
At School	36	Musician	2
Banking	5	Newspaper Editor/Deputy Editor	5
Brewery Worker	1	Nurse	3
Businessman	1	Office Clerk	6
Chief Constable/Officer	3	Optical Assistant	1
Civil Servant	4	Philanthropist	7
Credit Agent	1	Politician	54
Deputy Town Clerk	1	Pre-School	4
Diplomatic Service	7	Publisher	2
Director of MI5	1	Religious Minister	10
Doctor	5	Restaurant Owner	1
Domestic Servant	2	Royalty	3
Engineer	2	Shop Assistant	1
Espionage	1	Soap Broker	1
Farm Labourer	3	Solicitor	3
Gardener	1	Solicitor's Clerk	2
Inland Revenue Clerk	1	Stockbroker	1
International Trade	1	Stores Clerk	1
Journalist	11	Suffragette/Activist	7
Labour Activist	3	Teacher (including Headmaster)	8
Landed Lady	3	Textile Industry	4
Librarian	1	Trade Apprentice	5
Lord Lieutenant	3	Unknown/Unavailable	112
Lord Provost of City Council	1	University Lecturer	10
Lunatic Asylum Clerk	1	University Student	15
Managing Director of Printing Works	1	Vice-Chancellor of University	1
Mechanics Trade	2	Writer (including playwright/poet)	21
		TOTAL	441

Location of Utilized Diaries, Memoirs, and Journals
(Published and Unpublished)

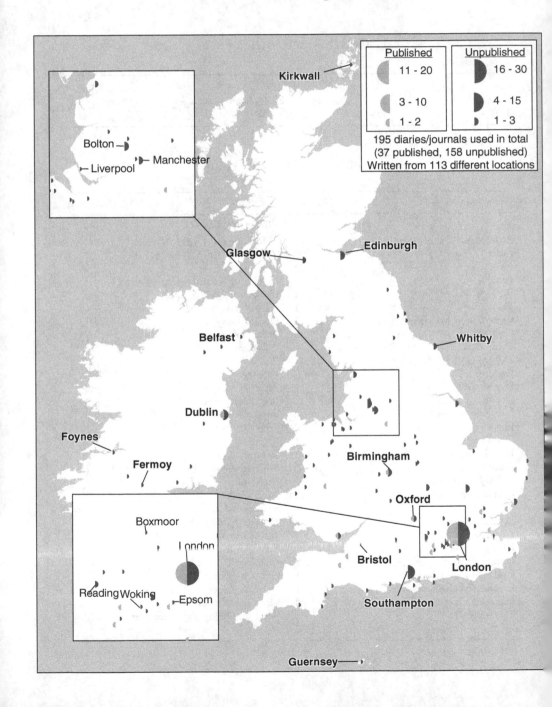

Published | Unpublished
11 - 20 | 16 - 30
3 - 10 | 4 - 15
1 - 2 | 1 - 3

195 diaries/journals used in total
(37 published, 158 unpublished)
Written from 113 different locations

Kirkwall

Bolton
Liverpool
Manchester

Glasgow
Edinburgh

Belfast
Whitby

Dublin

Foynes

Fermoy
Birmingham

Oxford

Boxmoor
London
Reading Woking
Epsom

Bristol
London

Southampton

Guernsey

Anti-German Riots and Western Military Events, October 1914

Date	Actual Western Front Chronology	Events on the Western Front as reported in *The Times*	Belgian Refugees in Britain, as reported in *The Times*	Spies in Britain, as reported in *The Times*	Major Anti-German Riots
02-Oct-14	Churchill visits Antwerp				
03-Oct-14			Lord Charles Beresford blames sinking of three British ships on 22 Sept on German spies		
04-Oct-14					
06-Oct-14	More British Naval troops land at Ostend for the defence of Antwerp				
08-Oct-14	Consulates and Belgian government transferred to Ostend				
09-Oct-14				Government reassures British people that all spies have been rounded up	
10-Oct-14	Fall of Antwerp				
11-Oct-14		Fall of Antwerp; Fighting at Ghent; Germans advance to Ostend	Many Belgians have arrived in London		
12-Oct-14	Ghent occupied	Attempts to reassure British public over loss of Antwerp	Over 10,000 arrivals in past three days		
13-Oct-14		British people should expect the fighting to develop towards northern France	Appeals from Lord Gladstone, War Refugees Committee, to help the refugees; 6,000 landed in Folkestone from Ostend		

Date	Actual Western Front Chronology	Events on the Western Front as reported in The Times	Belgian Refugees in Britain, as reported in The Times	Spies in Britain, as reported in The Times	Major Anti-German Riots
14-Oct-14	Consulates and Belgian government transferred to Le Havre (France)	Germans advancing from Antwerp; Belgian government evacuated from Ostend	More Belgians arrive		Aberystwyth
15-Oct-14	Bruges occupied	Is a German invasion of Britain possible?		Home Office is complacent over the issue of spies.	
16-Oct-14		German armies pushing northwards	10,000 Belgians arrived on 14 Oct	German spies will assist an invasion of Britain. Press campaign begins to boycott all German workers.	Saffron Walden, Essex
17-Oct-14		Ostend occupied by the Germans; Germans have emerged on the shores of the North Sea	British people are to be commended in the way they have helped the poor Belgian refugees	Police raid at Willesden Junction, London—twenty Germans seized and marched to prison in front of 'hooting' crowds	Deptford, London
18-Oct-14	First Battle of Ypres begins	British casualties at Antwerp published			
19-Oct-14		Churchill defends the British strategy at Antwerp		German spies are reported on the Scottish coast; Calls for all spies to be rounded up	
20-Oct-14		Allied forces advancing into Belgium, holding the line of the Yser from Nieuport to Dixmude	Belgian refugees most be removed from East Coast owing to espionage threat	German spies at Dover	
21-Oct-14		The Fight for the Coast: A major struggle is underway		Alien enemies ordered to leave Brighton; German and Austrian waiters sacked	

Date	Actual Western Front Chronology	Events on the Western Front as reported in *The Times*	Belgian Refugees in Britain, as reported in *The Times*	Spies in Britain, as reported in *The Times*	Major Anti-German Riots
		to gain control of the French/Belgian coast		from London hotels; German spy at Worthing; Suspicious wireless in Kirkcaldy; Suspicious German Works along south-west coast	
22-Oct-14				Arrests of alien spies throughout the country	
23-Oct-14		German forces in Belgium have taken the offensive		Spies are a major threat and should be removed; Government finally responding to real and dangerous threat	
24-Oct-14	Belgian army stops further German advance. End of Battle of Aisne and 'Race for the Sea'	Great Battle for the Coast: German forces making violent attempts towards Calais		Press calls for internment of all aliens	Crewe

* Sources: *The Times* and the *Times History of the War* (1914)

Sources and Bibliography

ARCHIVAL SOURCES

Please note that owing to the large amount of material consulted during the research of this book I will only list the archives, not the individual collections, I consulted. Specific references to individual items are recorded in full in the footnotes.

England

Devon
Devon Record Office, Exeter
North Devon Record Office, Barnstaple
Plymouth and West Devon Record Office, Plymouth

Essex
Colchester and North Essex Record Office, Colchester
Essex Record Office, Chelmsford

Kent
British Cartoon Archive, Canterbury

Lancashire
Bolton Archives and Local Studies Centre
Greater Manchester Record Office, Manchester
Imperial War Museum North, Salford
John Rylands University Library, University of Manchester
Lancashire Record Office, Preston
Liverpool Record Office, Liverpool
Manchester Archives and Local Studies Library, Manchester
North West Sound Archives, Clitheroe
Oldham Local Studies and Archives
Salford Diocesan Archives, Burnley
University of Liverpool, Special Collections

Leeds
Liddle Collection, Brotherton Library, University of Leeds

London
Bethnal Green Museum of Childhood
British Library Manuscripts Collection
British Library Newspaper Collection, Colindale
Imperial War Museum, Department of Printed Books
Imperial War Museum, Documents Collections
Imperial War Museum, Photographic Collections
Imperial War Museum, Sound Archives

National Archives, Kew
Senate House Library, Playne Collection

Midlands
Birmingham Archdiocesan Archives, Birmingham
Birmingham City Archives, Birmingham
Birmingham Local History Library, Birmingham
City Sound Archive, Birmingham Museum, Birmingham
Record Office for Leicestershire, Leicester and Rutland, Leicester
University of Birmingham, Special Collections, Birmingham
West Midlands Police Museum, Birmingham
Worcestershire Record Office, Worcester

Oxford
John Johnson Collection, Bodleian Library, University of Oxford
Modern Political Papers, Bodleian Library, University of Oxford

Windsor
Royal Archives, Windsor Castle, Windsor

Scotland
Edinburgh
Edinburgh Central Library
Edinburgh City Archives
National Archives of Scotland, General Register House, Edinburgh
National Archives of Scotland, West Register House, Edinburgh
National Library of Scotland, Edinburgh
University of Edinburgh, Special Collections
Scottish Catholic Archives, Edinburgh

Glasgow
Glasgow Caledonian University Archives
Glasgow Diocesan Archives
Mitchell Library, Glasgow
University of Glasgow, Special Collections

Wales
Aberystwyth
National Library of Wales

Cardiff
Glamorgan Record Office

Carmarthen
Carmarthenshire Archives Service

Hawarden
Flintshire Record Office
St Deiniol's Library

Swansea
South Wales Miners' Library, Hendrefoelan House, University of Swansea (Audio, Visual, and Printed Material)
South Wales Miners' Library, Singleton Park Campus, University of Swansea (Manuscripts)

Ireland
Belfast
Public Record Office of Northern Ireland

Dublin
National Archives of Ireland
National Library of Ireland, Department of Printed Books
National Library of Ireland, Manuscripts
Trinity College Dublin, Department of Early Printed Books
Trinity College Dublin, Department of Manuscripts
University College Dublin, Archives Department

France
Archives du Ministère des Affaires Etrangères, Paris

United States of America
National Archives of the United States of America, College Park, Maryland Campus, Washington, DC

Newspapers
Aldershot News
Barrow News
Belfast Evening Telegraph
Belfast Newsletter
Birmingham Gazette
Brighouse Echo
Bristol Times and Mirror
Cambridge Daily News
Church of Ireland Gazette
Cork Constitution
Cork Examiner
Cork Free Press
Cork Weekly News
Daily Citizen
Daily Graphic
Daily Mail
Daily Mirror
Daily News
Devon and Exeter Gazette

Eastern Daily Press
Edinburgh Evening News
Enniscorthy Guardian
Essex County Standard
Evening Standard
Forward
Freeman's Journal
Glasgow Herald
Grimsby Daily Telegraph
Hampstead Record
Huddersfield Examiner
Irish Independent
Irish News
Irish Times
Irish Volunteer
Irish Worker
John Bull
Keighley News
Kentish Gazette
Labour Gazette
Labour Leader
Lancashire Daily Post
Leitrim Advertiser
Leitrim Observer
The Lepracaun
Liverpool Courier
Liverpool Echo
Liverpool Post and Mercury
Longford Leader
Manchester Evening News
Manchester Guardian
Merthyr Pioneer
Midland Evening News
Midland Reporter
New Statesman
New York Times
North-Eastern Daily Gazette
North Wales Observer and Express
Northern Whig
Pall Mall Gazette
Peterborough Citizen
Pontypridd Observer
Punch
Roscommon Journal
Roscommon Messenger
Sinn Féin
Sláinte
Sligo Champion
Sligo Independent

South Wales Daily Post
The Times
Tyrone Constitution
Ulster Guardian
War Illustrated
Western Evening Herald
Western Mail
Western Nationalist
Westmeath Examiner
Wiltshire News
Worthing Gazette

OFFICIAL PUBLICATIONS

Census of England and Wales, 1911, Preliminary Report: Session 1911, Vol. LXXI, Cd. 5705.

Census of Ireland, 1911 (available online at <http://www.census.nationalarchives> i.e. via the National Archives of Ireland, Dublin).

Census of Ireland, 1911, Preliminary Report: Session 1911, Vol. LXXI, Cd. 5691.

Census of Scotland, 1911, Preliminary Report: Session 1911, Vol. LXXI, Cd. 5700.

Session 1914–1916, Vol. XXVIII, Cd. 7939: *Report of the Departmental Committee Appointed to Inquire into the Conditions Prevailing in the Coal-Mining Industry due to the War*.

Session 1914–1916, Vol. XXI, Cd. 7703: *Report of the Board of Trade on the State of Employment in the United Kingdom in October 1914*.

Session 1914–1916, Vol. XXI, Cd. 7755: *Report of the Board of Trade on the State of Employment in the United Kingdom in December 1914*.

Edmonds, Brigadier-General J. E. *Military Operations: France and Belgium, 1914*. Edited by Historical Section of the Committee of Imperial Defence. 2nd ed. 2 vols. Vol. 2, *History of the Great War Based on Official Documents*. London: Macmillan, 1925.

Hansard Parliamentary Debates, 1914.

HMSO. *Statistics of the Military Effort of the British Empire during the Great War, 1914–1920*. London: HMSO, 1922.

Les Communiqués officiels depuis la déclaration de la guerre. Du 15 au 31 août (Paris & Nancy: Berger-Levrault, 1914) (series: Pages d'histoire, 1914, no. 7).

Mac Giolla Choille, Breandán, ed. *Intelligence Notes, 1913–1916*. Dublin: Chief Secretary's Office, 1966.

PUBLISHED PRIMARY SOURCES

Addison, Christopher. *Four and a Half Years: A Personal Diary from June 1914 to January 1919*. Vol. 1. London: Hutchinson, 1934.

Angell, Norman. *The Great Illusion: A Study of the Relation of Military Power in Nations to their Economic and Social Advantage*. London: Heinemann, 1910.

Arthur, Max. *Forgotten Voices of the Great War*. London: Ebury Press, 2006.

—— *When This Bloody War Is Over: Soldiers' Songs of the First World War*. London: Piatkus, 2002.

Asquith, Margot. *The Autobiography of Margot Asquith*. 2 vols. Vol. 2. London: Thornton Butterworth, 1922.

Aston, Sir George. *Secret Service*. London: Faber and Faber, 1930.

Begbie, Harold. *On the Side of the Angels: A Reply to Arthur Machen*. London: Hodder and Stoughton, 1915.

Bell, Tom. *John Maclean: A Fighter for Freedom*. Glasgow: Communist Party, Scottish Committee, 1944.

Bennett, Arnold. *The Journals*. Middlesex: Penguin, 1932, 1971.

——*Liberty: A Statement of the British Case*. London: Hodder and Stoughton, 1914.

Bernhardi, Friedrich von. *Germany and the Next War*. New York: Edward Arnold, 1912.

Birrell, Augustine. *Things Past Redress*. London: Faber and Faber, 1937.

Bishop, Alan, ed. *Chronicle of Youth: Vera Brittain's War Diary 1913–1917*. London: Victor Gollancz Ltd, 1981.

Blades, D. P. 'Editorial', *The Student* XII, no. 1 (1914).

Blunt, Wilfred Scawen. *My Diaries: Being a Personal Narrative of Events, 1888–1914*. 2 vols. Vol. 2. London: Martin Secker, 1920.

Brittain, Vera. *Testament of Youth*. London: Victor Gollancz Ltd, 1933.

Brock, Michael, and Eleanor Brock, eds. *H. H. Asquith: Letters to Venetia Stanley*. Oxford: Oxford University Press, 1982.

Brooke, Rupert. *'1914': Five Sonnets*. London: Sidgwick and Jackson, 1915.

Callanan, Frank. *T. M. Healy*. Cork: Cork University Press, 1996.

Cambon, Paul. *Correspondance 1870–1924: Tome Troisième (1912–1924)*. Paris: Éditions Bernard Grasset, 1946.

Carlisle, Christopher, ed. *My Own Darling: Letters from Montie to Kitty Carlisle*. London: Carlisle Books, 1989.

Chesney, George Tomkyns. *The Battle of Dorking: Reminiscences of a Volunteer*. Edinburgh: William Blackwood and Sons, 1871.

Childers, Erskine. *The Riddle of the Sands*. London: Heinemann, 1903.

Clemens, Samuel. *King Leopold's Soliloquy*. London: T. Fisher Unwin, 1907.

Cole, Margaret I., ed. *Beatrice Webb's Diaries, 1912–1924*. 2 vols. Vol. 1. London: Longman, 1952.

Colvin, Ian. *The Life of Lord Carson*. 3 vols. Vol. 2. London: Victor Gollancz Ltd, 1934.

Coppard, George. *With a Machine Gun to Cambrai*. London: Papermac, 1969, 1986.

Connolly-O'Brien, Nora. *Portrait of a Rebel Father*. London: Rich and Cowan, 1935.

Cox, Jane, ed. *A Singular Marriage: A Labour Love Story in Letters and Diaries: Ramsay and Margaret MacDonald*. London: Harrap, 1988.

D'Arcy, Charles Frederick. *The Adventures of a Bishop: A Phase of Irish Life: A Personal and Historical Narrative*. London: Hodder and Stoughton, 1934.

David, Edward, ed. *Inside Asquith's Cabinet: From the Diaries of Charles Hobhouse*. London: John Murray, 1977.

Dolden, A. Stuart. *Cannon Fodder: An Infantryman's Life on the Western Front, 1914–18*. Poole: Blandford Press, 1980.

Donnington, Robert, and Barbara Donnington. *The Citizen Faces War*. London: Victor Gollancz Ltd, 1936.

Edmonds, Charles. *A Subaltern's War*. London: Peter Davies, 1929.

Elton, Lord. *The Life of James Ramsay MacDonald*. London: Collins, 1939.

Emanuel, Walter, and John Hassall. *Keep Smiling, More News by Liarless for German Homes*. London: Nash, 1914.

Evans, George Ewart. *The Strength of the Hills: An Autobiography*. London: Faber and Faber, 1983.

Ewart, Wilfrid. *Way of Revelation: A Novel of Five Years*. London: G. P. Putnam's Sons, 1921.

Fitzgerald, Desmond. *Desmond's Rising: Memoirs, 1913 to Easter 1916*. London: Routledge, 2006.

Forster, E. M. *Goldsworthy Lowes Dickinson*. London: Edward Arnold, 1934.

Graves, Robert. *Goodbye to All That*. London: Penguin, 1929, 2000.

Gwynn, Stephen. *The Irish Situation*. London: Jonathan Cape, 1921.

——*John Redmond's Last Years*. London: Edward Arnold, 1919.

Hartley, L. P. *The Go-Between*. London: Hamish Hamilton, 1953.

Haselden, W. K. *The Sad Experiences of Big and Little Willie during the First Six Months of the Great War*. London: Chatto & Windus, 1914.

Healy, Timothy Michael. *Letters and Leaders of My Day*. Vol. 2. London: Thornton Butterworth, 1928.

Higgins, D. S., ed. *The Private Diaries of Sir H. Rider Haggard, 1914–1925*. London: Cassell, 1980.

Hobson, J.A. *The Psychology of Jingoism*. London: Grant Richards, 1901.

Hulse, Sir Edward Hamilton Westrow. *Letters Written from the English Front in France between September 1914 and March 1915*. Privately Printed, 1916.

Keatley Moore, H., and W. C. Berwick Sayers. *Croydon and the Great War: The Official History of the War Work of the Borough and its Citizens from 1914–1919*. London: Central Public Library, 1920.

Kettle, Thomas M. *The Ways of War*. London: Constable and Company Ltd, 1917.

Laurence, Dan H., ed. *Bernard Shaw: Collected Letters, 1911–1925*. 3 vols. Vol. 3. London: Max Reinhardt, 1985.

Le Queux, William. *The Invasion of 1910 with a full account of the Siege of London*. London: Eveleigh Nash, 1906.

——*Spies of the Kaiser, Plotting the Downfall of England*. London: Hurst & Blackett, 1909.

Lee, Jennie. *To-Morrow is a New Day*. London: The Cresset Press, 1939.

Link, Arthur S., ed. *The Papers of Woodrow Wilson*. Vol. 30. Princeton: Princeton University Press, 1979.

Lloyd George, David. *War Memoirs of David Lloyd George*. 4 vols. Vol. 1. London: Ivor Nicholson and Watson, 1933.

MacDonagh, Michael. *In London During the Great War*. London: Eyre and Spottiswoode, 1935.

——*The Irish at the Front*. London: Hodder and Stoughton, 1916.

Machen, Arthur. *The Angel of Mons: The Bowmen and Other Legends of the War*. London: Simpkin, Marshall & Co., 1915.

Mackerness, E. D., ed. *The Journals of George Sturt, 1905–1927*. 2 vols. Vol. 2. London: Cambridge University Press, 1967.

Marcus, Geoffrey. *Before the Lamps Went Out*. London: George Allen & Unwin, 1965.

Martin, F. X. *The Irish Volunteers, 1913–1915: Recollections and Documents*. Dublin: James Duffy & Co, 1963.

Miles, Hallie Eustace. *Untold Tales of War-Time London: A Personal Diary*. London: Cecil Palmer, 1930.

Morel, E. D. *King Leopold's Rule in Africa*. London: Heinemann, 1904.

Munson, James, ed. *Echoes of the Great War: The Diary of the Reverend Andrew Clark, 1914–1919*. Oxford: Oxford University Press, 1985.

Nicolson, Nigel, ed. *The Question of Things Happening: The Letters of Virginia Woolf, Volume 2: 1912–1922*. London: Hogarth Press, 1976.

Ó Buachalla, Séamas, ed. *The Letters of P. H. Pearse*. Gerrards Cross: Colin Smythe, 1980.

O'Neill, Elizabeth. *The War, 1914: A History and Explanation for Boys and Girls*. London: T. C. & E. C. Jack, 1914.

Pankhurst, E. Sylvia. *The Home Front: A Mirror to Life in England during the First World War*. London: The Cresset Library, 1932, 1987.

Peel, Mrs C. S. *How We Lived Then, 1914–1918: A Sketch of Social and Domestic Life in England During the War*. London: John Lane, 1929.

Pinney, Thomas, ed. *The Letters of Rudyard Kipling*. Vol. 4. London: Macmillan, 1999.

Playne, Caroline E. *The Pre-War Mind in Britain*. London: Allen and Unwin, 1928.

——*Society at War, 1914–1916*. London: Allen and Unwin, 1931.

Purdon, C. B., ed. *Everyman at War: Sixty Personal Narratives of the War*. London: J. M. Dent and Sons Ltd, 1930.

Royle, Stephen, ed. *From Mons to Messines and Beyond: The Great War Experiences of Sergeant Charles Arnold*. Studley: K.A.F. Brewin Books, 1985.

Roynon, Gavin, ed. *Home Fires Burning: The Great War Diaries of Georgina Lee*. Stroud: Sutton, 2006.

Rudkin, Mabel. *Inside Dover, 1914–18: A Woman's Impression*. London: Elliot Stock, 1933.

Sandhurst, Viscount. *From Day to Day, 1914–1915*. London: Edward Arnold, 1928.

Shaw, Bernard. *John Bull's other island; and Major Barbara; also How he lied to her husband*. London: A. Constable, 1907.

Thomson, Basil. *Queer People*. London: Hodder and Stoughton, 1922.

Tracy, Louis. *The Invaders*. London: Pearson, 1901.

Trevelyan, Janet Penrose. *The Life of Mrs Humphry Ward*. London: Constable, 1923.

Tuohy, Ferdinand. *The Crater of Mars*. London: William Heinemann, 1929.

Van Emden, Richard, and Steve Humphries. *All Quiet on the Home Front: An Oral History of Life in Britain During the First World War*. London: Headline, 2004.

Verney, David, ed. *The Joyous Patriot: The Correspondence of Ralph Verney, 1900–1916*. London: Leo Cooper, 1989.

Walsh, Oonagh. *An Englishwoman in Belfast: Rosamond Stephen's Record of the Great War*. Cork: Cork University Press, 2000.

Weiss, Samuel A., ed. *Bernard Shaw's Letters to Siegfried Trebitsch*. Stanford: Stanford University Press, 1986.

Wells, H. G. *Mr Britling Sees It Through*. Leeds: Morley-Baker, 1916, 1969.

Whittaker, James. *I, James Whittaker*. London: Rich and Cowan, 1934.

Wilson, Jean Moorcroft, ed. *The Collected Letters of Charles Hamilton Sorley*. London: Cecil Woolf, 1990.

Wilson, Keith, ed. *The Rasp of War: The Letters of H. A. Gwynne to The Countess Bathurst, 1914–1918*. London: Sidgwick & Jackson, 1988.

Wingfield-Stratford, Esmé. *Before the Lamps Went Out*. London: Hodder and Stoughton, 1945.

Wood, Frances. 'The Increase in the Cost of Food for Different Classes of Society Since the Outbreak of the War'. *Journal of the Royal Historical Society* LXXIX, no. 4 (1916), 501–8.

Woods, Edward S., ed. *Andrew R. Buxton: The Rifle Brigade: A Memoir*. London: Robert Scott, 1918.

Zytaruk, George J., and James T. Boulton, eds. *The Letters of D. H. Lawrence: Volume II, June 1913 – October 1916*. Cambridge: Cambridge University Press, 1981.

SECONDARY LITERATURE

Abrams, Mark. *The Condition of the British People, 1911–1945*. Bath: Cedric Chivers Ltd, 1970.

Allport, G. W. and L. J. Postman. *The Psychology of Rumor*. New York: Holt, Rinehart and Winston, 1947.

Anderson, Benedict. *Imagined Communities: Reflections on the Origin and Spread of Nationalism*. London: Verso, 1991.

Andrew, Christopher. *The Defence of the Realm: The Authorized History of MI5*. London: Allen Lane, 2009.

Armitage, F. P. *Leicester 1914–18: The War-Time Story of a Midland Town*. Leicester: Edgar Backus, 1933.

Arnot, R. Page. *The Miners: Years of Struggle: A History of the Miners' Federation of Great Britain (from 1910 onwards)*. London: George Allen & Unwin, 1953.

Atkin, Jonathan. *A War of Individuals: Bloomsbury Attitudes to the Great War*. Manchester: Manchester University Press, 2002.

Audoin-Rouzeau, Stéphane, and Annette Becker. *1914–1918: Understanding the Great War*. London: Profile Books, 1999, trans. from French 2002.

Badsey, Stephen. 'The Boer War as a Media War'. In *The Boer War: Army, Nation and Empire*, edited by Peter Dennis and Jeffrey Guy. Canberra: Army History Unit, 2000, 319–419.

Barlow, Robin. 'Some Aspects of the Experiences of Carmarthenshire in the Great War'. PhD, University of Wales, 2001.

Baylen, J. O. 'The "New Journalism" in Late Victorian Britain'. *Australian Journal of Politics and History* 18, no. 3 (1972), 367–85.

Beazley, Ben. *Four Years Remembered: Leicester During the Great War*. Derby: The Breedon Books, 1999.

Becker, Jean-Jacques. *1914: Comment les Français sont entrés dans la guerre*. Paris: Presses de la Fondation Nationale des Sciences Politiques, 1977.

—— *The Great War and the French People*. Oxford: Berg, 1985.

—— '"That's the Death Knell of Our Boys . . . "'. In *The French Home Front, 1914–1918*, edited by Patrick Fridenson. Oxford: Berg, 1992, 17–36.

Becker, Jean-Jacques, and Gerd Krumeich. *La Grande guerre: Une histoire franco-allemande*. Paris: Tallandier, 2008.

Beckett, Ian. 'The Territorial Force'. In *A Nation in Arms: A Social Study of the British Army in the First World War*, edited by I. F. W. Beckett and Keith Simpson. Manchester: Manchester University Press, 1985, 126–163.

Berghahn, Volker R. *Militarism: The History of an International Debate, 1861–1979*. Leamington Spa: Berg, 1981.

Bidwell, Shelford, and Dominick Graham. *Fire-Power: British Army Weapons and Theories of War 1904–1945*. London: George Allen and Unwin, 1982.

Billig, Michael. *Banal Nationalism*. London: Sage, 1995.

Bilton, David. *The Home Front in the Great War*. Barnsley: Pen & Sword, 2004.

Boghardt, Thomas. *Spies of the Kaiser: German Covert Operations in Great Britain during the First World War Era*. Basingstoke: Palgrave Macmillan, 2004.

Bond, Brian. 'Judgement in Military History'. *The RUSI Journal* 134, no. 1 (1989), 69–72.

Bourke, Joanna. *Dismembering the Male: Men's Bodies, Britain and the Great War*. London: Reaktion Books, 1996.

Bourke, Joanna. *Fear: A Cultural History*. London: Virago, 2006.

—— *Working-Class Cultures in Britain, 1890–1960*. London: Routledge, 1994.

Bowman, Timothy. 'Composing Divisions: The Recruitment of Ulster and National Volunteers into the British Army in 1914'. *Causeway* 2, no. 1 (1995), 24–9.

—— 'The Irish Recruiting Campaign and Anti-Recruiting Campaigns, 1914–1918'. In *Propaganda: Political Rhetoric and Identity 1300–2000*, edited by Bertrand Taithe and Tim Thornton. Stroud: Sutton, 1999, 223–38.

Brazier, R. H., and E. Sandford. *Birmingham and the Great War, 1914–1919*. Birmingham: Cornish Brothers, 1921.

Brown, Kenneth D. *Labour and Unemployment, 1900–1914*. Newton Abbot: David and Charles, 1971.

Brown, S. J. '"A Solemn Purification by Fire": Responses to the Great War in the Scottish Presbyterian Churches, 1914–1919'. *Journal of Ecclesiastical History* xlv (1994), 82–104.

Burn, William Laurence. *The Age of Equipoise: A Study of the Mid-Victorian Generation*. London: George Allen and Unwin, 1964.

Calahan, Peter. *Belgian Relief in England During the Great War*. New York: Garland, 1982.

Callan, Patrick. 'Recruiting for the British Army in Ireland during the First World War'. *The Irish Sword* 17, no. 66 (1987), 42–56.

Campbell, Fergus. *Land and Revolution: Nationalist Politics in the West of Ireland, 1891–1921*. Oxford: Oxford University Press, 2005.

Carroll, Claire et al. 'The Approach of War, July and August 1914.' *Times Past* 7 (1990–91) 3–5.

Ceadel, Martin. *Living the Great Illusion: Sir Norman Angell, 1872–1967*. Oxford: Oxford University Press, 2009.

Clarke, I. F. 'The Shape of Wars to Come'. *History Today* 15, no. 2 (1965), 108–16.

—— *The Tale of the Future from the Beginning to the Present Day: A Check-list of those satires, ideal states, imaginary wars and invasions, political warnings and forecasts, interplanetary voyages and scientific romances—all located in an imaginary future period—that have been published in the United Kingdom between 1644 and 1960*. London: The Library Association, 1961.

Cockayne, Emily. *Hubbub: Filth, Noise and Stench in England, 1600–1770*. London: Yale University Press, 2007.

Codd, Pauline. 'Recruiting and Responses to the War in Wexford'. In *Ireland and the First World War*, edited by David Fitzpatrick. Dublin: Trinity History Workshop, 1986, 15–26.

Colley, Linda. *Britons: Forging the Nation 1707–1837*. London: Yale University Press, 1992.

Connelly, Mark. *Steady the Buffs! A Regiment, a Region, and the Great War*. Oxford: Oxford University Press, 2006.

Coogan, Oliver. *Politics and War in Meath, 1913–1923*. Dublin: Folens and Co., 1983.

Cosson, Olivier. 'Les expériences de guerre du début du siècle: Guerre des Boers, guerre de Mandchourie, guerres des Balkans'. In *Encyclopédie critique de la Grande Guerre, histoire et culture*, edited by Stéphane Audoin-Rouzeau and Jean-Jacques Becker. Paris: Bayard, 2004, 97–108.

Cronin, Gerald. 'Representations of Combat: The British War Correspondents and the First World War.' PhD, Trinity College, Dublin, 1998.

Cunningham, Hugh. *The Volunteer Force: A Social and Political History, 1859–1908*. London: Croom Helm, 1975.

Dalley, Stuart. 'The Response in Cornwall to the Outbreak of the First World War'. *Cornish Studies* 11 (2003), 85–109.

Dangerfield, G. *The Strange Death of Liberal England*. London: Serif, 1935, 1997.

De Groot, Gerard J. *Blighty: British Society in the Era of the Great War*. London: Longman, 1996.

Denman, Terence. '"The Red Livery of Shame": The Campaign Against Army Recruitment in Ireland, 1899–1914'. *Irish Historical Studies* 29, no. 114 (1994), 208–33.

Dewey, P. E. 'Military Recruiting and the British Labour Force During the First World War'. *The Historical Journal* 27, no. 1 (1984), 199–223.

Donnachie, I., C. Harvie, and I. S. Wood, eds. *FORWARD! Labour Politics in Scotland 1888–1998*. Edinburgh: Polygon, 1989.

Douglas, R. 'Voluntary Enlistment in the First World War and the Work of the Parliamentary Recruiting Committee'. *Journal of Modern History* 42, no. 4 (1970), 564–85.

Downes, Margaret. 'The Civilian Voluntary Aid Effort'. In *Ireland and the First World War*, edited by David Fitzpatrick. Dublin: Trinity History Workshop, 1986, 27–37.

Durr, Peter. 'The Governance of Essex Police, 1880–1920.' MA, Open University, 2003.

Echevarria II, Antulio J. 'The "Cult of the Offensive" Revisited: Confronting Technological Change Before the Great War'. *Journal of Strategic Studies* 25, no. 1 (2002), 199–214.

Farry, Michael. *Sligo 1914–1921: A Chronicle of a Conflict*. Trim: Killoran Press, 1992.

Ferguson, Niall. *The Pity of War*. London: Penguin, 1999.

——'Political Risk and the International Bond Market between the 1848 Revolution and the Outbreak of the First World War'. *Economic History Review* LIX, no. 1 (2006), 70–112.

——*The World's Banker: The History of the House of Rothschild*. London: Weidenfeld & Nicholson, 1998.

Fitzpatrick, David. 'The Logic of Collective Sacrifice: Ireland and the British Army, 1914–1918'. *The Historical Journal* 38, no. 4 (1995), 1017–30.

——'"The Overflow of the Deluge": Anglo-Irish Relationships, 1914–1922'. In *Ireland and Irish Australia: Studies in Cultural and Political History*, edited by O. MacDonagh and W. F. Mandle. London: Croom Helm, 1986.

——*Politics and Irish Life, 1913–1921: Provincial Experience of War and Revolution*. Dublin: Gill and Macmillan, 1977.

Flood, P. J. *France 1914–1918: Public Opinion and the War Effort*. London: Macmillan, 1990.

French, David. 'Allies, Rivals and Enemies: British Strategy and War Aims during the First World War'. In *Britain and the First World War*, edited by John Turner. London: Unwin Hyman, 1988, 22–35.

——'The Rise and Fall of "Business as Usual"'. In *War and the State: The Transformation of British Government 1914–1919*, edited by Kathleen Burk. London: George Allen and Unwin, 1982, 7–31.

——'Spy Fever in Britain, 1900–1915'. *The Historical Journal* 21, no. 2 (1978), 335–70.

Gassert, Imogen L. 'Collaborators and Dissidents: Aspects of British Literary Publishing in the First World War, 1914–1919'. DPhil, University of Oxford, 2002.

Geary, R. *Policing Industrial Disputes: 1893 to 1985*. Cambridge: Cambridge University Press, 1985.

Geppert, Dominik, and Robert Gerwarth. 'Introduction'. In *Wilhelmine Germany and Edwardian Britain: Essays on Cultural Affinity*, edited by Dominik Geppert and Robert Gerwarth. Oxford: Oxford University Press, 2008.

Gooch, John. 'Attitudes to War in Late Victorian and Edwardian England'. In *War and Society: A Yearbook of Military History*, edited by Brian Bond and Ian Roy. London: Croom Helm, 1977, 88–102.

——'Haldane and the "National Army"'. In *Politicians and Defence: Studies in the Formulation of British Defence Policy 1845–1970*, edited by Ian Beckett and John Gooch. Manchester: Manchester University Press, 1981.

——*The Plans of War: The General Staff and British Military Strategy c.1900–1916*. London: Routledge & Kegan Paul, 1974.

——*The Prospect of War: Studies in British Defence Policy, 1847–1942*. London: Frank Cass, 1981.

Good, Kit. 'England Goes To War, 1914–15.' PhD, University of Liverpool, 2002.

Grant, Kevin. *A Civilised Savagery: Britain and the New Slaveries in Africa, 1884–1926*. London: Routledge, 2005.

Gregory, Adrian. 'British "War Enthusiasm" in 1914: A Reassessment'. In *Evidence, History and the Great War: Historians and the Impact of 1914–18*, edited by Gail Braybon. Oxford: Berghahn Books, 2003, 67–85.

——*The Last Great War: British Society and the First World War*. Cambridge: Cambridge University Press, 2008.

Gullace, Nicoletta F. 'Friends, Aliens, and Enemies: Fictive Communities and the Lusitania Riots of 1915'. *Journal of Social History* 39, no. 2 (2005), 345–67.

——'White Feathers and Wounded Men: Female Patriotism and the Memory of the Great War'. *Journal of British Studies* 36 (1997), 178–206.

Halifax, Stuart. '"Over by Christmas": British Popular Opinion and the Short War in 1914'. *First World War Studies*, Issue 1, no. 2 (2010), 103–121.

Harris, Henry. *The Irish Regiments in the First World War*. Cork: Mercier Press, 1968.

Harris, Tim. *London Crowds and the Reign of Charles II: Propaganda and Politics from the Restoration until the Exclusion Crisis*. Cambridge: Cambridge University Press, 1987.

Harrison, R. 'The War Emergency Worker's National Committee, 1914–1920'. In *Essays in Labour History 1886–1923*, edited by A. Briggs and J. Saville. London: Macmillan, 1971, 211–59.

Healy, Maureen. *Vienna and the Fall of the Habsburg Empire: Total War and Everyday Life in World War One*. Cambridge: Cambridge University Press, 2004.

Hennessey, Thomas. *Dividing Ireland: World War One and Partition*. London: Routledge, 1998.

Herwig, Holger H. *The First World War: Germany and Austria-Hungary, 1914–1918*. London: Arnold, 1997.

Hickling, Lieutenant-General Frank. 'Introduction'. In *The Boer War: Army, Nation and Empire*, edited by Peter Dennis and Jeffrey Grey. Canberra: Army History Unit, 2000.

Higonnet, Margaret Randolph, and Patrice L. R. Higonnet. 'The Double Helix'. In *Behind the Lines: Gender and the Two World Wars*, edited by Margaret Randolph Higonnet, Jane Jenson, Sonya Michel, and Margaret Collins Weitz. New Haven: Yale University Press, 1987, 31–47.

Hobsbawm, Eric J. *Age of Extremes: The Short Twentieth Century, 1914–1991*. London: Michael Joseph, 1994.

Holmes, Colin. *Anti-Semitism in British Society, 1876–1939*. London: Edward Arnold, 1979.

——*A Tolerant Country? Immigrants, Refugees and Minorities in Britain*. London: Faber and Faber, 1991.

Hopkin, Deian. 'Domestic Censorship in the First World War'. *Journal of Contemporary History* 5, no. 4 (1970), 151–69.

Horn, Pamela. *Rural Life in England in the First World War*. Dublin: Gill and Macmillan, 1984.

Horne, John. 'Social Identity in War: France, 1914–1918'. In *Men, Women and War*, edited by T. G. Fraser and Keith Jeffery. Dublin: Lilliput Press, 1993, 119–35.

Horne, John, and Alan Kramer. *German Atrocities, 1914: A History of Denial*. London: Yale University Press, 2001.

Horne, John N. *Labour at War: France and Britain, 1914–1918*. Oxford: Clarendon Press, 1991.

Horrall, Andrew. *Popular Culture in London c.1890–1918: The Transformation of Entertainment*. Manchester: Manchester University Press, 2001.

Howard, Michael. 'Men Against Fire: The Doctrine of the Offensive in 1914'. In *Makers of Modern Strategy: From Machiavelli to the Nuclear Age*, edited by Peter Paret. Oxford: Clarendon Press, 1986, 510–26.

Howie, David, and Josephine Howie. 'Irish Recruiting and the Home Rule Crisis of August–September 1914'. In *Strategy and Intelligence: British Policy during the First World War*, edited by Michael Dockrill and David French. London: Hambledon, 1996, 1–22.

Howkins, Alun. *Poor Labouring Men: Rural Radicalism in Norfolk, 1870–1923*. London: Routledge, 1985.

Hynes, Samuel. *The Edwardian Turn of Mind*. Princeton: Princeton University Press, 1968.

Jeffery, Keith. 'The Irish Military Tradition and the British Empire'. In *'An Irish Empire'? Aspects of Ireland and the British Empire*, edited by Keith Jeffery. Manchester: Manchester University Press, 1996, 94–122.

Jones, Heather. *Violence Against Prisoners of War: Britain, France and Germany, 1914–1920*. Cambridge: Cambridge University Press, 2011.

Jones, Spencer. 'The Influence of the Boer War (1899–1902) on the Tactical Development of the Regular British Army 1902–1914'. PhD, University of Wolverhampton, 2009.

Kaye, Harvey J., ed. *The Face of the Crowd: Studies in Revolution, Ideology and Popular Protest. Selected Essays of George Rudé*. Hemel Hempstead: Harvester Wheatsheaf, 1988.

Keiger, J. F. V. 'Britain's "Union Sacrée" in 1914'. In *Les sociétés européennes et la guerre de 1914–1918*, edited by Jean-Jacques Becker and Stéphane Audoin-Rouzeau. Nanterre: Université de Paris X, 1990, 39–52.

Kennedy, Paul M. *The Rise of Anglo-German Antagonism 1860–1914*. London: George Allen and Unwin, 1980.

Keogh, Dermot. *Jews in Twentieth Century Ireland: Refugees, Anti-Semitism and the Holocaust*. Cork: Cork University Press, 1998.

Kynaston, David. *The City of London, Volume II: Golden Years, 1890–1914*. London: Pimlico, 1995.

——*The City of London, Volume III: Illusions of Gold, 1914–1945*. London: Chatto & Windus, 1999.

Larner, Christina. *Witchcraft and Religion: The Politics of Popular Belief*. Oxford: Blackwell, 1984.

Lefebvre, Georges. *The Great Fear of 1789: Rural Panic in Revolutionary France*. London: NLB, 1973.

Lewis, Geoffrey. *Carson: The Man Who Divided Ireland*. London: Hambledon and London, 2005.

Lynn-Jones, Sean M. 'Détente and Deterrence: Anglo-German Relations, 1911–1914'. *International Security* 11, no. 2 (1986), 121–50.

Lyons, F. S. L. *John Dillon: A Biography*. London: Routledge, 1968.

——'The Revolution in Train, 1914–1916'. In *Ireland Under the Union, II: 1870–1921*, edited by W. E. Vaughan. Oxford: Clarendon Press, 1996.

Lyons, J. B. *The Enigma of Tom Kettle: Irish Patriot, Essayist, Poet, British Soldier 1880–1916*. Dublin: The Glendale Press, 1983.

Macdonald, Lyn. *1914—The Days of Hope*. London: Michael Joseph, 1987.

Marder, Arthur J. *From the Dreadnought to Scapa Flow: The Royal Navy in the Fisher Era, 1904–1919. The Road to War 1904–1914*. 5 vols. Vol. 1. Oxford: Oxford University Press, 1961.

Martin, Kingsley. *The Triumph of Lord Palmerston: A Study in Public Opinion in England Before the Crimean War*. 2nd ed. London: Hutchinson, 1963.

Marwick, Arthur. *The Deluge: British Society and the First World War*. London: Bodley Head, 1965.

Maurice, Major General Sir Frederick. *History of the War in South Africa, 1899–1902*. 4 vols. London: Hurst and Blackett Ltd, 1906–1910.

McCartney, Helen B. *Citizen Soldiers: The Liverpool Territorials in the First World War*. Cambridge: Cambridge University Press, 2005.

Mercer, Eric. 'For King, Country and a Shilling a Day: Recruitment in Belfast during the Great War, 1914–1918'. MA, Queen's University, Belfast, 1998.

Mitchinson, K. W. *Defending Albion: Britain's Home Army, 1908–1919*. Basingstoke: Palgrave, 2005.

——*England's Last Hope: The Territorial Force, 1908–1914*. Basingstoke: Palgrave Macmillan, 2008.

Moon, Howard Roy. 'The Invasion of the United Kingdom: Public Controversy and Official Planning, 1888–1918'. PhD, University of London, 1968.

Morgan, Dafydd Densil. '"Christ and the War": Some Aspects of the Welsh Experience, 1914–1918'. *Journal of Welsh Religious History* 5 (1997), 73–91.

Morgan, Kenneth O. *Wales in British Politics, 1868–1922*. Cardiff: University of Wales Press, 1970.

Mòr-O'Brien, Anthony. 'Patriotism on Trial: The Strike of the South Wales Miners, July 1915'. *Welsh History Review* 12, no. 1 (1984), 76–104.

Morris, A. J. A. *Radicalism Against War, 1906–1914: The Advocacy of Peace and Retrenchment*. London: Longman, 1972.

Nasson, Bill. *The South African War, 1899–1902*. London: Arnold, 1999.

Neilson, Keith. *Britain and the Last Tsar: British Policy and Russia 1894–1917*. Oxford: Clarendon Press, 1995.

Novick, Ben. 'The Advanced Nationalist Response to Atrocity Propaganda, 1914–1918'. In *Images, Icons and the Irish Nationalist Imagination*, edited by Lawrence W. McBride. Dublin: Four Courts Press, 1999, 130–147.

O'Brien, Joseph V. *William O'Brien and the Course of Irish Politics, 1881–1918*. London: University of California Press, 1976.

Offen, Karen. *European Feminisms 1700–1950: A Political History*. Stanford: Stanford University Press, 2000.

Offer, Avner. 'Going to War in 1914: A Matter of Honour?' *Politics and Society* 23, no. 2 (1995), 213–41.

O'Halpin, Eunan. *The Decline of the Union: British Government in Ireland 1892–1920*. Dublin: Gill and Macmillan, 1987.

O'Riordan, Manus. 'The Justification of James Connolly'. In *James Connolly, Liberty Hall and The 1916 Rising*, edited by Francis Devine and Manus O'Riordan. Dublin: Irish Labour History Society, 2006.

Osborne, John Morton. *The Voluntary Recruiting Movement in Britain, 1914–1916*. New York: Garland Publishing, 1982.

Panayi, Panikos. 'Anti-German Riots in Britain During the First World War'. In *Racial Violence in Britain in the Nineteenth and Twentieth Centuries*, edited by Panikos Panayi. London: Leicester University Press, 1996.

——'Anti-German Riots in London during the First World War'. *German History* 7, no. 2 (1989), 184–203.

——'Anti-Immigrant Violence in Nineteenth and Twentieth Century Britain'. In *Racial Violence in Britain in the Nineteenth and Twentieth Centuries*, edited by Panikos Panayi. London: Leicester University Press, 1996.

——*The Enemy Within: Germans in Britain During the First World War*. Oxford: Berg, 1991.

——'"The Hidden Hand": British Myths About German Control of Britain During the First World War'. *Immigrants and Minorities* 7, no. 3 (1988), 253–72.

Parker, Peter. *The Old Lie: The Great War and the Public School Ethos*. London: Constable, 1987.

Parry, Cyril. 'Gwynedd and the Great War, 1914–1918'. *Welsh History Review* 14, no. 1 (1988), 78–117.

Pennell, Catriona. '"The Germans Have Landed!": Home Defence and Invasion Fears in the South East of England, August to December 1914'. In *Untold War: New Perspectives in First World War Studies*, edited by Heather Jones, Jennifer O'Brien, and Christoph Schmidt-Supprian. Leiden: Brill Academic Publishers, 2008, 95–118.

Porter, Bernard. *The Absent-Minded Imperialists: Empire, Society, and Culture in Britain*. Oxford: Oxford University Press, 2004.

Price, Mark David. 'The Labour Movement and Patriotism in the South Wales Coalfield during the First World War: The Case of Vernon Hartshorn, 1914–15'. MA, University of Wales, Aberystwyth, 1999.

Pugh, Martin. *State and Society: British Political and Social History 1870–1992*. London: Edward Arnold, 1994.

Pugh, Martin D. 'Politicians and the Woman's Vote, 1914–1918'. *History* 59 (1974), 358–74.

Purseigle, Pierre. 'Beyond and Below the Nations: Towards a Comparative History of Local Communities at War'. In *Uncovered Fields: Perspectives in First World War Studies*, edited by Jenny Macleod and Pierre Purseigle Leiden: Brill, 2004, 95–123.

Raithel, Thomas. *Das 'Wunder' der inneren Einheit: Studien zur deutschen und französischen Öffentlichkeit bei Beginn des Ersten Weltkrieges*. Bonn: Bouvier, 1996.

Ramsay, Clay. *The Ideology of the Great Fear: The Soissonnais in 1789*. Baltimore: John Hopkins University Press, 1992.

Reader, W. J. *At Duty's Call: A Study in Obsolete Patriotism*. Manchester: Manchester University Press, 1988.

Readman, Paul. 'The Liberal Party and Patriotism in Early Twentieth Century Britain'. *Twentieth Century British History* 12, no. 3 (2001), 269–302.

Robbins, Keith. 'Local History and the Study of National History'. *The Historian* 27 (1990), 15–18.

Roberts, Robert. *The Classic Slum: Salford Life in the First Quarter of the Century*. Manchester: Manchester University Press, 1971.

Rudé, George. *The Crowd in History: A Study of Popular Disturbances in France and England, 1730–1848*. New York: John Wiley and Sons, 1964.

Rueger, Jan. *The Great Naval Game: Britain and Germany in the Age of Empire*. Cambridge: Cambridge University Press, 2007.

Ryan, Michael W. 'The Invasion Controversy of 1906–1908: Lieutenant-Colonel Charles à Court Repington and British Perceptions of the German Menace'. *Military Affairs* 44, no. 1 (1980), 8–12.

Schaepdrijver, Sophie de. 'Occupation, Propaganda and the Idea of Belgium'. In *European Culture in the Great War: The Arts, Entertainment, and Propaganda, 1914–1918*, edited by Aviel Roshwald and Richard Stites. Cambridge: Cambridge University Press, 1999, 267–94.

Schneider, Eric F. 'What Britons Were Told About the War in the Trenches, 1914–1918'. DPhil, University of Oxford, 1997.

Schramm, Martin. *Das Deutschlandbild in der britischen Presse, 1912–1919*. Berlin: Akademie Verlag, 2007.

Secker, Jane-Louise. 'Newspapers and Historical Research: A Study of Historians and Custodians in Wales'. PhD, University of Wales, 1999.

Seldon, Anthony, and Joanna Pappworth. *By Word of Mouth: 'Elite' Oral History*. London: Methuen, 1983.

Sheffield, Gary. *Forgotten Victory: The First World War, Myths and Realities*. London: Headline, 2001.

Silbey, David. *The British Working Class and Enthusiasm for War, 1914–1916*. London: Frank Cass, 2005.

Simkins, Peter. *Kitchener's Army: The Raising of the New Armies 1914–1916*. Manchester: Manchester University Press, 1988.

Sisman, Adam. *A. J. P. Taylor: A Biography*. London: Sinclair-Stevenson, 1994.

Smith, Iain. *The Origins of the South African War, 1899–1902*. London: Longman, 1996.

Spiers, Edward. 'The Late Victorian Army, 1868–1914'. In *The Oxford History of the British Army*, edited by David G. Chandler and Ian Beckett. Oxford: Oxford University Press, 1994, 187–210.

Spiers, Edward M. 'Between the South African War and the First World War, 1902–1914'. In *Big Wars and Small Wars: The British Army and the Lessons of War in the Twentieth Century*, edited by Hew Strachan. London: Routledge, 2006, 21–35.

——*Haldane: An Army Reformer*. Edinburgh: Edinburgh University Press, 1980.

Staunton, Martin. 'Kilrush, Co. Clare and the Royal Munster Fusiliers: The Experience of an Irish Town in the First World War'. *The Irish Sword* 16, no. 65 (1986), 268–72.

Stevenson, David. *1914–1918: The History of the First World War*. London: Penguin, 2005.

Stibbe, Matthew. 'The Internment of Civilians by Belligerent States during the First World War and the Response of the International Committee of the Red Cross'. *Journal of Contemporary History* 41, no. 1 (2006), 5–19.

Strachan, Hew. 'The Boer War and its Impact on the British Army, 1902–1914'. In *'Ashes and Blood': The British Army in South Africa, 1795–1914*, edited by Peter B. Boyden, Alan J. Guy, and Marion Harding. London: National Army Museum, 1999, 87–9.

——'Economic Mobilization: Money, Munitions and Machines'. In *The Oxford Illustrated History of the First World War*, edited by Hew Strachan. Oxford: Oxford University Press, 2000, 134–48.

——*The First World War, Volume One: To Arms*. Oxford: Oxford University Press, 2001.

——*From Waterloo to Balaclava: Tactics, Technology, and the British Army, 1815–1854*. Cambridge: Cambridge University Press, 1985.

——'Introduction'. In *Big Wars and Small Wars: The British Army and Lessons of War in the Twentieth Century*, edited by Hew Strachan. London: Routledge, 2006.

Swartz, Martin. *The Union of Democratic Control in British Politics During the First World War*. Oxford: Clarendon Press, 1971.

Tabili, Laura. '"Having Lived Close Beside Them All The Time": Negotiating National Identities Through Personal Networks'. *Journal of Social History* 39, no. 2 (2005), 369–87.

Taylor, A. J. P. '1914: Events in Britain'. *The Listener* LXXII, no. 1842 (1964), 79–82.

—— *The Trouble Makers: Dissent Over Foreign Policy, 1792–1939*. London: Pimlico, 1993.

Terraine, John. *The Smoke and the Fire: Myths and Anti-Myths of War, 1861–1945*. London: Leo Cooper, 1992.

Thompson, F. M. L. *The Rise of Respectable Society: A Social History of Victorian Britain, 1830–1900*. London: Fontana, 1988.

Thompson, Paul. *The Edwardians: The Remaking of British Society*. St Albans: Paladin, 1975, 1977.

—— *The Voice of the Past: Oral History*. Oxford: Oxford University Press, 1988.

Thompson, Paul, and Natasha Burchardt, eds. *Our Common History: The Transformation of Europe*. London: Pluto Press, 1982.

Thorpe, Andrew. *A History of the British Labour Party*. 3rd ed. Basingstoke: Palgrave Macmillan, 2008.

Tierney, Mark, Paul Bowen, and David Fitzpatrick. 'Recruiting Posters'. In *Ireland and the First World War*, edited by David Fitzpatrick. Dublin: Trinity History Workshop, 1986, 47–58.

Todman, Dan. *The Great War: Myth and Memory*. London: Hambledon Comtinuum, 2005.

Tombs, Robert and Isabelle. *That Sweet Enemy: The French and the British from the Sun King to the Present*. London: William Heinemann, 2006.

Travers, Tim. *The Killing Ground: The British Army, the Western Front and the Emergence of Modern Warfare 1900–1918*. Barnsley: Pen & Sword, 1987.

Tuchman, Barbara W. *The Guns of August*. London: Robinson, 2000.

Turner, John. *British Politics and the Great War: Coalition and Conflict, 1915–1918*. London: Yale University Press, 1992.

Urquhart, Diane. '"The Female of the Species is More Deadlier Than the Male"? The Ulster Women's Unionist Council, 1911–1940'. In *Coming into the Light: The Work, Politics and Religion of Women in Ulster*, edited by Janice Holmes and Diane Urquhart. Belfast: Institute of Irish Studies, Queen's University Belfast, 1994, 93–123.

Veitch, Colin. '"Play Up! Play Up! Play Up! and Win the War!" Football, the Nation and the First World War, 1914–1915'. *Journal of Contemporary History* 20 (1985), 363–78.

Verhey, Jeffrey. *The Spirit of 1914: Militarism, Myth and Mobilization in Germany*. Cambridge: Cambridge University Press, 2000.

von Strandmann, Harmut Pogge. 'The Role of British and German Historians in Mobilizing Public Opinion in 1914'. In *British and German Historiography 1750–1950: Perceptions and Transfers*, edited by Benedikt Stuchtey and Peter Wende. Oxford: Oxford University Press, 2000, 335–71.

Waites, Bernard. *A Class Society at War: England, 1914–1918*. Leamington Spa: Berg, 1987.

Wall, Richard, and Jay Winter, eds. *The Upheaval of War: Family, Work and Welfare in Europe, 1914–1918*. Cambridge: Cambridge University Press, 1988.

Wallace, Stuart. *War and the Image of Germany: British Academics 1914–1918*. Edinburgh: Donald, 1988.

Watt, D. C. 'British Reactions to the Assassination in Sarajevo'. *European Studies Review* 1, no. 3 (1971), 233–47.

Webb, Dominic. 'Inflation: The Value of the Pound 1750–2005'. London: House of Commons Library, 2006. Available at <http://www.parliament.uk/documents/commons>.

Weinroth, H. 'Peace by Negotiation and the British Antiwar Movement, 1914–1918'. *Canadian Journal of History* X, no. 3 (1975), 369–92.

Wheatley, Michael. *Nationalism and the Irish Party: Provincial Ireland 1910–1916.* Oxford: Oxford University Press, 2005.

Wiel, Jerome Aan de. 'Archbishop Walsh and Mgr. Curran's Opposition to the British War Effort in Dublin, 1914–1918'. *The Irish Sword* 22, no. 88 (2000), 193–204.

—— *The Catholic Church in Ireland 1914–1918: War and Politics*, Dublin: Irish Academic Press, 2003.

Wilkinson, Alan. *The Church of England and the First World War.* London: SCM Press Ltd, 1996.

Wilkinson, Glenn R. '"The Blessings of War": The Depiction of Military Force in Edwardian Newspapers'. *Journal of Contemporary History* 33, no. 1 (1998), 97–115.

Williamson, Samuel R. *The Politics of Grand Strategy: Britain and France Prepare for War, 1904–1914.* Cambridge, Massachusetts: Harvard University Press, 1969.

Wilson, Trevor. *The Myriad Faces of War: Britain and the Great War, 1914–1918.* Cambridge: Polity Press, 1986.

Winter, J. M. *Socialism and the Challenge of War: Ideas and Politics in Britain, 1912–1918.* London: Routledge, 1974.

—— *The Great War and the British People.* London: Macmillan, 1986.

Winter, Jay. 'Paris, London, Berlin 1914–1919: Capital Cities at War'. In *Capital Cities at War: Paris, London and Berlin, 1914–1919*, edited by Jay Winter and Jean-Louis Robert. Cambridge: Cambridge University Press, 1997, 3–24.

—— 'Propaganda and the Mobilization of Consent'. In *The Oxford Illustrated History of the First World War*, edited by Hew Strachan. Oxford: Oxford University Press, 2000, 216–26.

—— *Sites of Memory, Sites of Mourning: The Great War in European Cultural History.* Cambridge: Cambridge University Press, 1995.

—— and Jean-Louis Robert, eds. *Capital Cities at War: Paris, London and Berlin, 1914–1919.* 2 vols. Vol. 1. Cambridge: Cambridge University Press, 1997.

—— —— eds. *Capital Cities at War: Paris, London, Berlin, 1914–1919: Volume 2, A Cultural History.* 2 vols. Vol. 2. Cambridge: Cambridge University Press, 2007.

Yapp, M. E. *The Making of the Modern Near East, 1792–1923.* London: Longman, 1987.

Young, Derek Rutherford. 'Voluntary Recruitment in Scotland, 1914–1916'. PhD, University of Glasgow, 2001.

Index

Printed in the USA/Agawam, MA
February 6, 2018

669229.099